# ALASKA

# Alaska
## A HISTORY OF THE 49TH STATE

Second Edition

by
Claus-M. Naske
and
Herman E. Slotnick

University of Oklahoma Press   :   Norman and London

By Claus-M. Naske

*An Interpretative History of Alaska* (Edmonds, Wash., 1973)
*Alaska: A History of the 49th State* (Grand Rapids, Mich., 1979)
*Edward Lewis "Bob" Bartlett of Alaska: A Life in Politics* (Fairbanks, Alaska, 1980)
*Anchorage: A Pictorial History* (Norfolk, Va., 1981)
*Fairbanks: A Pictorial History* (Norfolk, Va., 1981)
*Alaska: A Pictorial History* (Norfolk, Va., 1983)
*Alaska* (Toronto, Canada, 1984)
*A History of Alaska Statehood* (Lanham, Md., 1985)
*Paving Alaska's Trails: The Work of the Alaska Road Commission* (Lanham, Md., 1986)
*Alaska: A History of the 49th State*, 2d ed. (Norman, 1987)

Library of Congress Cataloging-in-Publication Data

Naske, Claus-M.
  Alaska, a history of the 49th state.

  Bibliography: p. 321
  Includes index.
  1. Alaska—History.   I. Slotnick, Herman E.,
1916–      . II. Title.
F904.N37   1987      979.8           87–40215
ISBN 0–8061–2099–1

# CONTENTS

# ILLUSTRATIONS

# MAPS

# ACKNOWLEDGMENTS

Historians contemplating the writing of a book believe that they are able to offer something that does not yet exist in published form. Much has already been written about Alaska. Even a casual survey of the available literature is overwhelming. There are, for example, the accounts of Russian, English, American, French, Spanish, and German explorers; secondary accounts dealing with Russian America; and many volumes describing Alaska as the American possession acquired in 1867. Voluminous federal government reports examine everything from the number of salmon to the conditions of the aborigines. The literature of the Klondike gold rush alone is vast, and eager writers in all fields have added substantially to this body of written work about Alaska.

Still, in spite of all that has been written, the authors feel—or know, depending on their frame of mind at the moment—that yet another book on Alaska is both desirable and necessary. This book is designed to present a narrative account of Alaska's major historical developmental strands from early times to the present, with an emphasis on major developments in the twentieth century. The authors consulted works both

lengthy and authoritative but did not attempt to survey all of the available literature.

The works of many specialists contributed to this volume. The holdings of the Skinner Collection in the University of Alaska, Fairbanks, and the Pacific Northwest Collection in the Suzallo Library at the University of Washington in Seattle were particularly useful.

The William B. Eerdmans Publishing Company, of Grand Rapids, Michigan, published the first edition of this volume. The public received it well, and after it went out of print, the University of Oklahoma Press agreed to publish this revised and updated version.

The authors are grateful to a wonderful group of persons who typed the various drafts and revisions at the University of Alaska. We thank Louise Flood, of the School of Engineering, for her efforts on our behalf. She unfailingly caught mistakes in spelling and corrected awkward sentences. Sheri Layral, the administrative assistant of the Department of History, skillfully managed our time, urged us on, and typed many pages. Linda Ilgenfritz typed much and caught many errors. Chris Bennett, of the School of Management, ever cheerful, typed portions of the manuscript during her lunch breaks and on weekends. We thank all of you. We are also grateful to our colleagues in the Departments of History and Political Science for the stimulating intellectual atmosphere they provide.

As on previous occasions, our wives, Dinah and Mary, helped with valuable suggestions and encouragement. We would also like to thank Renee Blahuta, of the University of Alaska, Fairbanks Archives, for her valuable help.

*Fairbanks, Alaska*    CLAUS-M. NASKE
*Seattle, Washington*  HERMAN E. SLOTNICK

Alaska

# ALASKA

# 1. THE GREAT LAND AND ITS NATIVE PEOPLES

Americans became aware of the great natural resources of the North as early as the 1840s, when New England whalers ventured into the Bering Sea in pursuit of their prey. After the United States acquired Alaska from Russia in 1867, restless and adventurous men went north in search of fortune. They soon found gold, and by 1890 Alaska's mineral production was valued at nearly $800,000. By 1904 gold production exceeded $9 million in value. This relatively rapid development attracted public attention and led to demands for government-sponsored and financed explorations, surveys, and other investigations. In a few years both public and private enterprise combined to produce a great amount of material on the geography, geology, and mineral resources of Alaska.[1] In short, Americans were becoming aware of Alaska's land and natural resources. Yet even as they found that the hardy could reap fabulous wealth from Alaska, they also discovered that the land itself was dangerous.

Alaskans were harshly reminded of the danger on June 6, 1912, when snow-covered, glaciered, and seemingly dormant Mount Katmai, on the Alaska Peninsula, blew up in a series of violent explosions that threw more than 5 1/2 cubic miles of debris into the air. For hundreds of square miles around, the eruptions destroyed the country. The city of Kodiak, 100 miles away, was plunged into total darkness for sixty hours while volcanic ash covered everything to a depth of several feet. The accompanying thunder and lightning convinced the terrified residents that the end of the world had come. In Juneau, about 750 miles away, the explosive sounds of the erupting mountain were plainly heard. In Seattle and Port Townsend, over 2,000 miles from Katmai, cloth fabrics disintegrated from the effects of sulfuric acid rain, which fell for days.[2]

Alaskans were again reminded of the geologically unstable nature of their land at 5:36 P.M. on Good Friday, March 27, 1964, when one of the greatest earthquakes of all time struck south-central Alaska. Measuring between 8.4 and 8.6 on the Richter scale, it released at least twice as much energy as the 1906 earthquake which destroyed San Francisco, and it was felt over almost a half million square miles. The motions lasted longer than those for most other recorded earthquakes, and more land surface was vertically and horizontally dislocated than had been moved by any previous known tremor. Not only was the land surface tilted, but an enormous mass of land and seafloor moved several tens of feet toward the Gulf of Alaska.[3]

The earthquake left 114 people dead or missing, and Alaska's governor estimated property damages at between one-half and three-quarters of a billion dollars. Even at that, Alaskans had been lucky. If the earthquake had occurred during the school and business day, many more lives would have been lost. And if the seismic sea waves accompanying the earthquake had struck the coastal communities of south-central Alaska at high instead of low tide, the loss of life and property would have been even greater. As it was, the sea waves traversed the Pacific.

A compilation by geophysicist T. Neil Davis, of the Geophysical Institute at the University of Alaska at Fairbanks, shows that between July, 1788, and August, 1961, about 880 earthquakes measuring 5 points or more on the Richter scale occurred in Alaska.[4] It is obvious that Alaska's geological setting, while promising great wealth in mineral resources, also holds great danger. Although geologists have worked in Alaska since the latter part of the nineteenth century, this huge landmass is not well known geologically. Complete geological mapping on a scale of one mile to the inch, comparable to that done in much of the lower forty-eight contiguous states, would require more than a century of intensive work and substantial expense. The present geological mapping has been done only at a reconnaissance level.

## THE GEOLOGICAL HISTORY OF ALASKA

Theories about Alaska's early geological history are in a state of flux. The geology of Alaska was once thought to be simple, based on its great regions of ancient rocks and ancient shallow seas, but in fact was poorly known. The data from research begun in the early 1970s are revealing the complex forces at work and leading geologists to rethink former concepts.

Present knowledge indicates that the Alaskan subcontinent is made up of many fragments of continental and oceanic materials which were rafted from the Pacific area on the backs of the major crustal plates and which coalesced to form the terrain we see today. An agglomeration of geologically different fragments would explain many of the dramatic changes in rock type across Alaska. It is not known when the various fragments became joined to each other and to ancestral Alaska, but it appears certain that the process is continuing, for the evidence indicates that one fragment, known as the Yakutat block, is now in the process of "docking." Just as the major earthquakes in the Gulf of Alaska and the Yakutat region testify to movements of the crust in our time, so do the very high, very young mountains of the Wrangell–Saint Elias Range bear mute testimony to earlier arrivals.

The other mountain ranges of Alaska are also thought to have resulted from collisions brought about by the movement of the major plates and of the geological flotsam they carried. The Brooks Range is perhaps the oldest of these mountain ranges, having been uplifted in the late Jurassic or early Cretaceous period, about 140 million years ago. Parts of today's Alaska Range were still basins as recently as the Miocene epoch, about 5 to 24 million years ago, and parts of the Chugach and southernmost ranges have arisen since then.

Scientists consider Alaska to be a key to understanding the geological relationships around the northern Pacific and the geology of the circumarctic areas. Alaska is crucial in evaluating the ancient histories of the Arctic and northern Pacific oceans through the study of its continental margins. It also serves for the testing of various theories of continental drift and seafloor spreading in the Arctic.[5]

## THE REGIONS AND CLIMATES OF ALASKA

The Aleuts call the Alaskan subcontinent Alaxsxag, which literally means "the object toward which the action of the sea is directed."[6] The Russians called their American possession Bolshaya Zemlya, the Great Land, and justifiably so.[7] Sweeping across four time zones, it encompasses 591,004 square miles, or 378,242,560 acres, about 2.2 times the area of Texas, the largest of the lower forty-eight states. Surrounded by fellow Americans from the Southwest working on the Trans-Alaska Pipeline, Alaskans often countered Texans' boastings about the size of Texas by threatening to "split in two and make you third in size."

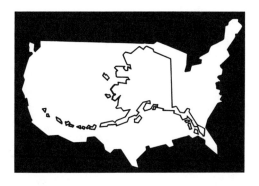

Outline map of Alaska superimposed on the contiguous forty-eight states to illustrate the subcontinental size of the Forty-ninth State

Alaska extends from 51° to 71°25′ north latitude and from longitude 129°58′ west to longitude 172°22′ east, thus occupying both the Western and the Eastern hemispheres. A map of Alaska superimposed on a map of the contiguous United States would touch the Atlantic and Pacific oceans and the Canadian and Mexican borders; Barrow, Alaska's northernmost settlement, would be situated near Lake of the Woods, in northern Minnesota, while Ketchikan, Alaska's southernmost city, would be situated in the vicinity of Charleston, South Carolina. Alaska measures about 1,420 miles from north to south and about 2,400 miles from east to west. The Aleutian Islands reach westward toward the Komandorskiye Islands of the Soviet Union, forming the stepping stones from Kamchatka that the Russian fur hunters followed in their quest for the sea otter.

The diversity of this lonely and lovely subcontinent is as incredible as its size. Alaska possesses arctic plains, great forests, swamps, glaciers, ice fields, broad valleys and fjords, the highest mountain of North America, active volcanoes, twelve major river systems, three million lakes, and countless islands. Alaska boasts 50 percent more seacoast than that of all of the contiguous states combined—about 33,900 miles—and its coasts are washed by two oceans and three major seas. Yet the entire state has about 523,048 people (Alaska Department of Labor estimate as of July 1, 1984), fewer residents than San Francisco.

The overwhelming majority of Alaskans are urban dwellers. According to the 1984 estimates, 240,602 Alaskans (46 percent) live in the town of Anchorage, and 69,633 (13.3 percent) reside in the Fairbanks North Star Borough. About 75,000 (14.3 percent) live in small urban centers from Ketchikan to Barrow and from Seward to Kodiak. The remaining 137,813 inhabitants (26.4 percent) live in the approximately 220 villages scattered throughout the state. Thus about 385,235 (73.6 percent) of Alaska's inhabitants are urbanites. The influx from the contiguous states to the north settles mostly in the urban centers, and many Natives are leaving their villages for the towns as well. On the other hand, many Natives, disillusioned with urban life, are returning to their villages. High birthrates among the native population also help keep the village populations stable.

Geographically there are six regions—the Arctic, the Panhandle, and south-central, southwestern, western, and interior Alaska—each with a distinctive topography and climate. The climates range from temperate to frigid and from desertlike aridity to almost continuous rainfall and snowfall. Barrow, Alaska's northernmost settlement, is not as cold as Fairbanks, in the interior, though it is only a comparatively short distance from the arctic ice pack and the North Pole. Alaska's southernmost point in the Aleutians is at about the same latitude as London, England, and has a similar climate.

Approaching Alaska from Seattle by ship, the traveler enters the so-called Panhandle, a narrow, 400-mile strip of land that crowds closely against the coast of British Columbia. It is cut off from the main body of the Alaskan landmass by the great Saint Elias Mountains. Juneau, Alaska's capital, is in the Panhandle, as is Ketchikan, self-proclaimed "Salmon Capital of the World" 'and also the site of one of the region's two pulp mills. Sitka, the former capital of Russian America, is situated on Baranof Island amid forested mountains overlooking the sound; it is the home of the second of the region's pulp mills. At the

In the decade 1929–39, Robert Marshall, forester, conservationist, and author, explored the remote, uninhabited Central Brooks Range (Endicott Mountains), above. He described a series of needlelike peaks extending about eight miles in a horsehoe around a creek rising in a glacier. The Eskimos called the range Arrigetch, which means "fingers of the hand extended" and admirably describes the mountains. Photograph by John Kauffman. Courtesy U.S. National Park Service.

upper end of the Panhandle lies Skagway, where thousands of argonauts disembarked in 1898 for their difficult climb over the Chilkoot Pass and their subsequent journey down the Yukon River to Dawson.

Many islands, steep valleys, and rugged peaks ranging to 10,000 feet stretch all along the Panhandle, and the seashores teem with marine life. The climate is moderate, with warmer temperatures than those found in most of the rest of Alaska and with a good deal of rain and cloudiness. Temperatures seldom dip below 10° F and often climb to the 60s and 70s during the summer. Annual rainfall varies from 25 to 155 inches, which produces lush forest growth. As a result the region contains most of the state's commercially marketable timber, western hemlock and Sitka spruce being the two major species.

The southern side of Alaska confronts the Pacific Ocean in a wide-sweeping arc of about 700 miles, flanking some of the highest mountains in North America. Within this arc lies the Gulf of Alaska. One of the arms of the arc is formed by the Alaska Peninsula, while the other is formed by the Panhandle and the coast of Canada. At the very center of this geographical formation lies the Kenai Peninsula, where Alaska's modern oil boom began in the mid-1950s. Set off from the mainland by Cook Inlet, this peninsula is mountainous, dotted with lakes and indented with fjords. Resurrection Bay, on the peninsula's east side, is long, deep, and completely sheltered. At the head of the bay lies Seward, the starting point of the Alaska Railroad. For many years Seward was the shipping and rail terminus for cargo coming into Alaska from the "outside." In recent years it has been superseded in importance by the port of Anchorage.

Since the 1950s, Anchorage has been the economic and social center of south-central Alaska. It also has become Alaska's largest city, with an estimated population of 240,602 in 1984. Situated on Cook Inlet, Anchorage began its existence as a tent city in 1915, when construction of the Alaska Railroad began.

Cordova, on Prince William Sound, southeast of Anchorage, is today a small fishing town, but it was once the terminus of the Copper River & Northwestern Railway, which carried copper ore 200 miles from the Alaska Syndicate mine in the Chitina Valley to tidewater. In one corner of Prince William Sound lies Valdez. Completely devastated in the Good Friday earthquake of 1964, Valdez was relocated on stable ground and has since become famous as the terminus of the 798-mile Trans-Alaska Pipeline originating at Prudhoe Bay, on Alaska's North Slope.

Kodiak Island, lying south of the Kenai Peninsula, is a mountainous region within the rich fishing waters of the North Pacific. Home of the gigantic Kodiak brown bear, it also processes millions of pounds of king and tanner crabs, as well as shrimp, halibut, and salmon.

Southwestern Alaska includes the Alaska Peninsula, the Katmai National Monument, and the great sweeping arc of the Aleutian Islands. It is a region of contrasts, stretching southwest from the lightly wooded hillsides and rugged mountains of the Alaska Peninsula and then curving westward through the barren and volcanic Aleutians almost to Siberia. The Aleutians form the dividing line between the Pacific and Bering seas. The distance from Mount Katmai, at the head of the Alaska Peninsula, to Attu, westernmost of the Aleutians, is nearly 1,500 miles. The international date line makes a sharp angle to the west to take in the last of the Aleutian Islands and keep all of Alaska within the same day. There are actually only a few large islands in the Aleutian chain; in order from east to west along the chain they are Unimak, Unalaska, Umnak, Atka, Adak, and Attu. Thousands of rocks and islets dot the ocean between Unimak and Attu.

The foggy Aleutians are stormy and rainy, swept alternately by the cold winds of the Arctic and the humid winds of the Pacific. Close to the Aleutian Islands flows the Japan Current, which brings a warm front from the south into conflict wth the cold winds from the north and accounts for the continuous fog, rain, and snow of the region. Temperatures rarely drop below 0° F in winter or rise above 55° F in summer, but the climate is characterized by "frequent, often violent cyclonic storms and high winds, countered by dense fogs and eerie stillness."[8] There is no major vegetation on the Aleutians other than grasses and moss. The islands are mostly of volcanic origin. Spread along the Aleutians are a number of military installations, weather stations, airports, and fish-processing and supply settlements.

The heart of Western Alaska, also referred to as the Bering Sea coast region, is a broad lowland where the Yukon and Kuskokwim rivers flow the last 200 miles to the Bering Sea. To the north the region extends across high hills and low mountains to the Seward Peninsula. To the south it covers the Ahklun and Kilbuck mountains and the southwestern extensions of the Kuskokwim Mountains and extends across the Nushagak River to Bristol Bay and the lowlands on the western side of the Alaska Peninsula along Bristol Bay. Cool, rainy, foggy weather with temperatures in the 50s and low 60s characterizes the summers. Winter temperature readings average around 0° F, but the wind-chill-factor temperatures are much lower. Annual snowfall in the lowland areas ranges from 40 to 90 inches; annual precipitation totals about 20 inches. Much of the Bering Sea coast is treeless tundra underlain by permafrost and contains thousands of lakes, ponds, and sloughs and almost unmoving rivers, such as the muddy mouths of the Kuskokwim and Yukon rivers.

Alaska's interior lies south of the Brooks Range and generally north of the Alaska Range and extends west from the Canadian border to an imaginary north-south line a distance of 40 to 200 miles from the coast of the Bering Sea. The Tanana, Yukon, and Kuskokwim rivers lie in the heart of the wide-open spaces of the interior. On the north and west lie the low mountains of the Tanana-Yukon upland and the Kuskokwim Mountains. The Yukon is the longest river in Alaska at 1,875 miles. Approximately 1,400 of these flow westward across the entire breadth of Alaska into the Bering Sea; the remainder flow in Canada. Along this river and is tributaries are situated most of the settlements and towns of interior Alaska. Fairbanks lies on the Tanana River, a tributary of the Yukon. Fairbanks with its environs has a population of approximately 69,633. It has been the metropolis and supply center for interior and northwest Alaska particulaly since the 1970s and the North Slope oil boom.

Temperatures in the interior often drop to −50° and −60° F, and ice fog hovers over Fairbanks and some other populated and low-lying areas when the temperatures falls below −20° F. Winters are cold and clear, and summers are generally hot and dry, with light rainfall of approximately 12 inches a year. Snowfall, because of the extreme cold, often consists of dry, powdery flakes that blow and drift easily. Fairbanks, however, has much fairer weather and enjoys long hours of splendid daylight during the spring and summer months, reaching temperatures in the 80s, which balances the long, dark winter when days seem grimly short.

The Arctic extends from the southern flanks of the Brooks Range, which rises to over 9,000 feet in the east and forms a mighty barrier between the interior and the slope. It extends from Kotzebue, north of the Seward Peninsula, to the Canadian border. The slope, about 750 miles long and 250 miles wide, consists of large areas of rolling uplands and coastal plains which stretch northward from the Brooks Range.

The whole Arctic Slope region is devoid of timber except for the occasional dense thickets of alder, willow, and resin birch in many river valleys. Tundra stretches across most of the area, and during the short summer months the profusion of flowering plants makes the Arctic a place of beauty. It is a place of nightless summers and sunless winters. Temperatures are low because of the prevailing northerly winds during all seasons of the year. The average July temperature at Barrow is 40° F, while the average January temperature is −17° F. Total annual precipitation averages agout 5 inches, making the area a desert. For much of the year, the shores of the Arctic are ice-locked. The Arctic Slope achieved sudden fame when several oil companies discovered vast oil and gas deposits at Prudhoe Bay. The Prudhoe Bay oil fields lie alongside the Sagavanirktok River delta, about 70 miles west of the Arctic National Wildlife Range. The slope has now become potentially the most wealthy region in the state.[9]

## ALASKA PREHISTORY

No one knows just when human beings discovered America, and the subject continues to be debated by many scholars. The disagreements arise anew with the unearthing of skulls, bones, burial sites, hunting camps, and utensils. Some people have suggested that Egyptians first saw America, while others supported the various claims of the Greeks, Etruscans, Hindus, Chinese, Buddhists, Japanese, and Irish. The Spanish scholar and writer Fray José de Acosta, in his volume *Historia natural moral de las Indias,* published in 1589, hypothesized that the first Americans walked across a land connection with Asia. The present consensus, following Acosta's theory, is that the first people who saw what is today called America were following Ice Age mammals migrating east from Siberia into present Alaska in search of more food. In time these hunters and gatherers, still following the game, wandered into the woodlands and grasslands of western and interior America, then east to the Atlantic shores of Canada and south across the deserts, through Central America, and finally down the spine of the Andean highlands to the tip of South America, reaching Tierra del Fuego more than 12,000 years ago.

These early hunters and gatherers may well have entered Alaska on the so-called Bering Land Bridge, about 1,000 miles wide, when Pleistocene glacial ice sheets locked up much of the earth's supply of water and lowered the sea levels. As the ice receded, the sea levels rose again until, about 1,000 to 2,000 years ago, Alaska and Siberia were again parted by the waters. Today 56 miles of stormy water separate Siberia's Chukchi Peninsula from the Seward Peninsula of Alaska at a point where the United States and the Soviet Union meet each other most closely. How long the Americas have been inhabited by human beings is simply informed guesswork, but most scientists agree that it has been at least 20,000 years, and possibly 30,000 years. Excavations elsewhere in the Americas have confirmed this approximate date. Perhaps it can be safely stated that, long after humankind had settled the continents of Asia, Africa, Australia, and Europe, America was unknown to any people.

In the last few years American and Soviet scientists have been involved in research which has shown that in the ABO blood-group system the predominant Asian blood type is O, with B also occurring among Asians at a relatively high rate of frequency in recent times. Since these blood groups are determined by separate genes and are not directly affected by the environment, one would expect to find a continuation of the high percentge of the B type east of the Bering Strait all the way to Tierra del Fuego. This is not the case, however. Only small numbers with B-type blood have been found in the recent Native (Eskimo and Aleut), populations on the eastern side of the strait, and practically none occur south of Alaska, where only blood types O and A are found. This suggests that the progenitors of the Indians reached America before the blood type B evolved in Asia and the progenitors of the Eskimos and Aleuts afterward. Still, most genetic and morphological traits reflect the biological affinities of Asians and Native American Indians. Biological evidence suggests that there were several migratory waves across the land bridge.[10]

The first to migrate were those who were later called Indians. Of particular interest are those who eventually settled along the shores of northwestern North America from Yakutat Bay, in southeastern Alaska, to Trinidad Bay, in present northern California. All developed and participated in a unique and rich culture based on the tre-

mendous wealth of the natural resources of their area. These consisted of the five species of Pacific salmon plus halibut, cod, herring, smelt, and the famous oil-rich eulachon, or candlefish, among others. The sea also furnished large quantities of edible mollusks in addition to such marine animals as the hair seal, sea lion, sea otter porpoise, and occasional whales. Land game abounded, and various vegetable foods were easily obtained. Nature provided in abundance what in most other parts of the world people had to work out of the earth through farming and raising livestock. There was, in short, a surplus of foodstuffs which allowed these people much leisure time to devote to the improvement and elaboration of their cultural heritage.

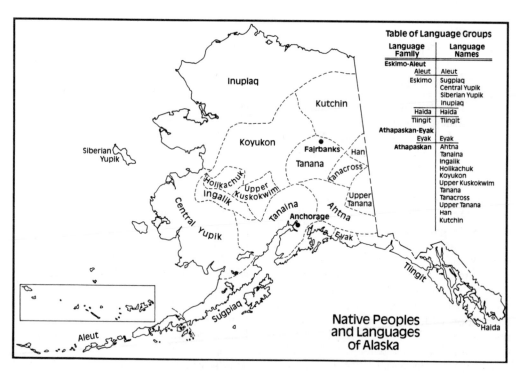

Native peoples and languages of Alaska. Map by Michael E. Krauss, director, Alaska Native Language Center, University of Alaska, Fairbanks.

## THE COASTAL INDIANS

Three distinct native groups—the Tlingits, Haidas, and Tsimshians—occupied an area in Alaska which lies approximately between Yakutat in the north and Prince Rupert in British Columbia in the south. The Tlingits, the most numerous, were scattered throughout the region in many permanent villages. They spoke a language that is believed to be related to the Athapaskan of the interior of the continent. Consisting of some fourteen tribal divisions, the Tlingits had been pressing westward just before making limited contact with the Russians in 1741 and ongoing contact after Captain James Cook's visit in 1777. The Yakutat Tlingits had probably driven the Chugachmiut Eskimos off Kayak Island, and they, or some related tribe, established an outpost among the linguistically related Eyaks at the mouth of the Copper River. Tradition has it that the Tlingits originally migrated north to Alaska from the Skeena River while some Athabaskan-speaking groups, following the Stikine River, moved from the interior to the coast.

The Haidas inhabited the Queen Charlotte Islands and the southern part of Alaska's Prince of Wales Island. Tradition has it that the Alaska Haidas were moving north in the 1700s, in the process driving out some of the Tlingit tribes.

The Tsimshians, divided into three major subdivisions, lived on the mainland and the islands south of southeastern Alaska. Those tribes wintering in villages along Metlakatla Pass near the modern town of Prince Rupert shifted their quarters to Fort Simpson after the Hudson's Bay Company built it in 1834. In 1887 a large group, primarily from Fort Simpson, led by the energetic Anglican missionary William Duncan, moved to Annette Island, in Alaska, after some church-related disagreements.

The Tlingits, Haidas, and Tsimshians shared certain physical characteristics. They were stocky, averaging 5 feet 8 inches in height, and had broad, muscular chests and shoulders; most had broad foreheads and faces and light skin color; their hair was very dark brown and coarse. All three groups had adapted themselves extremely well to coastal life. They used fish traps, nets, and dip nets for fishing, and for both fishing and hunting sea mammals they used harpoons with detachable heads connected to the shaft with a short line. They also used hooks for angling, particularly for cod and halibut. All three groups constructed fine canoes of various sizes for different purposes. For land hunting, the bow and arrow were standard equipment, but snares and deadfalls were used as well.

The Indians used wood as a primary material for most of their manufactures, which were distinguished by fine workmanship and elaborately carved and painted decorations. The cutting blades of their tools were made from stone and shell, while tough, hard, bright-green nephrite stones were used for adze blades. They built large, rectangular, gable-roofed houses in which the individual timbers were carefully joined together, and each house was occupied by several families.

The matrilineal type of organization—in which descent is traced exclusively through the maternal line—was the social framework among the Tlingits, Haidas, and Tsimshians. Each of the Tlingit and Haida tribes had two major moieties (subdivisions), and each individual had to marry a member of the other moiety. In some tribes, such as the Tlingits, the moieties were composed of clans—smaller unilateral social divisions, whose members traced their relationship from a legendary common ancestor.

All these matrilineal societies, however, were built up around lineages consisting of a nucleus of males related through females. They were composed of a group of brothers and some maternal cousins, their sisters'

Sitka Tlingit dancers at a Klukwan potlatch in the early 1900s. Courtesy Historical Photograph Collection, Alaska and Polar Regions Archives, Elmer E. Rasmuson Library, University of Alaska, Fairbanks, Alaska.

sons, and the sons of the sisters of the second generation. This social unit was usually politically independent; it claimed fishing, hunting, and berrying grounds, it had its own houses and chiefs, and it operated socially—and usually ceremonially as well—as an independent unit. It also had its own crest, personal names, and songs and dances for entire ceremonial occasions. Warfare was a well-established practice aimed at driving out or even exterminating another lineage, or family, to acquire its lands and material possessions. These matrilineal societies also separated individuals into levels of status, such as chiefs, nobles, commoners, and slaves. It was a flexible system, however with a good deal of mobility among levels.

Religious belief played an important part in everyday life. The fundamental principles that characterized these religions included a value notion of a disinterested supreme being or beings, the immortality of certain economically important animals together with ritual practices designed to ensure the return of these creatures, and the possibility of lifelong assistance from a personal guardian spirit. But the religions lacked a systematization of beliefs in creation, cosmology, and deities.

The elaborately carved totem poles, actually comparable to crests, are famous. There were several varieties of totems with different functions. Memorial poles were usually erected by the heir of a deceased chief as part of the process of assuming his predecessor's titles and prerogatives. Mortuary poles and house-portal poles were other varieties. All consisted of symbols that belonged to a particular lineage or family and referred to events in its past.[11]

## THE ATHAPASKANS

While the coastal Indians enjoyed nature's bounty, the Athapaskan Indians occupied the difficult and demanding expanse of arctic and subarctic lands stretching across the northern edge of the American continent. This vast area, greatly varied in topography, is not richly endowed with sustenance for life, and the Athapaskans had to search diligently for the resources they needed for survival.

The northern Athapaskans inhabited the drainages of the Yukon River just short of where it empties into the Bering Sea and also those parts of northern Canada drained by the Mackenzie River. Mountainous and for the most part covered by northern coniferous forests, this huge area has great environmental contrasts and many natural barriers between tribal groups. Long, cold winters and short, warm summers characterize the region. The archaeological evidence indicates that the ancestral Athapaskans crossed the Bering Land Bridge into Alaska about 10,000 years ago, near the end of the last great glacial period. As the glaciers receded, some of these people moved east and south through the Yukon Territory and interior British Columbia and on into the present state of Washington.

Though the area occupied by the ancestral Athapaskans initially consisted of treeless tundra, some 8,000 to 10,000 years ago most of central Alaska was covered with spruce forests. The faunal population of this area included moose, caribou, black and grizzly bears, sheep, and a variety of small game and fish.

Unlike the coastal Indians, the Athapaskans had only limited organizational structures within their bands. Anthropologists

A bull moose in the late fall. Courtesy Alaska Department of Fish and Game.

have therefore described northern Athapaskan culture as continuous, carried on by a series of interlocking bands whose lifeways differed in only minor details from those of their immediate neighbors.

The Athapaskans were hunters and gatherers who exhibited considerable resourcefulness. They relied on fish and caribou as the staples for their survival. Depending on the area, they fished for salmon with dip nets and basket-shaped traps; they also caught other fish, such as trout, whitefish, and pike, employing a variety of fishing methods. Caribou, abundant at certain times of the year, were driven between two long, converging rows of wooden sticks that led to a large enclosure of branches, where the hunters had set up snares of partly tanned moose or caribou hide; once caught, the animals were easily killed with bows and arrows. The hunters also employed water drives; driven into a lake or stream, the animals were quickly killed with lances or stabbed with knives. The larger moose were tracked down and shot or sometimes caught in deadfall traps. Bears, wolverines, and smaller fur-bearing animals were also caught in deadfalls, shot with bow and arrows, or captured in rawhide nets. Snares sufficed for hares and ptarmigans (grouse). Spruce hens, ducks, geese, and roots and berries supplemented their diet. Periods of starvation were not uncommon, however, because of the cyclicity of some of the major animal species on which they relied for food.

During the aboriginal period all winter hunting was done on foot, since dogs were not yet used for pulling sledges or toboggans. Snowshoes were therefore important, and many northern Athapaskans made two types. The hunting snowshoes were long and rounded in front for walking over fresh snow, while the travel snowshoes were shorter, with pointed and sharply upturned front ends.

The Tanaina Indians in the Cook Inlet–Susitna River basin were the only Athapaskans who lived on the seacoast. Influenced by their Eskimo neighbors, they became sea-mammal hunters, borrowing the necessary material-culture traits required for coastal life. Their low population density suggests, however, that they never became as skillful as the Eskimos in hunting sea mammals.

The more mobile a particular group of Athapaskans, the simpler its dwellings; conversely, sedentary groups employed more complex forms of construction. The shelter reflected the subsistence activities characteristic not only of particular times of the year but also of climatic variations. Athapaskans of every group built log or pole houses of various sizes covered with animal hides. There were many differences among the dwellings constructed, but all were built with the same basic materials. The more sedentary groups, such as the Ingalik, in the Yukon and Kuskokwim basins, occupied permanent winter villages and summer fishing camps. Living near Eskimos, they built winter houses that closely resembled the semisubterranean earth-covered Eskimo houses of southwestern Alaska.

Most aboriginal northern Athapaskans spent most of the year in small bands consisting of a few nuclear families. If resources permitted, small groups came together and combined into a regional band, to hunt caribou, for example. And although adult males made decisions together, leaders often emerged who attained prestige and influence by demonstrating their superior abilities, particularly as hunters. The northern Athapaskans engaged in both offensive and defensive warfare, often producing a war leader who demonstrated great physical strength. Generally, then, leadership was not hereditary but acquired, and once a leader lost his special abilities, he ceased to exert any influence.

As in all other Alaskan groups, the Athapaskan nuclear family constituted the basic unit of social organization. Furthermore, Athapaskan extended kinship was characterized by the matrilineal sib organization.

An Athapascan woman and child. Courtesy Eva Alvey Richards Collection, Alaska and Polar Regions Archives, Elmer E. Rasmuson Library, University of Alaska.

These sibs were held together by reciprocal social obligations, and a member generally had to find a mate outside his or her sib.

Among many Athapaskans the potlatch was given for a variety of reasons and constituted an important feature of social organization. When someone died, it was given so that the living would socially forget the death, and it also helped assuage grief. It was also given to mark the killing of the first game of each kind by a child; to mark a deed or an unusual accomplishment; to celebrate the return, recovery, or rescue of a relative or friend; and to pay for an offense or a transgression of some rule. A small potlatch could include just the members of the band, but, depending on the wealth of the giver, invitations to a larger potlatch might be sent to other villages. The larger the potlatch, the more ceremonial it was, and the number and quality of the ritual elements were directly related to the amount of wealth expended or the number of guests. The same potlatch could be given for several reasons. Often less wealthy people took advantage of the occasion to give away a few blankets while most of the other expenses were paid by the main host. Two or several men or women might join together to give a potlatch for the same person. The contributions each individual made, like the money given away, the amount of food contributed, and the number and kinds of gifts, were all recorded. Each giver had his or her own pile of blankets or other gifts, and long speeches were made to specify exactly who gave what.

Giving potlatches was also a means of achieving prestige within one's own group as well as in neighboring ones. For example, a man was expected to potlatch at least one and preferably three times before he married. If he aspired to leadership, he had to celebrate whenever possible, and the death of even a distant relative provided an excuse. It was necessary for him to have a sufficient supply of food, rifles, calico, blankets and other items to give away on these occasions. The individual who gave such large potlatches had to give away all the property he owned and could not accept aid from anyone for a year following the ceremony.

James W. VanStone, author and anthropologist with the Field Museum of Natural History, in Chicago, has noted that some authorities believe that the Athapaskans borrowed the potlatch directly from the more elaborate Northwest Indians. The Tlingit influences are apparently obvious in the ceremony as it is performed by the Upper Tanana. Recent studies of Athapaskan culture have revealed that some of these shared elements are common to much of the interior region and to all the western Athapaskan groups. Therefore, it is possible that many of the cultural elements common to the western Athapaskans and the Tlingits may be traits that were part of an earlier cultural level shared by the people of both areas. The western Athaspaskans, however, transformed the potlatch from the community rite it was among the Tlingit and other northwest coast groups to an essentially individualistic one. Perhaps this was related to the limited availability of surplus food.

The Athapaskans' belief in reincarnation in animal form blurred their distinction between animals and human beings and stressed the importance of placating animal spirits to enable the people to continue using the natural environment. The religion of the northen Athapaskans also emphasized individual rather than community rites, because the survival of hunters depended largely on individual skills. Their complex mythology provided answers to most of the questions concerning the origin of the world and man; they lived in a many-spirited world which they believed influenced every aspect of their lives and destinies. Shamans—the individuals with the greatest personal power in the culture—were the only religious practitioners. They used certain magical-religious rites to control the spirit world, prevent and cure disease, bring game to hunters, predict the weather, and foretell the future. In fact, Athapaskan leaders and shamans were coequal but on a different level.

As with other Native Americans, many of the early beliefs and practices that characterized the life cycle of the northern Athapaskan Indians either are no longer carried out or have changed greatly.[12]

## THE ALEUTS

Like other Native groups, the Aleuts adapted themselves superbly to life in the harsh marine environment of the Aleutian Islands. The ancestors of the Aleuts, relatives of the Eskimos, settled on the fog-shrouded and windswept islands nearly 10,000 years ago. They developed a rich culture and secured a well-balanced livelihood from the rich fauna of the sea. But neither their culture nor their livelihood long survived the first European contact, that with the Russians in the 1740s.

The Russian anthropologist Vladimir Jochelson described the Aleutian Islands in 1928:

All of the islands are of volcanic origin, and are covered with high mountains, among which are both active and extinct volcanoes. The shore line is irregular, the rocky mountains sloping abruptly to the sea. The bays are shallow, full of reefs, and dangerous for navigation. The vegetation is luxurious though limited to grasses, berry-bearing shrubs, creeping [plants], and varieties of low willows.

Alpine mosses and lichens covered the mountain slopes, Jochelson wrote, while

in the narrow valleys between the mountain ridges and on the low isthmuses with insufficient drainage are fresh-water lakes with hummocky shores. . . . The absence of arboreal vegetation is due not to climate, which is comparatively mild, but to the constant gales, and to the fogs and mists that are en-

countered in Aleutian waters, and that deprive the plants of much sunlight.

The Aleutian weather is the result of the meeting of the cold waters from the Bering Sea on the north side and the warm Japan Current on the south. "There are only two seasons," wrote Jochelson, "a long autumn and a short, mild winter. Both the incessant winds and gales cause the slightest cold to be felt and, in summer particularly, the constant fogs hide the sun."[13] On the eastern side of the Bering Sea lies the relatively shallow continenal shelf, while on the south the extremely deep Aleutian Trench under the Pacific parallels the islands. The upwelling of nutrients where these shallow Bering Sea and deep Pacific Ocean waters meet creates one of the richest marine environments in the world.

The aboriginal Aleut population has been estimated to have been as much as 15,000 to 25,000, although no exact demographic information exists. Margaret Lantis, an American anthropologist, has concluded that at least 80 percent of the Aleut population was lost in the first two generations of Russian-Aleutian contact: "A few were taken to southeast Alaska and California; most, however, were not merely lost to their homeland, they were totally lost.[14] Smallpox, measles, tuberculosis, venereal diseases, and pneumonia—as well as Russian guns—drastically reduced the Native population to 2,247 in 1834 and to 1,400 in 1848. In 1848 a smallpox epidemic struck, further reducing the number of Aleuts to approximately 900. By 1864, following intermarriage with the Russians, the population had increased to 2,005, but the 1890 census indicated a decline to 1,702 persons, 968 Aleuts and 734 mixed bloods.[15]

The many explorers who visited the Aleutians provided an adequate picture of Aleut home life but told little about the social structure. According to these observers, the typical Aleut house was large and built underground, containing several related nuclear families. Villages were composed of related individuals. Large villages might have as many as four such dwellings occupied at any one time. These were the permanent settlements, usually situated on the northern, Bering Sea side of the island because of the more abundant fish resources and larger supplies of driftwood there. The Aleuts also built seasonal dwellings, and they bathed in the sea to harden themselves against the climate.

Households usually included a man and his wife or wives, older married sons and their families, and sometimes a younger brother and his family. The adolescent sons of the household head were sent to their mother's village to be reared by her older brother or brothers. Women owned their houses. Although anthropologists have been unable to determine the Aleuts' rule of descent, many assume matrilineal descent. Aleuts were generally permissive regarding sexual relations and marriage, but incest was well defined and prohibited.

The Aleuts, living in an ice-free maritime region, developed sophisticated open-sea hunting techniques which enabled them to harvest the sea otter, hair seal, and sea lion and seasonally the migrating fur seals and whales. They encountered walruses only rarely, but different species of whales were especially abundant in the area from Unimak Island eastward to Kodiak, as were fur seals and other sea mammals. Therefore, it was there that most of the population resided.[16]

The Aleuts shared with the southern Eskimos a great number of subsistence tools, such as the two-holed kayak and bone and antler tools, but in place of the toggling harpoon used by the Eskimos for large sea mammals, the Aleuts used a multibarbed harpoon head.[17] The Aleuts also fished for cod and halibut with hook and line. They fastened bone hooks to braided strips of the stalks of giant kelp,

and they caught salmon in nets or traps as the fish ascended the streams to spawn. They derived a major portion of their diet from the shoreline itself. Women, old men, and children shared in the food-gathering activities. They took clams and other mollusks and also consumed huge quantities of green spiny sea urchins. Gathering the sea urchins at low tide, they rubbed off the spines and then broke the shells. Inside were clumps of bright-yellow eggs which they ate raw or steamed. They also ate several species of kelp and seaweed found along the coast.

Birds and their eggs also furnished much food. During the summers millions of birds nest in the Aleutians. The Aleuts hunted cormorants, murres, ducks, geese, loons, ptarmigans, gulls, and several other waterfowl. In fact, more than 140 species of birds are found in the islands, and it is not surprising that the people not only used the birds for their meat and eggs but also utilized their skins for parkas and for decorations. On the ground the Aleuts captured birds in nets or with snares and in flight caught them with bolas. The bola consisted of four to six strings about three feet long and tied together at one end; to the free ends were attached small stones for weight. As a bird flew over, the hunter twirled the bola and threw it into the flock, each string swinging out like a spoke on a wheel. The lines wrapped around the bird and brought it down.

The Aleuts also perfected the art of using the throwing stick, or atlatl, a long, narrow board with one end carved to fit the hand and with a small peg inserted at the other end to hold the butt of the spear shaft. The throwing spear or dart was laid on the board and then thrown. The device extended the length of the arm, thereby giving more power and distance to the cast.

The Aleuts also gathered large amounts of salmonberries, blueberries, crowberries, and roots, which contributed to their diet.

Land animals were not abundant and therefore played a very small part in the people's diet. On Unimak Island and father east along the tip of the Alaska Peninsula, some bear and caribou were killed.

At death the body of a highly honored person, often a whaler, was mummified, and slaves were occasionally killed to show the grief of the principal survivor. Aleut society, according to its eighteenth- and early-nineteenth-century observers, was divided into three classes: honorables, common people, and slaves. Despite the information available, however, the cultural and historical place of the Aleuts among the peoples of their region is still not clearly understood. Anthropologist Lantis observed that the Aleut and Pacific Eskimo cultures were related and that the Aleuts shared with the Tlingits their regard for wealth and status. There may also have been cultural links with various Siberian groups.[18]

It is clear that the Aleuts, over thousands of years, developed a functional society that enabled them to wrest a very adequate living from their difficult environment. The aboriginal culture was threatened with rapid extinction under the Russians; however, individuals as well as parts of the old culture survived, and with the help of the Russian Orthodox church the Aleuts began to develop a new culture.

## THE ESKIMOS

Much has been written about the Eskimos, particularly the Greenland and Canadian Eskimos, because of their adaptations to a far-north arctic environment. But most Alaskan Eskimos did not face the same rigors. They inhabited a great diversity of environments, and, contrary to popular conception, many did not live in a bleak, dark, snow-driven landscape in igloos (snow houses), eating only blubber and muktuk (whale fat and skin).

Today many experts agree that the Arctic-Mongoloid peoples arrived in the Bering Sea area approximately 10,000 years ago. They were the progenitors of the Eskimos and the Aleuts as well as of various Paleo-Siberian groups.[19] Eskimo culture developed in western Alaska, and it was also in Alaska that the division into Eskimo and Aleut stocks occurred. In time the Eskimos developed techniques that allowed them to exploit the arctic seas. The so-called arctic small-tool tradition represents the technological base for Eskimo culture in Greenland and Canada. Reaching back to Siberia, it crystallized in Alaska and spread across the Arctic from Alaska to Greenland about 4,000 years ago.

Proto-Eskimo is the ancestor of all Eskimo languages. About 2,000 years ago the proto-Yupik and proto-Inupik languages replaced all intermediate dialects. Eventually the Alaskan Yupik speakers became separated from Siberia when Inupik speakers occupied the Seward Peninsula, and in time the Yupik languages developed into Sugpik Aleut and Central and Siberian Yupik.[20] Throughout prehistoric times there were countless and mostly unknowable population shifts within the area. It follows that known Alaskan Native groups were the latest wave of perhaps hundreds or even thousands of groups that occupied the area at one time or another from prehistoric times onward. In historic times, for example, Eskimos were extending their control inland along rivers flowing into the Bering Sea and the western Arctic Ocean and in the process acculturating and assimilating Indian groups. On the southern fringe, however, the Aleuts successfully encroached on the peninsular Eskimos from the west.

Unfortunately, original Eskimo culture no longer exists. Anthropologists have painstakingly tried to reconstruct it and have pointed out that Eskimos and Aleuts form a cultural unit. The Danish anthropologist Kaj Birket-Smith pointed out that one of the most characteristic features of Eskimo culture is the difference that existed in some

An aerial view of ancient arctic house sites on the beach at Cape Krusenstern National Monument. Photograph by Keith Trexler. Courtesy U.S. National Park Service.

basic points between the Aleuts and Pacific Eskimos on the one hand and all remaining groups on the other; the inhabitants of Bristol Bay and the Yukon-Kuskokwim Delta occupied an intermediate position. This difference expressed itself in articles of clothing, in the shape of the blubber lamp, in the preference for the spear instead of the harpoon for whaling, and in the mummification of bodies, which were interred in caves in a crouched position. In fact, the Yukon formed a cultural dividing line.[21] So far this dualism in Eskimo culture has not been explained satisfactorily.

There were other differences as well. For example, the Central Eskimo culture in arctic Canada occupied a special position in relationship to the Western and Eastern Eskimos—in Alaska and Greenland, re-

spectively. In the coastal areas and Arctic Archipelago between Alaska and Greenland which form the central regions, certain cultural elements were lacking which were present in the western and eastern parts of the Eskimo area. These include the umiak (a large skin boat), the seal net, and gutskin frocks. They were found rarely in the central regions, and then in a modified form. Other elements were widely disseminated, particularly throughout the central area; examples are the special tools used for harpooning seals through breathing holes in the ice.[22]

From Alaska's north coast to Greenland the Eskimos hunted large sea mammals— whales, walruses, and seals. There were, however, some small groups whose lifeways had a markedly inland character and for

A-Pa-Look and Wy-Ung-Ena, Cape Douglas, Alaska. The two were married at Teller, Alaska, on April 10, 1905. They have traditional facial decorations: he has labret scars just below his lips, and she has tattoo marks on her chin. Her parka is made of reindeer or caribou skin, while his is made of ground-squirrel skins. Both parkas have wolverine-fur ruffs. Photograph by F. H. Nowell. Courtesy Smithsonian Office of Anthropology.

whom caribou hunting provided the mainstay of their existence. These groups included the Caribou Eskimos in the Barren Grounds west of Hudson Bay and smaller groups along the Colville and Noatak rivers in northern Alaska and in the Yukon-Kuskokwim Delta. In addition, certain Eskimo cultural features were the result of varying degrees of influence of Indian and Siberian peoples. In return the Eskimos influenced other groups.[23]

Despite these differences, recent Inupik Eskimo culture was fairly uniform. This came about when, about 1,000 years ago, the Thule culture spread from Alaska all the way to Greenland, in the process unifying Inupik Eskimo culture. The Thule culture Eskimos were a maritime people. Experts considered it to be essentially a prehistoric culture of Alaskan origin that had disappeared from the Central Canadian Arctic, to be replaced by that of the modern Central Eskimo. Anthropologist James W. VanStone showed that the modern Central Eskimo culture probably was a direct outgrowth of Thule.[24]

Eskimo social life centered around the nuclear family as the primary unit. But in a culture with an overwhelming emphasis on subsistence activities, men were obligated not only to their households and kindred but also to voluntary associations such as organized whale-hunting crews. Among the Yupiks the *kashgees* (ceremonial houses for men) were very important in the individual lives of all males; consequently, the *kashgees* were patricentric, while the households were matricentric. Adult males taught traditional skills to the boys in the *kashgee*, while mothers taught their daughters in the homes. Most marriages took place within the community.

Physical survival depended on the hunters' ability to take game and fish. These animals therefore occupied an important place in tribal religions, and Eskimo supernaturalism was based to a great extent on charms that aided individuals. More complex, but still individually based, were the family charms passed down a patrilineal line among some groups and, among Pacific Eskimos, the knowledge required to hunt whales. There were also many taboos, such as the prohibition against combining land and sea products; the Bering Sea Eskimos, for example, developed an intense

involvement with the species taken. The so-called bladder feast was the most complex of the various cults and focused primarily on the seals. The arctic hunters and fishermen, on the other hand, did not develop rituals as complex as those of the Bering Sea peoples or the whalers.

In short, Eskimos displayed many traits that were also found among other peoples In Alaska the term Eskimo therefore stands for much subcultural diversiy. Like other aboriginal inhabitants of Alaska, the Eskimos evolved ingenious and highly flexible techniques and lifeways which enabled them to live in a rugged arctic and subarctic environment.

Little is known about the early migrants who traveled eastward across the Bering Land Bridge from Asia in prehistoric times. Evidence of human occupation in Alaska is not as ancient as elsewhere on the American continent and dates back only about 12,000 years. More than 2,700 archaeological sites have been identified in Alaska, but

Inupiak Eskimo walrus or whale hunters in a umiak, about 1908. Courtesy Lusk Album, Alaska and Polar Regions Archives, Elmer E. Rasmuson Library, University of Alaska.

Pacific walrus hauled out on an ice floe. Courtesy Alaska Department of Fish and Game.

the age of only a few of them has been determined because of the high cost of fieldwork and analysis in these remote regions.[25]

What is clear is that Alaska's Eskimos, Indians, and Aleuts developed widely varying lifeways that were superbly adapted to their respective environments. Living in harmony with the land and seas, they flourished, despite occasional famines among various groups brought about by the cyclicity of game animals, until they encountered the industrial and technological culture of the Caucasians. A long decline ensued, and today only fragments of their once rich cultures remain.

# 2. THE EARLY RUSSIAN PERIOD

Alaska appeared on the world scene rather late. At the beginning of the eighteenth century the North Pacific was the least-known area of the world. Perhaps because of its remoteness, Alaska early developed that mystique that breeds legend. One legend holds that a Russian settlement was established as early as the seventeenth century. In 1648 the Siberian explorer Semyon Ivanov Dezhnyev headed an expedition which was to sail for the Anadyr River, but one or more of his boats were blown off course and carried to Alaska.[1] There is no evidence, however, of such a settlement or settlements. It was the Danish navigator Vitus Bering, serving Russia, who made Alaska known to the world on his historic voyage in 1741.

Following Bering, Russian influence in Alaska was felt in varying degrees, but at no time was there ever more than a fraction of the Native population or land under Russian control. Those Russians who came were mainly private individuals interested in the fur trade. Few settled permanently. They, more than the frequently unstable Russian government, gave Russian America its unique character.

Bering's voyage was the culmination of a great Russian eastward expansion. With little government assistance, Russian fur hunters—the *promýshlenniki*—had gradually penetrated Siberia and brought a great territory under control. Since Russia had been the first European state to establish herself on the Pacific, it is not suprising that her crews and not those of the more advanced naval powers, England or France, were the first to come to Alaska. At the time of Bering's expedition Russia was still feeling the effects of changes initiated by the explorer's first sponsor, Czar Peter the Great.

## PETER THE GREAT'S INTEREST IN EXPLORATION

When Peter and his half brother, Ivan V, came to the throne as corulers of Russia in 1682, many Europeans viewed Russia as a backwater of civilization inhabited by a people more Asiatic than Western. Its ruler was absolute, the administration of the government and judicial system was haphazard, and the armed forces reportedly were undisciplined. In contrast to the population of the West, where serfdom had almost died out, over half of the Russian population was in a state of bondage. Historians have given various explanations for Russia's differences from the West: her heritage was Byzantine, not Roman; her Christianity had been imported from Constantinople; the subsequent Tatar invasion and conquest had shut Russia off from the West for two centuries and stunted her development; and she had not experienced either the Renaissance or the Reformation.

Even before his reign Peter had experienced some Western influence. His interest in the West had been stimulated through contact with foreigners in what the Russians called the "German quarter" of Moscow. From them he had learned that Europeans looked on Russia as inferior in its development and regarded the Russian people as almost barbarians. After coming of age and assuming personal rule, Peter traveled to the West to see for himself. His journeys took him to England, Holland, Prussia, and the Hapsburg Empire. Much impressed, Peter was convinced that Russia must modernize—that change was absolutely essential if she was to survive as an independent state, let alone become a great power.

Some of the ways Peter chose to achieve his goal of making Russia a great power kept the country in a constant state of turmoil throughout his reign. With the exception of a single year, from 1719 to 1720, the nation was at war. In his haste to reform Russia, Peter resorted to a number of what today are called "crash programs," which frequently conflicted with each other. Although Peter's personal inclinations were not directed toward cultural affairs, he nevertheless became a patron of the arts and literature because he believed that the Russians must first learn to think and act like Westerners before they could master the superior political, technological, and military skills of the West. He ordered the people to wear Western clothing even though the Russian long coats gave much better protection during the severe Russian winters than did the shorter ones worn in milder climates. Westerners were brought in not only to train Russian soldiers but also to teach etiquette and table manners to the nobility, who were also encouraged to hold soirees.

Peter did not care a whit whether his edicts violated the most sacred of Russian traditions and beliefs. He abolished the office of patriarch and placed the Orthodox church under the control of a civil official. Russian men were told that they must shave, though to the devout this was tantamount to committing sacrilege, for all their icons showed the Deity wearing a beard. Saint Petersburg was built as a Western City, replacing Moscow, the symbol of Holy Russia, as the capital of the country.

Peter's role and influence in Russia have aroused bitter controversy. To his admirers he was the founder of modern Russia and the architect of its greatness. His critics point out that his reforms were not well planned and that they bore most heavily upon the poor, serfdom having increased during his reign. Peter's rule, it was said, left Russia more divided than ever.

The controversy concerning Peter extended to his sponsorship of the Bering expedition. According to the traditional view, Peter was motivated primarily by scientific interest. He had brought together at Saint Petersburg a nucleus of scholars to form the Academy of Sciences. From them and from other savants whom he encountered in his travels abroad he learned that the North Pacific, which touched upon his realm, was the least-known area of the world. He readily fell in with the suggestions that he outfit a voyage of exploration to determine the relationship of America to Asia. One of the goals was to discover whether the two continents were separated from each other or joined; another was to find a waterway, if one existed, from the Arctic to the Pacific.[2]

This traditional interpretation has been challenged in recent years by both American and Soviet scholars. Peter's instruction to Bering, they point out, clearly stated that he wanted the expedition to sail to America. Bering was told to go to Kamchatka, there to build one or two decked ships, and to sail "along the land which goes to the north," which, "according to expectation (because its end is not known), that land, it appears, is part of Ameica." Once having reached the place "where it is joined with America," the directive continued, Bering was "to go to any city of European possession" or if he saw "any European vessel to find out from it what the coast is called and to write it down and to go ashore . . . and obtain first-hand information, and placing it on a map, . . . return here." Nowhere was there any suggestion that the explorers should seek to resolve the relationship of America to Asia or to find an Arctic–Pacific passage.[3]

In characteristic fashion Peter simply ordered Bering to journey to Kamchatka and there to build the ship or ships that were to sail to America. Nowhere did he suggest how this was to be done or mention the obstacles involved. Peter died soon afterward, in January, 1725. His widow and successor, Catherine I, gave her blessing and support to her husband's project.

## BERING'S VOYAGES—ALASKA DISCOVERED

To reach Kamchatka, the great Siberian peninsula on the Pacific, which had finally been brought under control in 1697 and was still largely unexplored, Bering and his men had to travel across Siberia to Okhotsk, and from there across the Sea of Okhotsk. Okhotsk, their immediate goal, was a mere hamlet about 5,000 miles from Saint Petersburg. Neither this village nor any other place in Siberia had facilities for shipbuilding; Bering had to bring with him the skilled workers, equipment, and supplies for the job. They were literally trailblazers. In winter dog sleds provided the main source of transportation. Whenever possible they utilized waterways, the men constructing their own boats.

More than a year elapsed before all the men (who had been divided into three

groups for the arduous journey) finally arrived at Okhotsk. There they built a craft to carry them across the sea to Bolsheretsk, a tiny port on the west coast of Kamchatka. Kamchadals, as the Natives of Kamchatka were called, were pressed into service to carry the supplies and equipment five hundred miles to a site on the Pacific near the mouth of the Kamchatka River. There Bering's men built a sailing vessel, the *Gabriel*, to take them on their Pacific voyage.

In July, 1728, the *Gabriel* started northward on its course, keeping close to the shore. After sighting Saint Lawrence Island, the ship passed through the strait that now bears Bering's name. On August 16, after reaching north latitude 67°18′, Bering turned back, fearing that the ship would be trapped by ice if it advanced any farther. He further justified his decision to return by claiming that he had endeavored to comply with Peter's directives to go to the place where America and Asia were joined but had become convinced as a result of his observations that the two continents were separate. The seamen could no longer see land to the north and had already passed the point where the Asiatic coast disappeared from view to the west, while to the east there was not a glimpse of land.[4]

On the return voyage poor weather conditions in the strait limited visibility and prevented confirmation of Bering's observations. On September 2 they were back at Kamchatka, never having reached America. The following spring the *Gabriel* was blown off course during another attempt to reach America, as a result of which Bering accidentally discovered the southern boundary of Kamchatka, thus enabling the men to sail directly back to Okhotsk and avoid a land journey across the peninsula.

When Bering returned to Saint Petersburg on March 1, 1730, Russia had a new ruler—the third in five years—the empress Anna. A daughter of Ivan V, she had been forced by the nobility to accept severe limitations on her authority as the price for their recognition of her right to the throne. Within two years the power of the nobility had been broken, but Anna, unlike Peter a passive ruler, generally followed the advice of others and did not exert leadership.

Bering was absolutely convinced that America lay close to Kamchatka. In his written petition to the Admiralty College asking its members to support his request for financial aid in organizing a new expedition, he explained his reasons for thinking as he did, citing evidence obtained from observations made during the first voyage. As the ship had sailed eastward from the Kamchatka Peninsula, he pointed out, the ocean waves were lower, indicating a proximity to land, while the pine trees thrown ashore on the not too distant Karagin Island were of a different species than those to be found on Kamchatka. From this he concluded that the American mainland or nearby islands were only 150 to 200 miles away. There was no question but that the enterprise, if approved, would be successful.[5]

Bering was aware that successful exploration involved more than merely outfitting a ship. In his proposal he dwelled on the need to strengthen the Russian position in eastern Siberia so that it would be freed from the threat of attack by Natives, and he emphasized that Kamchatka and Okhotsk must become less dependent upon faraway European centers for supplies and personnel. He urged that steps be taken so that the iron, timber, and other natural resources used in shipbuilding could be produced locally. His suggestions called for settling skilled artisans in the region, supporting agriculture and cattle raising to provide food for a growing population, building the facilities needed to make Okhotsk a real port, and giving more attention to the improvement of transportation.[6]

After some discussion Bering received a favorable reply to his proposals. Although a report of the Admiralty College had

termed his findings that America and Asia were separate as having been based on inconclusive evidence, the government, nevertheless, thought well enough of his work to promote him to the rank of captain commander and to give him a reward of 1,000 rubles. Bering had the powerful support of three prominent officials of Anne's government in his campaign to secure aid for his project. They were Andrei Osterman, the most outstanding member in the empress's cabinet of ministers; Count Nikolai F. Golovin, of the Admiralty College, who became its president in 1733; and Ivan K. Kirilov, the senior secretary of the Administrative Senate. All "had risen to positions of influence and authority under Peter" and were apparently interested in carrying out the late czar's ideas.[7] In 1733, Bering was appointed the administrative head of a great expedition to coordinate the work of scientists, explorers, scholars, and government officials engaged in a wide variety of activities with different objectives, some of which had been proposed by Bering and others by the Russian Senate. The task of one group was to explore and map the arctic coast. Another, under the leadership of the scientists Gerhard Müller and Johann Gore, was to undertake a thorough reconnaissance of Siberia by studying its plant and animal life as well as the customs, language, and folklore of the people. Martin Spanberg was directed to sail to Japan and there establish trade relations. Bering's special assignment was, as he desired, the exploration of the American coast.

Almost a year was spent in assembling the men and in securing the necessary supplies. Bering had to devote most of his attention to housing and feeding the men and their camp followers, soothing ruffled feelings, and mediating quarrels. He received little cooperation from officials in Siberia. Little had been done, despite his recommendations, to improve the conditions of travel to Okhotsk. Bering had greatly underestimated the costs of the expedition, and each request for additional funds resulted in angry retorts that money was being squandered recklessly with no visible results. Finally, after Spanberg's departure for Japan, Bering and his men were able to leave for Okhotsk in 1737 to begin the work of building oceangoing vessels, which were completed in the summer of 1740.

After wintering in Kamchatka at Avacha Bay, the two ships set sail into the Pacific from the port of Petropavlovsk on June 4, 1741. Each had several scientists on board. Bering himself commanded the *Saint Peter* with seventy-five men on board, and Aleksey Chirikov the *Saint Paul* with a complement of seventy-six men. Desipte the efforts of their captains to maintain close contact, on June 20, the two vessels became separated.

The honor of the discovery of Alaska on the voyage properly belongs to Chirikov and his men, who sighted land on July 15 at what is believed to be the Prince of Wales Island in the Alexander Archipelago. Bering's ship, which had sailed in a more northerly direction, came upon Kayak Isand the next day. He named the great mountain that could be seen in the distance Saint Elias in honor of the saint whose day it was.

Throughout the voyage the crews of both ships suffered severely from scurvy. When near the mainland Chirikov sent one of his small boats ashore to get fresh water. When the men did not return, the remaining boat was sent in search of them, and it too disappeared. After spending several days in a vain effort to find them, Chirikov gave the command to return to Kamchatka and arrived at Petropavlovsk on October 8. Several of his men perished from scurvy on the journey back to Kamchatka. Chirikov himself never recovered from the effects of the voyage and died of tuberculosis not long after his return to Russia.

Meanwhile, on board the *Saint Peter,* Georg Wilhelm Steller, the ship's surgeon, a noted German scientist, persuaded Bering to allow him to go ashore on Kayak Island to look for antiscorbutic plants to help alleviate the misery of those suffering from scurvy. Steller had barely obtained some native artifacts, gathered specimens of a few plants, and captured a few birds before Bering, a nonscientist who looked on such activities as a waste of time, ordered him to return immediately to the ship or be left behind. Steller's rejoinder was that the expedition had apparently been planned "merely to carry some water from America to Asia," since "10 years of preparation" had led to but "10 hours of exploration."

Bering's men suffered greater hardships than Chirikov's had: the *Saint Peter,* beset by storms and fog, was wrecked on one of the Komandorskiye Islands, which lie just east of Kamchatka. Bering, who had mistakenly believed that he had reached Kamchatka, died on the island (which now bears his name). Several of his men also perished. The survivors, including Steller, wintered on Bering Island and kept alive by eating fish, sea cows, and seals. In the spring of 1742 they managed to build a crude forty-foot ship out of timber from the *Saint Peter's* wreckage and made their way back to Kamchatka in September.

The survivors of the *Saint Peter* and the *Saint Paul* who returned to Saint Petersburg over the next few years found a new ruler on the throne of Russia. Elizabeth Petrovna, the daughter of Peter the Great, had become empress after a palace revolution in 1741 in which the infant Ivan VI had been dethroned. Although she did much to make Saint Petersburg a modern city, Elizabeth tended to be indolent and less concerned with matters of state than with her personal appearance (she was said to possess 15,000 dresses). Neither she nor her advisers were much interested in the American discoveries. They directed that Russia's energies be spent in the European power struggle (the War of the Austrian Succession) being waged on the Continent. Since the country had a small population and possessed the vast territory of Siberia, even less populated, overseas colonies were unnecessary.

Except for issuing a directive that the Natives pay a tax called the *yasak* (a tribute in
furs) and that they be well treated, Elizabeth's government virtually ignored Alaska.

## THE FUR TRADE AND
## INTERNATIONAL RIVALRIES

For most of the next half century the rulers
of Russia showed little interest in Alaskan
affairs. The Russians who ventured to
Alaska were private individuals lured on by
the profits to be made in the fur trade.
When Bering's survivors returned to Russia,
they took with them the pelts of animals,
notably the sea otter, one of the finest fur-
bearing animals. A ready market developed
for their skins, especially in China. Russian
wholesale merchants, limited to trading
with China only through the town of
Kyakhta, on the Mongolian border, were
there able to turn a tidy profit on their furs.

Sergeant Yemelyan Basov, of the Okhotsk
detachment, who made voyages in 1743
and 1748, was the first Russian to exploit
the furs of the Aleutian Islands. Following
him, Russian fur merchants sent men and
ships to the islands to procure the animals.
The Russian fur hunters, or *promýshlenniki,* quickly made themselves masters of
the islands. A rough, hard-drinking lot,
many of them illiterate, quarrelsome among
themselves, unrestrained by either government or their leaders, they made virtual
slaves of the Aleuts. The Aleut men were
forced to do the hunting while the Russians
dallied with the women. On several occasions the Aleuts tried to revolt, and these attempts were repressed, sometimes with
great cruelty. Later writers, while acknowl-
edging that atrocities were committed,
claim that the numbers have been exaggerated and point out that "the Russians
lacked the weaponry to effect the mass
murder attributed to them in popular
literature."[8]

Russian penetration of the Aleutians

roughly followed a pattern of exploiting one
group of islands of the chain until the supply of animals became exhausted and then
moving eastward to the next group, eventually reaching the mainland. As the distance from Kamchatka increased, the cost
of operations went up, making it difficult
for the smaller companies to survive. By
1770 a few merchants— Grigory Ivanovich
Shelikhov, Pavel Sergeyevich Lebedev-
Lastochkin, and G. Panov—dominated the
Aleutian fur trade.

These changes in the nature of the business enterprise were accompanied by increasing government awareness of the region. Elizabeth died on Christmas Day,
1762. The rule of her nephew and successor, Peter III, was brief. Within a year of
his accession his wife, Catherine II, a member of a German noble family, organized a
coup d'etat and had herself installed as sovereign of Russia. Far more enterprising
than Elizabeth, Catherine was steeped in
the writings of the Enlightenment and
corresponded with some of its leaders—
Voltaire, Diderot, and d'Alembert. She devoted much of her time to government business and proclaimed her intention of being
an enlightened ruler, but she brought about
little reform; serfdom in Russian actually
increased during her reign. She issued directives demanding better care and treatment of the Aleuts but provided no means
of enforcing her decrees except that the fur
tax imposed on the Natives was finally terminated in 1769. Catherine was interested
in building up the Russian navy, which had
declined after Peter's death, but its strength
was focused in European waters. Navy men
were ordered to give help to Russians in the
Aleutians but to give it surreptitiously.
Catherine had no desire to involve Russia in
a conflict with others powers by openly an-
nexing territories in the Pacific.[9]

Russian activities in the North did not
pass unnoticed, however. Spain, in particular, was aroused. Ever since 1493 she had

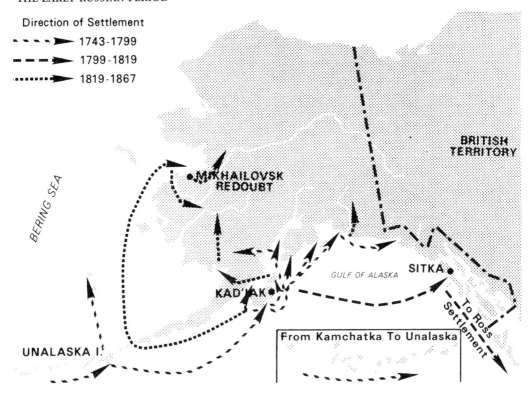

Direction of Settlement
- ▸ 1743-1799
- ▸ 1799-1819
- ▸ 1819-1867

BRITISH TERRITORY

BERING SEA

•MIKHAILOVSK REDOUBT

GULF OF ALASKA

SITKA•

KAD'AK•

To Ross Settlement

From Kamchatka To Unalaska

UNALASKA I.

Routes and times of settlement of Alaska by the Russians. From Svetlana G. Fedorova, *The Russian Population in Alaska and California: Late 18th Century–1867*, trans. and ed. Richard A. Pierce and Alton S. Donnelly (Kingston, Ont.: Limestone Press, 1973), p. 109. Reproduced by permission.

laid claim to all the territory on the Pacific, a right recognized by the pope and confirmed in 1494 by the Treaty of Tordesillas with Portugal, the other great exploring nation of the time. Spain, which had no settlements on the Pacific Coast north of Mexico, was stirred to action in the 1760s by an apparent fear of Russian expansion southward. Alta California, which the Spaniards had talked of settling for two centuries, was now occupied by José Gálvez, whom King Charles III of Spain had commissioned to inspect the Viceroyalty of New Spain. Galvez made use of the alleged Russian menace to the Spanish possessions in the south to win royal support for establishing presidios at San Diego and Monterey and for founding other California settlements. Meanwhile, the viceroy of Mexico sent expeditions to Alaska in 1774, 1777, 1778, and 1790 to see what the Russians were doing and, perhaps, to take possession of the territory for Spain, but the Spaniards were unable to hold any Alaska territory. Spanish power had been declining for more than a century. In a controversey that developed with England after a Spanish sea captain seized an English settlement on Vancouver Island at Nootka Sound, the Spaniards not only gave up possession but also acknowledged that the nationals of other states had the right to trade in the Pacific. Apart from giving a few place names to Alaska—e.g., Bucareli, Valdez, Cordova, Revillagigedo, and Malaspina—the Spaniards made no impact.

Concurrently with the Spanish expeditions, the British, French, and Americans also explored Alaska, but they did not make any serious effort to acquire any territory. Captain James Cook sailed north in 1776 intent upon finding a passage from the Pacific to the Atlantic, leading some Russians to fear that his real interest lay in making territorial claims, but this fear proved groundless.[10] Interested primarily in gathering knowledge, Cook visited the Aleutians, there exchanging information with the Russians, and mapped the Alaskan coast, a work which became the standard guide for over a century. Cook sailed from Alaska with sea-otter pelts obtained from the Natives, and although he was killed on Hawaii in 1779, his men proceeded under the leadership of Captain Charles Clerke to sail to Canton, where they sold the pelts at fabulous prices. Subsequently, Britain's interest in Alaska centered on trade, and British fur traders continued their activities despite the efforts of the Russians to keep them out. Like the Spaniards, the British contributed place names to Alaska—Cook Inlet, Prince William Sound, Prince of Wales Island, and Bristol Bay, among others. The French sent one expedition to Alaska in 1785 under the ill-fated Comte de La Pérouse (Jean-François de Galaup), killed on his way home in 1788, but further interest in Alaska was cut short by the outbreak of the French Revolution in 1789. That same year saw the initial voyage to Alaska of the Americans, who were to rival the British in the fur trade.

Catherine, called upon by some of her subjects to let these nations know of Russia's might in the North Pacific, responded by sanctioning two expeditions, both of which proved fruitless. Under the command of Joseph Billings, an Englishman in Russia's service who had sailed with Captain Cook, the expedition was sent to find new islands east of Unimak and bring "newly discovered people" under Russian control by "kind persuasion," but the results of his voyage were apparently of little consequence.[11] The other and more ambitious expedition, in which Captain G. I. Mulovsky would sail from the Baltic around Africa and eastward to the Pacific, proposed to annex the coastal areas of North America above 55° north latitude.[12] Russia, however, became involved in a war with the Ottoman Porte before Mulovsky sailed, and his expedition was canceled.

## FUR MERCHANT GRIGORY SHELIKHOV

The Russian companies engaged in the fur trade in Alaska had become increasingly disturbed by the foreign competition. They especially feared the British, who could offer the Natives better and cheaper goods than the Russians'. Among the Russian merchants was Grigory Ivanovich Shelikhov, a Siberian resident. He and his partner, Ivan Golikov, set up a special company and used the money they raised to build several ships, whereupon Shelikhov set sail for the Aleutians. Among the passengers was his wife, Natalya, reportedly the first white women to arrive in Alaska.

Shelikhov, his wife, and a party of 192 men proceeded from the Aleutians to Kodiak Island in 1784 and made a settlement on the northeast end of the island at Three Saints Bay on August 3. The Eskimos, a people more warlike than the Aleuts, first left them in peace, but later in August they grew suspicious of the designs of the newcomers and decided to attack. Shelikhov, however, struck the first blow. He ordered the bombardment of the rock where the Natives had gathered and frightened them into submission. He thus succeeded at Three Saints Bay in establishing the first permanent Russian settlement, a move that he considered necessary to strengthen the Russians against foreign competition.[13]

In 1788 he and Golikov went to Saint

Petersburg, where he pleaded in a letter to Catherine to be given a monopoly of the fur trade. He argued that only a single powerful Russian company could resist the inroads of the British and Americans and end their reckless competition, which was causing a very serious depletion of fur-bearing animals. He asked Catherine to approve a loan of 200,000 rubles to the company and to send a detachment of one hundred men to Kodiak and Afognak islands. Catherine was not convinced, and feared that a single strong company, intent on combating the foreigners, would involve Russia far more deeply in Pacific affairs than she cared to risk. Russia's wars with Turkey and Sweden were straining the government's resources. She informed Shelikhov that she was opposed to monopolies and believed in free trade and advised the merchants that they would have to "carry on their trade with the savage North American peoples at their own expense." But in appreciation of Shelikhov's and Golikov's services, the empress bestowed gold medals and silver sabers on the partners and presented them with citations.[14]

By 1786, Grigory Shelikhov could point with pride to his accomplishments in America. He had become the leading fur merchant there, holding shares in the rival Lebedev-Lastochkin Company a well as the controlling interest in his own organization. While a poet's allusion to him as a Russian Columbus has a hollow sound, since he was no seaman and not much of an explorer, with his settlement on Kodiak the Russian occupation of America had taken on an air of permanency. On his departure from Alaska in May, 1786, he left a pacified Kodiak. He entrusted the management of the enterprise first to the Cossack Konstantin Alekseyevich Samoilov and then to Yevstraty Ivanovich ("The Greek") Delarov, a seafarer and agent of the Golikov-Shelikhov Company, until he finally found the man he wanted—Aleksandr Andreyevich Baranov, a Siberian fur merchant.

Aleksandr Andreyevich Baranov. Courtesy Historical Photograph Collection, Alaska and Polar Regions Archives, Elmer E. Rasmuson Library, University of Alaska.

## THE BARANOV ERA

Baranov is probably the outstanding personality of Russian America. His long tenure first as manager of the Golikov-Shelikhov enterprise and later as head of the Russian-American Company has been fittingly called the "Baranov era." He had little formal education and was neither by training nor by inclination an administrator. He had no ambition to be an explorer or a colonizer, though he did a little of both. He was first and foremost a businessman whose main objective was to make a profit for his employer.

Shelikhov had met Baranov, a Siberian fur merchant in Okhotsk, and had asked him several times to become manager of his company in America, but each time Baranov found reasons why he could not accept. Baranov was born in Kargopol, near the Finnish border, the son of a small trader in a country where rank counted for much. He was short and slight of build. At the age of thirty-three he moved to Siberia, leaving behind in Russia a wife and a daughter, neither of whom he ever saw again. It was only after suffering severe financial losses that he agreed, in 1790, to work for Shelikhov, and then for a period of only five years. The journey itself was enough to discourge a lesser man, for he became ill en route and later was shipwrecked on Unalaska, an island of the Aleutian chain, before finally arriving in Kodiak in 1791, having completed his journey in a skin boat called a *baidara*.

By 1790 the initial phase of the Russian era in Alaska was coming to an end. The large Russian companies had displaced the small traders, were spread over a much larger area, and were becoming increasingly better organized. Russian America was then very vaguely defined, with scattered settlements isolated from each other; the largest, on Kodiak Island, was an unprepossessing village. The Lebedev-Lastochkin Company had agents on Cook Inlet and controlled the Pribilof Islands, with their valuable seal rookeries, while other Russians were operating in the Aleutians. Disputes among the rival companies were frequent, and with no existing government agency to resolve their differences, violence sometimes erupted. On one thing all Russians were in agreement: foreign competition had to be curtailed. Not only did the Americans (whom the Russians called "the Boston men") and the British have better and cheaper goods to sell, but also they were not burdened with maintaining costly settlements. What was much worse, they sold arms to the Natives. The Russian residents feared that these weapons might be used against them.

In coming to America, Baranov found that he not only had unfriendly neighbors to deal with but also faced a formidable task in meeting the problems of life on Kodiak. Not long after his arrival he moved the settlement from Three Saints Bay to Pavlovsk, on the northern side of the island, which had a better harbor and an abundance of forests to facilitate the construction of necessary buildings and fortifications. Relocating the site was an easy job compared to obtaining the commodities needed to exist. Much of the food and almost all finished goods had to be imported. Shelikhov made many promises to send supplies, but the fault was not entirely his that these were not readily forthcoming. Russian ships sailing to America were few and far between. Since Siberia had so little to offer, most of the vessels sailed from the Baltic on a voyage that was long, difficult, and expensive. To add to the difficulties, there were few trained Russian navigators, and the number of ships lost because of their inexperience was high.[15]

Supply was a problem that was to plague the Russians almost throughout their tenure in America. Baranov's solution was to trade with the foreigners, although he was forbidden to do so. He realized that the British, and especially the Americans, his hated business rivals, were the only ones able to furnish him with the goods he needed, and they demanded that he sell them furs in return. To lessen his dependence on them, Baranov secured the services of an experienced English ship builder, James Shields, to construct a vessel for his company. The work was done on the mainland on Resurrection Bay, where the quality of timber was adequate. Since many materials needed were unavailable, substitutions (not always of the best quality) were liberally made. When finished, the *Phoenix*, as the vessel was called, was used mainly in American waters, but it did make two voyages to Siberia before it sank in the vicinity of the Aleutian Islands. For Baranov the chief value of the *Phoenix* may have been symbolic, a demonstration of what could be accomplished in the colony.

Labor was also a key problem throughout the Russian period. Russian America never had enough workers, skilled or unskilled, for shipbuilding, taking care of the various tasks of the colony, or providing the proper defense. With serfdom an ever-present factor, few Russians were free to emigrate. Many of those who went to America were illiterate, a few were convicts who had been promised freedom, and more than one man crossed the ocean unwillingly; agents of the company, stationed on Okhotsk, were alleged to have waited outside tavern doors to seize the unwary who had had too much to drink and who, upon awakening the next morning, might find themselves on a ship bound for the New World. And newly arrived workers quickly found that life in Alaska had its drawbacks. The men's quarters were primitive, and their diet consisted mainly of dried fish, supplemented in summer with vegetables and occasional fresh meat when the hunters were lucky. Tea and sugar were luxuries dependent on the arrival of ships. Grain for bread making was frequently unavailable. Each worker signed a contract of employment to stay for seven years and was given a share in the company's stock, his income being dependent on the profits realized. The cost of living was high, and when accounts were settled at the end of the contract, many found that they had spent more than they had earned. Those in debt had no alternative but to sign up for another seven-year term.

Baranov had perceived from the moment of his arrival in 1791 that he was very much on trial. His predecessor, Delarov, had left him a complement of fifty men, roughnecks by any standard. Any weakness on Baranov's part could prove his undoing. To win the men's respect, he joined in their most dangerous activities. As the company's chief officer responsible for law and order, he drew up a code of conduct and rigidly enforced discipline. Each Sunday he lined up the men for parade. Punishments varied with the alleged crimes: the lash for

stealing and transport to Siberia for those accused of murder, who had to stand trial in a government court.

To get the men to work and to keep them from destroying one another while suffering the hardships and monotony of life in America, something more than discipline was needed—so their pleasures became his pleasures. Baranov personally took charge of brewing a drink in which crab apples, rye meal, and cranberries were basic ingredients. He invited each man to take as much as he could hold, but he forbade drinking during working hours. With facilities for amusement virtually nonexistent, any occasion—saints days, of which there were so many, birthdays, the arrival of a ship—all furnished the excuse for a party. Baranov usually took the lead in the singing. Every so often, overpowered by the combination of food and drink, he lost control of himself, struck out with his fists at whoever came in reach, and then attempted to make amends the next day by presenting his victims with gifts.

The Russians, who were not race conscious, invited Natives to these festivities. Baranov, who very much appreciated the role played by Native women in helping many a Russian adjust to life in the New World, himself took a mistress, the daughter of a Kenai chief. While encouraging these liaisons, he set down regulations governing the relations of the two races. Prostitution was forbidden. Once a Russian took a girl to live with him, he was obligated to provide for her even after they had lost interest in each other. Children of these unions were recognized as belonging to the mother, but many a Russian decided to remain in America after his contract had expired rather than be parted from his offspring, and perhaps from their mother.[16]

Natives made up much of the work force. Like his predecessors, Baranov utilized the superior skills of the Aleuts in hunting sea animals, while the promýshlenniki and the workers were employed in trapping, curing skins, guard duty, and a variety of chores. He learned to converse in some of the Native languages. The Aleuts, already a conquered people, were frequently sent on long expeditions far from home despite their protests, yet Baranov was fond of telling visitors that these were his children whom he protected and cared for in their old age. With the Tlingits, who resisted encroachments, it was a different story—Baranov had to be constantly on the alert for an attack.

In his dealings with the Natives Baranov sought to impress upon them that he had been sent by the czar, the great father across the waters, to be their overlord and protector. He soon found himself put to the test. Complaints began to come in from residents of Cook Inlet accusing employees of the Lebedev-Lastochkin Company of attacking women, robbing men of their furs, and burning dwelling places. Baranov appealed to Shelikhov, a stockholder in the offending organization, to use his influence in bringing these outrages to a halt. He received no replies to his entreaties. When Baranov tried to explain that he had no jurisdiction over the Lebedev-Lastochkin Company, his primitive audience reminded him of his previous assertions of supremacy. Knowing that he could not avoid the challenge any longer, Baranov led a party of men to Cook Inlet and there confronted Grigory Matveyevich Konovalev, the leader of the alleged wrongdoers. Reminding Baranov that he was simply a lackey of the Shelikhov Company without governmental authority. Konovalev jeered and defied him to do his worst. Baranov responded by ordering Konovalev and seven of his followers seized and placed in irons. They were sent to Siberia, where a court acquitted them of all charges. Fortunately for Baranov, the Lebedev-Lastochkin Company retired soon after from business in America and made no further trouble.

In 1794, not long after the Cook Inlet affair, eight monks arrived in Kodiak.

Baranov, although not a practicing Christian himself, believed that religion had a salutary influence and had requested Shelikhov to send him a village priest, a man with a good understanding of human nature and experienced in working with people. Instead, intent upon impressing the empress, Shelikhov had gone to the Cloisters of the Valaam Monastery in Finland, where he recruited monks to concentrate upon converting the Natives to the Orthodox faith. Once in America, these men, as members of the superior white clergy, refused to take part in the work of the colony and constantly challenged Baranov's authority. They accused him of harshly exploiting the Natives and promýshlenniki and advised them not to take any orders from him. They condemned him as a drunkard and sinner, living with one woman while married to another, and wrote to some Russian officials requesting that he be removed from his position. The clergy claimed great success in converting Natives, but they continued to practice their ancient rites and adamantly refused to abandon polygamy. One of the monks, Father Juvenal, was killed by Natives at Lake Iliamna, where he had gone to preach.

## THE YAKUTAT AND MIKHAILOVSK SETTLEMENTS

When the furs on Kodiak Island began to decline, Baranov moved in a different direction in his quest for new sources of supply. The most ambitious of his undertaking was the Yakutat settlement, designed to serve the fur trade and to provide Russian America with food. Its founding represents the single Russian effort to bring permanent settlers to the New World. These settlers were serfs whom Shelikhov had obtained from Russia and also included some former convicts. Yakutat, located in a glacial area unsuitable for farming, was a failure from the very beginning. The serfs, accustomed as they were to taking orders

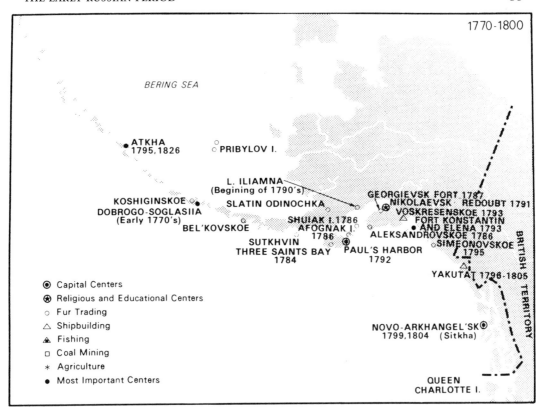

Russian settlements in Alaska and their economic functions, 1770–1800. From Fedorova, *The Russian Population in Alaska and California,* p. 128. Reproduced by permission.

almost from birth, made poor pioneers. They lived in constant dread of the fierce Tlingits (called the Kolosh by the Russians), who finally destroyed the village in October, 1805.

Far more important in the history of Russian America was the founding of Mikhailovsk, named after Saint Michael the Archangel, 6 miles north of present-day Sitka. Baranov had first visited the island, which today bears his name, in 1795. There, in what he regarded as Russian territory, he observed foreigners conducting a very lucrative trade with the Natives. Intent upon driving out the interlopers and having this profitable business for his own company, he paid the Tlingits a small sum for rights to the land. He returned in 1799, bringing

with him about a thousand Aleuts and a hundred Russians with their Native wives. About thirty canoes were destroyed by storms on the way. After seeing much of the new post completed, Baranov returned to Kodiak with most of the Aleuts and some of the Russians.

In June, 1802, while Baranov was away in Kodiak, the Tlingits attacked and destroyed Mikhailovsk, killing or taking captive most of the whites and Natives employed there. A few managed to escape to a British vessel anchored in the harbor. The vessel's commander, Captain Henry Barber, who had been accused of conspiring with the Indians against the Russians, took the escapees to Kodiak and there demanded a huge ransom from Baranov for having saved them. After some haggling, the two compromised on 10,000 rubles—about one-fifth the original request.

Baranov had no intention of capitulating to the Tlingits. In 1804 he returned to Sitka Island with a large contingent of Aleuts and Russians. There, aided by the Russian warship *Neva*, then in America on an around-the-world cruise, Baranov prevailed. The ship destroyed the Natives' village, and its occupants fled. Baranov banished the Natives from the island as punishment for their uprising, and near their village he set to work immediatley to build the settlement of New Archangel on the site of present-day Sitka. New Archangel became the largest town of Russian America, and after Baranov's retirement in 1818 the governors of Russian America used it as their capital.

## REZANOV AND THE FORMATION OF THE RUSSIAN-AMERICAN COMPANY

Meanwhile, unknown to Baranov, a decision had been made in Saint Petersburg by the new emperor Paul I affecting Russian activities in America. On Shelikhov's death in 1795 his dream of exclusive privileges in America had not been fulfilled. His son-in-law and successor as head of the company, Nikolay Petrovich Rezanov, had reached an agreement in 1797 with his leading rival, the Mylnikov Company, to amalgamate and form the United American Company, whose only competitors were a few small companies. Rezanov, who as a member of the nobility had much easier access to the royal court than had the merchant Shelikov, soon discovered that Paul was no admirer of the policies of his mother, whom he had succeeded in 1796. In 1799, Rezanov was successful in obtaining from Paul a charter granting a monopoly of the American fur trade to the new Russian-American Company, in which the majority of stock was held by the owners of the United American Company.

Nikolay Petrovich Rezanov. Courtesy Historical Photograph Collection, Alaska and Polar Regions Archives, Elmer E. Rasmuson Library, University of Alaska.

The Russian-American Company took as its model the British East India Company, a private business enterprise with limited powers of government. Advisers pointed out to the emperor that a single strong organization would strengthen the Russian position in America with minimum risk to the regime. Foreign competition could be better controlled, while the government, if challenged, could repudiate any action of the company as having been unauthorized. By its charter the company received extensive privileges and in turn assumed certain obligations. It was empowered to take possession of all territories already occupied by Russians north of 55° north latitude and to establish new settlements not only in that area but to the south as well, as long as this did not result in conflict with other powers. The company was given permission to cut timber from state forests and to buy arms and ammunition at cost from government arsenals. In return it promised to carry out an expanded program of colonization, to further trade relations with neighboring states in the Pacific, and to concern itself with making the Native peoples loyal subjects of the Russian state and members of the Orthodox church. When it was formed, the company's jurisdiction extended to the mainland of North America and to the Aleutian and Kuril Islands, subject only to the supervision of the Russian government.[17]

## REZANOV'S VISIT TO ALASKA

In the summer of 1805, Nikolay Rezanov visited New Archangel in his capacity as director of the Russian-American Company. An imperialist, Rezanov was as concerned about advancing Russian interests in the Pacific as about making a profit for the company and therefore differed from Baranov, his chief manager, whose interests were primarily commercial. Rezanov wanted to built up the population of the area and make it an outpost for further Russian expansion. He thus recommended that more attention be given to recruitment and to the improvement of working and living conditions, thereby inducing people to come and settle permanently.

Rezanov abolished the practice of giving the colonists shares in the company as payment for their services and replaced this system with an annual wage so that each man would know how much he could expect to earn in a year and could plan his expenditures accordingly. As a means of helping raise the standard of living, a major cause of complaint, Rezanov would offer generous bonuses to workers for jobs well done—a reform that would benefit the company as well. He recognized that the prices in the company stores were too high and believed that they could be lowered by more efficient management. Although certainly not a democrat, Rezanov proposed setting up homes for the aged, establishing schools for the children, and creating a people's court to act on minor offenses.[18]

Rezanov's zeal for reform ranged over a wide variety of subjects. He sought to uplift the colony's morals by restraining men from excessive drinking, which he felt contributed more than anything else to their poverty. He reprimanded the clergy for their interference in government affairs and for their lack of missionary zeal, particularly their failure to learn the language of the Native people, which would make their preaching more effective. Rezanov took upon himself the task of compiling a dictionary so that prayers and sermons might be more readily understandable. He also gave instructions to Baranov to organize a post for the defense of the colony. And in letters addressed to his fellow directors he urged them to petition the emperor to give his approval to freedom of emigration to the colony and that prospective settlers be required to undergo physical examinations to determine their ability to live in the New World.[19] Furthermore, along with wanting the colony to broaden its economic base, he warned against reckless overhunting as inevitably leading to the extinction of the fur-bearing animals they depended on.

Rezanov's visit gave him reason to value the wisdom of many of the policies of Baranov, whom he praised for his selfless devotion and primary concern for the colonies' welfare. Rezanov, after learning at first hand the problems facing the settlements, pledged his support in helping solve them. He admitted that he and his fellow directors had not always been well informed on conditions in America and promised to root out abuses that had crept into the company's operations and thus provide better service to the settlers. Rezanov agreed with Baranov that trade with foreigners was indispensable for supplying the colonies but thought that it was unwise to depend overmuch on the foreign sea captains to bring them what they needed. He advised Baranov to negotiate with the Americans and to buy ships from them, even if prices seemed too high, since the Yankee vessels were of much better quality than the Russians'. He left

Russian America about 1828: an early view of New Archangel, which later became Sitka. Baranov established the settlement as his headquarters in 1804. The fortified "castle" on the hill commanded the harbor and the area in which the town developed. Courtesy Historical Photograph Collection, Alaska and Polar Regions Archives, Elmer E. Rasmuson Library, University of Alaska.

when Baranov a letter of credit enabling him to purchase ships that would permit the colonists to go where and when they pleased in pursuit of trade.[20]

Rezanov was able to observe at first hand the consequences of the colony's dependence on others for their supplies. When he arrived in New Archangel late in August, 1805, the settlement of 192 Russians and an undetermined number of Natives was undergoing a food crisis. No Russian supply ship had come to the port for three years, while American vessels that docked were few, and the cargoes they brought were inadequate to meet its needs. George von Langsdorff, a German naturalist who had accompanied Rezanov on his voyage to America, reported that New Archangel was "in want of almost all the necessities of life" and described the physical condition of the workers as such that "all work was in dan-

ger of being stopped." Bread, a great staple of the Russian diet, was being rationed, each man being limited to one pound a week, and, it was feared, even that would come to an end by the first of October, when the supplies of grain would be exhausted. Fresh fish was no longer available since the hostile Tlingits controlled the coast and prevented the Russians from fishing. The only food to be had in the town was dried fish, sea lions, and seals. The men tried to supplement their meager diet by eating anything they could shoot or find, including eagles, crows, cuttlefish, and even vermin. Only those suffering from scurvy received millet with molasses and beer brewed from pine cones.[21] Rezanov assumed command of the post at New Archangel, superseding Baranov. In the fall he purchased a ship, the *Juno,* and its cargo from an American sea captain, which provided temporary relief. By the end of February, 1806, conditions in New Archangel had deteriorated to the point where Rezanov felt it necessary, he wrote to his fellow directors in Saint Petersburg, for him to go to California to secure supplies from the Spaniards.

Rezanov departed from New Archangel on the *Juno* early in March and reached San Francisco in April after a month's sailing during which he had attempted in vain to ascend the Columbia River to obtain provisions for the crew. Upon his arrival in San Francisco he was wined and dined but met with difficulties in attempting to get what he wanted. The governor was willing to enter into a regular trade agreement with the Russians but could not do so without the consent of his government in Madrid. Moreover, he and his leading officials were reluctant to deal with the Russians since relations between the two countries were strained: in 1806 the Spaniards were allied with France, then at war with Russia.

Rezanov was very much aware of the problems he faced and was eager to leave as soon as possible. He worked hard, using charm and persuasion to attain his objectives. He enticed the Spaniards by offering manufactured goods brought from Russia, which they sorely lacked, in trade for agricultural products. Most important, Rezanov, a widower, wooed and won the affections of doña Concepción Argüello, the daughter of the commandant of the presido of San Francisco, and, according to P. A. Tikhemenev, the historian of the Russian-American Company, "the very port and all those who were stationed there found themselves at his [Rezanov's] disposal." Even some of the governor's men were dispatched to help load the *Juno*.

Rezanov, after spending six weeks in California, set sail on March 8 with a cargo of grains, flour, dried meat, and small quantities of barley, dried peas, lard, and salt. He arrived in New Archangel early in June. He

found its inhabitants recovering from scurvy and malnutrition, which had claimed the lives of seventeen Russians and an untold number of Natives over the past winter. Their health had been restored thanks largely to the new supply of fresh food that became available when the run of herring began in March and fishing was resumed.[22]

That summer Rezanov sailed for Okhotsk en route to Saint Petersburg, where he hoped to receive permission from Emperor Alexander I to marry doña Concepción, a Roman Catholic. He returned to Siberia, and on September 24, 1806, he started out on his long overland journey to the Russian capital. Twice he was forced by illness to interrupt his journey and rest. At Krasnoyarsk he was overcome once again by sickness, and there he died on March 1, 1807. With him perished many of his far-reaching plans for the colony in America.

## BARANOV'S EFFORTS TO SUPPLY THE COLONIES

After Rezanov's departure Baranov resumed responsibility for affairs in the colonies. Several problems required his immediate attention: labor unrest in New Archangel, the hostility of the Tlingits, and the ever-present question of supply. Company spokesmen were frank in their admission that the Russians who came to the colonies were not an ideal lot. They were hard-drinking, savage, and given to debauchery. Their pay was low, they lived in squalor, and the food was bad and, as has been seen, far from plentiful. Discipline, according to Semen Bentsionovich Okun, the Soviet historian of the Russian-American Company, was severe. Baranov had been accused of punishing minor infractions of his rules by whippings and sometimes by exiling offenders to remote, thinly populated islands. In 1809 nine men led by the hunter Vassily Naplavkov plotted to assassinate Baranov and some of his aides, seize a ship,

Kodiak, showing the structure built under Baranov's direction. Now known as Erskin House, it is a museum. Courtesy Historical Photograph Collection, Alaska and Polar Regions Archives, Elmer E. Rasmuson Library, University of Alaska.

and sail for the South Seas. Baranov was warned in time by one of the conspirators about the matter and arrested the men. He sent five of them to Siberia for trial. The case dragged on for years. Some of the men died, while the others received long prison terms. The company, according to Okun, would have preferred to have the affair hushed up to keep conditions in the colonies from being revealed.[23]

The Tlingits posed a much greater threat to the Russians than had Naplavkov and his crew. Their destruction of Mikhailovsk in 1802 and Yakutat in 1805 thoroughly frightened the inhabitants of New Archangel, who were alerted by Baranov to the danger of surprise attacks. Men were warned to sleep with arms at their sides and never to go out alone. Baranov strengthened the fortifications of the town by erecting a high palisade around it. In 1806 the situation was so tense that not a single

hunting party put out to sea, and those that sailed in the next few years were subjected to a great deal of harassment. Still, during the Baranov era there were times when the Tlingits were allowed to come into New Archangel to trade furs and food—chiefly fish and vegetables they had grown—for Russian goods.[24]

After 1807, Baranov worked very closely with Americans. He found that he could depend on them to bring the supplies he needed, and was able to expand the Russian share of the Chinese fur market by contracting with the ships' captains to carry skins of the Russian-American Company to sell on a commission basis in Canton, the dominant market of the China trade, which Americans were free to enter and from which Russians were barred. There was one great drawback to this happy relationship. Americans persisted in coming into territory regarded by the Russians as their exclusive domain and to trade directly with the Natives, not only buying their furs but, what was worse, selling them arms and ammunition, which, according to the Russians, were used against them. Protests by the emperor's representatives in Washington, D.C., concerning this "illicit traffic" were to no avail. The American government maintained that its nationals were free to come and go as they pleased. Baranov lacked the manpower to keep the Americans out. And while he railed against the American intruders, he was most unwilling to terminate a connection that had been so valuable as a source of supply and in obtaining so many customers for the company's furs.[25]

Early in 1812, John Jacob Astor, the head of the American Fur Company, of Astoria, Oregon, came forward with a plan to resolve the differences between the Russians and the Americans. In May an accord was struck between him and representatives of the Russian-American Company defining their respective spheres of interest on the Pacific Coast. The Russians were acknowledged to have exclusive rights to hunt and to trade with the Natives in the area north of 55° north latitude, while the American firm was to have the same privileges south of the line. Both companies promised that they would not sell liquor, arms, or ammunition to the Natives and that they would work together and do what was necessary to keep rival concerns out of the territory. Astor agreed to supply the Russians with all the goods they needed, and they, in turn, designated him their sole agent to take furs to Canton to sell on a commission basis. The outbreak of the war between the United States and Great Britain in 1812 terminated the agreement. Astor sold his holdings in Astoria to the British-owned Northwest Company rather than risk their capture by the British navy.

Baranov was not at all unhappy to see the end of the Astor association. In the short period of their relationship he had become dissatisfied with the quality of the goods sent, the prices charged, and the unreliability of a service in which ships never arrived when promised and, when they came, did not bring much of what he had ordered. In 1813 he was in a very good position to make new arrangements, for he had accumulted enough provisions from his previous dealings with other American traders to last him for several years.[26]

Baranov took a very pragmatic approach to the international situation in 1813. Napoleon's invasion of Russia in 1812 had increased his isolation from home, but then he had never depended much on the mother country for support. The outbreak of the war between the Americans and the British he turned to his advantage. Once the British had taken control at Astoria, American ships sailed north to New Archangel to avoid capture. Baranov purchased several of the ships, leased others, and registered all of them under the Russian flag, rendering them safe from seizure by the British, who had become the czar's allies in the war against Napoleon. The American seamen, formidable competitors in the past, were much more efficient than the Russian crews, and Baranov used them to the utmost. For the next two years the company's profits soared froom the thriving commerce between Russian America and China, Hawaii, and California. One inconvenience did arise. The Russians, unable to use ships flying the American flag, could no longer send their furs to Canton but were forced to make the long overland journey to Kiakhta with its much inferior facilities for trade.[27]

The Russians had been attracted to California for at least two decades, some believing that it was the only place on the Pacific Coast where wheat could be grown successfully. In 1790, Shelikhov had yearned for the day when the Russians would rule in California, and for years Baranov had sent his Aleuts with Joe O'Cain and other American sea captains to hunt for sea otters there. Rezanov, in a letter written on June 17, 1806, after his return to New Archangel, noted that the settlement of California had not begun until 1760 and regretted that the [Russian] government had not given earlier thought to this part of the world." He was sure that if it had "continued to follow the perspicacious view of Peter the Great, who . . . had planned the Bering expedition with something definite in mind then one could positively maintain that New California would never have become a Spanish possession."[28] The expansionist Rezanov had even outlined a plan for the Russians to take over California.

With the permission of the emperor Alexander I, Baranov sent his trusted lieutenant, Ivan Kuskov, southward to establish a post on California land not occupied by the Spaniards. Kuskov made several voyages before choosing a site just north of Bodega Bay in 1812. He paid the Indians for rights to the land, which he named Fort Ross. Although the Spanish officials protested, they knew that Spain, engaged in a great struggle to rid her territory of the occupying French, was hardly in a position to help expel the Russians. For nearly thirty years the Russians remained at Fort Ross despite the efforts of Mexico, which had succeeded to ownership of California after overthrowing the Spanish rule in 1822, to secure their ouster. Fort Ross never fulfilled the expectations of its founders in either supplying food for Russian America and Kamchatka or becoming a center for hunting sea otters. Ross never had enough men for both purposes. Few of the Russians knew much about farming, and the site of the settlement apparently had been selected more for its defensive capabilities than for its usefulness for agriculture or its proximity to furbearing animals.[29] In 1841 the Russian-American Company sold Fort Ross to John Sutter, a Swiss entrepreneur, for about $30,000.

With Fort Ross unable to furnish many of their food supplies, in 1814 the Russians once again turned to Spanish California to supply their needs. Although the Californians refused to recognize the occupation of Fort Ross, they realized that common necessity made working together mutually beneficial. They had a surplus of meat and wheat to sell, while the Russians could bring them the manufactured goods that had been promised by Spain and Mexico but were seldom delivered. After the successful Mexican revolt in 1822 the Russians found it increasingly difficult to trade in California, and by the 1830s they were obliged to look for wheat elsewhere.[30]

Baranov had long been interested in the Hawaiian Islands as another source of food. Russians had been going to the islands for some time, and naval officers brought back tales of the abundance of fruits and vegetables grown on the islands and of the plentiful supply of pigs and cattle. They also noted that Hawaii was not under the control of a European power. Baranov saw the chance for his company to secure a degree of influence in Hawaii. In October, 1815, when Natives of the island of Kauai seized a cargo of furs from the *Bering*, a Russian ship that had been wrecked there in January, Baranov decided to dispatch his agent, the German Georg Anton Schaffer (Yegor Nikolayevich Sheffer), to the island to obtain the release of the cargo or, if that proved to be impossible, to negotiate for a cargo of sandalwood as compensation. Baranov cautioned the erratic Schaffer to "obtain trading privileges only." Schaffer, however, far exceeded his instructions and became deeply involved in the island's politics. He overreached himself when he persuaded one of the kings to cede his land to Russia, an act soon repudiated by the Hawaiian king. Baranov withdrew his support, and Schaffer was forced to leave Hawaii. Schaffer subsequently attempted to interest the Russian-American Company and Emperor Alexander I in schemes to annex the islands. The emperor, apparently fearful that Russia might thus come into conflict with England, which had some interest in Hawaii, let it be known that he was displeased, and the affair ended in May, 1819.[31]

## BARANOV'S FINAL YEARS

While Schaffer was still in Hawaii, the directors of the Russian-American Company, which had increasingly been coming under naval influence, met in Saint Petersburg in the summer of 1816 and decided that Baranov should be retired. It was noted that several times he had asked to be replaced. Twice a successor had been named, but each time the man had died before making the journey to America. By 1816 a number of charges for which Baranov was held responsible were brewing against the company. The chief manager's advancing years and illness, it was said, had been accompanied by a loss of the vigor which had distinguished him in his younger days, and that as a result the company's business had suffered.[32]

A navy man, Captain Leonty Andreanovich Hagemeister, was named as his replacement. The captain made a leisurely journey to New Archangel, arriving late in 1817. Without informing Baranov that he had come to take over his duties, Hagemeister spent two months investigating the company's affairs. An examination of the company's books relvealed some discrepancies, showing that there were actually more goods on hand than had been reported.[33] Baranov, informed in January, 1818, of the company's decision that he was no longer in its employ, was humiliated by the company's course of action, and the manner in which he was terminated smacked of an ouster. He was further distressed by the company's failure to vote him a pension. Captain Hagemeister, who apparently did not care much for New Archangel, remained in the colony only until autumn. He then turned the administration of the company's affairs over to Lieutenant Semyon I. Yanovsky, a naval officer who less than a year before had married Baranov's American-born daughter, Irina.

Like many other men who have devoted their lives to business, Baranov did not know what to do following his forced retirement. The two captains, Hagemeister and Vasily Mikhailovich Golovnin, the latter a persistent critic of Baranov, persuaded him to return to Russia, where he could give the company's directors the benefit of his counsel and experience. Their real motive, it has been alleged, was to get him out of Russian America, where he still possessed some influence.[34] In November Baranov sailed for Russia on board the *Kutuzov*, a ship commanded by Captain Hagemeister. He contracted a fever and died in the South Seas on April 12, 1819. His body was lowered into the waters of the Sunda Strait.

More than any other man, Baranov was responsible for making the Russian-American Company a viable commercial entity. Despite the lack of support given to him in a strange, primitive land, he had been able not only to keep the company afloat but also, thanks to his energy and resourcefulness, to see it pay handsome dividends in the later years. He had been entrusted with the responsibilities of a governor without the authority of one; thus, he could only protest when naval officers disobeyed his orders and decided for themselves what they thought was best for the colony. Baranov often found himself hard put to get his own men to do as he wanted; he could cajole, threaten, and sometimes use physical force, but there was no large labor pool from which he could choose others that might be more satisfactory. His relations with the Native peoples were of a mixed sort. He was sometimes harsh with the Aleuts, a conquered people who were often forced to go on long hunting trips without their consent, but he cared for them in their old age. With the Tlingits there was intermittent warfare, but mostly an armed truce. Although Baranov had been able to provide a degree of stability and permanence to the Russian occupation and had founded new settlements, most importantly New Archangel, he was not a great empire builder. He had carried out orders for overseas expansion in California and Hawaii but had lacked the means to be effective. The Russian settlements were primarily trading posts. Baranov did little to extend Russian civilization in the New World, probably because he was as much affected by the culture of the Natives as they were by his.

# 3. RUSSIAN NAVAL RULE AND THE SALE OF ALASKA

Baranov's retirement, coming in the last years of the Russian-American Company's charter, ushered in a new phase in the rule and development of Russian America, for his immediate successors were naval men. When the charter was renewed in 1821, two years after its expiration date, it stipulated that the chief managers—or governors, as they came to be called—must be naval officers. The navy had thus won its campaign to oust the merchants from control of the company, alleging abuses during the period of their rule and a failure to protect Russian interests in the Pacific.

Unlike Baranov, the naval officers had little inclination for business affairs; their emphasis on improvements in administration resulted in a considerable enlargement of the bureaucracy. Some of the governors, who usually served for terms of five years, were noted explorers. Others concerned themselves with the welfare of the Natives. None had had any experience in the fur trade, which was already declining in the later years of Baranov's tenure. In the words of the Soviet historian Semen B. Okun, there was "more order and less peltry" in the new regime.[1]

## THE FAILURE OF THE SECOND CHARTER TO STOP THE BRITISH AND THE AMERICANS

The announcement of the second charter in 1821 came at a time when the imperial regime had become increasingly active and conservative in international affairs. Emperor Alexander I, who had come to the throne in 1801 after the assassination of his father, Paul I, had played a leading role in the defeat of Napoleon and in the subsequent peace conference, the 1815 Congress of Vienna. Whereas in his early years as monarch Alexander had acquired the reputation of being inclined toward reform, after 1815 he became ever more conservative. As the chief architect of the Holy Alliance (1815), he, along with the rulers of Austria and Prussia, was pledged to intervene and put down by force, if necessary, any liberal innovations in the government systems of European states.

This ultraconservative Russian government was disturbed by disquieting reports concerning the activities of foreigners in Alaska—the Americans more than the British. The Americans were said to be gaining a disproportionate share of the Alaska fur market, and they, not the Russians, were profiting from furnishing the colonies with supplies. Russians were alarmed by speeches of American congressmen calling on the United States to prevent further Russian expansion in North America and asking protection for American traders in Russian America. Captain Vasily Mikhaylovich Golovnin warned that an American seizure of Russian territories was imminent and charged that the United States was supplying the Natives with arms to be used in an alliance against Russia.[2]

On September 16, 1821, Russia therefore announced new policies aimed against the foreigners and foreign influence. Alaska was to be cut off from outside influence: trade with non-Russians in the territory was absolutely forbidden, no furs were to be sold to them, and the colony was to be supplied only by Russian ships.

The Russian-American Company's second charter, confirmed on September 14, 1821, reflected this harder line taken by the imperial regime. In the belief that Russian naval officers would carry out the new policies the most firmly, they were offered inducements to enter the company's service. The charter declared the company's southern boundaries to be the 51st parallel. A ukase issued by the emperor forbade all foreign vessels from coming within 100 miles of Russian-claimed lands and vested in the company all fur-hunting, fishing, whaling, and commercial rights in the area. Both the British and the American governments protested the exclusion of their nationals from the northern fur trade.[3] Each reminded the imperial regime that the territory it claimed south of the 55th parallel lay within the Oregon country, then claimed and jointly occupied by the two under the terms of the Rush-Bagot Agreement. Stratford Canning, the British foreign secretary, proposed that the two nations act together in warning the Holy Alliance, Rus-

sia in particular, against further provocation. On the advice of Secretary of State John Quincy Adams, who was confident of British help in the event of trouble, which he did not really anticipate, President James Monroe issued the Monroe Doctrine, stating that the New World was no longer open for further colonization.

Even before the Monroe Doctrine, however, the Russian government had realized that its North American colonial policy was a failure. The prohibition against trading with the Americans had deplorable results. Furs which previously had found a market in the United States could not be sold after the ban on doing business with the Americans had been imposed, and since the furs could not readily be sold in Russia, many rotted. Neither Fort Ross nor Spanish California was able to provide enough wheat for the Russian settlers, some of whom went hungry. Goods shipped from the Baltic port of Kronstadt usually arrived late, often in poor condition, and cost more than twice what the Americans had charged, resulting in smaller profits for the company. Captain Matvey Ivanovich Muraviev, the Russian-American Company's chief manager in New Archangel, criticized the ban on trading with foreigners and asked the directors of the company to send more supplies. He also sent a vessel to Hawaii for food.[4]

By 1823, faced with its failing Russian America policy, unwilling to reduce its commitment to the play of European power politics to help the Russian-American colonies further, and unable to challenge England, the greatest naval power, Russia was ready to compromise. In 1824 the imperial government signed a convention with the United States (which England confirmed the following year) that recognized 54°40′ as the southern boundary of Russian territory. The negotiations with Great Britain were more complex, involving jurisdiction over a much larger area. After some haggling the Russians and British agreed that Russian territory would extend eastward to the 141st meridian, southward from the Arctic Ocean to the 56th parallel, and southward from there to include a narrow strip of land along the coast.[5] Britain's interests in acquiring land appeared to be minimal; she conceded territory to the Russians that they had not even explored. Her interests were primarily in the commercial aspects of the treaty. As in their agreement with the Americans, the Russians accorded the British the right to trade along the Alaska coast for a period of ten years. And, what was to be of even greater significance, they granted British ships the freedom to navigate the rivers flowing through Russian territory from British territory in the interior to the Pacific.

## THE UNBEATABLE HUDSON'S BAY COMPANY

With the ratification of these treaties Russian expansion in America formally ended. Trade and trading rights, however, continued to be major issues. A British organization, the Hudson's Bay Company, was set to challenge the Russian-American Company for control of the Alaska fur trade.

After amalgamating with the Northwest Fur Company in 1821, the Hudson's Bay Company had begun constructing a chain of trading posts at two-hundred-mile intervals, and by 1833 it had reached the southern boundaries of Russian America. Far more efficient than the Russians, the British utilized the services of trained and educated men as agents. These agents, who did no hunting or trapping themselves, had goods to sell or barter for furs. By selling its wares at low prices (sometimes even at a loss) and paying more for furs, the "Honorable Company," as it was called, succeeded in driving out of business smaller American firms with which it competed in the interior. The Russians, from motives of their own, decided to rid their territory of the competition of

small traders and completed the ouster of the Americans by informing U.S. citizens that the ten-year grace period allowing them to trade in Russian territory was over and that they must move.[6]

With the Americans no longer a factor in the fur trade, the Hudson's Bay Company was now free to take on the Russians. Company officials decided to build a post on the Stikine River near the edge of British territory to deal directly with the Natives, who in the past had sold their furs to coastal Indians acting as agents for the Russians. Upon learning of this, the governor of the colonies, Ferdinand Petrovich von Wrangell, took alarm. He knew that the Russian-American Company could not compete with the better-organized English firm, which had so much more to offer the Natives in the way of goods for trade. To prevent the British from capturing the area's business, Wrangell prepared to build a fort, the Redoubt Saint Dionysius, at Point Highfield, near the mouth of the Stikine River, to prohibit ships from going upriver to supply the Hudson's Bay Company's posts. When on June 18, 1834, a vessel of the company, the *Dryad,* approached the redoubt, then under construction, the Russian commander in the area, Lieutenant Dionisy Fyodorovich Zarembo, informed Captain Peter Skene Ogden that he had been instructed by Wrangell not to let any British ships enter the river. Ogden later claimed that the Russians had threatened to use force, which they denied, and that he had then turned back.[7]

The Hudson's Bay Company refused to be intimidated. It threatened to sue for damages because it clearly had the right under the Russo-British treaty of 1825 to navigate the Stikine. Although the Russian and British foreign offices took some part in the extended negotiations, the two companies settled their differences amicably by themselves in 1839. The Hudson's Bay Company dropped its suit; in turn the Russians agreed to lease to the British the mainland of their territory south of Cape Spencer for ten years at annual payments of 2,000 land-otter skins harvested by the British on the western slope of the Canadian Rockies. In addition the company promised to make available for sale to the Russians 2,000 or more otters from the same area at 23 shillings a pelt and 3,000 animals trapped east of the mountains at 32 shillings a pelt. Most important, the Hudson's Bay Company promised to supply not only Alaska but also Kamchatka with foodstuffs and manufactured goods at stipulated prices.[8] The benefits to the Russians were substantial: a nagging dispute had been resolved peacefully, income would be derived from an unoccupied area, stocks of furs and provisions were readily guaranteed, and the Redoubt Saint Dionysius could be closed, bringing about substantial savings.

A second European power had now come into Russian America. For almost thirty years, until forced out by the sale of the colony to the United States, the Hudson's Bay Company occupied a portion of the Russian colony subject only to the nominal jurisdiction of the Russian-American Company. Little friction occurred between the two organizations even though the British became guilty of squatting illegally in Russian territory. Chief Trader John V. Bell, while on an exploring expedition in 1844, came to the junction of the Yukon and Porcupine rivers. This location appeared to him to be a most suitable site for fur trading, especially since there were no Russians anywhere near the area. Alexander H. Murray, a clerk of the company, was ordered to build a post there, which was named Fort Yukon. The company instructed Murray that if he was challenged by the Russians for being on their land he should simply

The people of Fort Yukon in photograph taken in the early 1900s. All members of the group are in western clothing except the older man in the right front, who wears a shirt of small skins that resembles the traditional garment. Courtesy Historical Photograph Collection, Alaska and Polar Regions Archives, Elmer E. Rasmuson Library, University of Alaska.

reply that he was unaware of any wrong-doing and that the matter should be referred to the headquarters of both companies for resolution. Whether the Russians learned of the British presence at Fort Yukon is unknown. No challenge ever came.[9]

Officials of the Hudson's Bay Company did, however, disagree among themselves about how the leased territory should be organized. Dr. John McLoughlin, the company's chief factor on the Pacific, championed the use of trading posts. He established Fort Durham (usually referred to as Fort Taku) on the Taku River twenty-five miles south of present-day Juneau and, on the Stikine, replaced the Russian Redoubt Saint Dionysius with Fort Stikine. Sir George Simpson, the overseas governor of the company, at first enthusiastically supported the building of Fort Taku but soon changed his mind. He decided that the high cost of operating and maintaining the posts could not justify their continued existence, especially since the furs brought to them came mostly from the interior, which was in British hands. He became further disheartened when Indians attacked Fort Stikine, killing McLoughlin's son, and came to believe that only the timely arrival of the Russians prevented more British from being murdered.

The senior McLoughlin disagreed forcefully with Simpson. As the commandant at Fort Vancouver, he believed that he was in a much better position to judge the value of the posts than was Simpson, who only occasionally visited the area. He contended that the Indians would never wait for the British to come to them but would go directly to the Russians for any articles they wanted; moreover, once the stations were abandoned, British influence over the Natives would decline. But Simpson's views prevailed. Fort Taku closed in 1842, and Fort Stikine in 1847. For the remainder of the company's stay in southeastern Alaska, its trade was carried on by a steamer, the *Beaver*.[10]

## A PROFITABLE ARRANGEMENT

Both the Russian-American Company and the Hudson's Bay Company were apparently very much pleased with their new relationship, though as part of the bargaining process each pretended otherwise in an effort to make changes in the lease to secure some benefit. Together they drew up a new schedule of prices to be paid the Natives for their furs, prices that were considerably lower than those they had paid when they had been at loggerheads with one another.[11]

The farms of the Puget Sound Agricultural Company, a subsidiary of the Hudson's Bay Company, had become so productive that the parent organization was able to sell the Russians an additional 10,000 bushels of wheat. For the first time the Russian colony had an abundance of foodstuffs; moreover, the quality of the grain purchased was said to excel that previously received from California. To their delight the Russians found that the British goods were of the highest quality and were much cheaper than those they had been getting from the Americans. Since all goods coming into the colony were carried on British ships, the Russian-American Company was free to use its vessels for other purposes. Taken together, the Russians felt that they had gained the most from the deal, especially since the leased area was regarded as poor in furs.[12]

The Hudson's Bay Company also profited much from the agreement. Sales of grain from the Puget Sound Agricultural Company and the farmers of the Willamette Valley, in Oregon, resulted in a gain of about $3,125 a year, while their earnings from freighting amounted to almost $8,000 in 1844, and, best of all, the income from furs ranged from $8,000 to $10,000 a year.[13]

When the lease expired in 1849, it was renewed after some hard bargaining for another ten-year period, but not without substantial changes in the terms of the agreement. Although the Russians refused to lower the rental fee charged for the use of the territory, they recognized that changing conditions in the 1840s made it difficult, if not impossible, for the British to provide exactly the same service as that of the past. The Hudson's Bay Company, having lost some of its most productive farms as a result of the American annexation of Oregon in 1846 and plagued by a labor shortage brought about by the defection of many of its workers to the California gold fields in 1849, was no longer required to ship foodstuffs to the Russian colonies in Alaska and Kamchatka. The Russians also found that it was to their advantage to do business with others and not be dependent on a single supplier. Manufactured goods could be bought more cheaply by dealing directly with European firms, while transportation costs could be reduced by using chartered ships to carry goods to America.[14] Owing to the scarcity of animals, the new contract made no mention of the Hudson's Bay Company having to sell furs to the Russians.

In 1854 the Crimean War pitted Britain and France against Russia. The British and Russian foreign offices agreed to abide by the wishes of the Hudson's Bay Company and the Russian-American Company, both of which wanted the northern territory to remain neutral in the struggle. The Russians felt that they benefited the most since the British, who controlled the seas, could have readily attacked their settlements in North America. In 1859 the two companies agreed to a new accord to continue their association, but this time for only three years and payment of the rent to be in cash. The Russians reserved for themselves the right to use the ice, timber, coal, and fish found in the area as they saw fit. When gold was discovered in the neighboring Fraser River valley, some of the small independent traders, who had originally come to sell goods to the miners, became interested in the fur trade and invaded the leased area in 1861. There they competed with the Hudson's Bay Company and even sold liquor to

the Natives. The company complained to their landlord, demanding that the Russians expel the intruders, but to no avail. The Russians replied that they lacked the force to do so. From then until the American purchase of Russian America, the two companies, usually after some hesitation by the British, renewed the lease for periods of one to two years.[15]

Meanwhile, changes had been taking place in Russian America. The advent of the naval officers as chief managers of the company was accompanied by alterations of some consequence from Baranov's style of rule and direction of business affairs. The navy men, most of whom were members of the aristocracy, set themselves apart from the Natives and company workers. The rough democracy of the Baranov era gave way to a system in which rank and class standing were important. Government took on more formal aspects, with notable increases in the administrative staff. More accountants were hired. A staff was assembled to deal with employee problems. To help improve the management of the colonies, a new position was created, that of assistant chief manager. He could take charge and allow the chief manager to leave New Archangel from time to time to make the necessary inspections of the outlying settlements, and he could also help handle administrative details and supervise employees.

Colonial expenses increased with the construction of new buildings to house personnel, provide a home for the chief manager, install fortifications, and furnish barracks. Captain Matvey Muraviev was the first of the naval officers to exert any influence in the colonies, since neither Hagemeister nor Yanovsky, his predecessors, had stayed for any length of time. Muraviev was the great builder. The most important of his structures was a two-story arsenal. He also reversed Baranov's policies and allowed the Tlingits to come into New Archangel, subject to certain restrictions.[16]

Sitka about 1898, when a few tourists were beginning to arrive. The Sitka Trading Company is at right in one of the old Russian buildings. Just beyond is a small establishment advertising general merchandise and photographs by E. de Groff. The sign on the roof at the right of the church also advertises "Alaska Views, Curios." The Cathedral of Saint Michael, which dominates the town, was begun in 1844 and dedicated in 1848. The building burned in 1966, but the Orthodox church built a fireproof replica. Icons and furnishings that had been saved from the fire were reinstalled. Courtesy Historical Photography Collection, Alaska and Polar Regions Archives, Elmer E. Rasmuson Library, University of Alaska.

A strong governor such as Baron Ferdinand von Wrangell could advance the position of the company somewhat, but for the most part the chief managers found themselves burdened with directives yet given little more support from Russia than had been given Baranov. Russian America was still very much on its own and paid but little attention to the capital. Wrangell made some administrative changes. As an economy measure he closed all the shipyards in Russian America except the one at New Archangel and also built a sawmill at Ozerskoi Redoubt. He began a conservation program by limiting the number of seals that could be harvested on the Pribilof Islands.

Wrangell was an experienced explorer. He and his fellow governors gave a great deal of support to scientific studies and to expeditions conducted by naval officers and navigators of the merchant marine, whose accurate observations and maps supplanted the crude information that had been obtained by Baranov from the hunters and Natives. Their interest in exploration may have been stimulated by the need to advance knowledge, but perhaps it was motivated even more by the desire to find new areas for establishing trading posts and forts or to promote the fur trade.

Much of the work of exploration of the interior was done by Creoles, the offspring of Native women and Russian men. Some were almost illiterate, but others had been educated at the school in New Archangel,

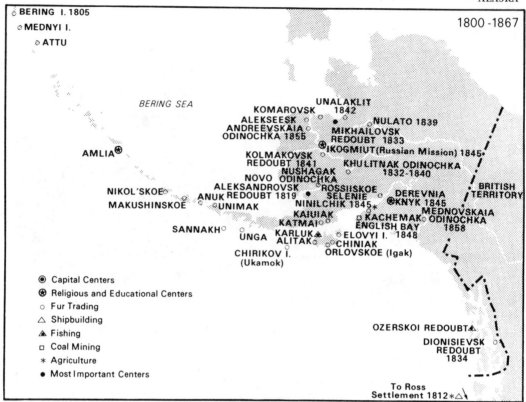

BERING I. 1805
MEDNYI I.
ATTU

1800 -1867

BERING SEA

UNALAKLIT
KOMAROVSK 1842
ALEKSEESK
ANDREEVSKAIA
ODINOCHKA 1855

NULATO 1839
MIKHAILOVSK
REDOUBT 1833

IKOGMIUT(Russian Mission) 1845

AMLIA

KOLMAKOVSK
REDOUBT 1841
NUSHAGAK
NOVO ODINOCHKA
ALEKSANDROVSK
REDOUBT 1819

KHULITNAK ODINOCHKA
1832-1840

ROSSIISKOE
SELENIE

DEREVNIA

BRITISH
TERRITORY

NIKOL'SKOE
MAKUSHINSKOE
ANUK
UNIMAK
SANNAKH

NINILCHIK 1845
KAIUIAK
KATMAI

KNYK 1845
KACHEMAK
ENGLISH BAY

MEDNOVSKAIA
ODINOCHKA
1858

UNGA
KARLUK
ALITAK
CHIRIKOV I.
(Ukamok)

ELOVYI I. 1848
CHINIAK
ORLOVSKOE (Igak)

⊚ Capital Centers
⊛ Religious and Educational Centers
○ Fur Trading
△ Shipbuilding
🔺 Fishing
◻ Coal Mining
* Agriculture
● Most Important Centers

OZERSKOI REDOUBT

DIONISIEVSK
REDOUBT
1834

To Ross
Settlement 1812 *△

Russian settlements in Alaska and their economic functions, 1800–67. From Fedorova, *The Russian Population in Alaska and California*, p. 129. Reproduced by permission.

and a few had been educated in Russia, usually in Saint Petersburg. Feodor Kolmakov, aided by the Creole Ivan Lukin, had been sent by Wrangell to explore the Kuskokwim River. The two established a post where the river joins the Khulitna, and it apparently exceeded all expectations in the profitability of furs harvested. Later they transferred the base to the river now known as the Kolmakov. The Creoles Andrey Glazunov and Pyotr V. Malakhov explored the Yukon. Malakhov was the first to reach the village of Nulato, where in 1839 he established a post representing the farthest settlement of the Russians in the interior.

Lieutenant Lavrenty Alekseyevich Za-

goskin transferred from the navy to the Russian-American Company because of his interest in exploration. His work has been praised as the single most noted "Russian achievement in interior Alaskan exploration," as well as the "outstanding source for the history, geography, and science of western Alaska under the Russian flag."[17] His travels took him as far as the Tanana River. According to the American geologist Alfred Hulse Brooks, Mikhail Tebenkov, first as an explorer and later as governor, "did more than anyone else to bring about a better knowledge of Alaska's coast" by compiling all available cartographic information and publishing a series of charts based on his compilations.[18]

## LABOR PROBLEMS: USE OF CREOLES AND COLONIALS

While the first love of Wrangell, Tebenkov, and some of the other chief mangers may have been exploration, they had to spend much of their time dealing with a most difficult labor problem. Russian America always had a shortage of personnel, never having enough men to take on the various tasks of skilled workers, hunters, traders, and common laborers or to provide for the proper defense of the colony. It was the responsibility of the chief manager to determine how his men could be used most efficiently, for he had to decide to which jobs they were to be assigned and which settlements were most in need of their services.

Critics of the company, while recognizing the difficulties of bringing men to America, have complained that it did too little in recruitment. Soviet historians have pointed out that the company only once brought serfs to America and was very reluctant to pay the high costs of transporting men to the colonies and then training them.[19] Captain Pavel N. Golovin had observed in his report of 1862 that the company would have to raise its wage scale if it wanted to attract skilled labor and a better type of workers, since the men could easily make as much at home and had little motivation to move to a far-off and little-known land. He thought that the company could do more to encourage foreigners to come to Alaska, for it was not necessary for emigrants to be of the Orthodox faith.[20]

In its second charter (1821) the company had made a great effort to keep those already in the colony from leaving. In this charter it had succeeded in bringing about changes that eliminated much of the complicated procedure the government had hitherto required of those who sought permission to remain in Russian America after their term of employment ended. Men no longer had to appear in person to make the request, a requirement which many had disliked, but could now have the company's representatives take care of the necessary paperwork for them. The second charter also granted employees of the company the same privileges accorded to those in state service, although this concession mainly benefited men in the upper ranks.

Of greater interest to the rank and file was the creation in 1835 of the class known as "colonial citizens"—to include workers who had been in the company's service for at least twenty years, widows of company employees, and those who because of poor health or for other reasons were no longer able to work. Colonial citizenship brought with it benefits of some importance: a guaranteed pension, the right to a small piece of land, and the right to sell the land's products as well as whatever was obtained in hunting, fishing, or trapping.[21] It is not certain how many workers remained to become colonial citizens—but certainly not enough to establish a large permanent population. According to Captain P. N. Golovin, colonial citizens were more of a burden than an asset and contributed little to the colonies' well-being.[22]

After 1821 the Russian population of the colony had increased, although it never attained much more than seven hundred at its height. Special conditions from time to time resulted in temporary increases. During the Crimean War, despite the proclamation of British neutrality, the fear of a British attack prompted the Russian government to send one hundred troops to its North American colony in 1855. These troops were soon withdrawn, but they were replaced by another one hundred in 1857 when it seemed that the Tlingits might cause trouble.[23] The beginnings of a coal-mining industry in 1855 also brought workers to Alaska. The coal miners usually remained for several years and were then replaced by a new group.

As the nineteenth century progressed,

Creoles became a more significant factor in colonial life, furnishing much of the needed labor, especially skilled workers. Some rose to positions of responsibility—for example, the explorers Andrey Glazunov, Peter Malakhov, Afansy Klimovsky, and Aleksandr F. Kashevarov—some were used as skilled navigators of company vessels, and others became priests. The company gave aid to those seeking to learn a trade or to acquire a rudimentary knowledge of science and navigation, sending a few to Russia for further education. A person who received any of these benefits had to promise that he would remain in the company's service for at least ten to fifteen years, depending on his position. Creoles constituted a separate element in colonial life, never fully accepted by the Russians and regarded with suspicion by the Natives; the Creoles in turn looked down on the Natives, frequently refusing to join with them in hunting parties even though it might mean a loss of income. Creole women usually married Creoles or Russians, while most of the Creole men reportedly wedded Aleut women.[24] By 1860 the Creole population of the colonies was more than three times that of the Russians.[25]

The governors after Baranov developed new policies in their dealings with the Native peoples in the hope of improving a relationship that retained many aspects of a truce, especially with regard to the Tlingits, who, unlike the Aleuts, were never conquered. Matvey Muraviev, upon his arrival in 1820 as the new governor, invited the Tlingits to come back to Baranov Island, from which Baranov had banished them in 1804, yet even Muraviev restricted them to a village just outside New Archangel, where they could be readily observed, and permitted them to be in town only during daylight hours. Spies in the village regularly reported on their activities. Captain Adolph Karlovich Etholen, who had served many years in the colonies before his promotion to governor in 1840, apparently

was convinced from his experience that new policies would have to be tried in dealing with the Tlingits. In 1841 he invited them to a fair in New Archangel at which entertainment, much to their pleasure, was provided, as well as facilities for them to exchange their furs, fish, and vegetables for Russian goods. In addition Captain Etholen began hiring Tlingits to work in the town and at the harbor. The board of directors commended him and expressed the hope that the fair would continue, perhaps on an annual basis. But the detente was short-lived. The Russians continued to regard the Tlingits with suspicion.[26] One of Captain Etholen's successors, Captain Nikolay Y. Rosenberg, governor from 1840 to 1853, put an end to the employment of Tlingits in the town. In 1855 the Tlingits attacked New Archangel but were beaten off.

Russian relations with the Aleuts can be roughly divided into three phases: the era of the *promýshlenniki,* the rule of Baranov, and the era of the naval officers who served as governors. In his 1862 report on the colonies, Captain Golovin is scathing in his denunciation of the promyshlenniki, who, almost totally free of government supervision, destroyed whole settlements and were responsible for causing the misery or death of thousands. During Baranov's tenure as chief manager the Aleuts' living conditions improved slightly. Baranov was said to think of the Aleuts as being no better than animals, and under him the Aleuts lost their last vestige of freedom when many were forcibly removed from their homes in the Aleutian Islands and resettled at Kodiak and New Archangel and on the mainland and were required to engage in expeditions that went as far south as California to hunt sea otters.[27] This harsh treatment and the spread of diseases among the Aleuts, which the whites were alleged to have brought, resulted in a steady decline of the population that continued until 1840.

The naval officers who came to the colonies as governors were guided by a spirit of paternalism. They were considered to be well educated, humane in their attitudes, and willing to do the best they they could for the people whom they ruled. During this period the company established schools and hospitals for the Aleuts and employed many, who were paid for their services. Some of the Aleuts learned trades, and a few became priests. An effort was made to teach them the rudiments of gardening so that they could grow vegetables and help supplement their diet. By the nineteenth century the Aleuts had grown accustomed to buying goods in the company stores, and it was considered necessary to place limits on their purchases of such "luxuries" as bread, tea, and sugar, lest they be left without enough money to obtain necessities.[28]

The Russians regarded the Aleuts as subjects of the emperor and thus protected by Russian law against arbitrary action. They were accorded the right of self-government, but this was limited primarily to the authority granted their elders, or *toyons,* as the Russians called them, who settled disputes among the people. Aleuts were not free to come and go as they pleased. No one was allowed to leave his or her place of residence without permission of the authorities. All males between the ages of eighteen and fifty were required to participate in expeditions organized by the company for hunting sea otters. But unlike the arbitrary exactions of the Baranov years, after 1820 the government placed a limit on the number of *baidarkas* the Aleuts were obliged to send out in a year and restricted the company from drafting more than 50 percent of the eligible men for duty on the hunt. Although many of the company's profits derived from sales of sea-otter skins, the hunts were justified as benefiting the Aleuts as much as the Russian organization.

The Aleuts were portrayed as a good-natured but inherently lazy people who worked only to satisfy immediate needs without concern for the future. They lacked the will to organize the large-scale expeditions needed to make the hunt successful, and the Russians lacked the skills to hunt the animals. "Thus in forcing the Alleuts [*sic*] to work," Captain Golovin wrote, "the company not only provides them with the basic necessities but also gives them the opportunity of improving their condition and way of life, and almost completely prevents them from starving to death."[29] But another Russian, Sergei A. Kostlivtsev, a state councilor who accompanied Golovin on his inspection trip, accused the company of evading the government's restrictions on the employment of the Aleuts by using more than the allowable quota. The Aleuts, he observed, "spend the best part of the year hunting sea otters and return home when all of the periodic fish have gone out to sea," and they "have no opportunity to lay in sufficient provisions for their families for the winter, which provisions consisted chiefly of dried or sun-dried fish."[30]

It was among the Aleuts that the Russian Orthodox church made its greatest progress in converting Alaska Natives to Christianity. Much of the credit belongs to Ivan Veniaminov, a man of great intellectual attainment who later became Metropolitan Innokenti of Kolomna and Moscow. Arriving in the Aleutians in 1824, he set about learning the language of the people. He devised an alphabet and wrote a grammar for the Aleut language, into which he translated many of the Orthodox religious books. Students at the school he founded received instruction in carpentry, metalwork, and other skills. Baron Ferdinand Petrovich von Wrangell persuaded him to come to New Archangel in 1834, but even Veniaminov met with little success in working with the Tlingits, though he was able to persuade some of them to submit to inoculation when smallpox threatened the area. Named the first archbishop for America and Kamchatka, Veniaminov remained in

The elaborately decorated interior of the Orthodox church at Unalaska, on the Aleutian Chain of Islands. Courtesy Charles E. Bunnell Collection, Alaska and Polar Regions Archives, Elmer E. Rasmuson Library, University of Alaska.

New Archangel until 1858, when the seat of the diocese was transferred to Siberia. While he was in Alaska, he recorded his observations of volcanoes and made detailed studies pertaining to meteorology. Later scholars have acknowledged their indebtedness to him for his studies of the Aleut culture. He labored hard to better the living conditions of the Native people and won the respect and admiration especially of the Aleuts, whom he visited often even after he moved to New Archangel.

Veniaminov was very much the exception among the Russian clergy who came to America, only a few of whom were well educated. In his 1862 report, Captain Pavel N.

Golovin complained (as Rezanov had earlier) about those clergy who had come to be missionaries but had not bothered to learn the language of the Native peoples. While he agreed that the missionaries could claim some success in making conversions, he criticized them for failing miserably both in teaching the true meaning of Christianity and in helping the Natives lead a "civilized" life. The colonies had seven parishes and thirty-five chapels. A special church had been built in New Archangel for the Tlingits, who, it was said, came into the building as a matter of curiosity, squatted down, and after a short visit departed.[31]

## SOCIAL GAINS AND DECLINING TRADE

Following the Baranov era life in Russian America took on some refinements. Thanks to Baroness Wrangell, the first of the wives of the chief managers to live in America, New Archangel acquired a more orderly social life. She and her husband inaugurated a custom of giving balls that was continued by later governors and their wives. Visitors to the colony expressed their pleasure at how much attention they were receiving and how well they were entertained. Some, however, like Sir George Simpson, the overseas governor of the Hudson's Bay Company, pointed out the great disparity in living conditions, particularly between the company officials' well-furnished quarters and the common folk's hovels. Simpson painted a dismal picture of the town, criticizing its odors and lack of sanitation and calling it the most miserable place he had ever visited.[32] Yet New Archangel did possess structures of some merit, notably the cathedral, rebuilt by Wrangell, and the governor's mansion, known as "Baranov's castle" because it was built on the site of the old chief manager's dwelling.

The capital also had several schools. One that gave boys some training in mathematics and navigation had been much improved when Lieutenant Adolph K. Etholen, later chief manager of the colony, became its director in 1833. Another, founded by his wife, served as a finishing school for girls. The church assumed the responsibility for educating the Natives and set up schools at New Archangel, Kodiak, and Unalaska; however, most members of the clergy (with the notable exception of Venaminov) tended to regard learning as secondary to their chief mission, the saving of souls. In addition to the schools, the company established infirmaries in New Archangel and Kodiak to care for the sick.

Meanwhile, as the colonies underwent a social transformation, the character of the Russian fur trade changed considerably. Overhunting, mainly in the era before 1820, had substantially reduced the number of animals, particularly the highly regarded sea otters. The market for furs was also declining. China, probably the company's best customer in the past but severely weakened by her conflicts with Western powers, curtailed her purchases drastically after 1830. Inept in the art of fur processing, the Russians found themselves at a marked disadvantage in competing for new customers in Europe and the United States with the Americans, British, and Canadians, all of whom provided quality furs for the markets.[33]

## THE THIRD CHARTER AND THE DECISION TO SELL RUSSIAN AMERICA

When the second charter expired in 1841, Czar Nicholas I, who insisted on personally reviewing all matters pertaining to administration, had delayed its renewal for three years before extending the Russian-American Company's authority for another twenty years. An extreme conservative, Nicholas I never disguised his antipathy for an organization some of whose directors had been implicated in the ill-fated Decembrist revolt at the beginning of his reign in 1825. But the real issue for him and his government centered on the very question of the existence of the company and the role it should play. The third charter, signed in 1844, stressed the government's role in administration and colonization, in the process slighting the company's commercial character. The new charter also ordered the employees to wear uniforms.[34] To avert the company's bankruptcy, the government granted it special privileges in the Russian tea trade, and by 1845 the income from tea far exceeded that from furs. According to Soviet historian Semen B. Okun, the czarist regime decided to subsidize the ailing company to put it to use in acquiring the Amur

A painting depicting the first and only Russian coal mine at Port Graham, on the Kenai Peninsula. Courtesy Historical Photograph Collection, Alaska and Polar Regions Archives, Elmer E. Rasmuson Library, University of Alaska.

River region in northeasten Manchuria. Company ships explored the river, and company agents travled overland, ostensibly on business but actually to learn more about the area and to win the support of the Natives in preparation for a Russian takeover in 1847. When this had been accomplished, Okun says, the Russian governent had no further use for the company.[35]

Meanwhile, in America concerned company officials, in an endeavor to keep the company afloat, initiated several new business ventures. Pyotr Doroshin, a mining engineer in the company's employ, had been sent to the colony in 1848. He spent four years prospecting in places where lignite coal occurs but was unable to find high-grade coal. The company hired Enoch Jhalmar Furuhjelm, a Finnish mining engineer, to mine coal at Port Graham using machinery purchased in Boston. At the time of its greatest activity the mine employed 131 men and produced 35 tons a day, more than enough to meet the company's needs. When coal shipped to San Francisco sold at a loss, the company abandoned attempts to develop an export trade. Governor

Nikolay Y. Rosenberg became discouraged when he discovered that the company could not compete with the more efficient Americans; for example, the Russo-Finnish Whaling Company went out of business in less than three years. Of all the enterprises the ice trade prospered the most—by 1859 the American-Russian Commercial Company, a San Francisco concern, had contracted to buy more than 3,000 tons of ice a year from the Russians. The Russians found petroleum, copper, and amber in their colony, but no industry developed. There was some mining of mica on the Kenai Peninsula, and some panning for gold took place. But in the 1860s, with the fur trade declining and the company's other enterprises either fading or being of too slight a character, there was, according to geographer James R. Gibson, "little choice for the Russians but to leave."[36]

Critics of the company had been calling on the Russian government to rid itself of its American possessions. Nicholas Muraviev, the governor general of eastern Siberia, believed that Russia's future lay in Asia, where it should concentrate its efforts. In an 1853 memorandum he predicted that the Americans, who already possessed California, would inevitably make themselves masters of the entire North American continent. He recommended ceding Russian America, which he regarded as irretrievably lost, to the United States. By this gesture, he reasoned, Russia would rid herself of a burden and, he hoped, gain a friend in the United States to give Russia support in her struggle against England.[37] When Russia became involved with England in the Crimean War in 1854, an agreement reached beforehand by the Russian-American Company and the Hudson's Bay Company to keep their territories neutral was honored by their respective governments, but it was nevertheless obvious that England, a great naval power whose ships had shelled the harbor of Petropavlovsk on the Kamchatka Peninsula, could easily have taken over the Russin holdings.

In 1843, U.S. Secretary of State William Marcy and Senator William M. Gwin, both ardent expansionists, asked Baron Eduard de Stoeckel, the Russian ambassador to the United States, whether the rumors they had heard about Russia planning to sell its colony were true. Stoeckel said no, but the question clearly indicated to the Russians that there was interest in the United States in purchasing the region.[38] For several years little was said in Russia about a sale. When Czar Nicholas I died in 1855, he was succeeded by his son, Emperor Alexander II, whose younger brother, Grand Duke Constantine, took the lead in advocating the sale of Russian America. Like Nicholas Muraviev, Constantine was convinced that the United States would eventually take over the territory. He believed that Russia's real interest lay in Asia, not America, and he argued that the continued possession of the colony was "a luxury that Russia could not afford." He suggested ceding the territory to the United States with or without compensation. Alexander himself became apprehensive when informed that the Mor-

mons, whose views on polygamy had made them unpopular in the United States, planned to move northward, and he noted that the question of the American possessions would have to be settled.[39] The outbreak of the Civil War in the United States in 1861, however, temporarily halted the informal talks that had been going on between Russians and Americans.

While the Americans were too busy fighting each other to worry about the Alaska question, the area was continuing to receive attention in Russia. Captain Pavel Golovin in his 1862 report on the Russian-American Company took it to task for its general ineptness, attributing its failure to develop the area's economy on the company's monopoly, which had thwarted individual initiative. He made many suggestions for changing policies but nowhere mentioned selling the colony.[40] A special committee formed to consider renewing the company's charter repeated many of Golovin's charges; it claimed that the company discouraged colonization and that its monopoly had prevented others from exploiting Russian America's resources. Like Golovin, the committee was not concerned with the possible sale of the colony but instead stressed the need to improve its administration and strengthen its defense, both of which would have required greater government expenditures.[41]

With Russia already burdened with debts incurred by the Crimean War and about to undertake a costly program of modernization emphasizing railroad building, neither the emperor nor his advisors wanted to spend money on the colony. Rather, they found the possibility of getting some money for the territory intriguing. Prince Aleksandr M. Gorchakov, the foreign minister, thought that Russian America was worth at least $5 million. At a meeting held in Saint Petersburg in December, 1866—attended by the emperor; his brother, Grand Duke Constantine; Gorchakov; Michael Reutern, the finance minister; Stoeckel, who was on a brief visit to Russia from the United States; and two other persons—the decision was made to sell the colony. The emperor instructed Stoeckel to begin negotiations immediately upon his return to Washington, D.C., and to have the Americans make the first offer.[42]

## THE SALE OF RUSSIAN AMERICA

After landing in New York, Stoeckel established contact with Secretary of State William H. Seward through an intermediary generally believed to be Thurlow Weed, a prominent political figure. They began their discussions on Monday, March 11, 1867, and met several times. In the course of their conversations Seward asked that residents of the Territory of Washington be

given fishing rights in Russian America, which Stoeckel declared that his government would not grant. According to the ambassador, Seward then inquired whether the colony was for sale but refrained from making a definite offer. Since Seward had first raised the question, Stoeckel felt that an affirmative answer would not be in violation of his instructions, and he said yes. Seward hurried with the news to President Andrew Johnson, urging him to agree to the purchase. Johnson replied that he had no opinions on the subject but would be guided by the views of the cabinet. Its members, upon being consulted, following Seward and voted their approval. After spending a week with Seward discussing details of the transaction, Stoeckel cabled his government for permission to sign a treaty with

A painting by Edward Leutze depicting the signing of the Treaty of Cession of Russian America to the United States, March 30, 1867. Left to right: Chief Clerk Robert S. Chew; William H. Seward; William Hunter, assistant secretary of state; Waldemar Bodisco; Eduard de Stoeckel, the Russian assistant secretaary; Senator Charles Summer, chairman of the Senate Foreign Relations Committee; and Frederick W. Seward, son of the secretary of state. Courtesy U.S. National Archives, Washington, D.C.

the United States for the sale of Russian America.[43]

According to the story as told by Seward's son Frederick, Stoeckel appeared at his father's home on Friday evening, March 29, and told Seward that the emperor had agreed to sell the colony to the United States. Stoeckel then proposed to come to Seward's office the next day to consummate the deal. Seward, impatient to conclude the business, asked why they should wait until the next day, and so before midnight the two men and their staffs met at the State Department offices, where they worked for several hours drawing up the treaty, which they then sent to their respective governments for ratification.

The price finally agreed on for the colony and the property of the Russian-American Company was $7.2 million. On October 18, 1867, the United States took possession of Alaska.[44]

## RUSSIAN ACCOMPLISHMENTS

The Russian phase of Alaska's history lasted 126 years. Russian activities were mainly limited to the coastal areas in southern Alaska. While there was some exploration of the interior, little settlement was undertaken there. Much of the mainland of southeastern Alaska had been leased to the Hudson's Bay Company since 1839. At its peak the Russian population numbered not many more than seven hundred persons; few Russians came to Alaska to make it their home, and, considering that the economic base of the colony was the fur trade, there was little reason that it should have been otherwise. The initiative for Russian expansion and settlement in the New World came from private individuals and groups, not from the government. Russian America and its interests received little support from the imperial regime, which was primarily interested in European and Asiatic affairs.

No single reason can explain why Russia decided to rid herself of the American colonies. Emperor Alexander II, after listening to his advisers, made his decision. In the opinion of some of the advisers it was only a question of time until the United States would take over Alaska, and it was best that something be done that would benefit Russia. A sale, it was argued, not only would bring needed revenues into the treasury but also would be of advantage to the Russian state. Relations between the United States and Russia, which had been strained by the activities of American traders and whalers there, would be strengthened, while those between the United States and Britain, Russia's great enemy during much of the nineteenth century, would be adversely affected by the friction that the Russians predicted would develop between the two nations once the Americans moved into territory north of British-held lands. Although the colony was known to possess valuable resources, vocal Russian critics of the area were concerned more with what they perceived to be its liabilities for Russia than with its assets. The fur trade, which had long been the economic base of the colony, had become unprofitable, and supplying the colony with goods continued to pose a most difficult problem. At a time when the Russian-American Company was being attacked for its ineptness, it was felt that the Russian government should not waste its energies assuming the responsibility for governing and strengthening the colony's defenses. A choice had to be made between retaining Alaska, which was termed a liability, or continued expanding in Asia, where the real interests of Russia lay.

The late Ernest Gruening, Alaska territorial governor from 1935 to 1953 and U.S. senator, devoted only a few pages of his history of Alaska to the Russian experience, declaring that it was of little significance. This view has been challenged by Soviet and Western scholars, who point out that the Russian phase brought forth some notable achievements. The Russians established the first settlements, took steps from the very beginning to develop the economy, and through the fur trade and shipping brought the region into worldwide commercial relations. After Baranov the governors introduced a semblance of European culture into Alaska, charted the coast, explored the interior, and made investigations of the region's natural history, resources, and ethnography. The Russians also converted the Aleuts and some of the Tlingits to Christianity, introduced the first educational and medical facilities, and strove to curtail warfare among the Natives and their use of slaves.

When the United States took over Alaska, it inherited something more than a wilderness. Compared to the policies of neglect followed by the British Hudson's Bay Company in southeastern Alaska and by the U.S. Congress in the early years of American occupation, the Russians accomplished much with limited means and few personnel.

# 4. AMERICAN PURCHASE AND SETTLEMENT OF ALASKA

When the United States took possession of Alaska in 1867, Americans were not much better prepared to administer and govern the territory than the Russians had been. Little in the American background provided the wisdom and experience needed in guiding the destinies of a land so distant and remote. The Civil War had just ended, and the minds of the people and their leaders were focused on the problems emanating from that conflict and how they should be resolved. Americans were generally far too excited about the great prospects opening at home in both industry and agriculture to give much thought to Alaska.

Although most Americans knew little about Alaska, it would be a mistake to infer that the area had been foisted on an unsuspecting public by a cabal led by Secretary of State Seward. Americans had been coming to Alaska for more than seventy-five years to trade in furs and sell supplies and later to hunt whales. Because of these traders' and hunters' activities not a small part of American foreign relations with Russia had centered on Alaska.

## WESTERN UNION'S TELEGRAPH SCHEME

In 1864 the Western Union Company, through its subsidiary, the Collins Overland Line, embarked on building a telegraph line to connect North America with eastern Asia. Starting from California, it would run to the Amur River by way of British Columbia, Alaska, and the Bering Strait. From there it would join the existing Russian facilities, thereby connecting with those of Europe and India. But since the primary purpose of the Collins Line was to establish telegraphic communication between the United States and Europe, the successful completion of an underwater cable by Cyrus Field on July 27, 1866, caused the Western Union Company to abandon the project.[1]

Western Union's effort did, however, play a role in stimulating interest in and enlightening Americans about Alaska. An exploratory expedition of scientists from the Smithsonian Institution sent ahead to obtain information brought back extensive data about the region's mineral resources, climatic conditions, and plant life. Harry Bannister, one of the members of the expedition, testified before the Senate in support of the treaty of purchase. He later noted that, while "the project of the Western Union Telegraph Company of an overland telegraph across Bering Straits was a failure, its greatest result was the annexation of Alaska."[2]

A painting (artist unknown) depicting a field camp for men engaged in the construction of a telegraph line to connect North America with eastern Asia and Europe. The project was abandoned in 1866 after Cyrus Field successfully strung an underwater cable. Courtesy Historical Photograph Collection, Alaska and Polar Regions Archives, Elmer E. Rasmuson Library, University of Alaska.

## SEWARD'S ROLE IN THE PURCHASE OF ALASKA

When Seward completed his work with Stoeckel in the early hours of March 30, 1867, he hoped to have the Senate ratify the treaty of annexation before it adjourned that day at noon, but he was unsuccessful. On Monday, April 1, a special executive session of the Senate was called to take up the matter. Seward faced a formidable task to secure ratification. Not only was there a great deal of prejudice and misinformation about Alaska, but there was the fear that any measure proposed by the administration of President Andrew Johnson, who was most unpopular with Congress, faced the likelihood of defeat. At first Charles Sumner, chairman of the Senate Foreign Relations Committee, asked Seward to withdraw the treaty from consideration because he was not sure that the proposal could secure the approval of two-thirds of the Senate needed for ratification.[3] A few newspapers were most vehement in their denunciation of what they called "Seward's Folly" and "Seward's Ice Box" and referred to Alaska as "Walrussia." Horace Greeley, the acerbic editor of the *New York Herald*, sneeringly advised European potentates with worthless territories to discard that they would find a ready buyer in the secretary.[4]

Seward carried on a vigorous campaign to gain support for the treaty. Most of the influential newspapers in the country ralled to his side. Congressmen were wined and dined by the secretary to secure their support. People of prominence, especially those familiar with Alaska, testified in behalf of ratification.[5] Most important, Charles Sumner, who had read the Smithsonian expedition's report and other materials on Alaska, became an advocate and made a three-and-a-half-hour speech on the floor of the Senate calling for ratification. He extolled the area's great wealth and its vast resources, emphasizing its fisheries, and pointed out that the climate was not as severe as was generally supposed.[6] By a vote of 37 to 2 the Senate accepted the treaty.

Difficulties arose in the House of Representatives. That body delayed appropriating the money to pay the Russian government, claiming that in a transaction involving millions of dollars it should have been consulted. Some time was spent by the legislators in taking up the claims of a Massachusetts sea captain against the Russian government before the lawmakers considered the appropriation. The opposition to President Johnson, who faced impeachment charges in 1868, was making itself felt.

Seward thought it necessary to commission a scientific expedition under the leadership of George Davidson to go to Alaska and bring back information that would justify paying for the territory.[7] He also selected and sent to the house 360 pages of "letters, reports, and speeches that put the treaty in the best possible light." Baron Stoeckel, the Russian ambassador, so feared that the United States might renege on the agreement that, it is alleged, he spent $30,000 securing the support of a few influential newspapers and lobbyists to obtain a favorable response from the congressmen. He is reported to have suggested that the emperor might shame the Americans into meeting their obligations by offering them the territory gratis. His majesty refused to consider the gesture, fearing, it is said, that it might be accepted.

On July 18, 1868, nine months after American troops entered Alaska, the House voted to pay the Russians for the land. Some congressmen admitted that they gave their consent only after having been persuaded that to do otherwise would offend an old friend, the Russian government.[8]

## THE AMERICAN TAKEOVER—BOOM AND BUST

In a ceremony at Sitka, General Lowell Rousseau, the official representative of the president, formally took possession of Alaska for the United States. A total of 250 American troops and a Russian company took part in the flag-changing ceremonies. A pulley rig was used to hoist a soldier up to untangle the Russian flag, which had been caught on the ropes in its downward descent. Princess Maksutova, the wife of the last Russian chief manager of the Russian-American Company, appropriately fainted as Russian rule of Alaska came to an end.

For the Russians the "unthinkable" had happened—Alaska had been sold.[9] They and the Creoles, who had been guaranteed the privileges of citizens of the United States, were given the opportunity of becoming citizens within a 3-year period, but few decided to exercise that option. Nor did the United States exactly roll out the welcome mat for them. General Jefferson C. Davis, who had been named as commander of the American troops in Alaska, immediately ordered the Russians out of their homes in Sitka, maintaining that these were needed for the Americans. The Russians complained of the rowdiness of the troops and reported a number of assaults. Many of the Russians returned to their native land; some went to California and the Pacific Northwest, where the opportunities were better. For the Natives, most of whom had never been under Russian rule, the change of regime appeared to be of little consequence. An American businessman, H. M. Hutchinson, of Hutchinson, Kohl and Company, of San Francisco, purchased the buildings, ships, equipment, and other movable properties of the Russian-American Company from Prince Maksutov, its chief manager.

He sold furs at bargain prices to Canadian and American merchants who had come to Sitka for the event.[10]

Soon after the ratification of the treaty, President Johnson recommended that Congress act to provide "for the occupation and government of the territory as part of the dominion of the United States." Unfortunately, the unpopular Johnson (who narrowly missed removal from the presidency by a single vote in the Senate) had no influence with the legislators, and Congress spent little time on the subject of Alaska. American laws governing commerce and navigation were extended to the territory, while the importation, manufacture, and sale of liquor were prohibited. General Davis, in command of the army troops stationed at Sitka, Fort Wrangell, Fort Kodiak, Fort Tongass, and Fort Kenai, became the virtual ruler of Alaska. The interior was left unpatrolled, however, and the posts at Kodiak, Tongass, and Kenai were soon closed. Nothing was done to establish a civil government, and for the next seventeen years Alaska remained under military rule. There were numerous proposals on how to change the status of Alaska. One would have made the area a county of the territory of Washington.[11] Even more striking was the suggestion that Alaska become a penal colony and serve the United States as another "Botany Bay."[12]

Sitka, the old Russian capital (New Archangel) and now the military headquarters of General Davis, immediately experienced a land boom and bid fair to continue as the center of American life. A number of enterprising Americans arrived almost simultaneously with the army, hoping to be first on the scene to exploit the region's reputed wealth. "Eager promoters," according to historian Ted C. Hinckley, "squatted over the whole vicinity of Sitka" and "preempted the governor's house and one godless individual even recorded a claim for the church and church lands."[13] These claims were illegal of course, but the optimists

Bvt. Maj. Gen. Jefferson Columbus Davis, Twenty-third Infantry, who commanded the troops who occupied the first noncontiguous dependency of the United States. When Davis was stationed in Alaska, he commanded a few hundred soldiers and several forts. Courtesy Historical Photograph Collection, Alaska and Polar Regions Archives, Elmer E. Rasmuson Library, University of Alaska.

were confident that Congress would enact laws confirming their title to land. The town's residents, with the blessings of General Davis, drew up a charter, elected a governing council, and named William S. Dodge, the collector of customs, as mayor. Thomas Murphy started a newspaper, the *Sitka Times*. A teacher was engaged at $75 a month. But Sitka's prosperity soon evaporated. The port's commerce steadily declined. Neither the soldiers nor the Natives provided enough business to sustain the merchants. People began to move out, and in the summer of 1873 the Sitka city council held its last meeting.[14]

Many of those who came and departed blamed the federal government for Sitka's decline and Alaska's misfortunes. Congress had failed to provide needed services; there was no regular mail delivery, no lighthouse was built to guide navigators in the tricky waters of Alaska, and no survey had been made of the land. People had left because they could not get title to land, and hence had no assurance that their work would not be in vain. The army had even been used to drive out people who had attempted to preempt lots for themselves. In its first edition the *Sitka Times* condemned military rule. Editor Murphy wrote that when Alaska had a civil government the region could "expect to hear of rich minerals having been fully developed by our latent industry but not before."[15]

When Seward visited Sitka soon after his retirement as secretary of state, he told his audience that civil government must come "because our political system rejects alike anarchy and executive absolutism," but he cautioned that, since fewer than two thousand whites lived among twenty-five thousand Natives, "a display of military force was needed." But how necessary? Alaska never experienced the wars between the races that marked much of early American history. Relations between whites and Natives in Alaska were characterized by personal incidents rather than by unending conflict. William S. Dodge, the special agent of the Treasury Department and the erstwhile mayor of Sitka, regretted the lack of discipline among the troops and complained that he had been called out on many a night by men and women, Russians and Natives alike, requesting protection from drunken soldiers. Misunderstandings were frequent. Americans had no appreciation of the Native culture, while the Natives found it difficult to comprehend the rules and regulations of the new masters of Alaska.[16]

One evening an intoxicated Native chief wobbled out of General Davis's house and entered the parade ground reserved for officers. He failed to stop when ordered to do so by the sentry on duty, and when he continued across the forbidden area despite a second challenge, a second sentry kicked him forcibly in the rear. Several followers came to their chief's defense. In the scuffle that ensued, one of the Tlingits wrested a rifle from a soldier and retreated to his village with the prize. Davis, who was no Indian hater, insisted that the Natives must be taught to respect the authority of the United States and sent a detachment of soldiers to apprehend and arrest the warrior and his chief. On another occasion, after the killing of two white men at Kake, the general sailed to the island to demand the surrender of the murderers. Upon being informed of his coming, most of the inhabitants fled. Davis then ordered their homes burned as a warning to all that lawbreakers must be punished.

The army never relished its Alaskan assignment. Both enlisted men and officers disliked their Alaskan tour of duty, suffering more from boredom than from attacks by the aborigines. In their annual reports army officials invariably recommended that the troops be withdrawn since the army possessed neither the authority nor the men trained to carry out the functions of civil government. Instead, they proposed that in view of Alaska's large area, long coastline, and interior rivers a revenue vessel be sent to perform the necessary police duties. In 1877 the War Department recalled its men from Alaska, stating that they were needed to suppress an uprising of the Nez Percé Indians in Idaho. After the army's departure Mottrom D. Ball, of the Treasury Department, was the only government official in the territory. Former territorial governor and historian Ernest Gruening has jocularly referred to this as the era when Alaska was ruled by a customs collector.[17]

When fighting erupted between Natives and whites, in February, 1879, resulting in several deaths, some residents of Sitka, fearful of an impending massacre, called on the navy to send a vessel for their protection. Since no immediate reply was forthcoming, they appealed to the British, who sent a warship, the HMS *Osprey,* from Victoria to Sitka. With the arrival of an American warship, the USS *Jamestown,* in April, 1879, the rule of the navy in Alaska began.

## THE ALASKA COMMERCIAL COMPANY

In the minds of many Alaskans in these early years the real power in Alaskan affairs was not the military but the Alaska Commercial Company. An outgrowth of the firm of Hutchinson and Kohl, the Alaska Commercial Company in 1870 bid and acquired a 20-year lease from the government, giving it exclusive rights to catch seals on their breeding grounds, the Pribilof Islands. Within a short time the company had extended its commercial empire to the Aleutians, Kodiak Island, and the Yukon River valley, having taken over the Hudson's Bay Company's post at Fort Yukon after the British had been ordered to leave American territory. A most efficient organizaton, it alone possessed the capital to build and maintain the ships needed to bring men and supplies to the different parts of the vast territory. As the company's economic power grew, so too did its role in the political and social affairs of Alaska. It provided schools and medical services in some communities and even took responsibility for the maintenance of what little law and order existed, especially in the interior.

Alaska Natives were said to have received better treatment from the company than from "petty traders who could be expected only to look after immediate profit." [18] The company's generosity and help has been acknowledged by "almost every explorer and scientist" who came to Alaska, while officials of the Smithsonian Institution have expressed their gratitude to the company for the many services extended to their agents, without any favors or compensation being asked in return. [19]

The company's critics are legion. They claim that the organization was motivated solely by considerations of self-interest and hold it responsible for much of Alaska's backwardness and for its failure to obtain self-government. After two years of work in taking the census, Ivan Petroff reported that there were only 430 white men living in Alaska in 1880; many attributed the decline mostly to the company's power in stifling individual initiative and discouraging people from settling the territory. There is no question that the company, because of its predominant interest in the fur trade, naturally enough desired the preservation of the wilderness and was generally opposed to settlement. [20] The company was equally adverse to government regulations and the payment of taxes, and it made its voice known whenever there was talk of extending government services to Alaska or organizing it as a territory. There was much muttering and protest when the company, despite having been the low bidder in 1870, was awarded the monopoly for exploiting the fur seal trade of the Pribilof Islands. The naturalist William Healy Dall accused its officers of seeking to crush all opposition in 1868 and of not having "hesitated at force, fraud, and corruption" to attain these ends. [21] A congressional committee called on to investigate these and other charges absolved the company of abusing its authority, conducting unethical practices against its competitors, showing a lack of concern for the Natives, or using its political connections to obtain favors. Complaints against the company continued, however, long after the committee issued its report.

In 1880 the Alaska Commercial Company paid a 100 percent dividend to its stockholders. [22] The company's profits, much of which came from the exploitation of the fur seal monopoly of the Pribilof Islands, clearly indicated that the fur trade was still lucrative in Alaska. But changes could be seen in the Alaskan economy in 1880. Men were engaged in various enterprises, some of which were eventually to surpass the fur trade in importance for the Alaskan economy.

The timber industry, which was not to experience its period of great expansion until the middle of the twentieth century, produced primarily for local needs in southeastern Alaska. Only a few sawmills operated, but with the development of mining and fishing, entrepreneurs built new mills and logging increased to meet the demands of these industries for lumber.[23]

Fishing, notably for salmon, which was to play a more spectacular role in the Alaskan economy than timber, was just entering its commercial era. In 1878 businessmen built the first canneries at Klawock and Sitka. By 1900 there were almost fifty in operation, but the industry did not experience its great growth until after the turn of the century. "In the early years" of the salmon business, economist Richard Cooley wrote, the "isolation of the fishing areas and the primitiveness of Alaska with its sparse population necessitated the importation of fishermen, cannery laborers, and supplies from the major population center to the south." San Francisco and later Seattle were "the main outfitting, employment, and financial centers for the Alaskan salmon industry." These cities, not Alaska, benefited most from the fisheries.[24]

## THE DISCOVERY OF GOLD

Mining—not fishing—gave the impetus to Alaska's first population boom. Small scale gold mining had been carried on in Alaska during the Russian era. Apparently fearful of an influx of gold seekers, the Russian-American Company chose to keep the knowledge of the existence of precious metals in their territory a secret.

Following the discovery of gold in California, prospectors began to work their way up the Pacific Coast in search of new areas for exploitation as the old mining centers became exhausted. They moved into British Columbia in 1859 to work the diggings near the Fraser River. They went to the Stikine River and from there rushed into the Cassiar region, and finally into Alaska. There placer gold was probably first found at Windham Bay in 1869 on a tributary of the Schuck River, about 70 miles south of the present-day city of Juneau. Veins of quartz containing gold had been found a few years earlier at Sitka. The census of 1880 listed eighty-two residents of Sitka as miners.[25]

In 1880 George Pilz, a German-born mining school graduate who had been working in Sitka, grubstaked two men, Joe Juneau and Richard Harris, to search for gold. In the course of prospecting in the vicinity of Gastineau Channel, they found placer gold in a stream they called Gold Creek, and also at Silver Bow Basin at the head of the creek. Since only shovels and relatively inexpensive equipment were needed for this type of mining, the area attracted hundreds of gold seekers. Historian Robert De Armond has stated that no mining district in the "western United States and Canada" was "so easy to reach at such an early date."[26] After about the end of March, 1881, there was a monthly boat available from either Portland or Victoria to the Harris mining district, so named after one of the prospectors. The town which grew up in the area was given the name Harrisburg; it was next called Rockford for a brief period, in honor of a naval officer who had assisted in organizing the district. Finally, the miners themselves decided upon the name Juneau.[27]

The Juneau area would probably have gone the way of most other mining districts after the placers had been worked out if it had not been for the discovery of lode, or hard-rock, deposits, which required expensive machinery to operate. John Treadwell, a California promoter, purchased a claim, called the Paris Lode, on Douglas Island,

A street scene in Juneau, about 1896. Courtesy Mrs. Rufus E. Rose Collection, Alaska and Polar Regions Archives, Elmer E. Rasmuson Library, University of Alaska.

from a prospector known as French Pete for a sum ranging from five to forty dollars, depending on one's source of information. According to the geologist Alfred Brooks, the site was worthless to French Pete, for he had "neither the experience nor the capital to develop a large body of low-grade ore." Treadwell recognized the area's potential, and by taking advantage of cheap ocean freight, the water-power sites, the abundance of timber, and a favorable climate, he succeeded in developing the Paris Lode—situated in the great pit known as the "Glory Hole," which eventually covered thirteen acres—into a very profitable enterprise.[28] The Treadwell Mine, as it was formally called, provided year-round employment and gave Juneau its economic base.

In 1890, Juneau had a population of 1,251, of whom 671 were white. It was a typically American town, with its variety of privately owned mercantile establishments, schools, and a hospital supported almost entirely by private subscription—and possessing, despite the edict of prohibition, nine saloons and two breweries.[29] It had thus grown from a small mining community whose inhabitants' chief interests in 1882, next to the taking of claims, had been "buying, swapping, [and] selling claims," as historian Robert De Armond has observed.[30]

In 1886, as at other places on the Pacific Coast, the area was swept with anti-Chinese riots. In 1884, John Treadwell, president of Alaska Mill and Mining Company, had begun hiring Chinese laborers to work in the mines. The white miners were not interested in employment at the mill and spurned jobs offered by Treadwell. They disliked quartz mining and were interested only in placer mining. The miners' antipathy to the Chinese, historian Ted Hinckley tells us, was not simply a dislike of the color of their skin. What they resented most was the docility of the Orientals, whose hard work and willingness to accept lower wages than those paid to the whites had made possible the wealth and great success of the hated Treadwell group, while the miners themselves suffered from the hard times.

A house in which Chinese were living was blown up in January, and when the Chinese did not leave Juneau, they were herded to the beach in August, put on two sailing vessels, and sent on their way. Upon hearing the news, Governor Alfred P. Swineford went to Juneau, but he was unable to persuade the officer in charge of the one small naval vessel on the coast of Alaska to bring the men back. The officer claimed that he lacked the force to "cope with the situation." Treadwell subsequently refused to press charges, and the matter was dropped. Oriental labor was never again employed in the mines at Juneau.[31] In 1889, Treadwell sold his interest, which by then included four mines, the Treadwell, the 700, the Mexican, and the Ready Bullion. By the following year this group of mines had yielded more than $3 million in gold.

The Yukon was opened up to mining largely through the efforts of Napoleon ("Jack") McQuesten, Arthur Harper, and Al Mayo, agents of the Le Roy Alaska Commercial Company. These men, though primarily interested in the fur trade, did some prospecting on their own, furnished supplies needed by the gold seekers, and even grubstaked a few of the prospectors. Mining on the Yukon had been confined almost entirely to the Canadian side of the river until 1886, when discoveries of gold near one of its tributaries, the Fortymile River, in American territory, triggered a new rush. Men left their Stewart River diggings and came to the Fortymile, as did a few individuals from Juneau.[32] In 1893 two men who had been grubstaked by McQuesten found gold in the Birch Creek area, which subsequently became the gold-mining cen-

ter in the Yukon and the most important mining camp there until the Klondike discoveries of 1896 and 1897.

Circle City grew up as the supply point for the area. Its population of five hundred made it the largest town on the Yukon. The settlement had an "opera house," where stage performances were given.[33] A decade after the discovery of gold in the Fortymile region, the value of mining from the Alaska Yukon increased from $30,000 in 1887 to $800,000 in 1896. On the coast mining at Juneau "plus the discoveries at Yakutat, Lityua, Yakataga, the Kenai," and elsewhere had raised the annual value of gold production along the coast from $20,000 in 1880 to $2 million. Since 1880 the white population of Alaska had increased from fewer than 500 to 8,000, most of whom were miners,[34] and of these about 1,000 were in the Yukon.

In the absence of a formal government structure, the miners of Juneau and the interior, like their counterparts in western America, drafted their own form of frontier democracy known as the miners' code. In their initial meetings they decided upon the boundaries for their mining district, drew up the rules for the staking of claims, and elected an official, known as the recorder, to register the site staked out by each man. They then prescribed the rules of conduct for the community: fines for minor offenses, banishment for stealing, and hanging for murder. A court composed of the miners themselves would sit in judgment and mete out the penalties.

## THE CLAMOR FOR SELF-GOVERNMENT

Although the navy was more popular than the army had been, the clamor for civil government became more articulate as the white population of Alaska increased. In 1881 the miners of southeastern Alaska met and elected as their "delegate to the congress," Mottrom D. Ball, the former collector of customs. Ball never was given official recognition, though the House of Representatives voted to pay his expenses. While in Washington, he condemned the American neglect of Alaska and warned the congressmen that Alaska would not advance in civilization or population until they passed laws to protect the rights of persons and property.[35]

Ball's views were contradicted by Henry Elliott, who had been a member of the Western Union's scientific project and was considered by many congressmen an authority on Alaska. A fervent champion of the Natives and of conserving the seals, Elliot saw no need for territorial government and its attendant services. He asserted in an article written for *Harper's Weekly* that agriculture would never thrive in Alaska and that the population would always remain small.[36] Elliott's colleague on the expedition, William Healy Dall, while enthusiastically extolling the potential riches of Alaska's mineral wealth, remained dubious about the advisability of immediate territorial government.

. Most influential of all the spokesmen on Alaska affairs was the Reverent Sheldon Jackson. Dr. Jackson, a Presbyterian minister, made the first of his voyages to Alaska in 1877, when he helped organize the Wrangell Mission, the first of his endeavors to bring Christianity to the Alaska Natives. Although he never became a resident, he quickly established himself as the authority on Alaska and spoke to hundreds of groups, primarily in the northeastern part of the United States. He appealed for their aid in his crusade against the evil influence of those whites who corrupted the Native men with drink and ravished the women. In Washington he was well known among members of Congress, being the intimate friend and fellow churchman of Benjamin Harrison, later president of the United States and author of the First Organic Act, which established civil government in Alaska.[37]

The Reverend Sheldon Jackson (1834–1909), a Presbyterian home-mission organizer. Courtesy Sheldon Jackson College Collection, Sitka, Alaska.

## ESTABLISHMENT OF CIVIL GOVERNMENT

While Dr. Jackson was mainly interested in securing fedeal support for educating the Natives, Harrison was concerned chiefly with government organization and administration, and together they were able to formulate Alaska's first civil government and obtain money for an Alaska school system. Harrison, chairman of the Senate Committee on Territories, had no illusions about the First Organic Act. He had introduced bills in previous sessions to no avail, but in the closing days of its first session in 1884, Congress and President Chester Arthur had apparently been persuaded that military rule should end in Alaska. Aside from agreeing that Alaska's government should be simple and inexpensive, they had no clear concept of the form it should take. The result ws a compromise, a hodgepodge of conflicting ideas and principles, a measure recognized as temporary until Congress could give more thought to establishing permanent institutions. Alaska was designated a "district." The term "territory" was deliberately omitted from its title because it implied certain constitutional forms and guarantees. The Organic Act of 1884 expressly forbade a legislature, and since Alaskans did not possess the right to vote for their representatives, they were not subject to taxation. Because laws were necessary for a civilized community, the act gave Alaska the code of Oregon, then the nearest state to Alaska (Washington was still a territory). This code was "declared to be law in said District of Alaska so far as . . . may be applicable, and not in conflict with the . . . laws of the United States."

The Organic Act of 1884 provided the first civil government for Alaska. President Chester Arthur appointed the first governor, John H. Kinkead, former governor of Nevada. Kinkead, seated, is shown in this photograph, taken in May, 1885. Other appointees are, standing, left to right: Edwin H. Haskett, U.S. attorney (from Iowa); Munson C. Hillyer, U.S. marshal (from Nevada); Ward McAllister, Jr., U.S. District Court judge (from California); and Andrew T. Lewis, U.S. District Court clerk (from Illinois). They posed in front of the U.S. Custom House in Sitka. The photograph was taken at the end of Kinkead's short term as governor. Courtesy Alaska Historical Library, Juneau.

The Organic Act gave the president the authority to appoint the officials of the Alaskan government, subject to the approval of the Senate. Of these officials, the most important by far was the district court judge who was given the onerous task of interpreting the Oregon code in Alaska. This judge also presided over major civil and criminal cases, holding court alternately at Sitka and Wrangell. He was assisted by commissioners sitting in Juneau, Wrangell, Unalaska, and Sitka, the latter serving as ex officio register of the Alaskan land office. A district attorney, a marshal and four assistants, and the clerk of the court comprised the staff engaged in law enforcement. The governor, aside from writing an annual report, had no real functions.

Many Alaskans protested that the act gave them no rights of self-government and dealt only superficially with their problems. No provision had been made for law enforcement in the interior. The act acknowledged that Alaska constituted a land district and should be governed by the mining laws of the United States, but it categorically denied that the American land laws extended to the region. It made no provisions for private ownership of property except for allowing the mission stations to retain up to 640 acres of land. Again, the Natives were not to be disturbed in their occupancy or use of land, but Congress reserved to itself the ultimate settlement of the Native claims to ownership of the land. Prohibition was retained. Congress appropriated $25,000 for the education of all children, Native and white, but this was not enough to erect the school buildings or to pay the salaries of more than a few instructors.

President Arthur, a Republican, appointed John Kinkhead, a former northern resident then living in Nevada, as governor, and named Samuel Ward McAllister of California and E. W. Haskett of Iowa as judge and district attorney, respectively. Almost immediately a conflict broke out between the officeholders and the Reverend Dr. Jackson, who had been appointed general agent of education for Alaska. Dr. Jackson and the missionaries who sided with him championed the cause of the Natives, who, they declared, were being exploited and corrupted by the whites. Kinkhead, like Dr. Jackson a Republican and a Presbyterian, was no enemy of the Natives, but he strongly supported the whites in their determination to develop Alaska. His opposition to prohibition aroused the resentment of the newcomers and of Dr. Jackson, who denounced him and the other presidential appointees as high-living, hard-drinking men whose interest in the Natives was minimal. In turn, Dr. Jackson's political enemies accused him of using the money entrusted to him as the General Agent of Education for Alaska solely for the benefit of the Natives and his church. Haskett, the district attorney, ordered Jackson's arrest on charges of attempting to convert a public road into the private property of the Sitka Industrial School, of which he was a sponsor, but soon dropped the case.[38] When Grover Cleveland was inaugurated as president, Dr. Jackson persuaded him to replace the Alaskan officeholders. The president complied, naming Alfred Swineford, a Democrat, as governor.[39] Swineford, a vigorous champion of self-government, became the inveterate foe of the Alaska Commercial Company, which he accused of wanting to control the territory—and, like Kinkhead, he also won the enmity of Dr. Jackson.

## THE LIQUOR CONTROVERSY

The controversy between the governors and Dr. Jackson, who represented the missionary group, was essentially a struggle for influence in the nation's capital over who should be consulted on Alaska legislation and political appointments. The two were definitely at odds over the liquor question and its control. Dr. Jackson was a strict pro-

hibitionist for whom alcohol was an evil and largely responsible for the depressed condition of the Alaska Natives. In Swineford's judgment, on the other hand, "prohibition served only to flood the territory with liquors most vile and poisonous to the enrichment of a few who have been engaged in their illegal importation." Moreover, Swineford felt that prohibition could not be enforced in Alaska. In his opinion the only way to control the liquor traffic was to limit the number of businesses allowed to sell liquor by requiring them to be licensed—and to establish rules, strictly enforced, for selling beverages.[40] Dr. Jackson was the immediate victor in the struggle. Prohibition continued in Alaska until almost the turn of the century, when a system of licensing along the lines advocated by Swineford was adopted. Dr. Jackson and Swineford also clashed on the issue of education. Swineford, according to historian Hinckley, "did not realize the appropriateness of a Christian leader as General Agent of Education;" he believed that Dr. Jackson was interested in foisting a system of education upon Alaska in which religious organizations would be dominant.[41]

## AMERICAN INFLUENCES ON WILDLIFE

The coming of the Americans affected the Native peoples more than the Russians had. The Americans had not only penetrated the interior but also gone into the Arctic regions. Their aggressive exploitation of Alaskan resources threatened the Native food supply in some areas.

Whalers, who had been present even during the Russian days, eventually decimated the whales. They then began hunting walruses for their highly valued ivory tusks and for their blubber, which was rendered into oil; the bodies were usually left to rot. In this reckless destruction, Eskimos soon took part. Some, having become enchanted with the goods that could be obtained from a commercial economy, discarded their age-old practice of killing only those animals needed for food. Their efficiency in slaughter was enhanced by the guns they obtained from the whites. Whole villages were threatened with starvation.[42] In the southeast, Natives complained that the white men were taking over the salmon runs and endangering the Indian economy.

## MISSIONARIES

While some missionaries believed that conversion to Christianity was the answer to Native problems, the Reverend William Duncan sought to lead the way by creating a model community. In 1887 he had brought a thousand Tsimshian followers from Metlakatla (Fort Simpson), in British Columbia, where his superiors in the Church of England had condemned his views on theology, to Annette Island. There, on land obtained through a congressional grant, he built a new Metlakatla designed to make the Natives self-sufficient. They were taught trades such as carpentry, seamanship, boat building, and other crafts. Their built their own sawmills and cannery and engaged in other enterprises. They lived in neat, orderly homes. But despite their prosperity the younger Tsimshians in particular became restless under Duncan's authoritarian rule and in 1912 successfully petitioned the government for a school, which he opposed.[43]

Dr. Jackson also threw his great energy into finding an answer to the Natives' economic problems so that they would not be dependent on charity or public assistance. His friend Captain Michael Healy, of the Revenue Cutter Service, suggested that the Eskimos might be taught the cultivation of the reindeer, which was the basis of livelihood for the Natives of the nearby Chukotski Peninsula, just across the Bering Strait. Dr. Jackson, very much taken with the idea, immediately began a campaign of public subscription and obtained enough

money to bring a small herd and instructors in 1891 to train the Eskimos in their care. Subsequently he secured a congressional appropriation to further the work. Thus began a new enterprise in Alaska, which, according to Brooks, prospered despite Jackson's mismanagement.[44]

American concern over another industry—the seal fisheries and in particular the hunting of seals on the high seas—brought about a diplomatic controversy with Great Britain. Each spring the seals made their way from southern waters to the Pribilof Islands to mate. There the Alaska Commercial Company, the lessees of the islands, designed a conservation program to keep the seal population stable. Since an adult bull has his own harem and keeps the younger males away from the females, the company killed only the three-year-old "bachelors." But other sealers made no distinction between male and female, young and old, and hunted them in the water where many seals drowned after having been shot. To stop this wanton slaughter, the United States declared the Bering Sea an American waterway on March 2, 1889, and prohibited all hunting of seals. American warships seized Canadian vessels and crews that refused to heed the edict. Great Britain protested on behalf of its Canadian subjects. An arbitration tribunal, meeting in Paris, awarded damages of slightly less than half a million dollars to the Canadians, but the two governments agreed to limit the number of seals taken in a single year.[45]

## ALASKA IN 1896

By 1896, the year of the great Klondike gold discoveries, Alaska bore the American imprint. Russian culture cannot be said to have been destroyed by the coming of the Americans, for there had been too few Russians in Alaska, and the area of their influence had been too slight to have had much lasting effect. The decline of Sitka and that small part of Alaska that could be called

76

Russian had taken place long before the American purchase of Alaska. Americans were free to come and go as they saw fit and were not required to obtain permission to engage in occupations of their choice. When the Americans came, they spread out far beyond the area that had been under Russian control. The white population of Alaska had increased tenfold since the Russian period. New communities had come into being, and mining was the industry that attracted most newcomers.

In the absence of civil government the miners had established their own codes to regulate affairs. When Alaska attained its first civil government, the miners' code con-

tinued to operate because the First Organic Act was fairly ineffective. Alaskans had a right to complain, because under the act they still did not have self-government, they could not obtain title to land, and they could not tax themselves to put into effect the services they needed. Alaskans were very much aware of the rudiments of American politics, for they had sent delegates to Washington, D.C., and even participated in national party conventions in 1888, but to little avail. Alaskan problems received little consideration from a far-off government in Washington that neither knew nor cared very much about them.

# 5. THE GREAT GOLD RUSH

With the discovery of gold in the Klondike, men flocked from all parts of the world to one of the greatest gold rushes, in which eventually more than $150 million gold was taken. Unaware that the Klondike is in the Yukon Territory of Canada, Americans clamored for information concerning Alaska and the North, and the trials and tribulations of the prospectors, most of whom were fellow countrymen, became front-page news stories for the "yellow press," then in its infancy. As the gateway to the Klondike, Alaska prospered; new towns and businesses sprang up to meet the needs of those going to the "great diggings." Alfred H. Brooks, the noted authority on Alaska geology, credits miners from the Klondike who pushed out in search of new mineral deposits with advancing the opening of Alaska's gold fields by many years.[1]

Although it was possible to make the journey to the Klondike entirely through Canadian territory, most of the gold seekers preferred the more accessible routes from Alaskan ports. Some went entirely by water, departing by ship from San Francisco or Seattle to Saint Michael, on Norton Sound, and there transferring to a river craft going up the Yukon to Dawson, the metropolis of the Klondike. This was the easiest but also the longest and most expensive route, and

late in the season it was threatened by a freeze of the river that could leave passengers stranded until the spring thaws. The most celebrated of the routes in legend and verse was the Trail of '98 from the head of Lynn Canal, in the Alaska Panhandle, across the White Pass or the Chilkoot Pass. The Chilkoot, accessible from Dyea, now a ghost town, was shorter but steeper. The White Pass out of Skagway had the advantage that animals could be used for transporting supplies. Hundreds of horses, frequently overloaded by incompetent or brutal masters who beat them, slid to their deaths on the slippery, boulder-strewn trail.

After crossing the passes, the thousands of gold seekers built boats and rafts along the headwaters of the Yukon River. They launched their homemade crafts, navigated across Lake Bennett, and proceeded down the Yukon to their destination. For many, the most difficult part of the journey was the climb to the summit of the passes. The Canadian government required that each man have at least one year's supply of food. The food, together with other necessities, such as medical supplies, tools, and camping equipment, might weigh several tons. It was common for two men to form a team, push part of their cargo on sleds, and carry as much as 150 pounds on their backs to the summit of the Chilkoot Pass. Then, after reaching the top, one man might go back for another load while the other stood guard, and so they would alternate until they had brought up all their possessions. The climb was dangerous as well as arduous. On April 3, 1898, a great snowslide took the lives of forty-three persons near Chilkoot Pass.

Almost overnight Skagway, the supply center for the Yukon, burgeoned into Alaska's largest town. For those finding employment there, Skagway was the end of the journey, while others waited sometimes for months on end for favorable weather to leave for Dawson or for a ship to take them home. The town achieved a great deal of notoriety largely as a result of the activities of Jefferson C. Smith and his gang. Because of the virtual nonexistence of formal government authority, "Soapy," as he was called, in the autumn of 1897 was able to make himself master of Skagway and terrorize its inhabitants. His men, stationed along Seattle's waterfront, advised travelers where to go and whom to see in Skagway. Upon arriving in town, the travelers would be met by other members of the gang, taken under Soapy's protection, and very often fleeced of their money either at gunpoint or in crooked gambling games. Returnees

Prospectors carrying their supplies over Chilkoot Pass about 1898. Hegg Photograph. Courtesy Anchorage Historical and Fine Arts Museum, Anchorage, Alaska.

Jefferson Randolph ("Soapy") Smith (with beard) in his saloon with some of his cohorts. P. E. Larss Photograph. Courtesy Alaska Historical Library, Juneau.

from Dawson might be treated in similar fashion. Newcomers to Skagway were encouraged to send telegrams to their loved ones announcing their safe arrival. Not long afterward they would be asked to pay an additional five dollars for return messages that had been sent "collect." The only problem was that no telegraph line existed in Skagway. Like a modern Mafia godfather, Smith was regarded by some as a great public benefactor, for as the head of the local welfare agency he was most generous to those in Skagway who found themselves destitute.[2] A patriot, Smith organized volunteers for service in the war against Spain. The secretary of war, however, politely declined their help.

Smith's rule came to an end in July, 1898.

Under the leadership of Frank Reid, a surveyor, angry townspeople formed a vigilante group to rid Skagway of the outlaws. Reid himself, at the head of the posse, challenged Smith. They exchanged shots, and Smith died instantly. Reid died a few hours later a martyr in defense of law and order.

## THE GOLD STRIKE AT NOME

Alaska soon experienced its own gold rush on the Seward Peninsula, the tip of which is only sixty miles from Siberia. Daniel Libby, a member of the Western Union Telegraph expedition, had found gold there in 1866, but it was not until 1897 that he returned to the area. With the backing of several men from San Francisco and accompanied by his brother-in-law Louis Melsing; H. L. Blake, who was a mining engineer, and A. P. Mordaunt, Libby left San Francisco on August 18, 1897, on board the steamer *North Fork* bound for Golovin Bay. The four organized the first mining district on the peninsula at Council City. On September 22, 1898, Jafet Lindeberg, Jon Brynteson, and Eric Lindblom, known as the "three lucky Swedes," although Lindeberg had been born in Norway, made their great strike at Anvil Creek, and the Nome Mining District came into existence.

No great stampede followed immediately. Prospectors had become leery of new El Dorados. Some of the newcomers came from Kotzebue, where they had pursued riches in vain. Others, returning from the Klondike by way of the Yukon River, decided after their arrival at Saint Michael that they had little to lose and made the 100-mile crossing to Nome to try their luck again. But after the ice had gone out in the spring of 1899, and ships arrived in Seattle laden with treasure from the peninsula, the rush was on. By October more than three thousand men were working at Nome.

Life at Nome was much different from life in the Klondike. Although the place was more readily accessible, living conditions there were more difficult. Most of the Seward Peninsula is barren of trees. Aside from driftwood, all lumber had to be imported, and it was almost imossible for miners to build cabins for themselves or secure fuel for heating. There was little game on the Seward Peninsula. Climatic conditions make vegetable growing impossible. A person unable to obtain lodging at Nome or its vicinity in winter had no choice but to leave.[3]

In the words of Alfred H. Brooks, Nome in the summer of 1899 "was anything but a contented community." Its problems were complicated by a general air of lawlessness combined with numerous instances of claim jumping. Professional claims takers, armed with powers of attorney, had been busy

filing claims for themselves and others, a practice contrary to American law, since no gold had been found at the time they made their applications. Their claims, as well as those held by foreigners, were challenged by newcomers, who were incensed to find that all the gold-bearing areas had apparently been staked. Mining had come almost to a standstill, and Nome appeared to be on the verge of civil war. Brooks believed that bloodshed was averted only by the prompt action of Lieutenant O. L. Spaulding, Jr., the commander of a small detachment of troops on the Seward Peninsula, in disbanding a meeting called by malcontents on July 10, 1899, for the purpose of taking over the disputed claims. But within a few days the discovery that the Nome beaches contained gold pushed these controversies to the background. Beach mining is easier than creek mining, for there is never any frozen material to thaw and the equipment needed is minimal. Access to the beaches was apparently open to all, though a mining company with adjacent claims tried to collect royalties. When the miners refused to pay, an attempt was made to evict them from the beaches, but the opposition was too great. By the summer of 1900, Nome was a tent city with more than 20,000 men working its "golden sands."[4]

Nome was wide open, condemned by moralists as comparable only to Skagway in its flouting of the law and disregard of convention. "Shootouts, muggings, and saloon brawls," according to historian William R. Hunt, "made life insecure." Brooks reported that, in all his years of travel throughout Alaska and the Yukon, Nome was the only place where he carried a gun or felt any apprehension of being robbed. In 1900 the town was filled with pimps, prostitutes, con men, and gamblers. It had fifty saloons, and that figure soon doubled.[5]

Respect for law and governmental authority in Nome was further undermined by the appointment of Arthur H. Noyes as the judge for the newly created Second Ju-

Freight and supplies being landed on the Nome beach, 1900. Courtesy Mulligan Album, Alaska and Polar Regions Archives, Elmer E. Rasmuson Library, University of Alaska.

dicial District of northern Alaska. Noyes, one of those whom novelist Rex Beach designated "spoilers of Nome," had been recommended to the position by Alexander McKenzie, a Republican national committeeman from North Dakota. McKenzie was also president of the Alaska Gold Mining Company, whose shareholders included Senator Henry C. Hansborough of North Dakota and Senator Thomas Carter of Montana. McKenzie and Noyes arrived in Nome on July 19, 1900, and within half an hour Noyes had appointed McKenzie administrator in charge of all mines in which a dispute over title to the claim existed.

McKenzie hired men to work the mines, dividing the profits with the judge, a district attorney, and a few other cronies. In the meantime, one of the original owners, Charles D. Lane, of the Wild Goose Company, made two trips to San Francisco in an effort to have the Ninth Circuit Court

of Appeals reverse Noyes' decision. Judge William Morrow, speaking for the higher court, directed that the claims be restored, and when McKenzie and Noyes refused to comply, Morrow sent marshals to enforce the order. McKenzie was taken to San Francisco for trial and sentenced to a year in jail. The sentence was subsequently commuted to three months by President William McKinley. Noyes continued as judge until the summer of 1901, when he was removed and fined $1,000 for contempt of court. The district attorney and an agent of the Department of Justice received sentences of four and twelve months, respectively, for their roles in the affair.[6]

The next great strike after Nome took place in the Tanana Valley and marked the beginnings of the town of Fairbanks. Two men, Felix Pedro, an Italian coal miner who had been prospecting in the area, and E. T. Barnette, merchant, promoter, and banker,

Felix Pedro, who discovered gold in the Tanana Valley near the site of present Fairbanks on July 22, 1902. Courtesy Historical Photograph Collection, Alaska and Polar Regions Archives, Elmer E. Rasmuson Library, University of Alaska.

are associated with the birth of the new settlement. Pedro first found gold on the hill above the valley that now bears his name, Pedro Dome. Barnette, on Pedro's advice, had established a trading post on the Chena River near the place where it joins the Tanana River. After the discovery of gold a minor stampede followed, ensuring the success of Barnette's venture. On September 27, 1902, the miners held a meeting and elected Barnette recorder of the district. Previously Judge James Wickersham had asked Barnette to name his trading post after Senator Charles W. Fairbanks, the senior senator from Indiana. Wickersham admired Fairbanks, a powerful figure in the Republican party who would become vice-president in 1904. Barnette agreed to Wickersham's suggestion, and in return for

the favor the judge promised to do everything in his power to help Captain Barnette succeed, no small promise from the most powerful government official within 300,000 square miles. Barnette later explained that both he and the judge thought the name Fairbanks for his trading post was a good idea, because should they ever need assistance in the nation's capital, they were assured of the friendship of someone who could help.

Barnette was eager to let people know of the gold discovery in Tanana Valley, and he invited friends to come to share in the good fortune even before there was much evidence of a great supply of the precious metal. Just before Christmas he sent his cook, Jujiro Wada, to Dawson with a load of furs to sell. Upon his arrival there Wada gave an interview to the *Yukon Sun* and told of the wonderful riches in the Tanana area. About eight hundred men were said to have left Dawson for the Tanana Valley in the dead of winter when the temperature hovered about −50°F. Before their arrival other men had come from the Rampart diggings. Many of the prospectors came to the new town of Chena, started near the mouth of the Chena River. But no great boom developed. For a time the area was threatened with starvation; supplies of food were dangerously low. There were threats to lynch Wada. By June, 1903, it seemed that "the bottom had fallen out of the stampede." Good town lots in Fairbanks were selling for ten dollars. What many miners did not realize was that conditions in Fairbanks made mining more difficult than in the Klondike. The gold was buried much deeper in the ground, some of it a few hundred feet down.[7]

Within a few months three great discoveries had been made near the town, at Cleary Creek, Fairbanks Creek, and Ester Creek. Miners slowly came back. By Christmas 1,500 to 1,800 were in the Tanana Valley, most of them employed by others at five dollars a day. Since expensive machinery and equipment were needed to thaw the ground and extract the metal from it, the individual prospector in time became a rarity, and the valley was dotted with a number of small companies.

Fairbanks was now well on its way to becoming the metropolis of interior Alaska. It called itself "the largest log cabin town in the world." Barnette had succeeded in persuading the Northern Commercial Company, the largest firm in Alaska, to buy a two-thirds interest in his store which they soon converted into total ownership. In 1904, after the ice went out, boats had come from Dawson bringing half the population with them. Construction work had begun on the Tanana Valley Railroad, a narrow-gauge line to connect Fairbanks and Chena with the mining camps and towns in the Tanana Valley. For years Fairbanks and Chena competed with each other to be the leading town of the district. Fairbanks won out, aided in part by Judge Wickersham, who moved the headquarters of the Third Judicial District Court to Fairbanks. All government buildings in the area—the courthouse, the post office, and the jail—were built in Fairbanks. Most people coming to the Tanana Valley chose to live in Fairbanks rather than Chena, where lots were more expensive. By 1915, Chena was almost deserted, and the Tanana River washed away most of the townsite; today only a marker indicates where the town once stood.

Many of the men who chose to settle in Fairbanks sent for their families to join them. As a consequence, the town acquired some domestic institutions such as schools,

A large outfit, with twenty-one mules and horses and forty-six sleds carrying twelve tons of whiskey and hardware, leaving Valdez for Fairbanks in 1905. The whiskey was an important component of the load, for there were many saloons in Fairbanks and the surrounding mining camps. Courtesy Anchorage Historical and Fine Arts Museum, Anchorage.

churches, and a hospital. By 1905 the population of Fairbanks had grown to five thousand. That it was still primarily a mining community, however, is emphasized by the statistics on gold production. In 1906 production reached more than $6 million, in contrast to the 1903 take of only $40,000. Also in 1906 a fire almost destroyed the town, but it was soon rebuilt.

Although churches thrived in this frontier town, they had to compete with the saloons for the miners' money. Saloons were open twenty-four hours a day. Gambling was wide open. Miners in from the diggings for a day or a week could find entertainment and solace on the "line," a section of the town set aside for the women who wanted their share of Alaska gold.

The women were not the only Fairbanks residents who acquired gold without digging for it. One of the most notorious characters in the area was a highwayman referred to as the "blue parka bandit" for the costume he wore. But the man had his principles. Once after robbing the Right Reverend P. T. Rowe, bishop of the Episcopal church, the highwayman returned the poke, explaining that he was, after all, one of the bishop's parishioners. Less principled and more notorious among the citizens of Fairbanks was its founder, E. T. Barnette, whose machinations resulted in the failure of the Washington-Alaska Bank. For many years the *Fairbanks News-Miner* carried headlines whenever there was a story of a bank failure in the United States or of a robbery involving a large sum of money, calling it "Barnetting going on still."[8]

Men mined gold throughout Alaska. New towns were founded; some were permanent, and others were as ephemeral as the mining camps. On the coast gold had been found in southeastern Alaska at Juneau and farther north on the Seward Peninsula at Nome. The discovery of gold in the Klondike profoundly influenced Alaska mining activities. When news came into the upper Yukon Valley of the Klondike bonanza, men left the diggings in the Fortymile country and Birch Creek for Dawson, and by 1897 Circle City had become virtually a ghost town. But once the Klondike boom had peaked, interest in Alaska was heightened. Of the thousands who had gone to Dawson, many crossed the border to try their luck in Alaska, some prospecting for new strikes, others joining established camps at Nome, Fairbanks, or more remote sites. Mining had begun at Rampart in 1893 but did not move into full swing until about four years later. At its height the town had about two thousand people, many of whom had been at Dawson, while others among the inhabitants had come up the Yukon on their way to the Klondike but had stopped at Rampart and never gone any farther. North of the Arctic Circle gold had been found in the vicinity of the Chandalar and Koyukuk rivers, where two towns, Coldfoot and Wiseman, came into existence. In the area of the Kuskokwim and Innoko rivers, Iditarod, McGrath, Bethel, Flat, and Ophir were communities of some size that had developed from mining camps.[9] Valdez and Eagle, although not mining towns, were very much affected by the activities of the miners. Eagle, on the Yukon River only a few miles from the border, served as the port of entry for those coming from Canada. The town had begun as a trading post on a site three miles from an Indian village. At its height Eagle "serviced more rich mining camps than any other American town along the Yukon River."[10] Men from the camps around the Seventymile, Nation, Charley, Tatonduk, and Fortymile rivers came to trade. Eagle became the terminus for a telegraph line from Valdez. Fort Egbert, the headquarters for the army in northern Alaska, was in Eagle, as was the seat for the Third Judicial District before its transfer to Fairbanks.

Valdez is an ice-free port. In 1898 prospectors on the way to the Klondike came to

Valdez and crossed the Valdez Glacier on their way to the Klondike. But most of those who used the trail to the interior went to the Copper River country, which had a good many mining camps, although the trail continued to Eagle. Valdez became increasingly more important with the development of Fairbanks. A trail built to connect the two towns became a wagon road after 1905.

## THE EFFECT OF THE GOLD RUSH

The gold rush focused attention on Alaska as nothing else had. Alaska and things Alaskan became front-page news. Rumors circulated that Americans in the Klondike and on the Alaska trails to the Klondike faced starvation. Congress responded and appropriated $200,000 to be spent for relief at the discretion of the secretary of war. Dr. Sheldon Jackson was sent to Norway to purchase reindeer for transporting supplies to the stricken miners. These "government pets," as critics of the expedition called the reindeer, were shipped to New York, then overland to San Francisco, and from there by boat to Skagway. The long voyage by sea took its toll. Many of the animals perished before reaching their destination. Upon their arrival in Skagway the surviving animals were taken over the White Pass trail, which is heavily wooded and not suitable for reindeer, which are native to the tundra and feed on lichens. More died. The relief expedition should not have been organized in the first place. Food had been provided by the Canadian government almost as soon as cries for help had been made, and no one went hungry.

Undeterred by the reindeer fiasco, Congress, for the first time since the purchase of Alaska, went on to deal more seriously with Alaskan problems. It appropriated money

Lapp reindeer herds, probably photographed in Scandinavia. Courtesy H. Levy Collection, Alaska and Polar Regions Archives, Elmer E. Rasmuson Library, University of Alaska.

for the U.S. Geological Survey to begin work on the survey and exploration of Alaska, and it extended the coal-mining laws of the United States to the district. The U.S. Army built posts at Eagle, Nome, and Haines, and at Tanana at the junction of the Yukon and Tanana rivers. The Department of Agriculture received money to examine the potential of farming in Alaska.

Congress also made the first changes in the Organic Act of 1884, a measure which even its supporters had looked upon as only a stopgap, enacting three pieces of legislation dealing with the economy and the Alaska political system. The first, passed in 1898, made it possible for railroad builders to obtain a right-of-way and gave settlers their first opportunity to receive title to land by extending the Homestead Act to Alaska. Alaskans, however, were restricted to 80 acres instead of the 160 acres customary in other parts of the United States. The prospective homesteader was also forced to have the land surveyed at his own expense.

Under the Organic Act of 1884 the Oregon Criminal Code had been extended to Alaska. In 1899, Congress recognized that Alaska had unique problems and enacted a few changes to make the code more responsive to Alaskan conditions. At the same time, taxes were levied on businesses, and the revenues collected went into the treasury of the United States, presumably to pay the costs of government in Alaska. Canneries were assessed $0.04 for each case of salmon packed (a case contained 48 one-pound cans). Railroads were taxed $100 for each mile in operation even before the lines were completed. Companies had to pay license fees for the privilege of doing business in Alaska, the charge varying with the nature of the enterprise; that for liquor was highest of all. The sale of liquor was legalized despite the objections of Dr. Sheldon Jackson, and Prohibition, which had been a dead letter in Alaska since its inception, was repealed. Even John Brady, Alaska's

governor and, like his mentor, Jackson, a staunch temperance advocate, recognized that the government's liquor policy had been a failure. He admitted that effective regulation of liquor could be achieved only through the payment of a high license fee that would limit the number of establishments engaged in the trade.[11]

In 1900, Congress revised the civil code and turned its attention to the government of Alaska. The Alaskan population had almost doubled in a decade as a result of the gold rush. Commensurate with this increase Congress added two new judicial districts. In southeastern Alaska the judge alternated in holding sessions at Skagway and Juneau. Saint Michael and then Nome served as the headquarters for the newly created northern division, while in the interior, first Eagle and then Fairbanks served as the seat of the judiciary. Congress also decreed that the capital was to be moved from Sitka to Juneau, a larger town, whenever "suitable grounds and buildings" were obtained; this move was not accomplished until a few years later.

Congress also gave Alaskans their initial taste of self-government when it provided for the incorporation of towns. Once a community had met the requirements of incorporation, it could elect a council of seven, one of whom served as mayor. The council had the power to furnish various services such as street improvements and police and fire protection and to provide for a school system. Towns were limited in their sources of revenue. Borrowing was expressly prohibited. Taxes on real and personal property were restricted to 1 percent of assessed valuation. The municipalities were permitted to impose license fees on businesses; half the money collected was to be used in support of education. Businesses thereupon protested that they were subject to a duplicate set of license fees. Congress responded by rescinding the authority of municipalities to impose license fees, and all the revenues the federal government collected from this source were turned over to the towns.[12]

## THE ALASKA-CANADA BOUNDARY DISPUTE

The era of the gold rush brought to a head the Alaska boundary dispute with Canada that had long been festering. It was generally agreed that the portion of the treaty of 1825 which had sought to define the limits of the Russian and British possessions south of 60° north latitude was very much clouded in ambiguity. On several occasions after the United States took possession of Alaska, disputes arose and suggestions were made, chiefly by the Canadians, to settle the controversy. Neither side, however, seemed to be willing to undertake the cost of a survey.

By 1898 the Canadian case extended to claims of ownership of Skagway and Dyea, which, if recognized, would give Canadians in the Yukon direct access to the sea without having to pass through American territory. Theodore Roosevelt, who succeeded McKinley as president following the latter's assassination in 1901, condemned Canada's claims as totally without merit. He refused to allow the matter to be decided by a board of arbitration because such bodies, he believed, invariably settled disagreements of this sort by dividing the disputed area equally between the rival contestants. Roosevelt instead proposed that a tribunal of six impartial jurists, three from each side, be constituted to examine the merits of the controversy. For the American delegation Roosevent named Henry Cabot Lodge, the ultranationalistic senator from Massachusetts; Elihu Root, secretary of war; and Senator George Turner of the state of Washington, who knew that the trade of the city of Seattle would be affected if the Canadian claims to Skagway and Dyea were upheld. None of them could be called impartial.

The British-Canadian delegation included Lord Alverstone, the lord chief justice of England; Sir Louis Jette, a former member of the Canadian Supreme Court; and Allen B. Aylesworth, a distinguished member of the Canadian bar.

By a vote of four to two the tribunal, with Lord Chief Justice Alverstone siding with the Americans, rejected the Canadian claims except for two small islands in Portland Canal. The Canadians accused Alverstone of having sold out their interests in behalf of British-American relations. The Alaska boundary was now clearly defined, but relations between the United States and Canada were long embittered by this dispute and its settlement.[13]

The gold rush has a prominent role in the history of Alaska, marking for some the beginnings of the modern era. It was indeed a time of great excitement. Thouands from all walks of life went to the territory for gold and adventure. With the new towns that sprang up came the first semblances of self-government, and Alaskans felt that they were beginning to receive the recognition that was their due. But the gold rush essentially remains an episode in Alaskan life and development, acting more as a stimulant than as a instrument of change. While it drew more people to the territory and resulted in a population that was to remain numerically stable until the great increase following World War II, those who went usually remained only a few years. But interest had been kindled, and indeed there was optimism concerning Alaska and its potential as the twentieth century opened.

## DEVELOPING ALASKA'S AGRICULTURE AND TRANSPORTATION

As Alaska's population grew, schemes were afoot to make the area less dependent on the outside for food. The Russians had considered the possibilities of farming and planted some vegetable gardens. During the American era travelers to the Yukon River valley had come back with tales of the tremendous cabbages grown there. But it was not until the advent of the gold rushes and the expectations of an increased population that Alaskan agriculture could no longer be considered a "fascinating oddity," in the words of historian Orlando Miller. In 1897 the U.S. Department of Agriculture sent three special agents to southeastern Alaska, the south-central region, Kodiak, the Alaska Peninsula, and the Yukon Valley. After mentioning the difficulties involved in farming in the north, they nevertheless indicated that a "variety of crops" could be grown and noted that cattle raising and vegetable gardening were already being undertaken. One of the investigators recommended encouraging men to settle on small plots and "engage in mixed fishing, lumbering and farming." He believed that

this would result in "settling the country with a hardy race of fishermen and others used to the water, from which we may secure seamen for the merchant marine and navy, and at the same time . . . develop other resources" and thus establish in Alaska "a great civilization." [14]

Acting on the agents' recommendations, the federal government established several agricultral experiment stations, first at Sitka in 1898 and then at Kenai, Kodiak, Rampart, Copper Center, Faribanks, and finally Matanuska in 1917. Danish-born C. G. Georgeson, appointed to head the station at Sitka, was an ardent promoter of Alaska agriculture. His constant refrain was that "the hope for the natives and the development of the territory [lies] in a prosperous agriculture, for it stands to reason that if the means to support life exist within the boundaries of the territory all other resources will become more valuable." [15]

A sternwheeler under construction in the Aleutian Islands in 1898. Courtesy M. Murphy Collection, Alaska and Polar Regions Archives, Elmer E. Rasmuson Library, University of Alaska.

The Fairbanks–Valdez Stage, run by Ed. S. Orr and Company, which carried passengers and freight along the Richardson Road (later Highway), named for the first president of the Board of Road Commissioners for Alaska. The approximately 360-mile trip was easiest in the winter after the mud of the trail and the creeks and rivers had frozen. Along the trail were many roadhouses of varying quality. In 1913, Robert E. (Bobby) Sheldon made the first trip by automobile between Valdez and Fairbanks, and soon "motor stages" took over. The roadhouses continued to operate because it was still a long, arduous journey. Courtesy Archie Lewis Collection, Alaska and Polar Regions Archives, Elmer E. Rasmuson Library, University of Alaska.

More immediate to the pressing needs of Alaska was a good system of transportation. Use of the inland waterways had been considerably improved in the Klondike era with the increase in the number of steamboats plying the Yukon and later the Tanana. Dogsleds were of importance almost everywhere, but there were few roads and trails. Although Congress had authorized private individuals to build and collect tolls on roads and bridges in 1898, few ventured to take advantage of such opportunities.

In 1904 another measure placed the burden of road building on the inhabitants of the territory. Each man was made liable to labor two days a year on the roads, or in lieu thereof pay a tax of $8. The U.S. commissioners appointed a supervisor in each district who was to receive $4 a day for his efforts at a time when the prevailing wage in the territory was $6 to $8 a day. But it was not until the passage of the Nelson Act in 1905 and the establishment of the Board of Road Commissioners for Alaska in the same year that road building in Alaska became a reality. The Nelson Act created the Alaska Fund, decreeing that 70 percent of all monies collected from license fees outside incorporated towns were to be used for road building, 25 percent for education, and the remaining 5 percent for the care of the insane. President Theodore Roosevelt appointed Major Wilds P. Richardson to head the board. Congress appropriated additional road-building funds annually. By 1920 about 4,890 miles of roads and trails, 1,031 miles of which were wagon roads, had been built; the most notable of these was the Richardson Road (now Richardson Highway), named for the first president of the board in 1919, which connected Valdez and Fairbanks.

While private companies had little interest in building Alaska roads, the lure of adventure in constructing lines in the Far North and the prospect of fabulous profits attracted railway men to Alaska. In the six months from September, 1897, to March, 1898, eleven companies reportedly petitioned for rights-of-way over 673 miles of land. Several more applied until the Panic of 1907 brought speculation to a halt. In 1903 the Alaska Central Railway began construction of a road to the interior; it went bankrupt in 1909 and reorganized as the Alaska Northern Railroad which completed construction to Kern Creek, mile 72, at the head of Turnagain Arm, where the track laying of the financially exhausted company ceased forever.

The Alaska Syndicate was to become famous, or infamous, depending on the sources consulted, in Alaska's economics and politics. Historian William H. Wilson has told of its involvement in railroads, copper, and coal. In 1900, Stephen Birch, who had accompanied an army expedition along the Copper River in 1898, bought a number of copper claims. He interested the Guggenheim mining family, who, with J. P. Morgan and Company and others, organized the Alaska Syndicate in 1906 to provide development capital. The syndicate's first interest was its rich copper-ore deposit. To move the ore to the Guggenheim smelter at Tacoma, Washington, the syndicate bought steamship and lighterage companies, which it consolidated under the Alaska Steamship Company. It also bought and sold canneries, creating various corporations.

The syndicate had decided that no other railroad would build to the interior in competition with its Copper River and Northwestern Railway from Cordova. That railroad had not crossed the mountains into the Tanana Valley, but its backers had decided that if or when any railroad traversed the mountains it would be theirs. When that time came, the Alaska Syndicate would extend its mining operations into the interior along with its railroad.[16]

The syndicate used various means to discourage competitors. Though violence was the least necessary and politically most damaging means, syndicate employees used it on two occasions. In one instance Copper River construction crews drove another railroad's workers from the Cordova area. On the more famous occasion the deputized leader of an armed band shot and fatally wounded a worker for a rival railroad attempting to build through the Keystone Canyon near Valdez, the site of an abandoned syndicate right-of-way. The event was particularly unfortunate because the challenging Alaska Home Railroad was a promotional line attempting a route the syndicate had already surrendered in all but title. During the subsequent trial of the deputy the syndicate lost much face as charges of bribery and other irregularities were aired. The Alaska Home Railroad was never built; it was merely a promotional scheme.

While several small narrow-gauge railroads served the needs of local inhabitants on the Seward Peninsula and in the Tanana Valley, only two of the larger lines prospered: the White Pass & Yukon Railway, built by Close Brothers of London, connecting Skagway, in Alaska, with Whitehorse, in Canada's Yukon Territory, and the 195-mile Copper River & Northwestern Railroad connecting the Kennecott mines with the port of Cordova.

Unfortunately for promoters, their interest in building railroads in Alaska came at a

The Alaska Home Railroad unloading one of its engines in Valdez in 1907. Courtesy Mrs. Mary Whalen Collection of P. S. Hunt Photographs, Alaska and Polar Regions Archives, Elmer E. Rasmuson Library, University of Alaska.

time when railroads in the United States, accused of having violated a public trust, were highly unpopular. Railroads had received large tracts of land from federal, state, and local governments; had been lent money at low rates of interest; and had been given other subsidies. Critics accused them of abusing their privileges by charging exorbitant rates, corrupting politics, and giving poor service. In Alaska the struggling companies faced tremendous problems of building in a rugged terrain and were hampered by severe climatic conditions. The federal government, however, not only refused aid but penalized the operators by imposing a tax of $100 for each mile the railroad had in operation, even though the construction of the line had not been completed. When President Roosevelt closed the coal fields of Alaska to further

entry, railroad builders felt that they had been struck another blow by being deprived of a cheap source of fuel.

Roosevelt stressed that the withdrawals of coal were temporary and asked Congress to enact laws that would make coal mining in Alaska workable. He further recommended that the United States should aid in building a railroad from the Gulf of Alaska to the Yukon. He also repeated the call that he had made to a previous session of Congress that Alaska be allowed to send a delegate to Congress who would be entitled to a seat in the House of Representatives and all the emoluments of a member of that body. The delegate could introduce measures of concern to himself and his constituents and take part in the debates but could not vote. There were those who believed that once Alaska had secured such a delegate, he would be listened to as an authority on Alaska affairs and would be able to influence Congress on the proper legislation for Alaska.

## THE PUSH FOR HOME RULE

A chain of circumstances enabled Alaska to secure a delegate. Following the war with Spain, the United States had come into possession of a number of islands inhabited by non-English-speaking peoples. In a series of decisions known as the Insular Cases, the U.S. Supreme Court ruled that these islands were unincorporated territories—simply possessions that belonged to but were not part of the United States. Alaska, by contrast, had been incorporated directly into the Union. In a case involving a Mrs. Rasmussen, who had been convicted by a six-man jury of running a house of ill fame in Fairbanks, the high court ruled that when the United States purchased Alaska it had guaranteed to the white inhabitants and persons of mixed blood the rights, privileges, and immunities of American citizens. As an Alaska inhabitant, therefore, Mrs. Rasmussen was a resident of an incorporated territory and entitled to the full protection of the Constitution. Her conviction by a six-man jury violated the Sixth Amendment and was therefore void. Congress reacted quickly to the Court's views on the status of Alaska and changed the official designation from "district" to "territory." It also enacted the measure which gave Alaska a delegate to Congress.[17]

In 1909, Roosevelt was followed as president by the man whom he had supported to be his successor, William Howard Taft. Soon after his inauguration Taft attended the Alaska-Yukon Exposition in Seattle, where Alaskans greeted him warmly and made him a member of the Arctic Brotherhood, a fraternal organization of Alaska pioneers. While he was in Seattle, Taft outlined his plans for governing Alaska. He advocated the creation of a legislative com-

mission to deal with Alaska problems. Its members were to be appointed by the president. This was the system that he had administered while he was governor-general of the Philippines. It had worked well there and would, he thought, be most suitable for Alaska, which lacked the population and resources for a legislature. Taft's remarks were greeted with cries of "No, no," and were generally interpreted by Alaskans as insulting. The president, they felt, thought they were not fit for self-government.[18]

Undoubtedly Taft would have been happier if he had never heard of Alaska and had not become involved in northern affairs. His administration was plagued by an Alaska issue that had far more serious consequences for him than the question of a territorial legislature for the territory. A controversy over the use of Alaska public lands developed between two members of his administration—Richard Ballinger, secretary of the interior, and Chief Forester Gifford Pinchot—that quickly became known as the Ballinger-Pinchot Affair. In fact, it became the leading political issue in American politics and led to a split in the Republican party between Taft and Roosevelt that helped elect Woodrow Wilson president in 1912. To understand the origins of the Ballinger-Pinchot Affair and its consequences for the Alaska home-rule movement, it is necessary to return to Roosevelt's withdrawal of the coal lands in 1906.

## WITHDRAWAL OF ALASKA'S COAL LANDS AND THE BALLINGER-PINCHOT AFFAIR

In 1906, Theodore Roosevelt, the first American president to become vitally interested in the conservation of America's resources, issued an executive order closing Alaska's coal lands to further entry, claiming that the existing laws limiting investors to 160 acres were unworkable and conducive to fraud. He asked Congress to enact legislation that would enable prospective coal-mine operators to obtain enough land to make mining profitable yet prevent any individual or group from securing a monopoly. The Alaska Coal Act, passed on May 28, 1908, permitted the consolidation of claims up to 2,560 acres. The act did not contain a leasing system, but it prevented the monopolization of Alaska coal lands and eliminated the use of dummy entrymen, that is, individuals who claimed lands with the intention of conveying them to someone else. Not until 1914 did Congress pass an Alaska coal-land leasing bill.

Among those who had attempted to obtain coal lands in Alaska before Roosevelt withdrew them were thirty-two persons who had given Clarence Cunningham the power of attorney to make selections for them. Acting on their behalf, Cunningham had taken an option on 5,280 acres of land in the Bering River area which Roosevelt incorporated in 1908 into the newly established Chugach National Forest. Cunningham's efforts to obtain patents for the land had been hindered by repeated delays. Rumors had circulated almost as soon as the necessary forms had been filed that the group had never intended to mine the coal themselves, as the law required, but that they had formed their association precisely for the purpose of transferring their claims to the Alaska Syndicate.

Richard Ballinger was a Seattle attorney whose connection with the Cunningham group antedated his appointment as secretary of the interior by President Taft in 1909. Ballinger had been the commissioner of the General Land Office when Cunningham first applied for patent on behalf of his clients. Following his resignation from government service, as a private attorney he had advised the Cunningham group on the procedures to follow in processing their claims. Louis Glavis, an agent of the Department of the Interior sent to Alaska to examine the Cunningham claims, soon became convinced that Ballinger was preparing to validate their transfer to the syndi-

cate. Glavis consulted Gifford Pinchot, an ardent conservationist, friend of Roosevelt, and head of the Bureau of Forestry. Pinchot advised Glavis to submit his findings to the president, which Glavis did. Taft, after reading Glavis's report, ordered Ballinger to dismiss him "for filing a disingenuous statement unjustly impeaching the integrity of his superior officers." Pinchot himself was later fired on charges of insubordination for having written a letter to Senator Dolliver highly critical of Taft's handling of the affair and his support of Ballinger. To the embarrassment of the administration, Dolliver read the letter on the floor of the Senate.

A joint congressional committee was formed to investigate the Department of the Interior for its handling of the Cunningham claims. It was also to examine the accusations made by Ballinger against some officials of the Bureau of Forestry who, he complained, "had inspired the charges against his department." Voting on strictly party lines, the majority, composed of stalwart Republicans, exonerated Ballinger of any wrongdoing, while the Democrats and one progressive Republican found him guilty of violating his trust. Ballinger resigned in the summer of 1911. His successor as secretary of the interior, Walter Fisher, vice-president of the National Conservation Association, soon afterward invalidated the Cunningham claims.[19]

Alaskans reveled in the publicity of the Ballinger-Pinchot Affair, which accelerated the movement for home rule in the territory. Its disclosures confirmed what proponents of home rule had been saying all along—that federal control had frustrated Alaska's development and that only Alaskans sitting in a legislature of their own could deal effectively with territorial problems. Supporters of the drive for a territorial legislature resented the total exclusion of Alaskans from matters of concern to them and were hardly mollified by the changes in the First Organic Act that gave Alaska two additional judges and allowed municipalities very limited rights of self-government. Nor would they agree that a delegate to Congress could be an effective representative for Alaska. Such a delegate, while useful, was only one voice among many with interests in Alaskan affairs. A minority of Alaskans, chiefly representing mining and fishing interests, were satisfied with Alaska government as it was. They argued that Alaska's population was too small and unstable to afford a legislature and feared that if such a body were constituted it would undoubtedly destroy existing Alaska industries by excessive taxation.[20]

## A NEW GOVERNMENT FOR ALASKA: JAMES WICKERSHAM AND THE SECOND ORGANIC ACT

James Wickersham, former judge of the third judicial district who had been elected as Alaska's delegate to Congress in 1908, took the leadership in the fight for a territorial legislature. Wickersham, a man of magnetic personality in contrast to his colorless predecessors, Waskey and Cale, had portrayed himself in his election campaigns as the enemy of the trusts and monopolies, particularly the Guggenheim family (the "Guggs"), whom he denounced time and again as enemies of Alaska self-government and possessed of an ambition to bring all the resources of Alaska under their control. Wickersham's enemies made much of a letter that had come to light revealing that the self-professed "trust buster" had once applied for a position with the syndicate and had been turned down. His enemies regarded his opposition to the syndicate as sour grapes and his recent conversion to home rule was equally opportunistic and insincere.

Wickersham waged an active campaign in the House of Representatives to secure a territorial legislature for Alaska. He used his influence to help defeat a bill, sponsored by Senator Albert J. Beveridge of Indiana, that embodied Taft's recommendations for a legislative commission to govern Alaska. He was unsuccessful in his early attempts, however, to have the House approve any proposals for Alaska home rule. By 1911 the political climate had changed considerably. President Taft, an adamant opponent of a territorial legislature, had lost control of Congress in the mid-term elections of 1910. The Democrats won a majority in the House of Representatives, while, in the Senate, Beveridge lost his seat, and a coalition of Democrats and progressive Republicans ousted the Republican stalwarts from control. But formidable opposition to home rule for Alaska remained. Wickersham was very much aware that he would have to make substantial concessions to different groups to get congressional approval for his bill and avoid a veto by the president. Although progressives were ideologically committed to home rule, there was fear among the conservationists that an Alaska legislature would be dominated by developers. Business groups, notably representatives of fishing and mining interests, opposed the idea that a territorial legislature regulate the industries. These interests also feared the high taxes that a legislature might impose. Crusaders for moral reform heard Alaska's delegate Wickersham branded a tool of the liquor and gambling interests by his enemies, and they questioned whether Alaskans were capable of undertaking the responsibilities of self-government.[21]

On August 24, 1912, President Taft signed the Second Organic Act, which created a new government for Alaska. Alaska had a legislature, but so many restrictions had been placed upon that body that Wickersham's many critics, including some who had opposed home rule, complained bitterly that he had sold out Alaska. The federal government still retained control of the use of Alaska's resources. The Alaskan Lobby, as the representatives of the mining and fishing interests were called, had succeeded in putting a clause in the Second Organic Act that expressly forbade the Alaska legislature "to alter, amend, modify and repeal measures relating to fish and game, or to interfere with the primary disposal of the soil." Congress retained for itself the exclusive right to legislate on matters relating to divorce, gambling, the sale of liquor, and the incorporation of towns and required that its approval be obtained before the Alaska legislature could set up a form of county government. Strict limitations were placed on the fiscal authority of the new government. The territory was forbidden to borrow money; its taxing power was restricted to 1 percent of the assessed valuation of property, except for towns, which were allowed 2 percent. Alaska's governor was a presidential appointee whose veto power extended to line items in appropriation bills.[22]

The Second Organic Act provided that the Alaska legislature was to consist of two houses: a senate of eight members and a house of representatives of sixteen members. Since Alaska had no political subdivisions, members of the Alaska legislature were selected in accordance with the judicial districts. Each district, regardless of population, elected four members to the house and two to the senate. Alaska was also unique among territories in not having a judiciary of its own; the president appointed the judges, whose numbers had been increased to four in 1909. Although the judges were federal appointees, their jurisdiction included both federal and territorial affairs. Congress agreed to pay the salaries of the legislators and the expenses of administration.

## THE FIRST ALASKA LEGISLATURE

Following the passage of the Second Organic Act, Alaskans held an election and organized the legislature. Most of the legislators regarded themselves as independents; party organization was still very weak. Al-

The first Alaska territorial House of Representatives, First Legislature, 1913. Courtesy Historical Photograph Collection, Alaska and Polar Regions Archives, Elmer E. Rasmuson Library, University of Alaska.

though severely limited by the restrictions of the act, the early legislature dealt with a wide variety of subjects. Lawmakers made substantial changes to bring civil and criminal codes more in conformity with the Alaska environment. Labor legislation included establishing an eight-hour day, defining conditions of employment in the mines, and providing for a system of old-age pensions. Alaska women were granted the right to vote. Native villages in southeastern Alaska were accorded some rights of self-government. Education received much attention. A territorial board was formed to coordinate the school system and give aid to schools.[23] Segregation of school-children by race, introduced with the passage of the Nelson Act of 1905, continued. Apologists for the dual system argued that putting Natives with poorer backgrounds in schools with whites not only would place them at a serious disadvantage but also would result in lowering educational standards for all.

## PRESIDENT WOODROW WILSON AND ALASKA

Democrat Woodrow Wilson was elected to the presidency in 1912 after a split in the Republican party between Taft and Roosevelt. He promised that Alaska's problems would receive the utmost consideration in his administration. Wilson was an activist, and his legislative program contemplated substantial reforms in the United States. On the subject of Alaska he was explicit. In his State of the Union address to Congress in 1913 (the first delivered in person by a president since the days of Thomas Jefferson) he emphasized that "a duty faces us with regard to Alaska," a duty that he found "very pressing and very imperative"—in effect a "double duty," for it concerned "both the political and material development of the territory." He urged that Alaska be given "full territorial government," and although he did not elaborate,

he undoubtedly was calling attention to the deficiencies in the Alaska system, for its people did not have the right to elect their governor and choose their judges, as the citizens of other territories did. He wanted the resources of Alaska unlocked and made available for use, but he counseled that they should not be "destroyed or wasted," for the "abiding interests of communities" must be placed above any "narrow idea of individual rights" that could bring about monopoly. A railroad should be built in Alaska and administered by the federal government "for the service and development of the country and its people.[24]

Although Congress refused to make changes in the Alaska system of government, it passed the Mondell Act, which reopened the Alaska coal lands to entry. In line with Wilson's suggestion, it instituted a method of leasing rather than outright ownership that could lead to monopoly. Prospective coal-mine operators were given the opportunity to obtain up to 2,560 acres of land, for which they paid a rental fee ranging from $0.25 an acre for the first year of operation to $1.00 after the fifth year. For each ton of coal mined, a royalty of $0.02 was paid. Alaskan coal thus could be available for use by the railroad recently authorized by Congress.

## BUILDING THE ALASKA RAILROAD

Even before Wilson took office as president, the groundwork had been laid for the federal government's sponsorship of a railroad in Alaska. As staunch a conservative as President Taft reluctantly admitted that private enterprise had faced too many obstacles in Alaska. While he agreed to the government's construction of the railroad, he insisted that it should be operated by a private company. In the debates about the railroad a few congressmen repeated the old canard that any expenditure in Alaska was a waste of money, while others were disturbed by the idea of government involvement in railroad building. But, as historian Edward Fitch pointed out, "a faith in railroads combined with a lack of faith in railroad personalities led Congress finally to adopt a program of government ownership and operation for a railroad in Alaska even though Congress disbelieved strongly in government ownership and operation."[25] Largely owing to the influence of Wickersham, regarded as an authority on Alaska affairs, the president was given the authority to choose the route of the railroad. Surveys of alternate sites had already been made by the Alaska Engineering Commission, established during the preceding administration. After some study and discussion Wilson directed that the line should run from Seward, on the tidewater, to Fairbanks, in the interior. Congress appropriated $35 million for the project. Construction began in April, 1915, but the project was not finished until 1923, because the difficulties in construction were formidable. Work was carried on sporadically and was marked by innumerable delays. Congress followed the practice of annual appropriations, allotting only a certain amount of money for each year's operation. When funds ran out, work stopped. During World War I the use of men and materials was drastically curtailed.

The immediate effect of the railroad construction was a boom in Alaska. More than 2,000 men were employed in construction in 1914, their numbers rising to a high of 4,500. Although the pay was only 37 1/2 cents an hour in the early years, the number of applicants for jobs far exceeded demand. Anchorage, now Alaska's largest city, owes its beginnings to the railroad. Begun as a construction site, it won out in competition with Seward to become the headquarters of the Alaska Engineering Commission. The commission built Anchorage, installing water, electrical, sewage, and telephone facilities; putting in streets; and providing fire-fighting services as well as a hospital and a school for the children of its em-ployees. An official of the railroad was named the townsite manager.

## THE JONES ACT AND ITS EFFECTS

In 1920, while the American government was building a railroad to improve Alaska's transportaon system, Congress passed the Maritime Act, usually called the Jones Act after its sponsor, Senator Wesley Jones of the state of Washington. The legislation placed new restrictions on Alaska's commerce. The Jones Act, the purpose of which was to build up the American merchant marine, made it mandatory that all ships engaged in commerce between American ports be American-owned and built in the United States. The act gave shippers the option of using either American- or Canadian-owned vessels to carry goods from a port in the United States to its destination somewhere in the Atlantic or the Pacific—with the exception of Alaska. Merchandise coming into or exported from Alaska had to be carried on American ships. American vessels had to be used even if shippers to Alaska could obtain better rates from Canadians. Alaskans protested that this discrimination violated the commerce clause of the Constitution. They brought suit to have the portion of the act excluding Canadian vessels declared null and void. Justice James Clark McReynolds, speaking for the Supreme Court, acknowledged that the act discriminated against Alaska commerce but pointed out that the Constitution clearly states that "no preference shall be given any regulation or commerce or revenue to the ports of one state over those of another."[26] Since Alaska was a territory, not a state, Congress had the power to discriminate if it so chose. That the act might be beneficial to Seattle, the chief port of Senator Jones's state, Washington, was not for the courts to decide.

In 1920, Alaska had a population of slightly more than 55,000 a loss of more than 14 percent during the previous dec-

The Fairbanks Exploration Company dredge on Gold Stream, near Fairbanks, in the late 1920s. The dredge, which floated in a small pond, dug the thawed ground with a bucket line (at the left) and after processing the soil to remove the gold, deposited the tailings behind the dredge. Courtesy Charles E. Bunnell Collection, Alaska and Polar Regions Archives, Elmer E. Rasmuson Library, University of Alaska.

ade. When the United States entered World War I, men had left Alaska to enter the armed services or to work in war industries. Following the war the United States experiencing a boom, and many had felt little inducement to return to Alaska, where the opportunities appeared to be more limited. The Alaska economy was still centered around the exploitation of its natural resources. Mining and fishing far outdistanced the fur trade, Alaska's mainstay in the Russian era. But the fisheries provided little employment for territorial residents, since the salmon packers brought their crews with them from the outside. The era of the great gold rush was over, and the primitive mining methods of the prospector had given way to the use of machinery. Dredges were now recovering the gold buried deep in the ground. Copper mining had come to rival gold but provided jobs for several hundred at most. Alaska agriculture had not flourished. In 1923, Alaska's chief agricultural regions, Fairbanks and Anchorage-Matanuska, had only ninety farmers, and they held 22,167 acres of land, only 11,421 of which were cultivated.

Alaska was still very much a colony of the United States. Her government was comparable to that of a British crown colony. She had been given a limited form of home rule, but control of her resources remained in the hands of Congress. The Alaska economy was colonial; the territory supplied raw materials to the mother country, from which she obtained most of her finished goods and the capital needed for investment in her enterprises. While Congress had finally appropriated money to build a railroad in Alaska, American lawmakers more often than not ignored Alaska's problems or passed laws that were ill-advised. Alaska's coal fields had been closed to entry for eight years because of congressional inaction. How much harm was done to Alaska commerce by the Jones Act is uncertain, but there is no doubt about the discriminatory nature of the legislation.

# 6. NORMALCY, THE DEPRESSION, AND THE NEW DEAL

Warren G. Harding succeeded Wilson as president of the United States in 1921. An exponent of the contemporary reaction, he repudiated the idealism of his predecessor, denounced the League of Nations, and declared in his inaugural address that it was a time for "normalcy and not nostrums." His brief tenure as president was an unhappy time for him, and his administration was

President Warren G. Harding driving the golden spike for the Alaska Railroad near Nenana, 1923. Courtesy Lulu Fairbanks Collection, Alaska and Polar Regions Archives, Elmer E. Rasmuson Library, University of Alaska.

plagued with scandals. He referred to the presidency as "this damned job," complained about the multiplicity of problems which he so little understood, and confessed his inability to make choices from conflicting advice, especially that of the economists.

On the subject of Alaska he was much more positive. The first president to visit the territory, he went to Nenana in 1923 to drive the golden spike symbolizing the completion of the Alaska Railroad. He spoke with feeling about Alaska, remarking that "if the Finns owned Alaska they would in three generations make it one of the foremost states of the Union." He urged that Alaska's resources should be used to benefit settlers and not for the advantage of outside speculators. He promised that his administration would work to the utmost to help develop Alaska. On his return trip to Washington he became ill in San Francisco and died shortly thereafter. With his death, wrote Ernest Gruening, governor of Alaska in the New Deal era and later elected U.S. senator from the new state, Alaska "lost a great friend at court."[1]

## THE SALMON FISHERIES

It was during Harding's administration that the federal government made its only serious attempt to deal with the problem of the Alaska salmon fisheries. The abundance of salmon in Alaska waters and the ease of catching them had enabled the Indians of the Panhandle, in whose diet salmon was the mainstay, to devote their talents to other pursuits and to develop a high culture. The Russians also depended much on the salmon for food, but the commercial era of the fisheries did not begin until the American period. The industry was dominated early by firms from outside the territory. There was little capital available in Alaska to make the heavy investments necessary for building canneries and carrying on fishing operations. The fishing grounds were usually in isolated areas, and the Alaska population was small and scattered. It was much easier for the great packers with headquarters in Seattle and San Francisco to bring their own crews to Alaska than to recruit labor in the territory.[2]

Even before the turn of the century, warnings were given that overfishing and reckless exploitation endangered the salmon supply. Government regulation, when it came, was sporadic and generally ineffective. In 1889, Congress passed a law that forbade the damming of streams to catch fish on their way to the spawning beds. Three years passed before the lawmakers appropriated the funds to hire an inspector and an assistant to see that the law was enforced. Since no commercial transportation existed, the inspectors had to depend on the ships of the packers whose activities they sought to regulate to take them where they wanted to go.[3]

In the 1890s several scientists of the U.S. Fish Commission became convinced that artificial propagation was the answer to the dwindling salmon runs. In May, 1900, the secretary of the treasury, whose department was charged with the regulation of the Alaska salmon industry, issued regulations requiring each company taking fish from

An aerial view of salmon traps in various stages of construction at Sunny Point, near Ketchikan. Courtesy Lulu Fairbanks Collection, Alaska and Polar Regions Archives, Elmer E. Rasmuson Library, University of Alaska.

Alaskan waters to establish hatcheries and "to return red salmon to the spawning grounds at the rate of at least four times the number of fish taken the preceding season." The regulation was not enforced, however, and its practicality for Alaska conditions was never tested. In 1903 the control of the Alaska fisheries was transferred from the U.S. Treasury Department to the newly created Department of Commerce and Labor, and the duties involved in regulating the industry were entrusted to the department's Bureau of Fisheries. In 1905 the bureau succeeded in getting appropriations for the construction of two hatcheries in Alaska but met with great opposition from the packers when it attempted to gain greater regulatory powers from Congress. The bill that became law in 1906 gave the secretary of commerce the authority to regulate fishing within five hundred yards of the mouths of rivers and streams instead of within the three miles that the bureau desired.[4]

By the turn of the century many Alaskans were fishing as a means of livelihood or to supplement their income. The bargaining over prices to be paid was spirited. In 1912 a major strike of fishermen took place. Many of the packers then decided to free themselves from dependence on the independent fishermen for the fish they needed, or from paying the high prices demanded, and so began to use more traps for catching fish. A trap was a huge permanent installation of log piles and netting that extended out from the shore for about a half mile across the paths fish travel on their way to spawning grounds in rivers and streams. In the fall the trap was dismantled and had to be rebuilt anew for each fishing season. The cost of construction was high, but it was easy to maintain; usually only a single watchman was employed to load the fish into a scow and guard against theft.

Traps were the most efficient method for catching fish, but their employment touched off a great political debate that ended only after Alaska achieved statehood

and the legislature made their use illegal. Although traps were blamed for having brought about the depletion of the salmon, the controversy surrounding the use of the traps, according to economist Richard Cooley, was basically an issue between labor and capital, and between resident and nonresident groups, about who should benefit from the exploitation of Alaska's salmon resources. Alaskans who wanted the fisheries used primarily to afford more people the opportunity of earning a livelihood and thus to encourage settlement feared that unless the traps were prohibited the packers would gain complete control of the industry and drive independent fishermen out of business. An article in the *Pacific Fisherman,* the trade journal of the packers, asserted that the trap was "the best and only friend the canners have in Alaska" and went on to say that "if this method of catching fish is prohibited it will mean almost the entire dissolution of the industry."[5]

The Bureau of Fisheries ignored the social aspects of the conflict. Its chief of the Alaskan division condemned all suggestions to restrict the use of traps as inimical to the competitive system on which the nation's economy was based. He preferred traps, because, unlike other fishing gear, they were stationary and could be inspected periodically, making regulation much easier. During the war years, when the price of fish was high and the supply low, robberies of traps became common. Vessels from several government agencies, including the navy, were sent to Alaska to help suppress what were regarded as acts of piracy.

The packers praised the Bureau of Fisheries and preferred federal to local regulation—at least in Alaska. Hearings on the use of the fisheries were usually held in Washington, and though few Alaska fishermen could afford the trip there, the representatives of the packers never missed a meeting. The packers' testimony was highly regarded. Members of Congress assumed that the packers knew more about the

Brailing, or emptying the fish trap. The tender takes the salmon to the cannery for processing. Courtesy Lulu Fairbanks Collection, Alaska and Polar Regions Archives, Elmer E. Rasmuson Library, University of Alaska.

problems of the salmon fisheries than anyone else, and it was unthinkable that their advice might not be in the best interests of the industry. When the bureau established a Pacific branch in Seattle, the office was conveniently housed in a building where twenty of the major salmon companies were located. The *Pacific Fisherman* was pleased by the continued federal control of the fisheries and, following the passage of the Second Organic Act, openly gloated that Alaskans had been given "a toy legislature to play with."

Both the Bureau of Fisheries and the Department of Commerce strongly resisted any suggestions that the territory be given a voice in the management of the salmon fisheries. William C. Redfield, secretary of commerce in Wilson's cabinet, feared that the territory would destroy the industry through high taxes and license fees and wrote that "not even the possibility of such a situation, much less the situation itself, should be allowed to exist." E. Lester Jones, deputy commissioner of the Bureau of Fisheries, lauded the "unusual training and experience" of the scientists in the Bureau of Fisheries and insisted that "any idea of transferring jurisdiction to the Territory or any other agency should be completely dismissed."[6]

Hugh Smith, a scientist, became commissioner of the fisheries in 1915. He stated that there was no cause for alarm concerning the depletion of the Alaska fisheries. He claimed that by expanding the program of artificial propagation through the maintenance of the fish hatcheries "the perpetuation of the Alaska salmon fisheries can be achieved . . . without any general or material curtailment of fishing operations or reduction of output." Economist Cooley points out that this was something the packers "wanted to hear," and Smith was hailed for his intelligence and practical wisdom. Artificial propagation was accepted as an act of faith, but no studies were carried out to see whether Smith's optimism had any validity.

Congress appropriated more money for the hatchery program than for any other aspect of the bureau's work. Only a pittance, however, was made available for its scientific studies and regulatory functions.[7] Warnings from Alaska fishermen and territorial officials that salmon were declining in great numbers went unheeded as long as the demand, accelerated by wartime government orders, continued. But with the conclusion of the conflict, not only were fish no longer needed in large quantities, but also, because the great armies and navies were rapidly being demobilized, governments were selling their surplus salmon stocks on the open market. Prices for salmon declined drastically. Spokesmen for the packers now admitted that overfishing had been taking place and that the need for conservation was manifest. "Even before Dr. Smith took office," an editorial writer in the *Pacific Fisherman* stated, "the approaching danger to the salmon fishery and the need of accurate knowledge were apparent to anyone interested in its future.[8] Smith resigned under a cloud in 1921. Three years later his successor as commissioner of fisheries, Henry O'Malley, told a congressional committee that artificial propagation was not the solution to the problem of the conservation of Alaska's salmon.

In view of the emergency, Herbert Hoover

secretary of commerce in the new Harding administration, took personal charge and held lengthy hearings on the plight of the salmon industry. When he was unable to secure legislation from Congress which he felt was necessary to restore the health of the salmon fisheries, Hoover recommended that President Harding issue an extensive order temporarily establishing the Alaska Peninsula Reserve, where fishing was to be by permit only. The president complied with Hoover's request and issued the executive order on February 17, 1922. Congress failed to provide relief for the fisheries even after the secretary warned that other fishery reservations would be created. Several months later, another executive order created the Southwestern Fishery Reservation, which included the Kodiak and Bristol Bay areas. Supporters of reservations maintained that the only way to halt overfishing was to limit the number of people allowed to fish. This restriction of the use of the fisheries by the Harding administration was indeed a revolutionary development, for it marked a break in the American tradition of a fishery free and open to all with the exception of a few areas open only to certain Indian tribes.[9]

Opposition to the reservations came quickly. Dan Sutherland, the Alaska delegate to Congress, charged that only employees of the large companies, and no Alaskans, were able to secure fishing places. He accused the administration of hypocrisy and declared that the goverment had never been interested in conservation as it now claimed but was really interested only in establishing a monopoly for the salmon packers. Several newspapers echoed his cry. Some predicted that a new Teapot Dome Scandal was in the offing—except that this time the subject was salmon, not oil. The administration, stung by the force of the criticism, sought to involve Congress, whose support it wanted, in finding a solution to the problem of the salmon fisheries.[10]

Secretary Hoover accompanied President Harding to Alaska for the ceremonies marking the completion of the Alaska Railroad. While they were there, he held hearings in several towns to "secure first hand information in regard to fishery conditions in Alaska." Bills based largely on his recommendations were introduced into the House by Wallace H. White of Maine and into the Senate by Wesley Jones of Washington. After considerable debate the two houses of Congress came to an agreement, and President Calvin Coolidge signed the measure known as the White Act in 1924.

The White Act was very much the product of compromise. Two controversial items that had been proposed—reservations desired by the packers and the outlawing of fish traps sought by the delegate from Alaska—were deleted. The act gave the secretary of commerce the authority "to limit or prohibit fishing in all territorial waters of Alaska" and allowed him to fix the size and character, but not the amount, of fishing gear. To achieve the desired goal of conservation of the salmon fisheries, Congress directed that at least 50 percent of the fish be allowed to escape to their spawning grounds. Nothing, however, was done to see that this objective was attained. Secretary Hoover spoke with pride of his achievement in getting Congress to approve the measure, which he believed had preserved the Alaska salmon runs. Shortly after the act was signed, he announced that fish had become so plentiful that foreign vessels were invading the Alaska fishing grounds. By 1925 the demand for salmon had increased significantly, and as the price rose, the salmon catch increased correspondingly. The packers hailed Hoover as the savior of the salmon industry, and as long as the total output continued to increase year after year, they considered the government's conservation program successful.[11]

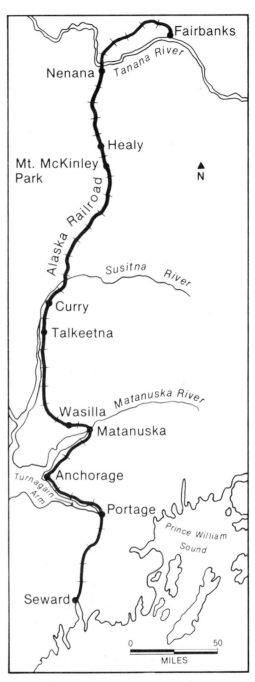

The route of the Alaska Railroad from Seward to Fairbanks, a distance of 470 miles. From Claus-M. Naske, *Paving Alaska's Trails: The work of the Alaska Road Commission* (Lanham, Md.: University Press of America, 1986), p. 64. Reproduced by permission.

## THE ALASKA RAILROAD AND THE GROWTH OF AVIATION

While Secretary Hoover was holding hearings in Alaska to save the salmon industry, Alakans, especially those from the interior, hailed his chief, President Harding, as he drove the golden spike at Nenana symbolizing the completion of the Alaska Railroad. The railroad, the first great construction project initiated by the federal government in Alaska, stimulated the Alaska economy by providing hundreds of jobs. Its construction was proclaimed as the advent of a new era of prosperity that would open up the interior for settlement and the development of its resources. Completed in 1923, the Alaska Railroad cost $65 million, almost twice the amount originally earmarked for its construction; inflation and delays accounted for most of the added expenditures. Successive managers of the railroad blamed the poor condition of the roadbed and the low quality of the equipment for the unusually high operations costs. Soon after service began, Congress appropriated an additional $17 million for improve-

ments, but much more was needed to make the railroad efficient. In its early years the Alaska Railroad seemed to be almost constantly under attack. The anticipated boom following its completion did not materialize. According to an authority on northern areas, "When the railroad was new, three out of four people one met along the Yukon maintained that the railway to Fairbanks had done harm to the Interior by competing with river traffic just enough to ruin the steamboat companies without supplying an alternative service more adequate to take their place."[12]

The railroad was plagued by almost continuous deficits. The cost of maintenance was high, and the number of passengers few, since the population of the rail belt remained small. While the mines benefited from the railroad, an export trade in coal failed to develop as the railroad planners had anticipated. This meant lower freight loads and not enough business to make the railroad a success. In Congress there was almost constant criticism of the railroad as an expensive luxury, and several members demanded that the line be closed. In 1928,

The Matanuska—Chickaloon train leaving Anchorage, 1929. Courtesy Lulu Fairbanks Collection, Alaska and Polar Regions Archives, Elmer E. Rasmuson Library, University of Alaska.

The Wien brothers were aviation pioneers in Alaska. Their early efforts led to the formation of a major Alaska airline. In the 1920s, Noel Wien landed near Circle Hot Springs at this airfield, which Frank Leach, the proprietor, had built using a team of horses. Taking off appears to have been a problem. Courtesy E. L. Bartlett Collection, Alaska and Polar Regions Archives, Elmer E. Rasmuson Library, University of Alaska.

Colonel Otto F. Ohlsen, a veteran railroad man with twenty-seven years' experience with the Northern Pacific Railroad, became general manager of the Alaska Railroad. Under his direction the line experienced its first profitable year in 1938.

Of much greater consequence for Alaska than the building of the Alaska Railroad was the beginning of the air age in the 1920s. Of all forms of transportation air travel was the most readily adaptable to the Alaska environment. Nature had placed great obstacles in the way of building roads and railroads in the territory. Its great size, its rugged terrain, and its severe climatic conditions together with the vast distances between communities made the building and maintenance of roads and railroads extremely expensive. Before World War II there were only 2,500 miles of road in Alaska, and only a single highway, the Richardson, connected Valdez to Fairbanks. Apart from the Alaska Railroad, 22.4 miles of the White Pass and Yukon Railroad, which ran from Skagway to Whitehorse,

passed through Alaska. Service on the Copper River and Northwest Railroad was discontinued in 1938.

The airplane made it possible for communities such as Nome, which previously had been almost completely isolated for much of year when the Bering Sea was frozen, to have year-round contact with the outside world. Bush pilots were able to fly into villages which previously had been accessible only by dogsled. Supplies could be taken into remote areas as needed by miners, fishermen, loggers, traders, and trappers. Thanks to the airplane, it became possible to bring the sick and the injured swiftly to the towns, where they could be treated in hospitals, or doctors and nurses could be sent into the field where help was urgently needed. Government agencies were able to use the airplane to great advantage. In the summer of 1929, navy fliers undertook an aerial survey in southeastern Alaska, mapping 10,000 miles of territory. Weather observations by plane were first made in 1930 and 1931. Planes were also used by the Bureau of Fisheries to check for violations of regulations.

Alaska played a prominent role in the early years of aviation and was the scene of some noteworthy flights. In 1920 many pilots made the first trip by air to Alaska from the United States; the flight began at Mineola, New York, with Nome as its final destination. Four years later the U.S. Post Office sponsored a flight by Lieutenant Ben Eielson to determine the practicality of establishing airmail service in Alaska. That year Alaska landing fields were used by army fliers who were making the first round the world trip by air. In subsequent years a flight was made from Spitzbergen to Alaska over the North Pole, and another over the same route originating in Alaska.[13]

Sir George Hubert Wilkins, Ben Eielson, Charles A. Lindbergh, Wiley Post, Harold Gatty, General Henry H. Arnold, and Howard Hughes particpated in the development of Alaska aviation, together with many bush pilots, such as to name but a few, the Wien brothers—Noel, Ralph, and Sig—Art Woodley, Merle ("Mudhole") Smith, Bob Reeve, Sam White, Bill Lavery, Jack Jefford, James Dodson, and Harold Gillam. By the 1930s planes were being used extensively in Alaska. Airmail service, which had been used intermittently for a number of years, was established in 1937 on a regular basis for many communities. That year planes carried almost 500,000 pounds of mail, and the Post Office ceased using dogsleds in many areas. Before World War II "Alaska had 116 times as many planes, which flew 70 times as many miles, carried 23 times as many passengers, carried 1,034 times as much freight and express and 48 times as much mail as the United States on a per capita basis." A report compiled in 1937 listed ninety-seven civilian airfields in Alaska. For the most part they had been built with money appropriated by the territorial legislature. Thirteen of these had more than one runway, while most had runways less than 1,500 feet long. Only the

fields at Fairbanks and Anchorage had lights, which consisted of rotating beacons and floodlights.[14] The federal government spent only a pittance in support of Alaska aviation; most of the money appropriated for transportation in Alaska went to the Alaska Railroad.

## THE "TWILIT TWENTIES"

Calvin Coolidge, who succeeded Harding as president of the United States, never exhibited his predecessor's interest in the welfare and development of Alaska. A firm believer in the dogma that "the business of America is business," Coolidge's chief concern seemed to be that the money spent in Alaska appeared to be "far out of proportion to the number of its inhabitants and the amount of production."[15] He whittled away at appropriations for the territory; as a result the agricultural experiment station at Rampart closed in 1925.

Except for agriculture, the Harding and Coolidge era was a period of prosperity for the United States. Alaska, which was not in the mainstream of American life, was little affected by the great advances made in manufacturing and commerce. The Alaska population remained almost static, growing by only a few thousand during the decade one writer has called "the twilit twenties." Aside from the building of the Alaska Railroad, which employed hundreds of men, Alaska's colonial economy followed with consistent "regularity . . . the seasonal harvesting of fish, canning of salmon, trapping of fur bearers and the mining of gold."[16] Mining production was lower because the great demand for copper of the war years had ended. In 1930, the fifteenth census listed 4,800 persons working in the mines, and it was estimated that an equal number were engaged in supplying and servicing the industry. After the postwar slump the demand for salmon increased again, attaining a new high in 1926 when more than 6.5 million cans were packed. Almost 6,000

Alaskans operated as independent fishermen, but they were only a small percentage of the workforce employed in the industry. The value of furs taken in Alaska slightly more than $2 million, was small compared to that of mining or fishing. But trapping provided most or all of the cash income for many Alaskans, especially the Natives. Ranches and farms had been established for breeding blue and silver foxes and minks for market. Many Alaskans lived off the land by hunting, fishing, and trapping. Alaska's timber resources were gradually being put to use. In 1913 the territory imported 84 percent of its timber; by 1925 this percentage had been reversed. Two years earlier a mill at Ketchikan had begun exporting to Seattle spruce which exporters then shipped to the United Kingdom and Australia. But with the onset of the Great Depression, the plans that had been made to build two pulp mills in southeastern Alaska were abandoned.[17]

## ALASKA IN THE GREAT DEPRESSION

Hoover, who as secretary of commerce had visited Alaska to find a solution to the problems of the salmon fisheries, had the misfortune to be president when the Great Depression struck the United States. Alaska, which had not shared in the American prosperity of the 1920s, suffered less from the traumas of the 1930s, although the depression had some effects upon the territorial economy. Employment in the mines declined: the number of copper miners was cut from 570 to 143. The value of salmon fell with the drop in commodity prices, and wages were cut. As has already been noted, the expansion of the lumbering industry halted. Federal appropriations for agencies in Alaska, which had never been very high, were cut. Because of its perennial deficits, the Alaska Railroad came increasingly under attack. A committee chaired by Senator Robert B. Howell of Nebraska demanded that services be cut and that rates

on the trains be raised 10 cents a mile for passengers and as much as 50 percent for freight to make the road more nearly self-supporting. These recommendations, however, when put into effect, resulted in a lowering of the railroad's income. After a few years a new, more realistic schedule of rates was adopted. As the Depression deepened in the 1930s, some Americans looked to Alaska as a place to escape from their economic woes. After all, there were plenty of moose, caribou, and salmon, and land, they believed, could be had for the asking.

An Eskimo woman and a helper from Ambler, on the Kobuk River, hauling a netful of fish from under the ice. From time immemorial Alaska's Natives have fished for subsistence. Courtesy U.S. National Park Service.

In the heart of the Depression the American people turned to Franklin Delano Roosevelt as their new leader. When Roosevelt took office, more than thirteen million Americans were unemployed, and many of those with jobs were not much better off. Wages ranged from $0.20 to $0.30 an hour in many basic industries, and it was not uncommon for men and women to receive less than $2.00 for ten hours of labor. Although Roosevelt had been much opposed to an extensive public works program, he reluctantly came to the conclusion that increased intervention by the federal government was necessary. In fact, more had to be done to keep people from starving even if that meant making direct relief payments, which Hoover had vigorously opposed. In essence, the New Deal was a composite of relief and reform programs which at times seemed to be working at cross purposes with one another. Alaskans shared in the New Deal, but since Alaska was a territory and not a state, its share was often small or even nonexistent.

Several actions of the Roosevelt administration benefited the territory, however. The president's decision to devalue the dollar by raising the price of gold stimulated an industry that had played a leading role in the development of Alaska. Beginning in 1936, gold production increased annually. The value of the mined ore rose from $10,209,000 in 1932 to $26,178,000 in 1940. Forty-eight dredges operated that year, mainly in the Nome and Fairbanks areas, an increase from twenty-eight, the average number in use during the Depression. More workers were being employed in the mines as the production of gold rose.

Some of the New Deal agencies were active in Alaska. Direct relief payments made by the federal government, besides aiding the recipients, were of some help in aiding the economy. The Work Projects Administration (WPA) gave employment to people on the relief rolls, paying them slightly more than the welfare grants they had been receiving but less than the prevailing wage. Another agency, the Public Works Administration (PWA), under the direction of Harold Ickes, secretary of the interior, sponsored public undertakings in which private contractors employed men and women at the prevailing community wage rates. As a result of these efforts a number of public buildings, roads, airfields, docks, and bridges were constructed; a guidebook to Alaska was published, improvements were made to harbors, and a hotel was established at Mount McKinley National Park. Governor Ernest Gruening and Anthony J. Dimond, Alaska's delegate to Congress, were unsuccessful in their efforts to have some of the money received from the WPA used for undertakings they considered more appropriate to Alaska conditions. Dimond, however, was able to get a bill through Congress authorizing the town of Skagway to issue bonds up to $40,000 so that it could obtain an equal grant or loan from the PWA to renovate its water system.[18]

The federal government, through the National Youth Administration (NYA), helped young people remain in school by making part-time jobs available to them. Of all the New Deal agencies the most innovative in Alaska was the Civilian Conservation Corps (CCC). The CCC, established for young men eighteen to twenty-three years of age without regular employment, provided work on projects to "conserve, protect and renew natural resources." In Alaska, the U.S. Forest Service rather than the army was put in charge of the CCC camps, and age restrictions were eliminated, since in Alaska the unemployed were middle-aged men rather than youths. A requirement of one year's residence in Alaska was instituted for enrollees. Under the direction of the Forest Service the CCC's work in Alaska took on many aspects. Men were used to build forest roads and trails, bridges, warehouses, small-boat facilities, a trout hatchery at Ketchikan, a dock and small boat harbor at Cordova, drainage ditches, community wells, and landing fields. Houses were erected for the Bureau of Fisheries, along with shelter cabins, floats, a salmon weir, and a fifteen-room biological laboratory.

A good part of the work of the CCC was devoted to planning and building recreational areas. CCC workers helped excavate and restore Old Sitka, the site of a fort by Baranov in 1799. One of the most impressive projects was the restoration of totem poles. Historian Lawrence Rakestraw has stated that "nowhere was the work of the CCC more appreciated than in the isolated Native villages and missions in the Interior." The employees of the CCC "built a muskox corral on Nunivak Island"; "razed the Army barracks at St. Michael"; helped clear the land at Galena, which had suffered extensive flood damage; built a telegraph line between Nulato and Unalakleet; and erected community houses and installed sanitation projects in many villages. Missionaries and teachers sent letters to the regional forester expressing their appreciation for the projects.[19]

## NEW FISHERIES PROBLEMS

The New Deal not only created new agencies of government but also used old ones in its attempt to bring the nation out of the Depression. Frank Bell, the newly appointed commissioner of the Bureau of Fisheries, who replaced Henry O'Malley, emphasized that the bureau not only intended to maintain the salmon resource but also was very much interested in bringing its policies into line with the social and economic objectives of the New Deal, especially the goal of spreading employment. He recommended reducing the number of fish traps and restricting their use so that local and independent fishermen could gain a larger share of the catch. He sought to relax some of the restrictions that had been placed on seiners and gill-netters and would "make other concessions to the desires of Alaska residents as long as such actions did not conflict with the fundamental principles of conservation." Commissioner Bell ran into considerable opposition when he attempted to put his program into operation. He was unable to get funds he wanted for seaplanes to use in enforcing the bureau's regulations and carrying out the agency's managerial functions. As general market conditions improved in 1934 and 1935, more fish were caught, and the packers were successful not only in having most of Bell's program nullified but also in having Congress kill a bill proposed by Delegate Dimond to abolish the use of traps.[20]

A conflict also developed between resident and nonresident independent fishermen about who should benefit from the use of the Alaska salmon fisheries. Both groups were organized in the Alaska Fishermen's Union, headquartered in San Francisco. The union insisted that packers should pay the nonresident fishermen four cents more per fish than they paid the residents and that the nonresidents should receive most of the available fishermen's jobs. George Lane, the union's secretary, declared that "if the Alaska Fishermen's Union is expected to permit Alaskan residents to usurp their just proportion of jobs from the men in the States, we will refuse to permit any fishing in the area." The Alaskans' attempt to organize their own union was unsuccessful because they were unable to secure recognition from the packers. According to economist Cooley, the feeling of hostility which developed in many Alaskans toward the outside forces of labor, capital, and government that controlled a basic industry did much to hasten the drive for statehood for Alaska.[21]

In 1939, Frank Bell resigned as commissioner of fisheries. His policies had come under attack from all quarters. The packers felt that he had gone too far in emphasizing the social responsibilities of the bureau, while the Alaska fishermen considered him ineffective. The Bureau of Fisheries was transferred from the Department of Commerce, which had always been more interested in promoting sales of salmon than their conservation and regulation, to the Department of the Interior, where it was merged with the Bureau of Biological Survey, an agency concerned with wildlife preservation, to become the Fish and Wildlife Service. In the same year Delegate Dimond succeeded in having the House of Representatives agree to an investigation of the administration of the Alaskan salmon fisheries. A subcommittee of the House Merchant Marine and Fisheries Committee, together with a joint committee of both houses of the Alaska legislature, traveled more than 3,700 miles and heard testimony both in Alaska and in the contiguous states before making its report. It strongly recommended that "the fisheries of Alaska should be administered by the United States not solely for the purpose of conservation as contended by some, but also as an Alaskan resource to be administered, controlled, regulated and operated in the interest of and for the benefit of the Alaskan people." But with the coming of World War II demand for salmon increased. "Groups that normally were at each other's throats on certain issues frequently found no difficulty in making expedient alignments in opposition to government proposals which might reduce their respective cuts of the pie." [22] Regulation of the salmon became virtually a dead letter after 1940.

## THE MATANUSKA VALLEY COLONY

Of all the New Deal activities in Alaska, the Matanuska Valley Colony excited the greatest interest, extending far beyond the boundaries of the territory. As originally conceived, the Matanuska colony was just one of the many resettlement projects of the Roosevelt administration designed to take people away from rural districts in which poverty had been prevalent long before the Depression and move them to places where they might lead more productive lives. No other settlement approached Matanuska in the publicity it received, and in no other were the expectations so high. The idea of creating a community in the wilderness stirred the imagination. Sponsors of the Alaskan colony included many who were not interested in relief and resettlement. Officials of the Alaska Railroad, who had long sponsored movement of people to Alaska, were delighted, for the colony meant more passengers and freight, which would help make the line self-supporting. Roosevelt himself was said to have expressed the view that the establishment of the colony would aid the military. For Alaskans, the Matanuska project meant that the government was doing something for Alaska. There was a widespread belief that the colony would clearly demonstrate that farming was feasible in Alaska and that a successful agricultural industry would help to free Alaska from dependence on outside sources for food supplies. [23]

Matanuska Valley is in the rail-belt area of south-central Alaska. Its leading settlement, Palmer, is about forty miles from Anchorage. Before the colony was established, there was homesteading in the valley, but few settlers had made farming their principal means of livelihood. The climate of the valley is much milder than the latitude might indicate. It is warmer there in winter than in many areas of the northern part of the United States, although it is much cooler in the summer. Rainfall averages about sixteen inches a year. The quality of the soils of the valley varies considerably.

President Roosevelt opened the way for the new settlement on February 4, 1935, when he issued an executive order banning further homesteading in the valley and reserving all remaining land for the colonists. The Alaska Relief and Rehabilitation Cor-

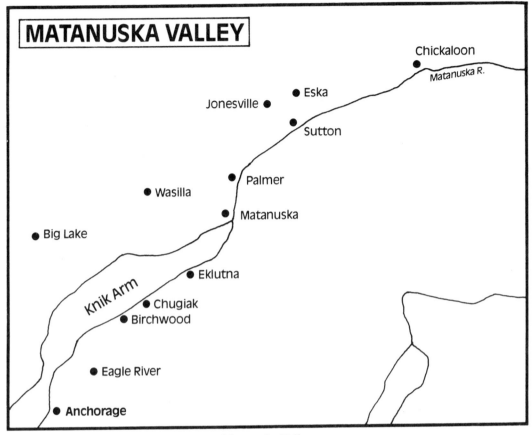

Matanuska Valley

poration, then a part of the Federal Emergency Relief Administration, later the WPA, was formed to manage the colony. Surveys were made, and the land was divided into 208 plots ranging from 40 to 80 acres, depending on the quality of the soil. Prices ranged from five dollars an acre for uncleared land to an unspecified amount in those places where it had been improved. Settlers were to make payments over a thirty-year period at an annual interest rate of 3 percent. The federal government agreed to build the houses and barns and pay for transporting families and up to 2,000 pounds of their household goods to Alaska. Farm machinery, equipment, livestock, and supplies were made available by the corpora-

tion to the colonists for purchase, lease, or payment for use. Supplies could be obtained as needed at cost until the colonists became self-supporting. Educational, cultural, recreational, and health services were to be provided by the corporation, while the colonists as their part of the contract agreed to observe the directives issued by the corporation relating to farm management and other affairs of the colony.

Selected from the applicants for a place in the colony were 201 families, all residents of northern counties of Michigan, Minnesota, and Wisconsin. These descendants of people of northern European stock, coming from an area where climatic conditions presumably most closely resembled those of the Matanuska Valley, would make the best colonists, it was believed. The locale from which they came, known as the "cutover region," had once been the scene of prosperous lumbering and mining industries. But with the decline of lumbering as a result of excessive cutting, and with the copper mines of the area no longer able to compete in the national market, employment had become irregular. Agriculture in the area was definitely submarginal.

Relief workers were given the task of selecting the colonists. Most of them worked hard to find suitable candidates for the colony and did not, as alleged, foist their most difficult cases on the Matanuska project, but they were limited in their selections. Successful farmers were not interested in going to Alaska and could not go even if they wanted to. Only people receiving welfare payments were eligible to be chosen. Lengthy questionnaires had been carefully devised to obtain information on the background of the applicants. But the replies were often not very accurate. Friends and neighbors frequently tended to show the applicants in their best light and exaggerated their qualifications. Few of those who went to Matanuska had farming experience.[24]

Great fanfare attended the movement of the colonists. They traveled by train across the country accompanied by newspapermen who interviewed them and reported on their activities. In San Francisco and Seattle they were entertained with dinners and speeches. Upon their arrival in Alaska they were greeted at the port of Seward. At Anchorage a half-day holiday was declared in their honor. Don Irwin, manager of the Matanuska Agricultural Experiment Station, warned them of the difficulties that lay ahead, and indeed their introduction to the valley was not a happy one—it was raining the day they arrived in May, 1935. During the next few weeks the rainfall was heavier than usual for that time of year. Because their homes were not ready, they lived

in tents, surrounded at times by a sea of mud. Some waited several months before their homes were ready for occupancy.[25]

Discontent was high. Some of the colonists complained that promises made to them had not been kept and sent letters and telegrams to members of Congress and to the newspapers airing their grievances. Nine families left in July, and they were followed by others. The government paid their transportation back to Seattle. Replacements for them were found; some of these were already living in Alaska. Opponents of the New Deal cited the colony as another example of bureaucratic foolishness. Senator Arthur H. Vandenberg of Michigan accused the Roosevelt administration of having planted "in net essence a complete commune under the American flag at Palmer, Alaska," and spoke of those "people . . . left stranded 5,000 miles from home in the face of a threatening calamity." The directors of the corporation heard themselves condemned for running the colony too loosely and for installing a dictatorship.

The colony had its defenders. Senator Homer T. Bone of Washington spoke glowingly of the Matanuska Valley's rich farmlands and contrasted the opportunities open to the colonists with the dismal life they had led on relief in their home states. Some of the colony's severest critics among the settlers in the early days changed their minds after a few months in Alaska. One announced that she was now "having the time of my life." When rumors began circulating that the colony might be disbanded, none of the remaining settlers appeared to be very happy with the prospect of being sent home.[26]

Of all the government resettlement projects Matanuska was by far the most expensive. Alaska labor costs were high. Almost everything needed—equipment, materials, and supplies—had to be imported into Alaska at great expense. "Above all," writes historian Orlando Miller, "the Matanuska project had to provide almost every facility that a new community would need." The project "built and equipped a general store or trading post, warehouses, shops, garage, community hall, dormitory, offices, staff houses, power plant, cannery, creamery, hatchery, hospital and school." If all the expenditures relating to the colony are taken into account—the transporting of families and goods, providing facilities, construction of roads and bridges to the Palmer area, the building of schools and hospitals, and loans made to colonists that were never repaid—the total cost would be over $5 million.[27]

Matanuska has been considered a qualified success. With the advent of World War II and the building of military facilities in the Anchorage area, a ready market became available for the colony's products. About 31 percent of the original settlers and 43 percent of the replacements were still living in the colony in 1948. Many who left found jobs or established businesses for themselves elsewhere in Alaska. Palmer benefited substantially from the founding of the colony, since people who were not members of the agricultural experiment moved into the town to avail themselves of the opportunities afforded by the establishment of a new community. The support of the government was undoubtedly a major factor in the Matanuska story.

Alaskans had mixed feelings about the Matanuska Colony. There was some appreciation that the federal government was at last doing something for Alaska, but some of the old-timers resented the special treatment and benefits conferred on outsiders who had never experienced the real problems of life in Alaska. And not all Alaskan were convinced that the Matanuska Colony was a success. According to his biogra-

This Matanuska Valley farm, with land cleared, cows grazing, and a neat farmstead in a scenic setting, appears to be the ideal that the colony was striving for. Courtesy Lulu Fairbanks Collection, Alaska and Polar Regions Archives, Elmer E. Rasmuson Library, University of Alaska.

pher Mary Mangusso, Anthony Dimond, Alaska's delegate to Congress, like many of his constituents, maintained an ambivalent attitude toward the project and usually kept a discreet silence when the subject was discussed. In later years Dimond referred to the settlement as "an experiment, a demonstration of the potential of agriculture in Alaska."[28]

Although many Alaskans spoke of the need to settle Alaska, they were usually reluctant, if not hostile, whenever there was any discussion of founding new settlements in the territory. Some said that they did not want another Matanuska. There was a great outcry of opposition in the territory when a bill was introduced in Congress that called for the settlement of unemployed Americans and refugees from Nazi persecution in Alaska. Opposition was based in part on the practical grounds of the difficulty involved in assimilating urban groups who did not have skills they needed to fit into the Alaska environment, but it was also mixed with some feelings of xenophobia and anti-Semitism. Nevertheless, there also was little enthusiasm for another proposal to bring Finns to Alaska after the Russo-Finnish War.[29]

## THE "NEW DEAL" FOR NATIVE PEOPLES

While attention centered on the newest settlers in Matanuska, Alaska's Native people were not entirely ignored. The Roosevelt administration promised a "New Deal" for them too. The president's chief advisors on Indian affairs rejected the policy of forced assimilation and recommended that the Indians' cultural heritage be preserved and that they be given more land on reservations as a means of furthering their welfare. The proposal, enacted into law as the Indian Reorganization Act of 1934, more commonly known as the Wheeler-Howard Act, was extended to

Alaska two years later and included Eskimos and Aleuts as well as Indian peoples.

Although Alaska never experienced the extensive warfare that had marked relations between the two races in the United States, the coming of the white man had seriously disrupted, and in some cases destroyed, the Native economy. The Natives' standard of living was much lower, they were subjected to social discrimination, and a separate school system had been established for their children.

Alaska's inclusion in the provisions of the Indian Reorganization Act enabled several Native American communities to incorporate and to draw up constitutions for self-government. Loans extended to a number of villages allowed them to set up canneries. Individual fishermen borrowed money to purchase boats and gear for themselves, while two of the Native canneries established businesses on a territory-wide basis. In 1938 the secretary of the interior was authorized to withdraw up to 640 acres of land for the use of the territory's schools and hospitals and for other purposes he might deem advisable. The most controversial aspect of the program was the one that contemplated the creation of reservations and a system of communal land tenure. This was regarded by its sponsors as the means of implementing the provisions of the First Organic Act of 1884 that "the Indians or other persons in the said District shall not be disturbed in the possession of any lands actually in their use or occupation or now claimed by them." Opposition to the reservations was most vehement. They were condemned as alien to the Native way of life, and their introduction was termed a step backward; the need of the people, it was said, was equality, not wardship. The very word "reservation," indicating restriction on the use of land, has always aroused strong feelings in Alaska. Land given to the Natives, it was feared, would be taken from the whites, and any large withdrawals for reservations would thwart Alaska's development. In the 1940s, following many protests, the plan for reservations was withdrawn. Not until 1971, more than a quarter of a century after the era of the New Deal, did Congress finally settle the Alaskan Native land claims.[30]

## ALASKA AND THE NEW DEAL

The New Deal's effect on Alaska was not profound, although Roosevelt had shown greater interest in the territory than had any of his predecessors, with the possible exception of Harding, whose secretary of commerce, Herbert Hoover, had succeeded in pushing through the Congress what, with all its faults, was the most comprehensive measure ever enacted by the federal government for the preservation of Alaska's fisheries. The New Deal spent more money on Alaska, though not much, and even provided the territory with a new settlement, but Alaska was never central to the New Deal or in the minds of its planners. A long-awaited study on Alaska, issued in 1937, prepared at the request of Congress concluded that "an appraisal of the national interests indicates that there is no clear need to speed the development of Alaska." Secretary of the Interior Harold Ickes, whose department was most concerned with Alaska, observed that "Alaska ought to do more for itself than running to Washington for everything."[31]

Ernest Gruening recalls in his memoirs that, just before he left Washington to take up his duties as governor of Alaska in 1939, Roosevelt told him that Alaska had "lost touch with the federal government" and that a "lot of the New Deal . . . hasn't come to Alaska."[32] But only a few months earlier, in January, Roosevelt had announced that in view of the threatening world situation the reform program of the New Deal was over. "Dr. New Deal" was giving way to "Dr. Win-the-War." It was not the New Deal but the war that broke out in September, 1939, that profoundly changed Alaska.

# 7. GUARDIAN OF THE NORTH

The army has been in Alaska for a long time. It first arrived on October 9, 1867, when Battery H, Second Artillery, and Company F, Ninth Infantry, reached Sitka in the transport *John L. Stephens* under the command of Bvt. Maj. Gen. Jefferson C. Davis, who had been designated commanding general, Military District of Alaska. On October 18 the USS *Ossipee,* under the command of Capt. George F. Emmons, U.S. Navy, arrived in Sitka bearing the commissioners who were to conduct the formalities of the transfer of Russian America to the United States: Brig. Gen. Lovell H. Rousseau represented the U.S. government, and Capt. Alexis Peshchurov the Russian imperial government. The transfer ceremonies took place the same day, and the military began governing the new acquisition.[1]

In the spring of 1868 the District of Alaska became the Department of Alaska under the Military Division of the Pacific. The same year also witnessed the arrival of four artillery batteries and the establishment of several new posts: at Fort Tongass, on a small island at the mouth of the Portland Canal; at Fort Wrangell, also in southeastern Alaska; and at Fort Kodiak, at Saint Paul Harbor, Kodiak Island. In 1869 the army built another establishment at the old Russian post Fort Saint Nicholas, 100 miles up Cook Inlet, and called it Fort Kenay and

also sent troops to the Pribilof Islands to help the Treasury Department regulate the fur-seal harvest. By 1870 the army had abandoned all forts but Sitka and had withdrawn four of the six companies, leaving fewer than 100 troops in the district. From 1870 until the army left Alaska in 1877, troops and post commanders were rotated about every two years. The army also had to administer the affairs of the district until Congress provided a civil government, yet throughout its stay the army's duties were neither set down in regulations nor authorized by law. In fact, during its ten-year tour of duty in the north the army had but a vague concept of what it was to accomplish. What it did, in essence, was prevent difficulties between arriving Americans and the Indians and enforce the provisions of the Indian trade laws, which consisted in the main of enforcing the prohibition against importing liquor.[2]

For several years before 1877 the army had recommended the withdrawal of the troops from Alaska because the military had neither the machinery nor the authority to administer a civil government. It recommended that a revenue vessel free to move around was better suited to carry out the necessary police duties. When the officers' quarters burned to the ground in Sitka on February 9, 1877, the army decided that it was cheaper to withdraw then to rebuild the structures. In June the troops left, and the Treasury Department assumed jurisdiction until 1879, when the USS *Jamestown* under Commander Lester Anthony Beardslee, U.S. Navy, arrived with instructions to "restore harmonious relations between settler and native, and in the admitted absence of law and government, to use his own discretion in all emergencies that might arise." The navy performed the role of district police until Congress passed the Organic Act of 1884, which provided Alaska with the rudiments of a civil government.[3]

Although the army had departed in 1877, it had not lost interest in the district. From 1874 through the 1880s the Signal Corps maintained weather stations in the Aleutians and the Yukon-Kuskokwim deltas, which worked in close harmony with the Smithsonian Institution. In fact, the Smithsonian nominated meteorological observers who were also trained naturalists. One of these, Lucien McShan Turner, of the Signal Service, arrived at Saint Michael, in Norton Sound, in May, 1874. Within a short time he had accumulated an ethnological collection later described as "one of the most striking ever contributed to the [Smithsonian] museum." Others followed Turner, but it was Gen. Nelson A. Miles, the commandant of the Northwestern Department of the Columbia, Division of the Pacific, who initiated a number of army explorations of Alaska, which began in 1883 and ended in 1885.[4]

In 1897 the army returned north in response to the discovery of gold in 1896 in Canada's Yukon Territory and the subsequent influx of argonauts. A subsidiary issue involved a dispute over the boundary between Alaska and Canada. Arising as early as 1871, the boundary issue became acute with the gold discoveries. To reach the gold fields, prospectors used the most accessible route through Haines Mission or Dyea, at the head of Lynn Canal, which Canada claimed. In August and September,

1896, Capt. D. D. Gaillard, of the U.S. Corps of Engineers, conducted a preliminary examination of the disputed area and concluded that the Canadian claims were not justified. Realizing the potential of the area, and to protect its interests until the matter was settled, the United States once again ordered the army to Alaska under the command of Col. Thomas M. Anderson. Troops were stationed at Dyea, Fort Wrangell, and Skagway in 1897. Soon thousands of argonauts were struggling across the mountain passes to reach the Klondike gold fields, and in 1898 both governments agreed to set up a joint commission to settle the boundary issue. No agreement was reached, however, and in 1903 negotiations were renewed. On October 20 of that year an arbitration tribunal decided in favor of the American claims. The tribunal awarded two small islands to Canada.[5]

In 1897 the army established Fort Saint Michael on Norton Sound, followed in 1899 by Fort Gibbon, on the north bank of the Yukon River opposite and a little below the mouth of the Tanana River; and at Fort Egbert, at the mouth of Mission Creek near Eagle City, on the Yukon. In the meantime, in February, 1898, the army also created the Lynn Canal Military District. It was to include Lynn Canal and all lands adjacent extending to the international boundary and within fifty miles in other directions. Colonel Thomas M. Anderson, of the Fourteenth Infantry, commanded the new district, headquartered at Camp Dyea.[6]

About a month before the outbreak of the Spanish-American War in 1898, the army organized three expeditions to explore Alaska. Specific orders stated that the expeditions were to collect "all the information valuable to the development of the country regarding topographical features, available routes of travel, feasible routes for railroad construction, appropriate and available sites for military posts, mineral resources, timber, fuel, products, capability of sustaining stock of any kind, animals, etc.," all of which was to be embodied in a report with maps and plates "to give the Department information on which to base its action, and the public as full an understanding as possible of the resources of . . . the country." Both military and civilian agencies benefited from the knowledge gained by the explorations of 1898. Others followed and in 1899 the army began construction of a military road from Valdez to Copper Center, whence it was to go by the most direct route to Eagle City. Another party under the command of Capt. Edwin F. Glenn was to explore the Cook Inlet region, and Lt. O. L. Spaulding and a squad of men were dispatched from Saint Michael to preserve law and order at Cape Nome.[7]

At the turn of the century the War Department reorganized the army in the north and created the Department of Alaska with headquarters at Fort Saint Michael, commanded by Col. George M. Randall. Only one company was still stationed at Skagway, and the Lynn Canal Military District had been discontinued some time earlier. In the meantime, the rush to the Nome gold fields began in 1899 and reached its peak in 1900. Since 1899 a detachment of troops had been stationed at Anvil City (Nome) to keep order. In 1900 construction began on Fort Davis, about two miles outside the tent city of Nome, and troops also built Fort Liscum, across the bay from Port Valdez. The temporary nature of the mining camps necessitated much flexibility by the army, which established and discontinued posts as circumstances required. Finally, on September 15, 1901, the War Department announced the abolition of the Department of Alaska and once again attached the district to the Department of the Columbia.[8]

Of long-range importance to Alaska was the development of a communication system tying the populated sections of the territory to the contiguous states. After Congress authorized construction of the system on May 26, 1900, the U.S. army Signal Corps began construction. Completed in 1904 against great odds, the system contained elements not previously combined into a single harmonious system. It totaled 1,497 miles of land lines, 2,128 miles of submarine cable, and a wireless, or radio, link of 107 miles. Within the next five years cables also tied in Seward, Wrangell, Ketchikan, and Cordova. In 1907 the Signal Corps began replacing the land lines in Alaska with a wireless system, and the U.S. Navy also built stations at Sitka and Cordova. Between 1917 and 1940 the communications system experienced growth and technical improvements. On May 15, 1936, the War Department changed the name of the system from WAMCATS to Alaska Communication System (ACS).[9]

Despite these activities the army's interest in Alaska and that of the nation as a whole declined during the first thirty-five years of the twentieth century. Eventually all forts and posts were closed, and only a token garrison at Fort William H. Seward (renamed Chilkoot Barracks in 1922), at Haines, near the head of Lynn Canal in southeastern Alaska, remained.

The 1930s were a troubled period for the United States as well as for Europe. On October 24 and 29, 1929, Wall Street stock-market prices plummeted, and by November 13 of that year about $30 billion in the market value of listed stocks had been obliterated. The "great crash" triggered the worldwide Great Depression. By the middle of 1932 market losses had mounted to approximately $75 billion. By 1933 about 15 million Americns had lost their jobs. America found itself in a desperate situation.

Europe and Asia did not fare well either. In Germany, Adolf Hitler had taken power, while in Italy Fascist dictator Benito Mussolini was riding high. After a bloody and bitterly fought civil war that lasted three years, the fascist dictatorship of General Francisco Franco replaced Spain's republican government in 1939. Russia boasted of a "dictatorship of the proletariat," which made the tyranny of the czars seem benevolent by comparison. Since 1931 economic penetration and military intervention had enabled the Japanese to bring a widening area of China under their control, and in September, 1940, Japanese forces occupied Indochina.

By 1939 war clouds rose ominously across the Atlantic and Pacific, and on September 1 of that year Hitler's armies, led by dive bombers and tanks, invaded Poland. Europe's major powers were soon embroiled in World War II.

## ALASKA'S STRATEGIC POSITION— EARLY WARNINGS

At the outbreak of the war Alaska's only military establishment was Chilkoot Barracks. An infantry post dating back to the gold-rush days, it was situated where it could observe traffic bound inland over the Dalton Trail or over three historic trails— the Chilkoot, Chilkat, and White passes. Eleven officers and approximately three hundred men armed with Springfield rifles manned the post. The installation did not have a single antiaircraft gun. The troops were immobilized because their only means of transportation was the venerable tug *Fornance*. Its engines were so feeble that, while returning from Juneau in December, 1939, with the commanding officer on board, it encountered a thirty-knot headwind, was unable to advance to Haines, and had to be rescued by the Coast Guard.[10] In essence, the territory was undefendable.

However, there had been voices reminding the United States of Alaska's strategic importance. As early as 1931 the territorial governor, George A. Parks, had reminded the secretary of the interior of Alaska's strategic position as the most feasible air route to Asia. Air traffic had increased considerably within the territory, and navigational facilities were badly needed. The governor

recommended that the army air corps station planes in Alaska if only to train pilots in flying conditions as they existed in northern latitudes. The pleas fell on deaf ears.[11]

In December, 1934, Japan denounced the five-power naval treaty of February 6, 1922. Under its terms the United States had agreed—among other things—not to fortify the Aleutians. Japan's action prompted Alaska's delegate to Congress, Anthony J. Dimond, to plead for bases at Anchorage or Fairbanks, and also in the Aleutians: "I say to you, defend the United States by defending Alaska." The delegate pointed out that the shortest distance between the United States and the Orient was the great circle route, located 2,000 miles north of fortified Hawaii but only 276 miles south of the Aleutians. The distance from San Francisco to Yokohama over the great circle route amounted to 5,223 miles, whereas the distance from Yokohama via Hawaii to the nearest point on the West Coast of the United States was 6,316 miles. Delegate Dimond reminded his colleagues that these geographical factors would invite an enemy of the United States, moving across the Pacific, to invade Alaska first. Dimond's measures to provide $10 million for an air base and another $10 million for a naval base died quietly in the House military committee and the naval affairs committee, respectively.[12]

Early in 1935, however, Congress named six strategic areas in which there would be an army air corps base. Alaska was one of the six areas. In subsequent congressional testimony, military witnesses unfailingly supported such an Alaskan base both for defensive-offensive purposes and for providing training in cold-weather aviation. Brig. Gen. William Mitchell, an advocate of air power, highlighted the various hearings with his testimony on February 13, 1935, in which he dramatically declared that Japan was America's most dangerous enemy in the Pacific. "They will come right here to

Alaska . . . [which] is the most central place in the world for aircraft, and that is true either of Europe, Asia, or North America. I believe in the future he who holds Alaska will hold the world, and I think it is the most important strategic place in the world."[13] It was to no avail; Congress did not appropriate the necessary funds.

Congressional inaction did not deter Alaska's Dimond. Year after year he warned his colleagues of the potential danger from Japan. In 1937 he pointed out that some Japanese, ostensibly fishing off Alaska's coast, were actually disguised military personnel seeking information on the depth, defenses, and landmarks of Alaska's harbors. At the same time, he attempted to secure a $2 million appropriation to begin construction of the air base near Fairbanks which had been authorized in 1935. If Hawaii constituted one key to the Pacific, Dimond pleaded, Alaska constituted the other. At the very least, he urged, army air corps pilots should be trained in cold-weather flying. Congress refused the necessary funds. In time Dimond made converts, most importantly Gen. George C. Marshall, the army chief of staff, and Maj. Gen. Henry H. Arnold, head of the army air corps.[14]

In 1940 an appropriation of $4 million allowed construction to begin near Fairbanks on a cold-weather testing station for airplanes. In the meantime, the navy proceeded in a leisurely fashion with its Alaska construction program. A year earlier, naval air stations at Sitka for $2.9 million and at Kodiak for $8.75 million were authorized. Delegate Dimond apprehensively declared: "We are starting defensive measures too late and proceeding with them too feebly."[15]

Included in the army's budget for fiscal year 1941 was a request for a base near Anchorage for $12,734,000. When the defense budget reached the full appropriations committee, however, the entire appropriation

for the Anchorage base had been eliminated. Despite testimony asking for a restoration of the funds by General Marshall, Major General Arnold, Delegate Dimond, and others, the House refused the monies on April 4, 1940.[16]

A few days later, on April 9, Hitler's armies invaded and occupied Norway and Denmark. Now, for the first time, many congressmen realized that the Scandinavian peninsula was just over the top of the earth from Alaska and that bombers able to fly such a distance existed. Both Generals Marshall and Arnold appeared before the Subcommittee on the War Department of the Senate Appropriations Committee on April 30 and once again asked for a restoration of the Anchorage base. Before the Senate subcommittee had finished its hearings on May 17, 1940, the German air force had bombed Rotterdam without provocation or warning, while the German army had seized the Netherlands. The Senate restored the Anchorage base, and the House concurred.[17]

Construction of bases had been underway at various locations, among them bases for seaplanes and submarines on Kodiak Island and at Dutch Harbor at the eastern extremity of the Aleutians. By September, 1941, Kodiak and Dutch Harbor had been commissioned as naval air stations and could even handle submarines.

The Civil Aeronautics Authority and the army engineers supplemented naval efforts by building a series of staging fields north from Puget Sound inland, and out to Cold Bay on the Alaska Peninsula.

In the mid-1940s the U.S. Army established the Alaskan Defense Command under Brig. Gen. Simon Bolivar Buckner, Jr. The navy soon followed with the creation of an Alaskan sector under the Thirteenth Naval District headquartered at Seattle and appointed Capt. Ralph C. Parker to the command.[18]

Yet, when the Japanese struck Pearl Harbor without warning on December 7, 1941, Alaska was hopelessly unprepared for war. Major General Buckner exclaimed in exasperation, "We're not even the second team up here—we're a sandlot club." There were a few tiny army garrisons, a scattering of airfields guarded by a few bombers and fighters, and a navy fleet of outmoded World War I vintage destroyers and wooden "Yippee" boats, which, in the opinion of their commander, Carl ("Squeaky") Anderson, "would sink if they got rammed by a barnacle."[19]

As early as May 5, 1942, Japanese imperial headquarters ordered that the "Commander-in-Chief combined fleet will, in cooperation with the Army, invade and occupy strategic points in the Western Aleutians and Midway Island."[20]

## THE JAPANESE ATTACK

On the night of June 2, 1942, a Japanese force of two aircraft carriers with eighty-two planes, two heavy cruisers, three destroyers, and an oiler steamed through the foggy North Pacific toward Dutch Harbor. Supporting the task group not far to the west cruised the ships of Vice Adm. Boshiro Hosogaya's northern force, including four cruisers, nine destroyers, and three transports carrying 2,500 Japanese army invasion troops. Submarines screened the fleet. The planes were to strike a paralyzing blow at Dutch Harbor while troops were to land on Adak, Kiska, and Attu and occupy those islands.

The Japanese carrier force had turned into a foggy, cold-weather front earlier in the day after Rear Adm. Kakuji Kakuta, the task force commander, had been alerted by the sighting of a patrol plane in the clouds overhead. The Japanese were uncertain whether it was an American PBY Catalina flying boat or a Russian plane. Not wanting to lose the element of surprise, the task force stayed with the leading edge of the storm.[21] On the morning of June 3, 1942, the carriers *Junyo* and *Rynjo* launched their planes for the attack on Dutch Harbor, less than 170 miles away. Unknown to the Japanese, however, their element of surprise had been lost. The flying boat Admiral Kakuta had seen at noon the previous day had been an American patrol plane.

When the planes of the carrier *Junyo* attacked Dutch Harbor early on the morning of June 3, 1942, they were met by the blazing antiaircraft guns of the alerted American base. The attack planes of the carrier *Rynjo* had lost their bearings in the dense fog and had turned back. From the very beginning both American and Japanese forces realized that despite all human courage and mechanical genius, the forces of nature called the shots in the Aleutians.

The two attacks on Dutch Harbor did not last very long, and the American defenders soon discovered that the base had weathered the opening skirmish of the Aleutian campaign without much physical damage or defense impairment.[22]

Although the attack on Dutch Harbor has been recorded in history as merely an "incident," it nevertheless powerfully influenced the course of the war. The Japanese assault on the Aleutians was designed to divert massive American naval forces north toward Alaska. According to the plan, the main body of Admiral Isoroku Yamamoto's combined imperial fleet was to intercept and destroy the American fleet at Midway Island on June 4, 1942. But because the Dutch Harbor attack diverted Japanese forces needed at the rendezvous, Japan lost the balance of power at Midway, a major battle there, and perhaps even the war.[23]

After regrouping and some indecisiveness, early on June 5, 1942, Vice Adm. Boshiro Hosogaya ordered Rear Adm. Sentaro Omori, commander of the Adak-Attu Occupation Force, who was then some 225 miles southwest of Adak, to turn back and proceed to Attu. On the morning of

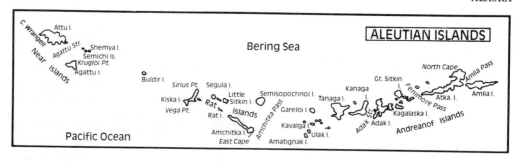

The Aleutian Islands

June 7, 1942, Omori landed his 1,200 troops on Holtz Bay, from where they marched overland through snow to Chichagof. The main part of the troops got lost and arrived at Massacre Bay by mistake. The remaining troops attacked the little settlement of Chichagof and made prisoners of its entire population of thirty-nine Aleuts and one teacher, a Mrs. Jones. The Kiska Occupation Force also made its landing on June 7 without opposition from the ten members of the temporary U.S. weather station.[24]

Subsequently, it has become clear that the Japanese had no intention of capturing anything east of Adak, that they had no plans to invade the Alaskan mainland, Canada, or the United States. Apart from its diversionary aspect, the Aleutian operation was principally defensive, designed to prevent an American invasion of Japan. Because of the loss at Midway, Kiska essentially had become worthless as the northern anchor of the new defense chain. Nevertheless, the Japanese high command decided to keep the island and develop it as an air base, partly to block a possible invasion and partly for nuisance and morale value.[25]

The Americans did not discover the occupation until June 10, when a Catalina— an amphibious plane—reported four ships in Kiska. This initiated a new phase of the war, with the Japanese attempting to hold what they had and the Americans trying to blast them out. The war for the Aleutians essentially became a contest of air power in which both sides were hampered by the foul weather.[26] The war quickly frustrated both sides. Nobody won fame or fortune, and none of the operations accomplished anything important or had any noticeable effect on the outcome of the conflict. American—and probably Japanese—sailors, soldiers, and aviators regarded stationing in this area of almost perpetual winds, fogs, and snow as little better than punishment. Distance and weather constantly impeded American as well as Japanese operations.

Vice Admiral Hosogaya, commander in chief of the Northern Area Force, was responsible for maintaining and defending Attu and Kiska. On the American side, Rear-Adm. Robert A. Theobald, commander of the North Pacific Force, had been instructed by Adm. Chester W. Nimitz to keep pounding the two islands until forces could be spared to recover them.

Hosogaya's base at Paramushir in the Kuril Islands lay 1,200 miles north of Tokyo and 650 miles west of Attu. Ships bound for Kiska had anothr 378 miles of steaming through reef-filled waters.[27] Admiral Theobald had established his headquarters at Kodiak. Rear Adm. William W. Smith commanded a cruiser task force, while Brig. Gen. William O. Butler commanded the Eleventh Army Air Force, consisting of medium bombers and fighters, a few Flying Fortresses, and a growing group of PBY's. Major General Buckner was the army commander of the Alaskan sector with a token garrison at Fort Morrow on the base of the Alaska Peninsula. Fort Glenn on Umnak Island, 536 miles east of Kiska by air and 660 miles by sea, was the westernmost American airfield. The only American naval and seaplane base in the Aleutians, inadequate and also damaged by the June 4 raid, was Dutch Harbor, about sixty miles eastward on Unalaska Island. Fort Randall at Cold Bay on the Alaska Peninsula possessed a good army airfield but was located another 155 miles eastward by air or 185 miles by sea. Alaska's main advanced military and naval base was on Kodiak Island, some 372 miles east of Cold Bay by air and 505 miles by sea. All needed supplies for the American armed forces had to come from Seattle, which meant a flight of 1,742 miles or a sea voyage of 1,957 miles to get reinforcements and material to Umnak.[28]

The Japanese also had a difficult time. On July 7 and 8, 1942, Admiral Yamamoto withdrew four carriers and other capital ships southward. This left Vice Admiral Hosogaya with an insufficient Northern Area Force for offensive operations. He therefore decided to build airstrips on Attu and Kiska from which land-based bombers could defend the Japanese Aleutians. Because of the lack of construction equipment capable of dealing with the spongy muskeg and the underlying frozen volcanic ash, work proceeded very slowly. For all practical purposes, Japanese offensive bombing in the Aleutian campaign ceased after a high-altitude attack on the morning of July 20, 1942.[29]

American forces, however, went on the offensive. Admiral Theobald ordered the construction of an airfield on Adak within fighter-plane distance of Kiska so that bombers could be escorted on the round trip. Construction crews found an almost ready-made airfield in the form of a flooded tidal basin. Army engineers drained and filled it and within ten days finished their job. On September 14, 1942, the first

Capt. Ira Wintermuth, left, and his navigator, Lt. Paul Perkins, studying the route before taking off to bomb the Japanese garrison on Kiska Island in World War II. #208-AA-5EE-1. Courtesy U.S. National Archives.

Kiska-bound fighter-bomber strike took off from Adak.[30]

In September, 1942, the Japanese abandoned Attu as an economy measure, concentrating their troops at Kiska. By early October of that year, the island, with its massive antiaircraft emplacements and network of underground bunkers, had become virtually impervious. Only Kiska's supply line remained vulnerable. And since the Japanese had decided to abandon the Aleutians at the onset of winter and fall back on the northern Kurils, they were satisfied with the maintenance of the status quo. Soon, however, the Japanese imperial headquarters changed its North Pacific policy and decided to hold on to the Aleutians.[31]

On October 29, 1942, the Japanese reoccupied Attu, and the American forces soon thereafter landed only forty miles from Kiska on Amchitka, where they built a forward air base which became operational in February, 1943.[32]

## AMERICAN DEFENSE EFFORTS

In the meantime, Major General Buckner's Alaska Defense Command had grown to 150,000 troops. With the help of two army reserve officers, Capt. Carl Schreibner and Maj. (later Lt.-Col.) M. R. Marston, Alaska's Governor Ernest Gruening had organized the Territorial Guard, a security force primarily intended to guard the long coastline and pass intelligence on to the armed forces in the absence of the National Guard. Dutch Harbor, the assembly point of the Aleutian theater of war, handled approximately 400,000 tons of shipping a month. Alaskan coal production had increased tenfold in 1942, and the army constructed the four-inch-wide Canol Pipeline to carry crude oil from Norman Wells on the Mackenzie River to a refinery in Whitehorse. From there a three-inch pipeline was to carry the various petroleum products to Alaska. Alaska's population had mushroomed under the stimulus of the military construction boom. And under the protection of the U.S. Navy and Coast Guard, Alaskan fishing fleets made record catches, most for export to the lower forty-eight states.[33]

A road connecting the contiguous United States with Alaska had been in the talking stage since the 1930s. The opening of the Alaska-Canada Military Highway (Alcan) on November 20, 1942, represented a major engineering achievement. Built to connect many of the landing fields on the air route to Alaska—via Great Falls, Montana; Lethbridge, Calgary, Edmonton, and Grand Prairie, Alberta; Fort Saint John and Fort Nelson, British Columbia; Watson Lake and Whitehorse, Yukon Territory; and Northway, Tanacross, Big Delta, Mile 26, and Ladd Field at Fairbanks, Alaska—the 1,420-mile pioneer road wound its way through the wilderness. Seven engineer regiments, aided by forty-seven contractors employed by the Public Roads Administration, worked toward each other from various points along the route under often harsh weather conditions and over extremely difficult terrain. They finished the pioneer road exactly nine months and six days after the start of construction.[34]

Although the road was crude, by December of 1942 army convoys crawled north to Alaska with supplies and materials for the Alaskan command and for the Soviet Union as well.

Marvin R. Marston, an Anchorage businessman and real estate developer. During the war he was a lieutenant colonel stationed at Elmendorf Air Force Base. As part of the war effort he organized the Eskimo Scouts for the Territorial Guard. The National Guard in Alaska developed from that scout unit and continues to play an important role in many villages in the state. Courtesy Anchorage Historical and Fine Arts Museum.

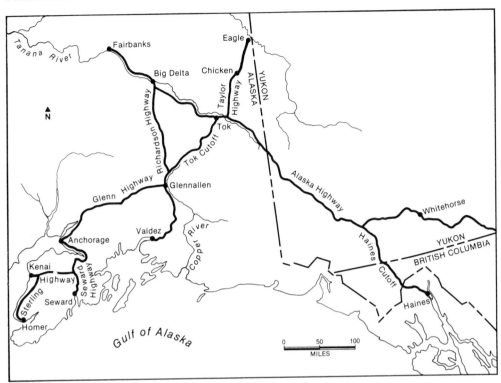

The Alaska Highway and connecting roads. From Naske, *Paving Alaska's Trails*, p. 241. Reproduced by permission.

## LEND LEASE AND INTENSIVE WARFARE

ALSIB—the Alaska-Siberia Lend Lease Route originated on March 11, 1941, when Congress passed H.R. 1776, known as the Lend-Lease Act—was designed to help hard-pressed Great Britain and any other nation at war with Nazi Germany. When Germany invaded the Soviet Union on June 22, 1941, that nation soon became a lend-lease participant.

As early as September, 1941, the United States suggested that lend-lease aircraft be delivered to Siberia via Alaska, using American pilots and crews. The Russians declined because they considered the route too dangerous.

The exigencies of the war finally made the use of ALSIB imperative, and from September, 1942 until the fall of 1945, some 7,926 combat and transport aircraft were delivered in Fairbanks to the Russians, who then flew them to Nome and Siberia.[35] ALSIB cut the travel distance from 13,000 miles via the Middle East to less than 3,000 miles. In addition, the Russians took over lend-lease destroyers and other ships at Cold Bay. Cargo shipped by sea from West Coast ports was escorted by the U.S. and Canadian navies through the Aleutians and on to Vladivostok, a major Russian seaport.

At the same time, American planes kept bombing the Japanese installations. The winter of 1942/43 turned into the worst one in thirty-four years. Fairbanks temperatures dipped to −67° in December, and

Late in September, 1942, this truck was driven up the Alaska–Canada Military Highway (Alcan) from Dawson Creek, British Columbia, to Whitehorse, Yukon Territory—the first truck to make the trip. Courtesy Anchorage Historical and Fine Arts Museum.

in the Aleutians it took crews two hours to get the ice off airplane wings, while blowtorches were used to thaw engines before they would start. Yet despite these handicaps, the bombers dropped more than a half-million pounds of explosives on enemy bases during the last three months of 1942.[36]

Early in January, 1943, Rear Adm. Thomas C. Kinkaid, a grizzled naval hero, arrived to replace Rear Adm. Robert A. "Fuzzy" Theobald as comander of the North Pacific Force, and Rear Adm. Charles H. McMorries relieved Rear Adm. William W. Smith as commander of the cruiser-destroyer group. With the arrival of these two men the Aleutian campaign went into high gear.[37]

On March 26, 1943, Admiral Hosogaya, who had decided to run the American blockade and resupply Attu, encountered a small task group under Rear Admiral McMorries. The subsequent engagement, named the "Battle of the Komandorski Islands," was to have no parallel in the entire Pacific War. Rear Admiral McMorries fought a retiring action against Admiral Hosogaya's forces, twice as large as his own and with double the firepower. The battle lasted continuously for three and one-half hours, and the opponents shot at each other at ranges of eight to twelve miles. No planes or submarines intruded, and neither side did the other great harm. The Japanese finally broke off the battle when Admiral Hosogaya became convinced that he was under air attack. What had happened was that the heavy cruiser *Salt Lake City*, having run out of armor-piercing shells, started shooting high explosives with white phosphor splashes that looked exactly like bombs dropping through the overcast sky.[38] The battle was decisive, because after

Pvt. Simeon Polotinkoff, an Aleut from Unimak Island, fought with the U.S. Army in World War II. He is shown aboard the transport that took him and other soldiers to Attu, which American forces retook from the Japanese after a fierce battle. In human lives it was the second-costliest American battle in the Pacific Theater, second only to Iwo Jima. Courtesy U.S. National Archives.

Hosogaya turned back, no further Japanese convoys were to reach the Aleutians.

On May 11, 1943, American troops landed on Attu, a forbidding, mountainous island some thirty-five miles long and fifteen miles wide. Bitter fighting raged for two weeks. On May 28, Col. Yasuyo Yamasaki took stock of his situation. Of the 2,600 men he had started with on May 11, fewer than 800 fighting men remained. Some 600 were wounded. He estimated American strength at 14,000 men. There would be no evacuation because the fleet of large transport submarines, called I-boats, had been turned back by the American destroyer screen. The colonel, therefore, decided to attack, in the hope—however remote—of raiding American supplies. That evening he sent his last radio message to Japan, burned his records, and prepared his soldiers for the assault. Lt. Nebu Tatsuguchi returned to his post that evening and made his last diary entry:

> At 2000 we assembled in front of headquarters. The last assault is to be carried out. All patients in the hospital are to commit suicide. . . . Gave 400 shots of morphine to severely wounded, and killed them. . . . Finished all the patients with grenades. . . .
> Only 33 years of living and I am to die here. I have no regrets. Banzai to the Emperor. . . . Goodbye Tasuko, my beloved wife.[39]

On the morning of May 29, Yamasaki made a banzai charge with his remaining men. The Japanese came close to taking back what the Americans had gained in nearly three weeks of bitter and bloody fighting. Individual Japanese soldiers held out in the hills; some were not flushed out until three months later. When finally cornered, every Japanese soldier chose to commit suicide.[40]

It had been an expensive battle. In proportion to the numbers of troops involved, it would rank as the second most costly American battle in the Pacific Theater, second only to Iwo Jima. Landing Force Attu had suffered 3,829 casualties: 549 killed, 1,148 wounded, 1,200 injuries due to the severe cold; 614 disease casualties, including exposure; 318 other casualties, which included self-inflicted wounds, psychiatric breakdowns, drownings, and accidents. The Japanese were practically annihilated. Only twenty-eight prisoners were taken, not one officer among them, and the American burial parties counted 2,351 Japanese bodies; several hundred more dead were presumed to have been buried in the hills by the Japanese during the three weeks of battle.[41]

## KISKA—ANTICLIMAX

American attention next turned to Kiska. From June 1 until August 15, army pilots flew 1,454 sorties and dropped 1,255 tons of bombs on Kiska. In addition, the navy bombarded Kiska from its cruisers and destroyers. Unknown to the Americans, however, the Japanese had decided to evacuate the Kiska garrison. At first thirteen big I-boat transport submarines were to be used, but seven of these were lost or crippled, while only 820 men were evacuated. On July 28 and 29 the enemy, under the cover of fog, skillfully brought a surface fleet into Kiska Harbor. Within fifty-five minutes, Rear Adm. Shozo Akiyama, officers, enlisted men, and civilians, numbering 5,183, crowded on board two cruisers carrying 1,200 each and six destroyers averaging 470 passengers each. The ships left undetected and safely reached Paramushir on August 1, 1943.[42]

Before the evacuation of Kiska, on July 23, the radar of a Catalina had contacted what were believed to be seven vessels some 200 miles southwest of Attu. The American command believed that these ships were a Japanese reinforcement convoy bound for Kiska. American warships rushed to the scene, and on July 26 the American fleet made radar contact and fought what was to become known as "The Battle of the Pips."

After expending 1,005 rounds, Rear Adm. R. C. Giffen gave the order to cease firing and at dawn circled back to the scene of the "battle." An observer plane found no debris, no wreckage, nothing but the gray waves of the North Pacific. Apparently return echoes from the mountains of Amchitka and other islands had shown up on radar some 100 to 150 miles distant.[43]

On August 14 the Kiska invasion proceeded on a colossal scale. Two days later the American troops reached the enemy's main camp and discovered all the signs of hasty departure, with food, stores, and weapons only partially destroyed. Yet the Americans suffered casualties. Patrols occasionally shot fellow Americans by mistake. Some twenty-five soldiers died and thirty-one suffered wounds from these errors. In addition, the navy lost seventy men dead or missing and forty-seven wounded.[44]

S. Sgt. Edmond Birdsell, of San Francisco, samples rice left behind when the Japanese evacuated Kiska in World War II. Courtesy Hanna Call Collection, Alaska and Polar Regions Archives, Elmer E. Rasmuson Library, University of Alaska.

## THE WAR'S EFFECT ON THE NORTH

After the Aleutians had been secured, military activities declined sharply. From 152,000 members of the armed forces in Alaska in 1943, the number declined to 60,000 in 1945 and to a mere 19,000 in 1946. Although military activities decreased rapidly after 1943, the war had a profound and lasting impact on the territory. It irrevocably altered the pace and tenor of Alaskan life. The residual benefits to the civilian economy and the development of Alaska were tremendous. Between 1941 and 1945 the federal government spent well over one billion dollars in Alaska.[45] The modernization of the Alaska Railroad and the expansion of airfields and construction of roads benefited the civilian population as well as the war effort. Many of the docks, wharves, and breakwaters built along the coast for the use of the Navy, the Coast Guard, and the Army Transport Service were turned over to the territory after the war. Thousands of soldiers and construction workers had come north, and as reflected in population statistics, many decided to make Alaska their home at the end of the hostilities. Between 1940 and 1950 the territory's civilian population increased from approximately 74,000 to 112,000.[46] But this influx put a tremendous strain on Alaska's already inadequate social services, such as schools, hospitals, housing, and local government.

In short, the war was the biggest boom Alaska ever experienced, bigger than any of the gold rushes of the past. Yet, at the end of the war, with the curtailment of defense spending, Alaskans once again were confronted with the problems of a seasonal economy.

## THE COLD WAR

The development of tensions between the United States and the Soviet Union after World War II, resulting in the Cold War,

U.S. Army paratroopers on maneuvers in Alaska in the 1960s. Courtesy Anchorage Museum of History and Art.

rescued Alaska from economic depression and obscurity. The territory's geographical position astride the northern great circle route from Asia to the United States gave it a strategic importance in the free world, an importance which once again was to bring thousands of troops and the expenditure of millions of dollars.[47]

By 1947 construction had commenced on what was then the largest airfield in the world, Eielson Air Force Base, twenty-six miles south of Fairbanks. Long-range bombers were to use this facility. The rebuilding and expansion of other major defense facilities at Fort Richardson and Elmendorf Air Force Base near Anchorage; Fort Greely near Big Delta; Kodiak; Shemya; Adak; and smaller bases and stations elsewhere got underway as well.

By 1949 military planners had become worried about Russian activities in Siberia and speculated that four-engined aircraft stationed on the Chukotski Peninsula could theoretically attack the atomic bomb plant at Hanford, Washington, and return to their bases. A limited radar network existed, but much had to be done to upgrade Alaska's defenses effectively. The construction and equipping of the electronic Distant Early Warning Line resulted, soon to be followed by the White Alice system, a tropospheric scatter radio communications network.

The Cold War quickly forced American strategic rethinking, and in the late 1940s military planners decided on the so-called heartland concept of Alaskan defense. This included a virtual abandonment of the Aleutian Islands and a massive strengthening of the military bases in and near Faribanks and Anchorage. The new concept coincided with a general realignment in the overall strategic emphasis from the Pacific to the Atlantic.[48]

Before the shift in emphasis could be accomplished, however, massive problems had to be overcome in Alaska. As the armed forces had discovered, Alaska was a region of magnificent distances, lethal cold, forbidding terrain, and a still totally inadequate system of communication and transportation. As on previous occasions, the territory challenged American technical imagination and ingenuity. For despite the intensive construction activity during the war, Alaska was still a primitive frontier that lacked housing and possessed no modern economic and social infrastructure to support the defense effort.

Supplies still came mostly by sea from Seattle to the ports of Seward, Whittier, Anchorage, or Valdez, each one insufficient in one way or another. The best was probably Seward, although wood worms had done severe damage to the docks, which required frequent replacements. Whittier, built during the war and located at the head of a fjord in a small glacial ravine, was plagued

The C-5 Galaxy, the largest airplane ever to fly in Alaska, lands at Eielson Air Force Base in the winter of 1970. Courtesy *Fairbanks Daily News–Miner*.

by high winds and almost continuous rain and snowfall in addition to inadequate docking and unloading facilities. With a glacier behind it, the sea in front of it, and 30 to 50 feet of snow on top of it in the winter, it was isolated, had no recreational facilities, and appeared to be the end of nowhere in Alaska for army personnel unfortunate enough to serve there. Large floating ice cakes and 36-foot tides plagued Anchorage.

The Alaska Railroad, which carried freight from the ports, was antiquated. Completed in 1923 after 8 years of construction, the railroad's average daily capacity of some 1,500 tons was insufficient even for normal civilian requirements. It had inadequate rolling stock and grades and a poor roadbed. In the so-called loop area between Seward and Portage the trains had to traverse a high ravine in nearly a full circle; the tracks were supported on high, wooden trestles which had been erected many years earlier and which were quite shaky by 1949. In addition, heavy snows and occasional avalanches between Seward and Anchorage often interrupted train service.[49]

The Alaska Highway connected the territory with the contiguous United States. Although open the year around, it had a maximum capacity of only 1,000 to 1,500 tons daily. Alaska's 2,500-mile road system was primitive, and not one road from any of the ports was consistently open all winter long.[50]

The territory's communication system was similarly primitive. Only one land line existed, running along the Alaska Railroad. The Alaska Communications System, run by the Army Signal Corps, relied on radio transmission, which was often blocked by ionospheric interference.[51]

Housing was abysmal throughout the territory, particularly for military personnel, thereby severely undercutting morale and causing an almost negligible reenlistment rate for the territory. Many of the single men among the 20,000–30,000

troops lived in overcrowded barracks and dark quonset huts. Family quarters were scarce and substandard, and rents were exorbitant. Packing-case houses, open walls, and outdoor privies predominated, in addition to severe overcrowding. Construction costs, two and one-half to three times above those in the contiguous United States, severely limited new housing starts, while exceedingly high prices for food, appliances, and services stretched already modest budgets to their limits. Compounding the problems was the lack of adequate recreational and social activity.[52]

In order to achieve the "heartland" concept of defense in Alaska, the military realized that vast expenditures would be needed to provide basic facilities. The Defense Department asked Congress for funding, and, though there were delays and cuts in various construction requests, military expenditures approached $100 million in 1949, starting the territory's postwar economic boom.[53]

## THE POSTWAR DEFENSE CONSTRUCTION BOOM

By June of 1950 it had become apparent that some $250 million worth of construction would be undertaken. All was not rosy, however, because carpenters, electricians, and other craft unions had gone on strike for higher wages. These work stoppages completely halted many projects and considerably slowed others. But workers, undeterred, had been flocking to the territory from the contiguous States since early spring. Hoping for quick employment at high wages, their resources were slim, and many suffered hardships because of the prolonged strike.

The influx of defense spending made prices soar. Housing in Fairbanks, always insufficient and mostly substandard, now fetched premium prices. Cabins without electricity or water rented for $150 per month, and rooms in hotels in Anchorage

were even worse because rental was anywhere from 10 to 20 percent higher than in
Fairbanks—and nothing was available.

Workers earned big money, and they
worked a good deal of overtime. Building
mechanics, for example, received weekly
paychecks that often exceeded $200, in ad-
dition to free board and room. The basic
daily wage of a waitress amounted to $8.60;
that of a cook, $18. Craft unions such as
the plumbers and steamfitters, electricians,
carpenters, and painters all made over
$3.00 per hour. But prices corresponded to
wages. Fruits and vegetables, all airborne,
were exorbitant. Restaurant meals were
high: a plain omelet or a lettuce and tomato
salad came to $1.50 or $1.75, and a piece
of toast cost 30¢ or 35¢. But despite the
prices, business boomed.[54]

Population, like prices, had also skyrocketed. In 1940 the territory boasted
75,000 residents, of whom some 1,000 were
military personnel. By 1950 Alaska's population had jumped to 138,000, of whom
26,000 belonged to the military services.[55]
Anchorage had been a sleepy railroad town
of 3,495 in 1940; in 1950 it had an estimated
11,060 residents—not including several
outlying suburbs which would have brought
the population to approximately 20,000.
Also not included were transients and military personnel stationed at the bases. The
population of Fairbanks jumped from approximately 5,600 in 1940 to 11,700 in
1950, and that of Seward, from 949 to 2,063
during the same decade.[56]

While contractors hurried to complete
military family quarters, barracks and official quarters, service clubs, warehouses,
and power plants, the influx of job-seekers
severely taxed Alaska's housing and social
services. Transients clogged the cities, and
although there was no spectacular increase
in major crimes in Fairbanks, Anchorage
police reported half a dozen murders during the first half of 1950. Police blamed the
increase in robberies in both cities on the
boom conditions. Gambling flourished in

the construction centers, and although it
was against territorial laws, officials over-
looked the games "so long as these are carried on in an orderly and gentlemanly fashion." The fact was that municipal taxes
from these activities had something to do
with official leniency. Prostitution flourished
despite the fact that red-light districts in
both cities had been closed some years earlier. The women now cautiously walked the
streets or operated outside the city limits.
Cab drivers often acted as steerers, directing customers to prostitutes for a fee.[57]

Despite many problems, Alaskans ultimately stood to profit from the turmoil of
the boom. As a result of military construction, the private business sector flourished.
In Fairbanks the Community Savings Bank
of Rochester, New York, financed the 270-
family Fairview Manor development with
$3,080,000. In Anchorage the Government
Hill Apartments, designed for 696 families,
took shape at a cost of $10 million, and
the Brady-Smalling Construction Company
built two 132-unit housing developments at
a cost of $3 million. In both Anchorage and
Fairbanks large and small modern houses
supported by Federal Housing Authority
(FHA) guarantees were built in new subdivisions. The Anchorage suburb of Spenard
numbered 3,000 residents, and a modern
shopping center was built on a tract that had
been part of Alaska's wilderness only five
years earlier. In addition, both Anchorage
and Fairbanks had new airports under construction. Increased demands stimulated the
professional and business communities to
expand services.

Considerable sums also went into the expansion of the small highway network and
Alaska Railroad extensions and improvements. In short, Alaska coped with its
problems.[58] The territory slowly built up a
backlog of social overhead. Despite worries
within Alaska's business community, the
defense boom continued unabated.

A fifty-three-day walkout of the Sailors'
Union of the Pacific of the American Feder-

ation of Labor (AFL) in the summer of 1952 slowed Alaska's boom somewhat, yet projects planned or already underway continued. Private building expanded significantly, but housing shortages still were critical even though the Alaska Housing Authority built or financed many units during that summer, among them 150 low-rental units in Anchorage and another 75 units in Fairbanks.[59]

Many began to recognize that the territory was quickly becoming a guardian of North American defenses. The massive infusion of military dollars stimulated tertiary growth; modern hotels and office buildings sprang up, and new radio stations gained permission to operate. Air transportation expanded vastly with new commercial airports and connections to most points in Alaska and to many international destinations. Modern subdivisions alternated with unattractive slum areas containing shacks and wanigans, largely the result of slipshod regulations and hurry-up building. In Fairbanks the number of bank deposits doubled between 1949 and 1952, while car registration in Anchorage increased 1,390 percent in a decade and school attendance increased nearly 1,000 percent within the same period. The population of the greater Anchorage area increased 52.1 percent between April 1, 1950, and December 31, 1951.

But despite the private building boom sparked by defense spending, much remained to be done. Both towns suffered from a shortage of school buildings, and Fairbanks was in dire need of a sewage dis-

The main thoroughfare of Anchorage in the spring of 1945, when it had a population of about 8,000. In 1940, the population had been 4,229. By the 1980s, Anchorage had become Alaska's largest town, with a population of more than 200,000. Military spending contributed significantly to the population increase. Courtesy Lulu Fairbanks Collection, Alaska and Polar Regions Archives, Elmer E. Rasmuson Library, University of Alaska.

posal system. For the first time Alaska offered bright opportunities for young professionals in addition to the customary seasonal employment for floating labor.[60] In short, the territory was in a period of transition, fewer and fewer people fled as soon as the weather turned cold or a fortune had been made. The accumulating social overhead made living easier and more comfortable.

By 1954 the territory had passed the peak of military construction. Military housing needs had largely been met, and Alaska's defenses were nearly completed with a network of radar defenses and massive military bases. The gains had been great. Within a five-year period from 1949 to 1954 the territory had become habitable on a year-round basis for a vastly increased population. Expenditures for defense and civilian construction combined had been approximately $250 million per year from 1949 to 1954.[61]

When construction for defense installations passed its peak in 1954, much had been accomplished. Alaska's road system had more than doubled, from a prewar mileage of 2,400 miles of dirt and gravel roads to 5,196 miles of high-grade paved highways and gravel roads in 1958. The Alaska Highway and the Haines cutoff had become all-year links. Highway construction received massive funding and was transferred to civilian program direction with the inclusion of Alaska in the federal aid-to-highways program in 1956.

The prewar Alaska Railroad had hauled freight and passengers along a single track 470 miles long from Seward to Fairbanks. Its equipment consisted of coal-burning locomotives and primitive wood-frame cars handed down from the Panama Canal construction project. By 1958 the Alaska Railroad right-of-way had been upgraded, the rolling stock completely modernized, and the coal-burning locomotives replaced by diesel engines.

The ports of Seward and Valdez had been rebuilt and now easily accommodated military and civilian freight, while the new military port, Whittier, provided an alternative for landing freight. An 8-inch, 625-mile-long pipeline from Haines pumped oil products to Fairbanks, while air fields aided commercial aviation, which progressed from single- to multi-engined propeller and then jet aircraft.

The development of the strategic bomber and the intercontinental missile reduced the warning time of an impending attack from hours to minutes, placing top priority on the creation of a distant early warning (DEW) system. Continuing a tradition dating back to World War II, the United States and Canada agreed on the construction of reciprocal continental defense and warning systems in the Arctic. Military planners envisioned a radar screen stretching along the coasts of Alaska's western and Canada's eastern Arctic. After considerable research construction began in the late 1940s in secrecy. By 1952 the project had become public knowledge, and a construction base was established in Anchorage early that year. Bell Laboratories, the prime contractor for the DEW Line system, furnished engineering expertise and assistance. In 1953 the first DEW Line station at Kaktovik (commonly known as Barter Island) became operational. By 1957 the entire northern sector of the early warning network in the United States was functioning, and two years later, on May 1, 1959, the Aleutian segment of the DEW Line was dedicated; it featured aircraft and warning detachments stationed between Nikolski and Port Heiden.[62]

In December, 1954, the navy reactivated an old oil-exploration camp at Barrow and renamed it the Naval Arctic Research Laboratory (NARL). For the next quarter century scientists from universities and research institutes from the United States and Europe used the facility as a base camp while accu-

A Distant Early Warning (DEW) line site at Barrow. Photograph by Claus-M. Naske.

mulating knowledge of arctic conditions and the northern military environment.[63]

Most important were the people who came to Alaska during and after the war. Most of them were members of a mid-twentieth-century American urban industrial society who expected—and demanded—the same standards of community living and service as those available in the lower forty-eight states. Prosperity induced by defense spending in the Far North made it possible slowly to meet these demands. In addition, the expansion and change in the composition of Alaska's population in the postwar period resulted in increasing political agitation for self-government and the eventual attainment of statehood in June, 1958. The culmination of the long statehood struggle came when President Dwight D. Eisenhower signed the official proclamation on January 3, 1959, which admitted Alaska to the Union as the forty-ninth State.[64]

By 1958, Americans were debating the threat of intercontinental ballistic missiles (ICBMs). The technology and delivery systems of these long-range weapons, many feared, had destroyed the geographical remoteness that had for so long shielded the United States from enemy attack and occupation. A few well-placed nuclear bombs or missile warheads could easily destroy northern defenses and allow the Soviets to occupy Alaska and install missiles targeted on American cities. As both superpowers increased their ICBM stockpiles as a part of their deterrence and containment policies, the nuclearization of the military made its impact on Alaska. In May, 1959, Maj. Gen. C. F. Necrason, chief of the Alaska Air Command, announced that Clear, about seventy-five miles southwest of Fairbanks, was to be the site for one of three Ballistic Missile Early Warning Sites (BMEWS), the other two to be built at Flingdales Moor, England, and Thule, Greenland. Where the DEW Line had been designed to protect the United States from a bomber attack, the BMEWS were developed in response to the ICBM threat.[65]

Throughout the 1940s and until at least the mid-1960s military construction and the maintenance of garrisons and uniformed personnel and their dependents made the military the major single element in the economic growth of Alaska. Compared with prewar expenditures of less than $1 million in the territory, military spending peaked at $512.9 million in 1953 and amounted to $354 million in 1970.

The military remained an important factor in the Alaska economy. In 1980, for example, total Department of Defense expenditures had once again risen from their $512.9 million peak in 1953 to more than $932 million. Throughout the 1970s and into the 1980s the Department of Defense consolidated and modernized the Alaska Command. The deployment of increasingly complex and sophisticated military hardware, such as enhanced "over-the-horizon" radar and satellite surveillance, resulted in decreasing troop strength. General James E. Hill, chief of the North American Air Defense Command, remarked in 1979 that Alaska would continue to be militarily important to the contiguous states. In 1980, perhaps in recognition of that importance, the air force replaced its aging combat fighter

aircraft with modern A-10 Skyhawks, close-air-support bombers, and state-of-the-art F-15 Eagles. The air force maintains a base at Galena, on the Yukon River, in service since 1943, featuring a 7,200-foot runway and modern installations. Operated on a twenty-four-hour alert status, fighter aircraft often scramble to intercept Soviet aircraft intentionally or inadvertently violating American air space. Bases at Clear; King Salmon, on the Alaska Peninsula; and Chemya, in the Aleutian Islands, have monitoring tracking, and intelligence-gathering capabilities.[66]

In November, 1983, President Ronald Reagan spoke briefly at Elmendorf Air Force Base en route to Japan and Korea. Like other chief executives before him, the president emphasized Alaska's crucial role in national security policy considerations, concluding that the state was America's "first line of defense," underscoring the postwar continuity of continental defense.[67]

Alaska's senior U.S. senator, Theodore F. Stevens, has vigorously supported President Reagan's defense policies, including increased military priority for Alaska. In 1983, Stevens, with the support of Lt. Gen. Lynwood Clark, chief of the Alaska Air Command, succeeded in his efforts when the air force increased the number of F-15 combat fighters from eighteen to twenty-four, based at Elmendorf, and provided a similar increase in A-10 Skyhawks based at Eielson Air Force Base, twenty-six miles south of Fairbanks. Despite Stevens's efforts, however, the navy has not increased its strength at its installation on Adak Island, in the Aleutian Chain.[68]

In April, 1984, the army announced plans to create several light-infantry divisions as one component of the Rapid Deployment Force. This was a response to changing strategic and tactical requirements in situations described as "low-intensity conflicts." The light-infantry-division concept grew from the necessity to develop more flexible conventional-force capability and the ability to respond quickly to trouble centers around the world. Alaska's congressional delegation, state politicians, and community leaders clamored to have one of the proposed new divisions based at either Fort Wainwright or Fort Richardson. Public hearings were conducted, and the army's Corps of Engineers prepared an environmental-impact statement. Many individuals, particularly in Fairbanks, expressed concern about the impact such a division would have on the quality of life and community services and predicted disruptions in the local economy. On September 11, 1984, Secretary of the Army John Marsch, Jr., and Senator Stevens jointly announced that one of the two new light-infantry divisions would be stationed in Alaska; the other was to find a home at Fort Drum, New York. After further deliberations the army decided to station the new unit at Fort Wainwright, near Fairbanks.[69]

The decision to base the light-infantry division in the Forty-ninth State reaffirmed the continuing strategic importance of Alaska because of its location on the air crossroads of the world. For this reason the state will continue to play an important role in the overall military strategy for the defense of American interests in the Pacific region.

Over the years close relationships have developed between the armed forces and the civilian communities. Cities like Anchorage and Fairbanks continue to derive substantial percentages of their annual revenues from military and dependent spending. Service families contribute to the social life of their adopted communities, and emergency medical and fire crews often respond off base

when needed. Because of Alaska's vast size and difficult geography and the isolation of most villages, the military performs tasks it would not normally undertake in the contiguous states. For example, in 1959 military planes bombed ice floes at Fort Yukon and Aniak, situated on the Yukon and Kuskokwim rivers, respectively, to prevent flooding. Each Christmas army and air force pilots deliver Christmas presents provided by military and civilian donors to families in rural areas. After the disastrous Good Friday earthquake of March 27, 1964, the military provided personnel and facilities, saving lives and helping victims. When the Chena overflowed its banks in Fairbanks in August, 1967, and inundated the town, the army lent a helping hand in evacuating civilian personnel to higher ground at the University of Alaska, six miles north of town. The armed forces have also helped in innumerable search-and-rescue missions to help find downed civilian planes or lost hunters.[70]

Over the years the armed forces have performed many functions in America's only arctic and subarctic province, ranging from serving garrison duty to exploring; from building wagon roads, trails, bridges, and tramways to stringing telegraph cables; and from evicting the Japanese from Attu to guarding the North against threats from the Soviet Union. The military contributions to Alaska's social, economic, and political history have been important and continue to be so. The size of the military contribution to Alaska's economic well-being is determined by the dynamics of international affairs, particularly the relationship between the United States and the Soviet Union.

# 8. ALASKA'S ROCKY ROAD TO STATEHOOD

World War II had revolutionized Alaska, and along with the influx of new residents came demands once again for the territory's admission into the Union as a state.

The idea of self-government had been discussed off and on since 1867, when Sitka residents had made the request: "Territorial government for the Territory [sic] of Alaska."[1] While on a world tour at the end of his services in the administration of President Andrew Johnson, William Seward visited Sitka. There the former secretary of state and architect of the purchase of Russian America predicted that "the political society to be constituted here, first as a Territory, and ultimately as a State or many States, will prove a worthy constituency of the Republic."[2]

No one on that August day in 1869 realized that it would take eighty-nine years for Alaska to achieve statehood. In the meantime, Congress provided Alaska with the rudiments of civil government when it passed the First Organic Act in 1884. Jack E. Eblen, a scholar of territorial government, has concluded that the organic act "provided a cruelly modified first-stage government and made no provisions for eventual representative government."[3]

It was not until 1906 that Congress finally passed a measure giving Alaskans a voteless delegate to Congress, in part, perhaps, to meet President Theodore Roosevelt's plea to "give Alaska some person whose business it shall be to speak with authority on her behalf to the Congress." So many different interests—lobbyists of mining, canned salmon, steamship, and mercantile interests, as well as the appointive governor and other civil, military, and federal officials—had claimed to represent northern interests that Congress was simply confused.[4]

Despite much effort and the accompanying acrimony, it was not until 1912 that Congress passed the Second Organic Act, which provided for an elected legislature for Alaska. The territorial legislature had many restrictions imposed on it: it could not, for example, regulate Alaska's fish, game, and fur resources or assume bonded indebtedness without congressional consent. Despite all of its apparent and real defects, however, the Second Organic Act of 1912 ended Alaska's vague legal and constitutional status. It specifically stated that "the Constitution . . . shall have the same force and effect within the Territory of Alaska as elsewhere in the United States." The distinction between a territory and a district was a crucial one, because the former was thought capable of exercising at least a limited measure of home rule through a locally elected legislature, while the latter was considered incapable of exercising self-government.[5]

Even the term "territory" was modified in the early twentieth century. As a result of the Spanish-American War of 1898, the United States acquired Puerto Rico, the Philippines, and other noncontiguous lands. The question soon arose whether or not these new acquisitions should become integral parts of the United States. The Supreme Court decided in the negative in a series of decisions known collectively as the "Insular Cases." The Court made a hazy distinction between "incorporated" and "unincorporated" territories. The former were to be subject to the "fundamental" and "formal" parts of the Constitution as well as all public laws applicable to them, while in legislating for "unincorporated" territories Congress was restrained only by the "fundamental" parts of the Constitution.[6] Secretary of War Elihu Root reportedly said of this rather nebulous distinction established by the Court that "as near as I can make out the constitution follows the flag but doesn't quite catch up with it."[7] Under these distinctions Alaska and Hawaii were declared to be "incorporated," whereas the Philippines and Puerto Rico were not.

Historically, statehood had been tied to the territorial classification and specifically, after the Insular Cases, to the incorporated status. The Court also decided that once an area had been incorporated it could not revert to an unincorporated status. Most important, the act of incorporation was consistently looked upon as a commitment by Congress ultimately to admit the incorporated territory as a state.[8]

These and other legislative restrictions soon led to demands for additional powers. As early as 1915 territorial legislators asked for changes in the Organic Act and even for statehood. Congress did not respond.[9]

## THE FIRST STATEHOOD BILL, 1916

While the territorial legislature debated the merits of full territorial government and statehood, Alaska's delegate to Congress,

James Wickersham, introduced a bill to enlarge the powers of the territorial legislature.[10] The most important feature of this measure would transfer management of Alaska's fish and wildlife resources to the territory. But the opposition of the commissioner of the United States Bureau of Fisheries killed the bill.[11]

Wickersham had given some thought to statehood as early as 1910, when he wrote an article for *Collier's* with the suggestive title "The Forty-ninth Star." In it he argued that Alaska was destined to become a state and had, as a matter of fact, "the constitutional right to Statehood." Wickersham also made known his intentions to introduce a statehood bill for Alaska late in 1910.[12] The promised statehood bill never appeared, and one can assume that he may have used the possibility of such a measure as a device to get the Organic Act through Congress.

The year 1916 was to be different. Wickersham drafted an enabling act for the proposed state. He patterned his bill after the 1906 measure that had gained admission for Oklahoma. That particular bill, he reasoned, was recent, contained many new ideas, and was liberal in its grants of money and land to the new state.[13]

On March 30, 1916, the date of the forty-ninth anniversary of the signing of the treaty of cession of Russian America, Delegate Wickersham officially introduced his enabling measure.[14] He had carefully chosen the date to emphasize Alaska's long apprenticeship as a possession of the United States. But it was more of a trial balloon than a serious measure.

The statehood bill, the first in a long line of such measures, was simple and skeletal. It contained the standard provision in enabling acts that the proposed new state would be admitted on an equal basis with the other states. The rights of Alaska's Indians, Eskimos, and Aleuts to lands claimed by them were protected in that the future state disclaimed all rights and title to any unappropriated public areas that were claimed by the various indigenous groups until Congress extinguished those rights.[15] Congress, however, did not act on the Wickersham measure.

In 1916, Alaskans reelected Wickersham on his own ambiguous platform, in which he favored extended powers for the territorial legislature and statehood "as soon as it can be organized in the interest and to the advantage of the people."[16] The issue of statehood was dead for the present, but it would soon reappear.

The year 1920 turned out to be a Republican year with the election of Warren G. Harding of Ohio to the presidency. In the race for the delegateship in Alaska, Dan Sutherland, a Republican, prevailed over his Democratic opponent, George Grigsby. The new president appointed Scott Bone, former editor of the *Seattle Post-Intelligencer* and director of publicity for the Republican National Committee, to the governorship of Alaska.[17]

In 1923, President Harding decided to visit Alaska. This was the first time a chief executive had visited the territory during his term in office. The visit was of utmost importance to Alaskans, and they looked on it as an opportunity to present their views to the president on a variety of matters. Harding was interested in, among other things, finding a solution to the administrative tangle in Alaska. At that time five cabinet officers and twenty-eight bureaus exercised authority over the territory. Many of the agencies were in bitter conflict over how best to develop and use the vast resources of the area. Secretary of the Interior Albert B. Fall, for example, consistently promoted a plan to concentrate the administration of Alaska into one department (presumably Interior), thus allowing private enterprise to exploit the natural resources as speedily as possible. Secretary of Agriculture Henry C. Wallace, in whose department was the conservation-minded Forest Service, objected to Fall's plan. President

Harding was torn between the conflicting opinions and wanted to investigate on the spot before making any decisions. This was also an opportunity to draw attention to the United States' neglected territory. The completion of the federal government's Alaska Railroad gave the president the opportunity to drive the official golden spike.

During his visit Harding evidently concluded that few important changes of policy or administration were necessary or desirable. He delivered his last major speech in the University of Washington stadium on July 27, 1923, a week before his death in San Francisco. He spoke of the future of Alaska and indicated that he opposed radical changes in its administration. He rejected the idea of a sudden exploitation of Alaska's resources that Secretary Fall had advocated, endorsing the conservative policies of his predecessors. The president said that he favored a slow, planned evolution that would protect the territory's natural resources and yet permit their gradual use. Equally important to Alaskans, Harding declared that the territory was destined for ultimate statehood. "Few similar areas in the world present such natural invitations to make a state of widely varied industries and permanent character," he said. "As a matter of fact, in a very few years we can set off the Panhandle and a large block of the connecting southeastern part as a State." Alaskans' reaction to the president's speech was overwhelmingly favorable.

## SECESSION MOVEMENT IN SOUTHEASTERN ALASKA

While Harding's Seattle speech and his subsequent death were still being discussed in the nation's press, the inhabitants of southeastern Alaska, the territory's most populous and developed section, were taking steps to secede from the rest of Alaska. Encouraged by the president's remark that their section would be the first to attain statehood, they wanted to speed that day by establishing a full territorial government for South Alaska. On November 6, 1923, a referendum was held in all the large southeastern towns except Sitka, which was not notified in time. A total of 1,344 citizens approved the plan; 89 rejected it.[18]

For three days, March 27–29, 1924, the House Committee on the Territories held hearings on a measure introduced by Chairman James Curry of California to reapportion the Alaska legislature. Soon after the hearings opened, Curry categorically declared that Alaska would not be partitioned or receive statehood.[19] That effectively ended the separationist movement in southeastern Alaska; the reapportionment bill also died.

## THE DEFEAT OF REPUBLICAN WICKERSHAM AND THE ELECTION OF ANTHONY J. DIMOND

On November 5, 1929, Delegate Sutherland announced his decision not to seek election for a sixth term. That very night James Wickersham declared his candidacy, and in January, 1930, he issued his platform, which included, among other items, support for "a more perfect form of Territorial Government" and territorial control over the fish and game resources. Wickersham won the nomination and defeated his Democratic opponent, George Grigsby, in the fall elections. At seventy-four years of age, the veteran again assumed a seat in Congress.

The Great Depression spelled disaster for many Republican officeholders, among them Wickersham. Unopposed in the primary for a second term in 1932, he faced Democrat Anthony J. Dimond, a tall, somber man, in the November election.[20] Dimond had moved to Alaska from Palatine Bridge, on the Mohawk River in New York, early in the century. He had taught high school and read some law. While he was on a prospecting trip in 1911, a shooting accident forced him to abandon gold mining.

He resumed his law studies, and not long after leaving the hospital in Cordova, he was admitted to the territorial bar and began the practice of law. He served as commissioner of the Chisana recording district in 1913 and 1914, as mayor of Valdez for ten years, and as territorial senator for two terms. After a vigorous campaign Dimond won the election by a substantial margin, and Alaska Democrats gained large majorities in both houses of the territorial legislature. The American public also voted for a national political change, and Dimond began his Washington career in an era of political ferment.[21] It was also he who initiated the modern drive for statehood.

Despite his largely unsuccessful attempts, the delegate accomplished no more for home rule than had his predecessor, Wickersham. However, changes in the governance of Alaska were made which affected the federal executive. Until 1934 federal relations with the territories had been conducted from the office of the chief clerk of the Department of the Interior. In that year the function shifted to the newly created Division of Territories and Island Possessions within the department.[22] Ernest Gruening became the first director.

Born in New York City in 1887, Gruening graduated from Harvard College and Harvard Medical School in 1912. Instead of practicing medicine, he pursued a career in journalism and became known for his editorship of a succession of Boston and New York newspapers as well as the liberal journal the *Nation*. In 1936 the energetic director visited Alaska for the first time, and within two weeks he had traveled approximately four thousand miles to familiarize himself with the North.[23]

It was the war that led to the rediscovery of Alaska and its rapid development, a circumstance neither foreseen nor planned by the federal government. A day after the outbreak of war in Europe on September 2, 1939, President Franklin D. Roosevelt announced that John Troy had resigned from

144

Ernest Gruening, Alaska's territorial governor, 1939–53, and Alaska's junior U.S. senator, 1958–68, in Barrow. Courtesy the Reverend and Mrs. Klerekoper Collection, Alaska and Polar Regions Archives, Elmer E. Rasmuson Library, University of Alaska.

the governorship of Alaska because of ill health and that Ernest Gruening would take his place.[24] In his inaugural address on December 5, 1939, Roosevelt predicted that Congress would be slow in granting statehood to the first noncontiguous territory and that hurrying the process would be desirable.[25]

## THE BEGINNING OF THE MODERN STATEHOOD MOVEMENT

In the 1941 progress edition of the *Daily Alaska Empire,* Dimond attempted to persuade Alaskans about the advantages of statehood. He pointed out that Alaska's population had increased substantially and that the federal government had initiated, if belatedly, a defense construction program. Dimond pointed out that statehood would enable Alaskans to manage their fish, fur, and game resources; have their own judicial system and police force; and gain federal matching funds for highway construction. Above all, it would bring voting representation in Congress.[26]

The war postponed any action on the matter, but early in 1943, Senator William Langer, a maverick Republican from North Dakota, drafted an enabling bill which he introduced with conservative Democratic Senator Pat McCarran of Nevada on April 2, 1943. It was a short measure, eleven pages long, and dealt with drafting a constitution, establishing a federal district court in the state, and disposing of public land.[27]

## ALASKANS REACT TO THE STATEHOOD BILL

Several organizations and newspapers in Alaska considered the measure. Some reacted favorably, while others objected to the cost of statehood, fearing it would be excessive.[28]

On December 2, 1943, Delegate Dimond, who had talked so much about statehood, introduced his own measure. Very similar to Langer's bill, it provided that the federal government convey to the state practically all public lands.[29]

Secretary of the Interior Harold L. Ickes conceded that ultimate statehood was desirable but objected to the general land transfer because he feared that special interests would resist adequate taxation, thereby tempting state lawmakers to allow wasteful exploitation of the lands to obtain needed revenues. None of the various executive departments most closely concerned with Alaska opposed the principle of statehood.[30]

Delegate Dimond decided to retire from Congress in early 1944, and shortly thereafter President Roosevelt appointed him federal district judge for the Third Judicial Division, an office he had wanted to occupy. His protégé E. L. ("Bob") Bartlett successfully overcame primary opposition and won the delegateship in the general election in September, 1944. He had made the issue of statehood one of his campaign planks.[31]

The territorial legislature met in early

Edward Lewis ("Bob") Bartlett, Alaska's last territorial delegate to Congress, 1944–58, and the new state's first senior U.S. senator, 1958–68. He died in office on December 11, 1968. Claus-M. Naske Photograph Collection, Fairbanks.

1945 for its biennial session. On the fourth day Governor Gruening delivered his annual message, reminding his listeners that the platforms of both territorial political parties as well as the two opposing candidates for delegate had endorsed statehood in 1944. Furthermore, he said, few if any Alaskans rejected statehood in principle; they differed only on the timing of admission. The governor thought that a referendum on the question should be held but that first the voters had to have information on the issue. This information should be assembled impartially, published, and distributed widely.[32]

Anthony J. Dimond, Alaska's delegate to Congress, 1933–44. Courtesy Lulu Fairbanks Collection, Alaska and Polar Regions Archives, Elmer E. Rasmuson Library, University of Alaska.

## CONGRESSMEN VISIT ALASKA

Several groups of congressmen toured Alaska in the fall of 1945. One group was composed of the House Subcommittee on Appropriations for the Department of the Interior. They reported that, although the majority of Alaskans favored statehood, the members seriously doubted the territory's ability to assume the burdens of statehood. The reasons mentioned were absence of an adequate tax law as well as inadequate social legislation. Representative John Rooney of New York amplified these views in a newspaper interview. Any people, he remarked, who allowed a major industry like fishing to take out about $60 million annually and retained only $1 million in taxes obviously were not ready for the responsibilities of statehood. Rooney observed that absentee fishing and mining interests controlled the legislature, but he blamed Alaskan citizens as much as the legislators for this state of affairs.[33]

## DEBATE ON THE EARLY STATEHOOD PROPOSAL

By mid-1945 the executive departments most concerned with the administration of Alaska had to take an official stand. Finally, on August 10, 1945, Secretary Ickes issued a statement on behalf of his department stating that statehood was now a part of the department's policy for Alaska. Ickes remarked that statehood would link Alaska more closely with the rest of the nation and encourage new settlers and the development of its resources. It would result in greater capital investment and bestow equality on territorial residents by giving them voting representation in Congress. The secretary dismissed as of no consequence the arguments used against admission, namely, the small population, lack of agricultural markets, seasonal unemployment, inadequate health services, underdeveloped economy, and higher costs of state over territorial government. He warned, however, that admission would not necessarily transfer the entire public domain to state control.[34]

Obviously an endorsement of statehood from this department was very important, since it had jurisdiction over mining, fish and wildlife, Native affairs, national parks and monuments, the Pribilof Islands' seal harvest, the Alaska Railroad, road construction and maintenance, the care and treatment of Alaska's insane, and the development, disposal, and surveying of the public lands. Its Division of Territories and Island Possessions generally supervised territorial affairs, and the president-appointed governor addressed his annual reports to the secretary. Governor Gruening was elated by the announcement and thought that if Alaskans voted affirmatively in the referendum admission to the Union would not be too far behind.[35]

The legislature had authorized a referendum, but no provisions had been made to inform the citizenry on the subject. Private citizens formed an Alaska Statehood Association and commissioned George Sundborg, a newspaperman and planner, to undertake a statehood study.[36]

In the meantime, Congress reassembled in 1946, and in his January address on the State of the Union President Harry S. Truman urged members to admit Hawaii and Alaska as states as soon as their residents had expressed their wishes. A short while later, on February 13, Harold L. Ickes resigned as secretary of the interior. The president appointed Julius A. Krug to the position.[37]

In August, 1946, the new secretary went on a ten-day tour of Alaska to listen and learn, but he nevertheless did much of the talking. Many Alaskans were impressed by Krug, a large, jovial man, because he seemed sincere and interested. Krug cautioned residents that statehood was not the answer to all territorial problems but was a step in the right direction. Upon returning to Seattle, he told newsmen that Alaska "should comprise at least one state and perhaps two or three." He also remarked that Congress always moved slowly on major decisions unless it was "against the gun. This is not an issue on which it is against the gun."[38]

A few weeks after Krug left the territory, Alaskans received the statehood report prepared by George Sundborg. Printed both as a pamphlet and as a newspaper supplement entitled *Statehood for Alaska: The Issues Involved and the Facts About the Issues,* it was widely distributed throughout the territory. For many years this study was the authoritative reference work for the statehood forces. As might be expected, it clearly showed the sympathies of its author and the sponsoring group: of fifty-six pages only five were devoted to arguments against statehood.[39]

## THE 1946 ELECTIONS AND RESULTS OF THE REFERENDUM

The report, combined with debates, speeches, meetings, and radio broadcasts, stimulated public interest. About a month after the distribution of the report Alaskans went to the polls. In the referendum 9,630 residents voted affirmatively and 6,822 negatively.[40] The 3 to 2 vote was decisive, but not a landslide as proponents had hoped. Only 16,452 ballots had determined the issue, less than 23 percent of the 1939 population, but low voting participation was characteristic of Alaska.

Foremost among the businessmen opposing statehood was Austin ("Cap") Lathrop, a entrepreneur whose interests in 1946 included apartment buildings, radio stations, motion-picture theaters, the Healy River Coal Company, and the *Fairbanks Daily News-Miner.* He was Alaska's wealthiest man and was esteemed by many because he reinvested his profits in Alaska rather than outside. On the day before the referendum, his eighty-first birthday, he explained that he objected to statehood because of the "terrific financial burden" it would impose on a very small group of taxpayers. Business investment was needed, but capital would have to come from outside. High taxes would discourage investments. Once Alaska had more people, statehood would come easily.[41]

Although businessmen generally shared Lathrop's views, many supported statehood nonetheless. Many of those living in incorporated towns firmly believed that statehood would be good for business because it would increase population and investment from outside the territory. A mass market would benefit everyone and also bring down the high cost of living. It was this perception which probably accounted for the widespread endorsement of statehood by chambers of commerce.[42]

Most Alaska politicians supported statehood, often because they believed in it and because it would expand the number of executive offices and judgeships, and also make available two U.S. Senate seats and one House seat. The prospect of reapportionment, however, did not appeal to the sparsely populated Second Judicial Division, where various politicians opposed statehood.[43]

While Sundborg had conjured visions of population growth and economic development, these were precisely the features that many Alaskans, particularly old-timers, did not want. They were content with the unhurried pace, leisure, independence, and outdoor life—untrammeled, for the most part, by regulations—that Alaska offered. If they had preferred the amenities of city life, they said, they would have lived in Seattle. In the last analysis, however, Alaskans were reluctant to close the door to statehood and also were dissatisfied enough with federal rule to cast a majority vote endorsing statehood.

## THE NATIONAL ATTITUDE TOWARD STATEHOOD FOR ALASKA

Alaskans had indicated that they wanted statehood, and an even larger proportion of the American people were ready to accept

Alaska as a state. On September 21, 1946, George Gallup, director of the American Institute of Public Opinion, announced that 64 percent favored admission, 12 percent opposed it, and 24 percent were undecided. Most of those who favored admission felt that Alaska was "vital to the defense of the nation" and that "it deserves equal representation in the body of states." In addition, dozens of national fraternal, business, labor, civic, patriotic, and other organizations supported statehood for Alaska. Foremost among organizations in the support it gave was the General Federation of Women's Clubs. As early as 1944 the federation had adopted a resolution favoring statehood for Alaska.[44]

If Congress had reflected popular sentiment, it would speedily have admitted both Alaska and Hawaii. But partisan and sectional interests in part motivated congressmen. Many members of the U.S. Senate, which had ninety-six members, did not favor the idea of diluting their power. If Alaska were admitted, Hawaii would not be far behind, making a total of four more senators. This consideration was not as important in the House, where the number of representatives was fixed at 435; still, the prospect of two or three representatives from Alaska and Hawaii would result in the consolidation of two existing districts. Additionally, six or seven new members would be added to the electoral college, which chose the president.[45]

Partisan considerations were important as well. During most of the 1950s the Democratic and Republican parties were almost evenly balanced in the Senate. The admission of only one territory might shift that balance in favor of one or the other party. Hawaii had been Republican since the presidency of William McKinley, but Alaska had reflected the nation at large and had gone Democratic in the 1932 election.

Sectional considerations were important as well. The West consistently and vigorously supported Alaska statehood, sharing with the territory many interests, such as extensive public lands, national forests, and extractive industries, that differed only in degree from those of the territory. In fact, in 1946 the Western Governors' Conference endorsed the admission of Alaska and Hawaii, and the National Governors' Conference followed suit in 1947.[46]

## SIDETRACKS TO STATEHOOD

There were many other delays and skirmishes on the way to statehood, some of which originated in Alaska while others came from Congress or the public. One of the disruptions in Alaska was the persistent regionalism intensified by a massive population shift. From 1939 to 1950 the population of the Juneau area increased by only 2 percent and that of Ketchikan by 16 percent, while the Fairbanks and Anchorage areas increased by 241 percent and 658 percent, respectively. Massive federal spending for military bases caused these population increases, and in time many Juneau residents worried that Alaskans from those areas, not Congress, would decide the location of the capital.[47]

## CONGRESSIONAL HEARINGS ON STATEHOOD

The House Subcommittee on Territorial and Insular Possessions of the Public Lands Committee dealt with Hawaii first and then, in April, 1947, held hearings on Alaska statehood. Acting Secretary of the Interior Warner W. Gardner recommended the enactment of the statehood measure but objected to the provisions which, with few exceptions, would have transferred to the new state title to practically all public lands. This, he stated, was contrary to the traditional practice which had been followed throughout the American West. Lands had always been retained by the federal government. Gardner proposed to grant Alaska about 21,000,000 acres for schools, approximately 438,000 acres for the University, and another 500,000 acres for various internal improvements. He also objected that Native rights were not protected in the measure and proposed that the state and its people forever disclaim both the right and the title to all land retained by or ceded to the federal government by the statehood bill and to all land owned or held by Natives or Native "tribes, the right or title to which shall have been acquired through or from the United States or any prior sovereignty." Not only the Department of the Interior but also James Curry, a Washington Attorney for the National Congress of American Indians and the Alaska Native Brotherhood, sought such a guarantee of Native rights.[48]

Numerous Alaskans flew to Washington, D.C. to testify at the hearings, and most of them spoke in favor of the statehood bill. While generally sympathetic, the congressmen worried about Alaska's willingness and ability to finance statehood. Eight days after the hearings ended, the members of the subcommittee voted 8 to 5 to defer reporting the measure until they had been able to visit Alaska personally.[49]

Between July 26, 1947, when the nation's lawmakers recessed, and November 17, when they reconvened, various groups of lawmakers visited Alaska and conducted statehood hearings. Five members of the subcommittee heard testimony from ninety-two people in various Alaska towns. Most of the testimony favored statehood, although some witnesses expressed fears about the added expenses.[50]

Another group touring Alaska consisted of Senator Hugh Butler and three members of the Senate Public Lands Committee. They did not hold formal hearings. Butler had made it clear in 1946 that he opposed statehood for offshore areas and that, although Alaska was not offshore but a part of the North American land mass, he had decided "to remain a member of the jury" until the enabling bill came before his com-

mittee. Their trip was a fairly leisurely one; they did listen to Alaskans but made no record of their observations.[51]

## DEBATE IN CONGRESS IN 1948

When Congress reconvened in January, 1948, Representative Fred Crawford of Michigan had become a crusader for Alaskan statehood. His trip to Alaska the previous year as a member of the House subcommittee had convinced him that statehood would correct much that was wrong in the North. Crawford called together the three colleagues who had toured the territory with him, and they decided to recommend statehood favorably to the full subcommittee. When the subcommittee met to draft the measure, the Department of the Interior repeated its earlier recommendation that the state receive 21,930,000 acres of public lands to be selected from any lands in the public domain rather than being restricted to certain sections in each township.[52]

Chairman Richard Welch then instructed Bartlett to negotiate the size of the land grant with officials of the Departments of the Interior and Agriculture. Eventually all agreed that Alaska was to receive four sections. On March 2, Bartlett introduced a revised measure, which the subcommittee reported unanimously to the parent committee on March 4. Under its provisions the future state was to receive about 39 million acres of land. After some further debate about Native rights which left them unaltered, the Public Lands Committee finally reported the bill favorably.[53]

In the meantime, on February 6, 1948, Senator Butler had reported his findings to his full committee. It was more important to develop Alaska than to push for statehood, he concluded, but he thought that the Panhandle might be split from the rest, since it would be ready for statehood within the foreseeable future.[54]

After a flurry of activity, Speaker of the House Joseph Martin, Jr., refused to bring up the Alaska statehood bill because, as he stated, he did not believe that the Senate would act on it. Since all measures not acted upon at the end of the two-year Congress died, the whole process of introduction and committee review would have to be started again in 1949.[55] Republicans Joseph Martin and Hugh Butler had stopped statehood progress in 1948.

The November elections returned Democrats to control of both houses of Congress and also retained President Truman in the White House. Many Alaskans were cheered when the Democrats pledged themselves to immediate statehood for Alaska and Hawaii, while the Republicans had promised only eventual admission. In Alaska also changes had occurred when voters rejected

the "anti-governor, anti-statehood, anti-progress" legislators who from 1941 through 1947 had blocked the enactment of a basic tax system for Alaska.[56]

## TAX REFORM AND A REVIVED STATEHOOD MOVEMENT

After the election the governor summoned a special session which convened on January 6, 1949, and was followed by the regular session on January 24. From it emerged Alaska's basic tax system.[57]

There were many parts to this new tax structure. The most important was a net income tax, which required individuals and corporations to pay the territory 10 percent of their federal income tax obligation,

Members of the Alaska Statehood Committee, early 1950s. Standing and holding flag, right to left: nonmember Barrie White, Chairman Robert B. Atwood, and Delegate Edward Lewis Bartlett; seated, right to left: Andrew Nerland, Victor Rivers, Warren Taylor, Percy Ipalook, Roy Peratrovich, Mildred Hermann, and William Baker. Courtesy E. L. Bartlett Collection, Alaska and Polar Regions Archives, Elmer E. Rasmuson Library, University of Alaska.

calculated before the deduction of territorial taxes. The tax reform was important because it sent a signal to Congress that Alaskans were willing to tax the special interests and themselves to meet the responsibilities of modern government.

The 1949 session also created the Alaska Statehood Committee. An abortive effort in this direction had been made in 1947, but this time the legislature responded and appropriated $80,000 for the committee's operation. The legislature assigned several tasks to the committee, among them research, preparation for a constitutional convention, planning for the transition from territorial to state government, and aiding the delegate to Congress in lobbying for the enactment of enabling legislation.[58]

## HOUSE APPROVAL BUT SENATE OBSTRUCTION

Meanwhile, the House considered Bartlett's new statehood measure, identical to the one approved in 1948 by the House Committee on Public Lands. In 1948 the House Subcommittee on Territorial and Insular Possessions had consisted of twenty members, but in 1949 it had only ten, the delegates from Alaska and Hawaii and the resident commissioner of Puerto Rico. All the Republicans were subcommittee veterans, while all the Democrats, including Monroe Redden of North Carolina, the chairman, were new.[59]

Redden asked the committee members to study the published materials from the past two years; he planned to hold hearings in March. On March 3 his subcommittee unanimously approved statehood for Hawaii, and on the next day it held brief hearings on the Alaska measure, made minor amendments, and voted for it unanimously. On March 10 the two bills were reported to the House. The Rules Committee, however, bottled up the measures for the remainder of 1949. Early in 1950 the House Public

Lands Committee voted to bypass the Rules Committee and instructed its chairman, J. Hardin Peterson, to take the necessary steps. Circumventing the powerful Rules Committee had become possible the previous year when, during the organization of the House, a reform was approved which barred the Rules Committee from holding for more than twenty-one days a measure which had been approved by one of the other committees. After the specified time period the chairman of such a committee could move for a bill's consideration on the floor. Speaker Sam Rayburn of Texas granted Peterson's request, and both statehood bills came to the floor of the House. On March 3, 1950, the Alaska measure passed by a vote of 186 to 146.[60]

The House had passed the Alaska statehood bill. Now the struggle shifted to the Senate, which until 1950 had seemed oblivious of the matter. One reason was that Bartlett was not a member of the upper house, and another was that Senator Hugh Butler had consistently obstructed action in his committee on the Alaska bills in 1947 and 1948.

## STATEHOOD HEARINGS IN THE SENATE

On June 10, 1949, Estes Kefauver of Tennessee and nineteen other senators introduced an enabling bill for Alaska. Not until March 27, 1950, however, did Senator Joseph O'Mahoney's Committee on Interior and Insular Affairs schedule hearings on the bill, because he wanted the House to act first.[61]

To present an effective case to the Senate, in April, 1950, the Anchorage Chamber of Commerce chartered a plane and flew interested Alaskans to Washington. They met with Bartlett and were told that it was essential to urge senators to approve the House-passed bill.[62]

On April 24, 1950, Alaska statehood

hearings opened in the Senate. They were to be the most important and productive hearings held so far. Since Senator O'Mahoney was ill, Clinton P. Anderson of New Mexico presided. He had been a general insurance agent and President Truman's secretary of agriculture before his election to the Senate. The various executive department heads testified, among them Oscar L. Chapman, the new secretary of the interior. Various Alaskans told Anderson that they desired the committee not to alter the bill substantially lest it be lost in the final rush for adjournment. Finally Anderson told Edward Davis, an attorney representing the Anchorage Chamber of Commerce, that he did not intend to rubber-stamp the version passed by the House.[63]

On the fourth day of the hearings Judge Winton C. Arnold, representing the Alaska Salmon Industry, Inc., a trade organization, appeared before the committee, and all that day and part of the next, supported by an elaborate exhibit of charts and graphs, maps, and tables, he presented a brilliant analysis of the measure. His arguments ranged widely from impairment of international treaties and noncontiguity to questions concerned with federal land policies in Alaska and their relationship to the transfer of public lands to the proposed state. The core of his testimony dealt with the natural resources provisions of the bill. Alaskans should oppose the measure because it "would doom the new State to perpetual pauperism and bureaucratic control." One reason was that the state could select only from vacant, unappropriated, unreserved public lands. This excluded about 27 percent of Alaska's land, because about that much had been withdrawn. Arnold also reminded the senators of his earlier warnings about the massive confusion the aboriginal land claims would cause.[64]

Arnold's testimony alerted senators to the inadequacy of the statehood bill under discussion and to the applicability to Alaska of the western model of the public land state, with its township-section selections. In any event, Arnold's testimony provided the basis for a unique and generous land selection formula which, even though enlarged in subsequent years, did not change in concept.[65]

The Senate hearings ended on April 29, and on June 29 the Senate Interior and Insular Affairs Committee completed its revision of the Alaska statehood bill and reported it favorably. Although the statehood measure died in that particular Congress, the Senate report marked a turning point in the land-grant formula. As Delegate Bartlett related to his listeners in territory-wide broadcasts in July, 1950, the Senate committee had "struck out in a novel and bold precedent shattering way in determining how land should be transferred to the new state." Instead of awarding to the new state sections 2, 16, 32, and 36 in each township, the Senate had granted the right to take from the public domain 20 million acres of vacant, unappropriated, and unreserved lands best suited to its particular needs. Additionally, the measure granted about 200,000 acres from the national forests, the same amount adjacent to established or prospective communities, and another 1 million acres for internal improvements. Title to subsoil mineral rights, except where it conflicted with prior established ownership, was to pass to the new state as well.[66]

Once the historical precedent for the traditional land-grant formula, with its small land grants and specific township-section requirements, had been broken, the way opened for increasingly generous land-grant provisions in succeeding statehood bills.

For the rest of 1950, however, the Southern Democratic-conservative Republican coalition prevented both the Alaska and Hawaii bills from coming to the floor of the Senate. This meant, of course, that the whole tedious process of getting a new bill through the House and then through the Senate had to be repeated.[67]

## THE STATEHOOD STRUGGLE CONTINUES

On January 8, 1951, Senator Joseph O'Mahoney submitted an Alaska statehood measure for himself and eighteen of his colleagues of both parties. With the introduction of three companion bills in the House the statehood struggle was joined again. Late in January, 1951, the Senate Interior and Insular Affairs Committee began its study of the Alaska measure, but since extensive hearings had been held the preceding year and there was little that could be added, committee consideration of the bill was cursory. In May the committee reported the measure favorably by the narrow margin of 7 to 6. But with the outbreak of the Korean War in June, 1950, national priorities had shifted, and Alaska statehood took very much a back seat. The years 1951 and 1952 were lean ones for the statehood forces, and even the Alaska Statehood Committee became somewhat moribund.[68]

With the end of the war in sight early in 1953, half a dozen new statehood bills were submitted, most of them identical to the 1951 bill. Delegate Bartlett doubled the land grant to 40 million acres in the measure he introduced on February 6, 1953. He also included 400,000 acres from the national forests, a like amount for community and recreational purposes, and 2,550,000 acres for internal improvements, a total of 43,350,000 acres. A few days later Representative John Saylor of Pennsylvania seconded Bartlett's bill with an identical measure of his own. The House Subcommittee on Territorial and Insular Possessions of the renamed House Committee on Interior and Insular Affairs held hearings on a number of these measures and finally reported the Saylor bill favorably in June, 1953, along with a number of amendments. The most important of the amendments increased the

proposed land grant from 40 million to 100 million acres. After this favorable treatment the Alaska measure promptly disappeared into the House Rules Committee.[69]

Despite lack of legislative progress, by 1954 both House and Senate measures proposed to bestow some 100 million acres of land on the new state. This constituted a substantial land grant; more important, it followed the new formula that allowed Alaska to select its acreage in large blocks rather than take what luck gave it in the traditional township-section pattern.

In his 1955 State of the Union message, President Dwight D. Eisenhower, as he had the year before, strongly recommended the admission of Hawaii. For the first time in such an address he mentioned the possibility of Alaska statehood, but only dubiously. Frustrated, various individuals began considering the possibility of holding a constitutional convention before the territory's uncertain admission into the Union. But most rejected the various alternatives to statehood that were suggested from time to time.[70]

One of the alternatives to statehood was the repeated proposal that Alaska and Hawaii become commonwealths. Senator Mike Monroney of Oklahoma was the chief proponent of this idea, first suggesting it in 1952 when Puerto Rico officially assumed that status. He revived the idea in 1954. Commonwealth status, as its backers envisioned it, would grant Alaska exemption from the internal revenue laws of the United States but not much else. In 1954, Senator Guy Cordon of Oregon destroyed the arguments for a commonwealth when he submitted a report from the Library of Congress which indicated that no incorporated territory had ever been exempted from federal taxes. Nevertheless, various small groups in Alaska supported the concept, still lured by the faint possibility of tax exemption. Delegate Bartlett remarked that commonwealth was mentioned only when there was a chance that Congress might approve

Alaska statehood. Once legislation failed, talk of commonwealth also subsided.[71]

At the national level the statehood movement did not fare well in 1955, though four statehood bills were introduced—one in the Senate and three in the House. The new Democratic-controlled House and Senate Interior and Insular Affairs committees prepared joint Alaska-Hawaii statehood bills, aware that it was important to satisfy President Eisenhower on this issue. The House again held hearings, primarily for the benefit of its new members. How to satisfy the president on statehood was a problem committee members faced. Secretary of the Interior Douglas McKay testified, favoring Alaska statehood with a "proper bill." The secretary desired to exclude northern and western Alaska from the proposed state. Asked whether a military reservation should be inside or outside the state, McKay stated that it made little difference. Congressman Arthur Miller subsequently had prepared an amendment meeting McKay's requirements.[72]

Bartlett disliked the amendment, pointing out that neither the Department of Defense nor the president had indicated that it met their objections. Above all, the delegate had been given no opportunity to analyze the provisions of the amendment. He urged the omission of the amendment, and the committee went along with him and voted it down.[73]

Soon thereafter the Defense Department reported on the twin statehood measures. It raised no objection to Hawaii's admission but cautioned that no change be made in Alaska's status at that time. After more debate Bartlett compromised, and an amendment acceptable to all was worked out. Thereupon the committee approved the twin bill by a vote of 19 to 6.[74]

In the upper chamber Senator James Murray and twenty-five of his colleagues had reintroduced essentially the same bill that that body had passed nine months earlier. Senator Henry M. Jackson's Subcommittee on Territories and Insular Affairs dealt with two markedly different executive reports. The Defense Department informed Jackson, as it had the House, that no changes should be made in the political status of Alaska, while the State Department asserted that admission of both territories would comply with the United Nations charter.[75]

After hearing testimony from various officials of executive departments, Senator Jackson and Congressman Miller wrote to the president asking him what sort of statehood legislation he would accept for Alaska. Eisenhower's answer was ambiguous. "I am in doubt," he wrote, "that any form of legislation can wholly remove my apprehension about granting statehood immediately. However, a proposal seeking to accommodate the many complex considerations entering into the statehood question has been made by Secretary of the Interior McKay, and should legislation of this type be approved by Congress, I assure your subcommittee that I shall give it earnest consideration." The president at last had indicated that he would at least consider Alaska statehood.[76]

The House sent its version of the twin bills to the Rules Committee, where Congressman Howard Smith of Virginia, the new chairman, was implacably opposed to statehood for either territory. After lengthy hearings the committee granted a "closed rule" under which no modifications would be permitted except for the fifty-six amendments reported by the House Committee on Interior and Insular Affairs. On May 10, 1955, after two days of debate, the House recommitted the tandem bill by a vote of 218 to 170. The Senate, waiting for the outcome in the House, did not act at all.[77]

## ALASKA'S CONSTITUTIONAL CONVENTION AND A NEW TACTIC

In the meantime, the sentiment for holding a constitutional convention to boost

Alaska's sagging fortunes found expression in measures introduced in the 1955 territorial legislature. Such a convention was finally convened, and after seventy-five days of labor the fifty-five delegates produced a document which experts considered a model constitution.[78]

During their deliberations the delegates attached the so-called Alaska-Tennessee Plan ordinance to the constitution. The idea had originated with George H. Lehleitner, a public-spirited businessman from New Orleans who had become an advocate of Hawaii statehood. Finding that Hawaii would make no progress, Lehleitner then made statehood for Alaska a personal crusade. During his research into American history Lehleitner had discovered that a number of territories had departed from the conventional procedures for seeking admission to the Union as states. Instead, these territories drafted state constitutions, elected two U.S. senators, and sent them to the nation's capital and asked for admission. Tennessee and six other territories had employed similar procedures.[79]

When the voters went to the polls in the general election on October 9, 1956, they elected three Democratic candidates for the positions described by the Alaska-Tennessee Plan: for U.S. senators, Ernest Gruening and William A. Egan; and for U.S. congressman, Ralph J. Rivers. Delegate Bartlett had agreed to the scheme even though, if it was successful and Congress seated the three, he would lose his job. The three men went to Washington, D.C., and although they were not seated, they lobbied hard for the cause.[80]

## THE LAST PUSH AND SUCCESS

The outlook for statehood had already brightened in 1956. In March of that year Secretary of the Interior McKay had resigned, and the president had appointed Fred Seaton to replace the Oregonian. Seaton, a publisher and broadcasting executive from Hastings, Nebraska, had served in that state's legislature from 1945 to 1949. Upon the death of Senator Kenneth Wherry in 1951, the governor had appointed Seaton to fill the vacancy. On February 20, 1951, Senator Seaton delivered his maiden speech in support of Alaska statehood. He had been persuaded to support Alaska's cause by Ernest Gruening, who also drafted the speech for him. Seaton did not run for election in his own right in 1952, but in 1953 Eisenhower appointed him assistant secretary of defense for legislative and public affairs, and in 1955 he became a presidential assistant. During his confirmation hearings Seaton mentioned that he favored statehood for Alaska. He also pledged to have the administration-requested defense withdrawals so that Alaska could join the Union.[81] True to his word, Seaton staunchly supported Alaska statehood.

On the territorial level B. Frank Heintzleman resigned as governor three months before the expiration of his term and was replaced by Fairbanks attorney Mike Stepovich. The new governor told Alaskans in his inaugural address that the time had come to close ranks on the statehood issue and work toward the admission of the territory, since that was what the majority wanted.[82]

In 1957, at the request of Bartlett and Delegate John Burns of Hawaii, Senator James Murray introduced separate statehood bills for the territories, and each delegate introduced companion measures in the House. The new Alaska statehood measures differed somewhat from previous ones in that they considered the Alaska Constitution an accepted fact and thus became admission rather than enabling bills. In March the House Subcommittee on Territories and Insular Affairs held ten days of hearings on the subject. The Senate counterpart, presided over by Senator Jackson, devoted two days to it. In general, the two hearings were perfunctory, because many members of the House and Senate committees felt that little new could be added to the record.[83]

As finally reported to the House, the Alaska measure provided the state with 182 million acres of vacant, unappropriated, and unreserved land to be selected within a period of twenty-five years after admission. Native land claims were protected and left to be dealt with by future legislative or judicial action. In August the Senate committee reported its Alaska bill favorably, granting the state the right to select 103,350,000 acres from the vacant, unappropriated, and unreserved public domain within twenty-five years after admission to the Union.[84]

In July, 1957, Speaker of the House Sam Rayburn, hitherto a foe of Alaska statehood, finally changed his mind at Bartlett's urging and promised to give the territory "its day in court" but advised him not to bring the bill to the House until 1958.[85]

In January, 1958, President Eisenhower for the first time fully supported Alaska statehood and again urged Hawaii's immediate admission. Soon after delivering his message, however, Eisenhower again dimmed the hopes of Alaska statehood proponents when he advocated that the Hawaii bill be brought up simultaneously with the Alaska measure. At this critical point Delegate Burns of Hawaii helped the Alaska cause when he asserted that "nothing should interfere with success in the consideration of [the] Alaska" statehood bill. He promised to remove the Hawaii measure from the Senate debate if that was necessary to ensure the success of the Alaska bill. The two bills were not combined.[86]

Toward the end of January, 1958, Bartlett again visited Rayburn and received the latter's assurance that the Alaska statehood bill would come to a vote in the House. Not long after his talk with Rayburn, Bartlett "had a long, long talk with [Senate Majority Leader] Lyndon Johnson. Lyndon told me then that he was ready. He was ready to permit Alaska statehood to come to the floor of the Senate for action there."[87]

At about the same time Rayburn told Congressman Howard Smith, chairman of the House Rules Committee, that he wanted a ruling on the statehood bill. Bartlett was elated. He was even more pleased when Lyndon Johnson told him that the Alaska bill would be brought to the floor of the Senate soon and would be passed as well. Liberal Democrats and friendly Republicans had also agreed not to make the Hawaii statehood bill title 2 of the Alaska measure.[88]

In the House, Congressman Smith had not changed his mind. Representative Clair Engle of California, chairman of the House Interior and Insular Affairs Committee, warned Smith that unless the Alaska bill was given the green light by the middle of March he intended to bypass the House Rules Committee by employing a little-used device under which statehood and a few other kinds of legislature were deemed privileged.[89]

In the meantime there were demonstrations for statehood in Anchorage and Fairbanks, and early in March the American television public saw an Alaska and Hawaii statehood debate on the CBS program "See It Now" with host Edward R. Murrow. Bartlett, Governor Stepovich, and Robert Atwood spoke in favor of Alaska statehood, while Winton C. Arnold, John Manders, and Senator George Malone spoke against it.[90]

In the House, Bartlett's friend Congressman Leo O'Brien announced that he would support four amendments to his bill. One would retain federal jurisdiction over Alaska's fish and game resources in the broad national interest. The others provided for a statehood referendum; a reduction of the land grant from 182,000,000 to 102,550,000 acres, with an additional 400,000 of public lands and another 400,000 acres of national forest lands, a total of 103,350,000 acres; and permission for the Federal Maritime Board to retain control of Alaska's seaborne trade with other states. Bartlett agreed to the other concessions but was unhappy with the federal retention of fish and game management.[91]

After the House Rules Committee stalled, the leadership decided to employ the bypass procedure. Representative Wayne Aspinall brought up the Alaska statehood measure as a privileged matter on May 21, 1958. Speaker Rayburn overruled various objections, and after lengthy debate and the adoption of four amendments, the House passed the Alaska statehood bill on May 26 by a vote of 210 to 166.[92]

Except for the likelihood of amendments being added to the bill, prospects looked bright in the Senate. However, if the Senate bill differed in important particulars from the House version, Bartlett worried, the statehood forces would "be catapulted into a morass." Bartlett and others therefore set up a meeting with Senator Henry M. Jackson, floor manager of the bill, who agreed to abandon the Senate bill and take the House measure instead.[93]

The Senate debated Alaska statehood in the latter half of May and throughout June. Southerners, realizing the futility of resistance, agreed to make only token speeches in opposition, and on June 30 the Senate passed the Alaska statehood bill 64 votes to 20. The long struggle had finally ended in victory.[94]

The struggle had been an extended one, involving many people in Alaska and Washington and throughout the rest of the nation. Bartlett, summing up the long fight, stated that "it took fifteen years for fruition, and I think that given the nature of the opposition, the size of the project, the fact that no state had been admitted since 1912, that actually it was a pretty successful campaign."[95] Bartlett might well have decided that it was fortunate that statehood had not been attained earlier under the meager bills then under discussion.

President Eisenhower signed the Alaska statehood measure into law on July 7, 1958, and on January 3, 1959, signed the proclamation officially admitting Alaska as the forty-ninth state of the Union.

Together with vast changes in its political structure, Alaska received a total of 103,350,000 acres, to be selected from the vacant, unappropriated public lands within a twenty-five-year period after admission. The magnitude of the federal land grant to the new state can best be understood in a comparison with the acreage turned over to the forty-eight contiguous states. The total area of the contiguous states is approximately 1,904,000,000 acres, of which 1,442,000,000 acres at one time were part of the public domain. The federal government disposed of 1,031,000,000 acres by various methods over a period of time. Land grants to the contiguous states totaled approximately 225,000,000 acres. The historical record shows that the public-land states—those carved out of the public domain—have not been treated uniformly as far as federal land grants are concerned. The midwestern and southern states have received a larger percentage of their total area than have the eleven western states. Florida ranks first with a grant of 24,119,000 acres of a total state area of 37,478,000 acres—an astounding 64.3 percent. Nevada, with a land grant of 2,723,647 acres of a total state area of 70,745,000 acres—3.8 percent—ranks last. In the overall list of states Alaska ranks seventh, with 27.9 percent of area granted, but it received by far the largest total acreage of any of the other public-land states.[96] Congress had been generous indeed.

# 9. TRANSITION TO STATEHOOD

Alaska entered the Union as the largest state, with an area of 378.3 million acres. Yet in 1958 the federal government owned 99.8 percent of Alaska's land mass, while only slightly more than 500,000 acres had passed into private ownership. Over the years various federal agencies had withdrawn and reserved for permanent public ownership more than 92 million acres, amounting to more than one-fourth of the total land area, while the remaining area, about 286 million acres consisted of vacant, unappropriated federal public domain lands under the stewardship of the U.S. Bureau of Land Management.[1]

The federal land-management policies had become the root of an increasingly bitter political controversy in Alaska. Most of the federal land-managing agencies seemed primarily interested in holding northern lands for some undetermined future use. Considering their role a custodial one, they had given little consideration to planning the future or coordinating the programs of the many federal agencies. Perhaps their attitude was conditioned by a lack of demand for the resources these lands could provide, but still many Alaskans had come to regard conservationists as a group of unscrupulous politicians retarding the settlement and development of the North through restrictive and unworkable land laws and the withdrawal and reservation of land.[2]

The statehood act was to change this land-ownership pattern, because Congress authorized the new state to select 103,350,000 acres of unreserved federal land over the next twenty-five years. Alaska's future, to a very large extent, would depend on the policies the state adopted for the selection, classification, and disposition of this vast potentially resource-rich acreage covered with forests, containing minerals and water resources, inhabited by many species of wildlife, and blessed with magnificent scenery. The congressional land grant represented less than one-third of Alaska's total acreage, but an area larger than California.

## THE CHANGING ALASKA ECONOMY

The large land grant promised future economic development, but the state of the economy in 1958 did not cheer anyone. Military spending had passed its peak in 1954 and had declined steadily since. Gold mining had never fully recovered from its virtual shutdown as nonessential for the war effort in the early 1940s, and salmon fishing faced a crisis brought about by years of federal mismanagement, overfishing, and recent high-seas salmon catches by the Japanese fishing fleets. Farm production was negligible, with only about 20,000 acres under cultivation, and so was the income derived from furs.

The future for the timber industry looked brighter. In 1954 the first large pulp mill opened in Ketchikan, and thereafter the annual timber cut increased considerably. In the years before 1954 the volume of timber cut in the Tongass National Forest had been modest, for it was primarily intended to meet local requirements for fish-trap pilings, packing cases, mine timbers, dock piles and timbers, and building lumber. In fact, the cumulative total of timber cut between 1909 and 1953, inclusive, amounted to 1,844,512,000 board feet as compared with 864,768,000 board feet harvested between 1954 and 1958, after the pulp mill started operations. In other words, during the first four and a half years of operation of the pulp mill the amount of timber cut amounted to 46.9 percent of the total cut for the entire previous forty-five years of small sawmill operations. In 1959 the Alaska Lumber and Pulp Company, financed in large part by the Japanese Toshitsugu Matusi Company, began operating a pulp mill at Sitka.[3]

Another hopeful development occurred when Richfield Oil Company discovered oil in commercial quantities at Swanson River, on the Kenai Peninsula; by 1959 three wells were producing. As exploration and development activities extended offshore to Cook Inlet, additional oil-and-gas fields eventually started production. Still, Alaskans looking at historical patterns feared that the traditional boom-and-bust economic cycles would repeat themselves.

How had Alaska's economy developed over time? George W. Rogers, Alaska's most astute economist, has conveniently summarized past development patterns in three broad phases, Native Alaska, Colonial Alaska, and Military Alaska. The central theme of each phase, he maintained, can be summed up and compared in terms of the differing attitudes toward use of natural resources and the attitudes, interests, and aims that each phase has contributed to Alaska's alternating drift and drive toward an ill-defined and hazy future.[4]

In Native Alaska land and marine resources were for subsistence—the survival of the people. Differences in living standards and the elaboration of their cultures were directly related to the variety and availability of natural resources in each region. Shared by all, however, was the primary interest in simple survival, which is still dominant today. For despite the existence of welfare programs assuring physical survival, individuals still struggle to preserve their cultures and identities while adapting to changing economic and social conditions.[5]

Native Alaska contributed the only stable and balanced element in the population, the only uniquely Alaskan art forms and culture, and the knowledge of how to survive and subsist in the more inhospitable areas of the land. Along with these assets came the problems arising from cultural differences and the economic, health, and welfare problems experienced by Native people in the throes of change.[6]

Colonial Alaska developed natural resources beyond the needs of subsistence. This phase was based primarily on the specialized and intensive exploitation of furs, salmon, and gold. Almost all the exploiters were nonresidents. Renewable and nonrenewable resources were usually exploited to the point of exhaustion. The raw materials and products were destined for nonresident markets, and capital, as well as much of the required labor, was imported. Industrial technology, too, was brought to Alaska, and this in turn stimulated some limited permanent settlement and local capital formation. In Alaska the absentee owners maintained a highly successful lobby which hampered and almost stopped the evolution of local self-government and the imposition of a tax system required to provide the capital for further development.[7]

At the core of Military Alaska was the defense of the nation. Remoteness from the "mother country" and vast spaces, liabilities in Colonial Alaska, became assets in this third Alaska. Strategic location, not natural resources, was its reason for coming into being. The basic activities of government and construction were carried on without concern for resources. Military Alaska produced an explosive expansion of the population, extension and improvement of surface and air transportation, and investment of more than $2 billion of public funds in defense construction. It also created local markets for some Alaska products, local capital, and labor pools. Military Alaska attracted people and produced employment and living amenities substantially beyond those that could have been supported from Alaska's own resources.[8]

Rogers concluded that upon attainment of statehood Alaska's dominant characteristic was the lack of self-sustaining basic economic activity. Consumption, not production, was characteristic of Alaska, and both public and private investment had been pri-

marily concerned with the improvement of living conditions rather than the fostering of solid economic development.[9]

## STATEHOOD BECOMES LAW

That was the situation in Alaska after the U.S. Senate passed the Alaska statehood bill on June 30, 1958. Even though most residents welcomed Alaska's admission to the Union as the Forty-ninth State, a few remained hostile. One of the diehards probably best summed up the sentiments of those remaining opposed by stating, "Wait till the honeymoon is over and the taxes arrive."[10] His forebodings proved to be prophetic.

Many Alaskans remained uneasy about the impending changes. They feared higher taxes, continuing problems with the fishing industry, the elimination of federal cost-of-living allowances, and the possible suspen-

President Dwight D. Eisenhower signing the Alaska statehood bill, July 7, 1958. Looking over his shoulder, left to right: Ralph J. Rivers, Ernest Gruening, Edward Lewis Bartlett, Secretary of the Interior Fred Seaton, Waino Hendrickson, unidentified, Mike Stepovich, and Robert B. Atwood. Sitting on the president's left is Vice-President Richard M. Nixon, and on the right Speaker of the House Sam Rayburn. Courtesy E. L. Bartlett Collection, Alaska and Polar Regions Archives, Elmer E. Rasmuson Library, University of Alaska.

sion of federal welfare payments. Some of those fears may have been quieted by assurances from the U.S. Civil Service Commission that the statutory authority for paying cost-of-living allowances to federal employees would be unaffected by statehood.[11]

Rumors circulated in a number of Eskimo and Athapaskan villages that statehood would bring reservations, restrictions of traditional hunting and trapping activities, the closing of Native hospitals, and the suspension of federal welfare payments. Secretary of the Interior Fred Seaton denounced these rumors and reassured the Natives.[12] Despite these trepidations, statehood was achieved. President Eisenhower signed the statehood measure into law on July 7, 1958.

## FIRST ELECTIONS

With the president's signature the statehood bill became the law of the land. It was now up to Alaskans to undertake the necessary steps to get the new state functioning. On July 16, Governor Mike Stepovich announced that candidates for political office had until July 28 to file. The primary election was to be held at the end of August. Candidates for the U.S. Senate were to run for either the A or the B term, neither term identified in regard to length. Forty-one days elapsed between the governor's proclamation and the primary elections. A seasoned observer characterized the period as one in which an epidemic had been "let loose in the land." George Sundborg, editor of the *Fairbanks Daily News-Miner,* was amazed and amused that so many were "willing to sacrifice personal gain and give their all for the people of the great state." "The same number," he caustically remarked, "feel they very likely deserve it— after all, didn't I write a letter to the editor about statehood back in 1953?"[13] In short, many felt called, filed for candidacy, and campaigned.

At the primary election the voters were also to decide on three propositions that had been inserted in the statehood bill: (1) Shall Alaska immediately be admitted to the Union as a state? (2) Shall the boundaries of the new state be approved? and (3) Shall all boundaries of the statehood act, such as those reserving rights and powers to the United States, as well as those prescribing the terms and conditions of the land grants and other property, be consented to? These were important propositions, and the Alaska Statehood Committee, Operation Statehood, and most candidates for office urged Alaskans to vote affirmatively.[14]

With no preregistration any Alaskan nineteen years of age or older simply had to appear at the nearest polling place and vote. Officials expected a record turnout of 35,000 people, but instead 48,462 voters streamed to the polling places and overwhelmingly approved the three propositions by votes of 40,452 to 8,010; 40,421 to 7,776; and 40,739 to 7,500, respectively. Many polling stations ran out of ballots and had fresh supplies flown in or used sample ballots.[15]

There was no primary contest for U.S. Senate because Democrats E. L. ("Bob") Bartlett and Ernest Gruening ran unopposed. For Alaska's single seat in the House of Representatives Democrat Ralph Rivers, former territorial attorney general, defeated Raymond Plummer, Alaska's former Democratic national committeeman, by a margin of 630 votes in the primary. Henry Benson, the Republican territorial commissioner of labor, won the Republican nomination and would oppose Rivers in November. The field of Democratic hopefuls for the governorship was more crowded. William A. Egan defeated the territorial attorney general, J. Gerald Williams, and the territorial senate president, Victor Rivers.[16]

Alaska's voters had spoken, and the candidates prepared for the November 25, 1958, general election. The two former territorial governors, Ernest Gruening and Mike Stepovich, dominated the thirteen-week campaign. Gruening knew that he had an uphill battle against Stepovich, who had enjoyed much public exposure in recent months and had received 5,721 more votes in the primary than had Gruening. Knowing that he would have to work extremely hard to win, Gruening launched a well-organized campaign that blanketed Alaska.[17] As befitting Alaska's new dignity as the Forty-ninth State, national political figures journeyed north to help. Republican Vice-President Richard M. Nixon, Democratic Senators John F. Kennedy of Massachusetts and Frank Church of Idaho, and Secretary of the Interior Fred Seaton ventured to Alaska to endorse their candidates. Republican Seaton, overeager to ensure Mike Stepovich's election, became controversial when in time-honored fashion he coupled his campaign with announcements of projects his department promised to undertake in the new state. In fact, Seaton's approach vastly overshadowed that of his protégé.[18]

On election day a record number of 50,343 of an eligible 65,000 Alaska voters went to the polls to elect E. L. Bartlett by 40,939 votes over 7,299 for Ralph Robertson. Despite the boost Secretary Seaton had tried to give him, Stepovich polled 23,464 votes to Gruening's 26,045, while Ralph Rivers comfortably outpolled his rival, Henry Benson, by a margin of 27,948 to 20,699. In the race for governor Democrat William A. Egan easily defeated Republican John Butrovich by 29,189 votes to 19,299. As many Republicans at the national level had sourly predicted, the voters gave Alaska's four top offices to Democrats. Voters favored Democrats just as decisively in the state legislature races when they won thirty-three of the forty house seats and seventeen of the twenty senate seats.[19]

The election was a disaster for the Republicans, probably because their Democratic counterparts were more experienced and better known. However, Alaskan Republicans had also been badly factionalized for the last two decades and had fought as much with each other as with the Democrats.

## TRANSITION TO STATE GOVERNMENT

After the votes were counted, the transition to state government lay ahead, and planning for it had already begun. In the transition the Alaska Statehood Committee again made substantial contributions, for one of its responsibilities was to gather information on how to bridge the gap between territorial and state government. Once before, in 1955, the Statehood Committee had engaged the services of the Public Administration Service of Chicago to help prepare for the constitutional convention. The committee hired PAS again and directed it to begin its work in the spring of 1958. During the summer the Statehood Committee enlarged the scope of the work and increased the initial contract from $25,000 to $35,000. PAS delivered detailed reports, outlining the organization of the executive, the judiciary, local government, and personnel administration.[20]

While all was being prepared in Alaska, President Eisenhower formally admitted Alaska as the forty-ninth state when he signed the prescribed proclamation on January 3, 1959, together with an executive order creating a new flag for the United States. Soon thereafter U.S. District Court Judge Raymond Kelly administered the oath of office to Governor-elect William A. Egan and Secretary of State-elect Hugh Wade in the governor's office in Juneau, Alaska.[21]

## STATEHOOD EXPENSES AND THE OMNIBUS BILL

Alaska had finally become a state, and, with two U.S. senators and one representative, it had also acquired modest influence and voting power in Congress. Soon enough the Alaska delegation found occasion to flex its

Delegates to the Alaska constitutional convention, which met at the University of Alaska from November 8, 1955, to February 6, 1956. The delegates posed informally in Constitution Hall, on the campus of the University of Alaska at Fairbanks, which had been turned over to them for the convention. Courtesy R. Griffin Collection, Alaska and Polar Regions Archives, Elmer E. Rasmuson Library, University of Alaska.

muscles in speeding the passage of the Omnibus Bill for the new state—an afterthought, as it were, to the statehood bill.

As early as July, 1958, the U.S. Bureau of the Budget had suggested to the president that a study was needed of the fiscal and administrative effects of Alaska's admission on federal legislation and activities. Similar studies had led to measures that had become law after the admission of Oklahoma, New Mexico, and Arizona. Since federal-state relations had been much simpler at that time, the bills reflected that simplicity.[22]

In May, 1959, the Bureau of the Budget presented the results of its studies to the House and Senate Interior and Insular Affairs committees. Basically the recommendations were designed to put Alaska on an equal footing with the other states. Among other things the apportionment and matching formulas of various federal grant-in-aid programs had to be revised. Equality of treatment also required that the federal establishment cease developing policies for and conducting governmental functions in Alaska that were exercised by state and local governments elsewhere. The Alaska congressional delegation realized that equality would cost money; so did the Bureau of the Budget, which recommended assistance of $27.5 million in the form of transitional grants over a five-year period. Under this proposal the state was to receive $10.5 million for the fiscal year 1960, $6 million each year for fiscal years 1961 and 1962; and $2.5 million each year for fiscal years 1963 and 1964. These monies were to be spent at the discretion of the new state government. The Bureau of the Budget believed that at the end of the five-year period enough revenue would be flowing into state coffers from oil-and-gas leases, the Pribilof fur-seal operations, and the sale of state lands that the state would be on its own.[23]

The state faced immediate expenses, such as the operation of the Anchorage and Fairbanks international airports and seventeen smaller airports. Built by the federal government at a total cost of $41,460,200, the nineteen airports were expected to cost $1,438,000 a year to maintain, while earning $1,215,000, producing a deficit of $223,000 a year. The two international airports were expected to earn most of the revenues, but they were as yet unable to accommodate jet traffic. Major improvements were needed, and the estimated cost was about $9.8 million. By using $3.4 million of the transitional money, the state could obtain $6.4 million in matching funds, enough for the needed construction, under the Federal Aid Airport Act.[24]

Road construction and maintenance loomed as a large item in Alaska's state budget. The Bureau of the Budget proposed that Congress turn over to Alaska the highways, rights-of-way, and whatever real estate and equipment it owned to build and maintain roads. Excluded were roads in Mount McKinley National Park and in the national forests and equipment used for their construction and maintenance. To assist Alaska, the Bureau of the Budget therefore recommended $4 million for each of the fiscal years 1960 to 1962. Equality with the other states required that Alaska match 86.09 percent of federal monies with 13.91 percent of state monies. In other words, if the state could raise $5,940,877 a year for road-building purposes, it would receive $36,768,519 in federal matching funds. The state was not permitted to use any of the matching funds for maintenance expenses.

State officials foresaw the budgeting strain Alaska would surely experience after the expiration of the transitional grants, and Acting Governor Hugh Wade, representing the desperately ill Bill Egan, pleaded for permission to allow the state to use matching funds for road maintenance. In return the state was willing to compute only two-thirds of the eligible land area to arrive at the matching formula, knowing full well that this would reduce the maximum yearly grant by approximately $9.5 million.[25]

The Bureau of the Budget, however, insisted that no exception be made for Alaska, particularly since other states from time to time had proposed using federal funds for maintenance. All requests had been denied because the basic purpose of the Federal Aid Highway Program was to speed road construction. In addition, because of the new state's vast land area, it would receive more funds than any other state and initially pay less in matching funds than any other state. The Bureau of the Budget was confident that the new state would be able to collect sufficient revenues within five years to pay for road maintenance. Another advantage Alaska had, Bureau of the Budget personnel pointed out, was freedom from bonded indebtedness. And Alaskans paid 3.5 percent of their income in state taxes, as compared with a national average of 4.5 percent.[26]

About $7,190,000 for mental and general health care, already managed by Alaska, were included in the transitional grant of $27,500,000, and no more monies were to be paid under the old authorization. This was also the case with $200,000 which Congress had authorized the Department of the Interior to spend on the construction of recreational facilities in Alaska during fiscal year 1960–61.[27]

The Eisenhower administration was determined to shorten the transition period from federal to state control and therefore had requested no funds for civilian airports, roads, mental and general health programs, or recreational facilities for fiscal year 1960. Instead, it had asked that Alaska receive the first installment of the $27.5 million transitional grants. The Omnibus Bill also provided that the state could ask the president for continued federal operation of various functions until the state's staffing needs had been met and the functions could be transferred to state operation. Transitional monies were to be used for such operations. The state also had the option of contracting with the federal government on a reimbursable basis to provide needed services. In addition, the measure gave the president until July 1, 1964, to lend or transfer outright to the state federal property that had become surplus because of the termination or curtailment of federal activities in Alaska. The new state also was

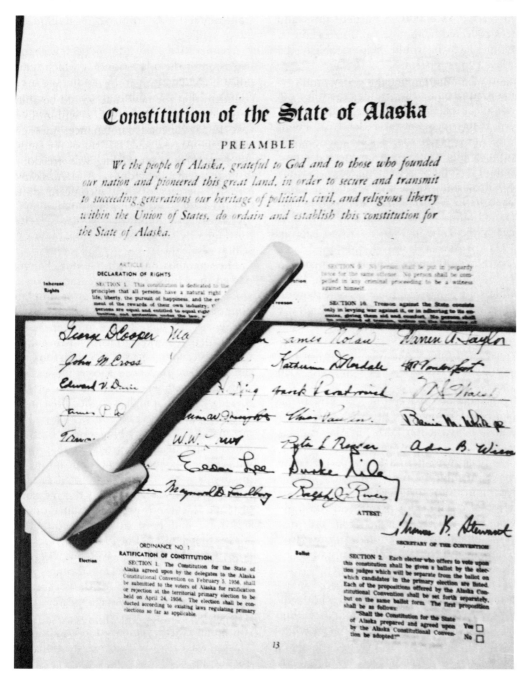

The completed constitution and the ivory gavel used by the presiding officer at the constitutional convention, 1956. Courtesy Historical Photograph Collection, Alaska and Polar Regions Archives, Elmer E. Rasmuson Library, University of Alaska.

to receive $500,000 in unspent fines and fees collected by the federal district courts, monies which would help establish the Alaska court system.[28]

Some statutory inequalities were to remain, justified on the grounds that they did not affect federal-state relationships or general requirements of the Federal Aid Highway Act of 1921 that a state's federal-aid primary highway system not exceed 7 percent of its total highway mileage outside urban areas and federal reserves in 1921. This presented no problem in the contiguous United States, since the total mileage was nearly the same in 1959 as it had been in 1921. In Alaska, however, there had been less than 2,000 miles of all kinds of road in 1921, and less than 4,000 miles in 1959. Unless it was waived, the 7 percent requirement would keep Alaska's primary highway system very short indeed. Precedent for making Alaska an exception existed, because the primary highway systems of Hawaii, Washington, D.C., and Puerto Rico were exempt.[29]

Still another exception concerned the National Housing Act. Because of the much higher construction costs in Alaska, Hawaii, and Guam, the federal housing commissioner was permitted to exceed the maximums on the principal obligations of federal insured mortgages by as much as 50 percent. Without this permission Alaskans would have been excluded from the program, unable to meet stiff federal standards of design and construction required for obtaining federal mortgage insurance.[30]

The Omnibus Bill also eliminated inappropriate statutory references to the territory of Alaska and included the state within the "continental United States." And while Congress considered the measure, members added several amendments, among them one by Ralph Rivers which increased the

transitional funds from $27.5 million to $28.5 million.[31]

Another Rivers amendment dealt with the provision of the admission act which temporarily retained federal jurisdiction over Alaska's fish and wildlife resources. Acting Governor Hugh Wade had already signed three pieces of legislation that met the state's responsibility. One of these created the Alaska Board of Fish and Game. Soon thereafter, Secretary of the Interior Fred Seaton reported to Congress that Alaska had met the requirements of the admission act, thereby transferring effective control over its fish and wildlife resources to the state on January 1, 1960.[32]

The Omnibus Bill, with a minor change, passed the House of Representatives on a voice vote on June 1, 1959, after only an hour of debate, and a few days later it passed the Senate in a mere twelve minutes. Senator Bartlett remarked to a friend that during the afternoon before the Senate took up the bill, there had been a briefing session with staff members of the Bureau of the Budget. "And that night I studied the whole proposition for over two hours. That makes me madder than anything else." Bartlett jested "that he had wasted all that time without a single word of opposition or inquiry."[33]

When the president signed the measure on June 25, 1959, Alaska's transition to statehood had been accomplished.[34] The Alaska Statehood Act of 1958 and the clarifying Omnibus Act of 1959 had become a compact between the United States and its people and the State of Alaska and its people transferring sovereign powers and responsibilities and agreeing on certain institutional rearrangements and conditions. Alaska was already creating its political institutions.

# 10. THE STATE OF ALASKA

Statehood, contrary to the expectations of many, did not solve all of Alaska's problems. It did not appreciably diminish the federal role in Alaska, it did not result in instant economic growth, and it did cost money, most of which Alaskans now had to raise themselves.

The first problem Alaskans faced was the implementation of the state's constitution. Recognizing that the territorial governor and the secretary of Alaska had been presidential appointees, that various other officials were popularly elected, and that many boards and commissions had been created over the years, the framers were determined to end "outside" control and executive fragmentation. The constitution provides for only one elected executive officer, the governor, while the secretary of state, today the lieutenant governor, is determined by being the governor's running mate. The framers limited the number of units within the executive branch to no more than twenty departments, each headed by a single person, appointed by and serving "at the pleasure of the Governor." In case the legislature created a board or a commission to head any department, the governor not only would appoint members to such a group, subject to legislative confirmation, but also would have the power to reject their nominee.

The constitution, following ample precedent, provides for a bicameral legislature composed of a senate of twenty members elected for four-year terms from sixteen districts and a house of forty members elected for two-year terms from twenty-four districts. Subsequent reapportionments have changed the number of districts. The state legislature convenes annually on the second Monday in January and is now limited to a 120-day session. A ten-member legislative council and a six-member legislative audit committee are permanent interim committees. The governor has the responsibility for reapportionment and redistricting.

The Alaska court system constitutes the third branch of state government. Like Alaska's constitution as a whole, the judiciary article is widely regarded as a good example of constitutional craftsmanship. The judicial system is efficient, independent, and accountable to the electorate. It is a unified system, which means that all the courts are part of a single state system. They are administered from one place, and all operate under the same rules. The state legislature finances the court system. The federal courts share this type of organization, but in most states the court system is fragmented. It may contain municipal courts and courts of special jurisdictions, county courts, and state appellate courts, each with its own peculiar jurisdiction, rules and procedures, administration, and source of finance. The members of the constitutional convention embodied in Alaska's constitution court reforms long sought in older states.

## LOCAL GOVERNMENT

Alaska has two forms of local government: boroughs and cities. Framers of the local government article of the constitution were acutely aware of the inadequacies of the traditional pattern of counties, cities, and towns to accommodate the growing needs of an urbanizing country. They believed that Alaska would eventually develop substantial urban areas and that continued growth would create increasing sophistication in local affairs. But the delegates also realized that most of the urban settlements in the Alaska of the 1950s were very small, few in number, and widely separated. So they fashioned a local government organization capable of serving both urban and rural areas, both as they existed then and as they might develop in the future. As a result the local government article was designed to provide a simple, flexible system of local self-government to allow maximum local self-government with a minimum number of local government units and to prevent duplication of tax-levying jurisdictions.[1]

The local government article of the constitution mandated a new form of government called the "borough." There were two forms of boroughs, the "organized" and the "unorganized." Standards for creating boroughs included population, geography, economy, transportation, and other factors. In short, each borough was to embrace an area and population with common interests to the maximum degree possible.[2] The borough is an areawide unit stronger than the traditional form of the county.

After statehood, local areas were reluctant to form boroughs in order to provide services already performed by the state or by limited, special-purpose service districts. At the time of statehood Alaska had about forty cities and twenty special districts. Fewer than half the cities had a population of 1,000 or more. In 1960, Anchorage and Fairbanks had populations of 44,000 and 13,000, respectively, accounting for more than one-fifth of Alaska's total population. Nearly another third of the residents lived in special districts and territory-serviced areas around the borders of these two large cities. There was practically no tax base except in the few populous areas. Federal and territorial agencies barely met the service, protection, and regulatory needs of settlements outside the larger cities.[3]

For the first few years after statehood neither residents nor officials thought much about the constitutionally mandated creation of boroughs. In 1961, the legislature passed a measure authorizing borough incorporations and providing broad guidelines for local action. It required that all special-service districts, including independent school districts, be integrated with organized boroughs, or cities, in the case of certain public utilities, by July 1, 1963.[4]

Only one borough, the Bristol Bay Borough, organized by initiative before the July, 1963, deadline. Containing 1,200 square miles and about 1,000 inhabitants, this small borough is situated in southwestern rural Alaska. When the legislature met in January, 1963, it seemed unlikely that any more boroughs would be formed before the deadline. The legislature, therefore, extended the life of the special districts for one year, and then it passed the Mandatory Borough Act. The measure required incorporation of boroughs in eight areas of the state containing public utility and independent school districts as of January 1, 1964.[5]

In 1963, under the threat of mandatory incorporation by the state, four local-option boroughs were established in Ketchikan, Sitka, Juneau, and the Kodiak Island region. Voters defeated incorporation proposals in the Fairbanks and Anchorage areas, whereupon those two areas and the Kenai Peninsula and Matanuska and Susitna valleys were mandatorily incorporated as boroughs on January 1, 1964. With the exception of Juneau's citizens, voters in the eight newly incorporated areas chose second-class rather than first-class status for their new boroughs, believing that, if boroughs had to exist, at least their powers should be limited. The majority of voters in all areas also preferred an elected chairman, later renamed mayor, to the appointed manager as the form of borough executive. Thomas A. Morehouse, a political scientist with the University of Alaska's Institute of Social and Economic Research in Anchorage and a specialist in local government, has stated that most Alaskans probably preferred the traditionally passive and weak mayor for their boroughs rather than the manager, which was popularly associated with more activist city governments.[6]

By 1972 there existed ten organized boroughs. The rest of the state, not part of an organized borough, was termed the "unorganized borough." There the state legislature exercised the powers and provided the services normally supplied by local government.[7]

Article 13 provides for the formal amendment of the constitution. Delegates desired to make the amendment process difficult enough to prevent hasty and destructive changes but easy enough to allow the constitution to accommodate the legitimate needs of a changing society. Delegates believed that, since constitutional matters are of fundamental importance, all changes should be ratified by the voters, as is the custom elsewhere. They designed a two-step process allowing for deliberation, attention to detail, and reflection. Proposals for change must come from a deliberate body, either the legislature or a constitutional convention convened expressly for studying changes in the state's basic law. Only then can the proposed changes go to the electorate for ratification.[8]

There should be few needs for fundamental changes to the constitution, because the delegates sought to reduce the need for amendments by leaving to the legislature many matters that are usually included in the constitutions of other states, such as the powers of local government and the organization of the executive branch. They also created automatic mechanisms to deal with anticipated changes such as legislative reapportionment.

Article 15 provided a schedule of transitional measures. It established the legal continuity between the territory and the state and set in motion the new machinery of state government. This article fulfilled its function, transitional measures have become history, and it therefore is no longer a working part of the constitution. The courts have ruled that provisions of Article 15 may be amended by statute, and it is therefore no longer a part of the constitution.[9]

## OWNERSHIP AND USE OF NATURAL RESOURCES

Another important consideration occupied the framers of the constitution: natural resources. In an effort to clear away the ambiguities of federal management policies, which sometimes favored exploitation by nonresidents, the state would "encourage the settlement of its land and the development of its resources by making them available for maximum use consistent with the public interest. The utilization, development, and conservation of all natural resources belonging to the State, including land and waters," were to be "for the maximum benefit of its people."

When Alaskans went to the polls and ratified the constitution by a vote of 17,447 to 7,180 in 1956, they also overwhelmingly accepted an ordinance providing for the abolition of fish traps for the taking of salmon for commercial purposes in the coastal waters of the state. That vote was a lopsided 21,285 to 4,004.[10]

Fishing scene near Hoonah, in southeastern Alaska. Photograph by Claus-M. Naske.

Alaska's salmon fisheries declined even after the abolition of fish traps and the transfer of management from the federal to the state government. Consequently, a 1972 constitutional amendment allowed the state "to limit entry into any fishery for purposes of resource conservation, to prevent economic distress among fishermen and those dependent upon them for a livelihood and to promote the efficient development of aquaculture in the State."[11] Designed to limit fishing gear in Alaska waters by an elaborate system of permits, this limited-entry amendment soon became embroiled in heated controversy. In 1976, Kodiak Island fishermen spearheaded an initiative drive to repeal limited entry. Voters, however, opted to keep the permit system. Aquaculture, designed to restore depleted salmon runs, has not been controversial among fishermen in general. Various hatcheries have been built with state aid, and the program has gotten off to a promising start.

## THE FIRST STATE GOVERNMENT

Alaskans chose Democrats William A. Egan and Hugh J. Wade as their first governor and secretary of state. These two men faced the stupendous task of translating the provisions of the state constitution into working political institutions. Egan was born on October 8, 1914, in the little Prince William Sound community of Valdez. He held a variety of jobs, including truck driver, bartender, goldminer, fisherman, and aviator. After wartime service in the army air corps in 1943–46, he returned to Valdez, where he became proprietor of a general-merchandise store. He was a member of the territorial house of representatives between 1941 and 1945 and again from 1947 to 1953. Elected to the territorial senate in 1953, he served one term. In 1955 fellow constitutional convention delegates chose Egan to preside over their deliberations. One observer later reported that "few deliberative assemblies have been so fortunate in their choice of chairmen" because he "presided with a combination of firmness, fairness, and humor" which helped to weld a group of comparative strangers, "inclined to be suspicious of one another, into a body of friends and co-workers united by their mutual respect and common purpose."[12]

The new administration got off to an inauspicious start when Egan became so ill that he required hospitalization and several operations in Seattle. Wade became acting governor, a difficult position for him to assume because Egan had not briefed his running mate. Wade recalled that Egan was essentially a "loner": "When I took over as Governor, on the first day, why, I hadn't talked with him for twenty minutes before or during the campaign." But Wade performed his duties as acting governor capably for more than three months, using the services of various territorial officials. Egan recuperated from his near-fatal illness, and in April, 1959, during the closing days of the first session of the first legislature of the state of Alaska, he returned to Juneau, where he resumed his duties as chief executive.[13]

The first session of the first Alaska state legislature convened on January 26, 1959, amid an atmosphere of confidence as Alaska bravely stepped into a new era. Lawmakers were not greatly concerned with state finances and budgets, because Alaska started life as a state with a comfortably large surplus in its treasury acquired during the last prosperous years as a territory, with the certainty of five years of generous federal transitional grants, and with the prospects of a growing oil-and-gas boom. Relieved of money worries, the first session turned its attention to organizing the new state government.

In the State Organization Act of 1959 the new legislature created twelve departments: administration, law, revenue, health and welfare, labor, commerce, military affairs, natural resources, public safety, public works, education, and fish and game. Each department was to be headed by an executive appointed by the governor. The principal executive officers of the departments of education and fish and game were to be appointed by the governor from nominations made by boards affiliated with these departments. The legislature also drafted land laws and created a division of lands within the department of natural resources. The division was to choose, manage, and dispose of the state's entitlement—more than 103 million acres—under the statehood act. The state wished to select the resource-rich lands in order to stimulate economic development and create a year-round local economy, but the process was slow. No adequate inventories of Alaska lands existed, and the Bureau of Land Management moved at a snail's pace in approving, surveying, and patenting state selections. Another inhibiting factor was awareness that landownership entailed expensive management responsibilities, such as classification, surveying, and fire control. The imposition of the land freeze in 1966 and the withdrawal of national-interest lands in the wake of the Alaska Native Claims Settlement Act of 1971 further impeded state land selections. As of March 31, 1971, the state had selected 68,818,500.[34]

An ARCO exploration drilling rig in Cook Inlet. Courtesy ARCO.

acres and patented a mere 9,759,136.37 acres of state selections. Obviously Alaskans' optimistic expectations that statehood would free the new political entity from the constraints of the federal government were misguided.[14]

Alaskans quickly found that the federal government continued to play an important role in the state's government and economy. The U.S. Department of Defense, for example, continued to spend hundreds of millions of dollars a year on manning, maintaining, and improving its defense installations in Alaska. It also continued to operate the state's telephone and telegraph system until it was sold to private enterprise in 1971. The U.S. Department of the Interior loomed large in managing the extensive public domain and providing a range of social and other services found in all the other states. The U.S. Department of Transportation operated the Alaska Railroad, and the Forest Service of the U.S. Department of Agriculture managed the state's two national forests. The list of federal agencies involved in Alaskan affairs seemed endless. A few figures illustrate the pervasive federal influence. Of a total employed work force of 62,900 in 1959, 16,800 were federal employees. Although federal employment slowed in subsequent years, in 1971 federal workers still numbered 17,300 of a total employed work force of 110,600. By 1971 government employees made up more than one-third of the total employed work force; that growth was attributable to the expanding needs of local and state government. In 1959 the former employed a modest 3,000 workers, and the latter 2,600. These figures had risen to 9,000 and 11,700, respectively, by 1971.[15]

## FACING UP TO THE ECONOMIC REALITIES OF STATEHOOD

Alaskans had desired statehood in part because they believed that it would bring fairly rapid and diverse economic development. In fact, to survive as a political entity capable of fulfilling the role of a self-supporting state, Alaska desperately needed basic economic development. It possessed a few small lumber operations, two pulp mills, a mining industry consisting of one underground operation and several relatively minor placer operations, and an ailing and seasonal salmon-fishery and fish-processing industry. The only bright prospects were the potential expansion of tourism and the hope that oil-and-gas production would increase.

Patrick O'Donovan, a British newspaper correspondent, perhaps best summed up the dream and reality of Alaska shortly after the statehood bill passed Congress:

> They like to call this the last frontier. It is not; it is the new sort of frontier and there are several of them in the world. A young man cannot come here with his hand and his courage and carve an estate out of the wilderness. You can get a 160-acre homestead from the Government for all but nothing. To develop it properly you are likely to need a capital of $25,000 or three generations of peasant labor. The banks will not be kind. You can work for a great corporation out in the wilderness, without women or drink, live like a Cistercian in a cell, have your cheeks scabbed by cold in winter, be fed each day like a prince hungry from the hunt and draw a salary of a bank manager. You can find temporary, chancy work in the city, but there is also unemployment. Alaska is a longterm, massive operation, conditioned by its inaccessibility, and its ferocious terrain. It is proper meat for the great corporations with capital the size of national debts and machines and helicopters and dedicated graduates from mining schools.[16]

Statehood proponents had been an optimistic lot, but soon after the attainment of their goal, many became convinced that they had attained a stage of political development before they had the economic base to support it fully. One tenacious opponent of statehood, Juneau lawyer Herbert L. Faulkner, strongly expressed the fears of many: "Well, I felt that Alaska was not ready for statehood, that it could not support it, that it would be much more expensive to have a state than to rely on the federal government for most appropriations to support what government we had." Faulkner also opposed new taxes to support the new state because "there's always got to be somebody opposing taxes or we'd be taxed out of existence." [17]

Statehood had been a means of accomplishing several goals: the achievement of full self-government accompanied by improved efficiency and responsiveness of local government, an increase of local control over natural resources, and the political means of severing the economic constraints of colonialism. But all of these goals would cost money, and Governor Egan called attention to this fact when he presented the first complete state budget in 1960. The governor explained:

> During the last half of the current fiscal year, we will have assumed full responsibility for the management of our fish and game resources, an excellent start will have been made on a State Land Management Program, the judicial and other purely state and local functions will have been fully assumed. How will we fare beyond June 30, 1961? Most immediately, we are faced with a progressive reduction of the transitional grants available under the Alaska Omnibus Act [a federal aid program] with those grants ending by June 30, 1964. At that time we will have to make up several millions of dollars if we are not to curtail services. [18]

By 1960 many Alaskans, as well as outside observers, began to share the doubts expressed for so long by Faulkner and others of his persuasion. Journalist Ray J. Schrick reported on "Alaska's Ordeal" in the *Wall Street Journal* in early 1960. Schrick observed that the "job of equipping the huge frozen back country with the political machinery for self-government is less than half-done."

A financial crisis loomed ahead, and

Alaska sectionalism had reasserted itself in bitter squabbling among numerous local factions over where highways should be located and how boroughs should be established. One group, centered in Anchorage, wanted to move the state capital from Juneau, while another wanted its region to secede from the new state entirely. Alaska's woes, Schrick continued, would affect American taxpayers because the federal government might well be called upon to foot "as much as 74% of the bill for a proposed $323 million state construction program in the next six years." [19]

Alaska's projected expenditures on highways alone for the next fiscal year amounted to $48 million, about $12 million more than the state general fund budget. Approximately $43 million of these monies would come from the federal government, but the state still had to raise $5 million as a match. The highway department had employed only 12 individuals in 1959; employment skyrocketed to nearly 1,000 when the state took over the functions hitherto performed by the federal Bureau of Public Roads. Every mile of road built added between $800 and $1,500 a year in maintenance expenses.

When the legislature met in 1961, it realistically considered Alaska's financial predicament and raised tax rates where they would do the least harm to future economic development. This legislature gave Alaskans the chance to do a fair job of managing the new state's financial affairs if spending restraints were used and the state encountered some luck along the way in the form of expansion in crude petroleum and gas production, income from competitive oil-and-gas lease sales, expansion in the fisheries through diversification, and expansion of the forest-products industries. And luck was with the new state. While defense spending, Alaska's major industry since the 1940s, steadily dropped during the 1960s, the value of the major natural resources rose encouragingly. Crude petroleum worth

$1,230,000 was extracted in 1960; by 1967 the value had risen to $88,187,000. Gas production rose from $30,000 in 1960 to $7,268,000 in 1967. Alaska's income from the oil industry had kept pace with expanding production. In 1960 the state treasury received a modest $3,372,000. By 1967 the figure had risen to a respectable $35,613,000.

On February 20, 1960, the state officially took over state civil and criminal cases, which meant opening eight superior courts and replacing four former federal district courts, appointing ten district magistrates, and trying to settle "over 3,000 unfinished cases from Uncle Sam." The Nome Chamber of Commerce complained that the administration had assigned only one state trooper and no full-time prosecutor to its area, which is as large as the states of California and New York combined. "We were better off under the federal government," concluded many of Nome's citizens. One state official told Schrick that "economically you can't even justify Alaska's existence but it's here—just like Washington, D.C." Alaskans, however, were determined to make statehood work. Pilot Jim Dodson, of Anchorage, a member of the antistatehood minority, perhaps best expressed this determination: "We created a monster up here. We weren't ready for it [statehood]. But now that we've got it, we're going to make a go of it."[20]

Statehood had put Alaska in the national limelight, however, and some Alaskans were cautiously optimistic about the future. An increasing flow of new settlers, investors, and tourists had arrived in the new state in 1959. New motels, hotels, and resorts were in either the planning or construction phase, and more oil had been found. Alaska now possessed four modestly producing wells, and oil companies intended to undertake substantial exploratory work. This was reflected in the state's first competitive oil-and-gas lease sale in December, 1959, when several companies paid approximately $4

million for a total of 77,000 acres. Japanese investment groups which, together with American capital assistance, built the second pulp mill at Sitka had interested other Japanese companies in examining Alaska's coal, iron, and oil potential as a possible source of raw materials for the Orient.[21]

But there were many uncertainties as well. Federal defense spending was tapering off, and the long-ailing salmon industry recorded a record low pack in 1959. The outlook for the salmon fisheries was obscured by continued fishing of Alaska-spawned salmon stocks by Japanese fleets in the Bering Sea and the mid-Aleutian area. And although the Japanese were fishing in international waters and west of a 170° longitude demarcation line set up by international treaty, negotiators subsequently discovered that they had not placed the dividing line far enough toward Kamchatka. They had discovered that Bristol Bay salmon had been using this mid-ocean area for a place to mature before returning to their home streams to spawn. Adding to the fishery worries was the fact that for the first time big Russian trawlers and factory ships were appearing in the Bering Sea, catching fish species such as sole, haddock, flounder, rockfish, and cod. Americans, who generally did not use those species, were afraid that the Russians would soon be dragging the halibut grounds.[22]

Alaska's chief executive drew attention to some of these problems and also to the general causes for the increased financial costs of statehood in his 1960 budget message. Governor Egan also warned that available revenues would fail to meet those costs by several million dollars, but he hoped that monies would be forthcoming "from increased state land revenues, mineral lease receipts, stumpage payments, and other sources."[23]

Then he presented a balanced budget to the legislature that included proposed tax increases of 2 cents per gallon on highway motor fuel and 1 cent per gallon on marine motor fuel sales, plus the expenditure of approximately $15 million of federal transitional grants and withdrawals from the general fund surplus. Such a combination of monies would normally not be available, and it was the Alaska State Planning Commission that more fully explained just how far beyond its means the state would be living. At current rates of income and expenditures, the committee predicted, Alaska would be about $30 million in debt on operating programs by the end of the 1966 fiscal year and $70 million in debt if the financing of a minimum—and sorely needed—capital improvement program was included.[24]

The 1960 legislature, together with the Alaska State Planning Commission, gave the first accurate assessment of the new state government. Transfer of functions from the federal government to the state had almost been completed. The most dramatic revelation concerned the shift in monetary terms; from a high of $38 million per year during territorial days the administration would be managing expenditures in excess of $104 million in 1961, and state employment was to increase from 3,900 to approximately 4,600, including the employees of the University of Alaska and the Alaska State Housing Authority. Even the most optimistic, looking beyond the year immediately ahead, could not help but be disturbed by the financial crunch that had to be faced soon.

Following the attainment of statehood, the abolition of fish traps, and the transfer of fish and game management control from the federal to the state government, significant advances were made. But much had to be learned about fish-management techniques, and fishermen eventually would have to diversify and begin utilizing the great offshore resources of bottom fish, which so far only the Russians and the Japanese har-

View of Juneau from Douglas Island, 1965. The large building on the left houses federal offices. Photograph by Claus-M. Naske.

Eskimo hunters cutting up a bowhead whale near Barrow, Alaska, in the spring of 1965. Photograph by Claus-M. Naske.

vested. There was a need to enforce international conservation agreements. For years the coast guard had been handicapped in that enforcement because of lack of equipment. Ever so slowly, however, Congress had been strengthening the coast guard. If much needed to be done, a great deal had been accomplished by 1967, including the creation of a vigorous king-crab fishery worth more than $10 million a year. In 1960 the wholesale value of the fish catch amounted to $96,689,000, and by 1965 it had risen to $166,572,000. In 1967, however, it declined to $126,696,000, primarily because of a drastic decline in the salmon runs.

In 1960 the timber industry had an estimated annual payroll of $18.3 million and turned out wood products with an estimated end-product value of $47.3 million. By 1967 these figures had risen to $25 million and $77.7 million, respectively.[25]

## PARTY POLITICS OF THE 1960S

While many Alaskans worried about the state's economic future, the Alaska electorate trooped to the polls on November 8, 1960, to participate for the first time in a presidential election. Most observers except for a few die-hard Republicans believed that the state's three electoral votes were securely in the Democratic column. There was ample ground for Democratic optimism in the Forth-ninth State, since the Republicans had been successful only twice since World War II, once in 1946 and again in 1952.

Party labels, however, mean little in Alaska, because issues important to the state do not fit traditional party molds. Voters from the left to the right on the political spectrum are freely distributed in both political parties, and notions of party loyalty are elusive at best. Within the state the Republican party made an astounding comeback, reducing the Democrats in the statehouse from thirty-four to twenty-one. In the senate the Republicans gained five seats. And although Alaska's congressional delegation was still Democratic and the

state legislature boasted a Democratic majority, the 1960 election clearly ended the overwhelming Democratic predominance and, in effect, made Alaska a two-party state. Actually, statewide elections between 1958 and 1972 showed a substantial drift toward Republican voting, although the Democrats were dominant for most of the period.[26]

Perhaps reflecting the Republican drift, the Alaska electorate in 1966 voted out veteran Democrat William A. Egan, who was seeking a third term as governor, and narrowly elected colorful and ambitious Republican Walter J. Hickel, an Anchorage real estate developer and hotel owner. The new governor, perhaps best remembered for his decision to authorize a winter haul road from Livengood on the Yukon to Sagwon on the North Slope to improve transporta-

Narvak Lake, in the Gates of the Arctic National Park and Preserve. Photograph by John M. Kauffman. Courtesy U.S. National Park Service.

tion to the oil fields, quickly abandoned the executive mansion when President-elect Richard Nixon nominated him as secretary of the interior.

On the same day, December 11, 1968, the most powerful Alaskan in the history of the territory or the state, Senator E. L. Bartlett, died after undergoing arterial heart surgery in a Cleveland hospital. Before Hickel's successor, Keith H. Miller, took over as governor, Hickel appointed Republican Theodore F. Stevens to fill Bartlett's position. This was an ironic choice, because Stevens had recently lost his bid in the primary for the U.S. Senate when he was defeated by Elmer E. Rasmuson, president of the National Bank of Alaska and one of the state's wealthiest men.

Governor Miller promptly named the winter haul road the Walter J. Hickel Highway. Hickel made a wise choice in appointing Stevens, for he sent to Washington a man who had extensive contacts in the Department of the Interior and was well versed in Washington's folkways. Hickel needed Stevens's help, because before his Senate confirmation the rough-hewn and forthright Hickel had made reckless statements to the press that had aroused the ire of many. The secretary-designate had stated that he opposed placing federal lands "under lock and key" just for the sake of conservation and that it would be wrong to set water-pollution standards so high that "we might even hinder industrial development." Senate foes held up Hickel's confirmation for weeks but eventually approved the new secretary. Unfortunately, the Hickel Highway turned into a canal in the spring of 1969 as the underlying permafrost began to melt and erode away. One observer called the highway, built to accommodate the trucking industry, "the biggest screwup in the history of mankind in the arctic." And then, to add insult to injury, President Nixon fired his secretary of the interior in 1970.[27]

## RESPONSES TO NATURAL DISASTERS

In retrospect, the first decade of Alaska statehood was an exciting and trying time for its citizens and its leaders alike. First there was the continuing struggle to attempt to provide for an ever-growing array of badly needed state services in the face of strictly limited monetary resources. The Egan, Hickel, and Miller administrations had limped from one oil-and-gas lease sale to another.

Then, suddenly, on Friday, March 27, 1964, one of the greatest recorded earthquakes of all times, measuring 8.4 to 8.7 on the Richter scale, struck south-central Alaska and in a few minutes caused damage almost beyond description. Fortunately, the loss of life was relatively low, but property damage was estimated at $380 million to $500 million.[28]

Quickly technicians and mechanics arrived to restore essential services, and medical teams and rescue units "fanned out through the 900-mile coastal arc ripped by more than 10 million times the force of an atomic bomb to minister to the injured and prevent typhoid epidemics." Space was made available for the two thousand homeless in Anchorage alone, while Abe Romick, the state's commissioner of commerce, predicted that many Alaskans would never recover economically from the disaster. Kodiak's famous crab and salmon canneries were shattered, buildings from the towns had floated as far as two miles out to sea, and Seward's shoreline looked as though it had been bombed. In Valdez the waterfront looked "as though it was sawed off"; docks had been shattered, and homes had been "snapped from foundations and shredded into kindling." Most of the office buildings in the center of Anchorage had been destroyed or severely damaged, and one store had sunk so far into a fissure that only its roof showed on the buckled street level.[29]

The massive Good Friday earthquake

Fourth Avenue in Anchorage after the earthquake on March 27, 1964. Courtesy U.S. Army Corps of Engineers.

was not confined to Alaska. Huge tidal waves called tsunamis battered the Pacific coast. Crescent City, California, experienced four such tsunamis, which severely damaged the town and killed ten (another fifteen were reported missing). And at Depoe Bay, Oregon, a tsunami killed four.[30] The eyewitness report of twelve-year-old Freddie Christofferson, of Valdez, illustrates the enormity of the earthquake. Freddie had gone to the town dock to watch the unloading of the freighter *Chena*, which hailed from Seattle. The boy had just left the dock when "the earth started shaking." His companion hollered "Earthquake!" and then took off running. "When I looked back," said Freddie, "I saw the ship up in the air. The water was up on the dock. The ship hit the dock. Then it blew the whistle and pushed off. The dock went up in the air after the ship left. It just exploded in a lot of planks. I never did see any of the people on it when it happened."[31]

Industry as well as government responded swiftly and generously. Commercial airlines and the military dramatically displayed their capabilities by airlifting to the disaster areas hundreds of tons of emergency supplies, including drugs, food, water, electrical insulators, oxygen, blankets, flashlight batteries, heaters, and even sterile baby bottles. They also airlifted engineers and architects to inspect and restore damaged buildings and electricians and natural gas workers to restore utilities. The example of one airline suffices to show the tonnages transported: the company reported that it flew 145,000 pounds to Alaska in a three-day period. Because of the swift response of the airlines and other industries, Alaska quickly returned to normal.[32]

At the urging of Senator Bartlett, President Lyndon B. Johnson established the Federal Reconstruction and Development Planning Commission for Alaska, headed by Senator Clinton P. Anderson (Democrat, New Mexico). A month later a careful assessment showed that earthquake damage had amounted to $205,811,771 rather than the expected $400 million, and on August 14, 1964, President Johnson signed into law legislation that generously assisted Alaska reconstruction.[33]

South-central Alaska quickly recovered, but a few years later, in August, 1967, the Chena River, which bisects the town of Fairbanks, overflowed its banks and put much of the city under about eight feet of water. Although confined to that one city, property damage was heavy; but once again the federal government lent a helping hand. The Small Business Administration, as in the earthquake disaster, extended necessary long-term loans at favorable interest rates to put Fairbanks back on its feet.

## THE EUPHORIA OF OIL AND PLANNING FOR THE FUTURE

Not all was disaster in Alaska. Early in 1968 the Atlantic-Richfield Company struck the ten-billion-barrel Prudhoe Bay oil field on Alaska's North Slope. In the subsequent oil-lease sale in 1969, the twenty-third since statehood, oil companies bid in excess of $900 million. Euphoria reigned, and there was hope that Alaska's perpetually rocky economy would now stabilize and diversify.

With over $900 million dollars in the bank, many citizens believed that Alaska's financial problems had been solved. The question clearly was, "What do we do with all the money?" The legislative council of the state of Alaska in association with the Brookings Institution scheduled a series of conferences in late 1969 with leading citizens to discuss directions for the future. In four successive meetings a broad cross section of Alaskans examined and dis-

cussed the financial foundations of the future Alaska, the use of human resources, the quality of the natural environment, and alternative futures for the state.

Throughout the sessions participants called for preserving the "unique" Alaska life-style, defining it as one which "affords the conveniences of technological innovation combined with the opportunity and values of living as close to nature as possible." Most agreed that compatibility between the oil industry and the Alaskan life-style could be achieved with "well enforced, proper regulation."[34]

Members of the Brookings Institution team and outside experts in socio-economic planning tried to warn the "representative" group of approximately 150 Alaskans that they probably could not eat their cake and have it too. The seminars certainly served to educate and inform the participants and the public, and the recommendations that were made were to serve as guidelines for legislators.

Not to be outdone by the legislative council, the office of the governor of Alaska contracted with the Stanford Research Institute to prepare planning guidelines for the state based on identified or projected physical, economic, and social needs of the state and the resources available to meet those needs over the next few years.

The institute recommended substantial upgrading of urban services such as water, sewers, and solid-waste disposal and improvements in education, manpower development, public welfare, and health. The consultants warned, however, that, far from transforming Alaska into an embarassingly rich state, the North Slope oil discoveries at best would help place the state on a more comparable basis with its fellow states in terms of financial position and the availability of adequate public services. The high living costs and other disadvantages of a relatively remote and sparsely populated land would persist. In fact, the consultants

Aerial view of part of Anchorage, Alaska's largest city, in the early 1980s, showing the industrial area and harbor in the front and the downtown area with its high-rises just beyond. In the background are the Chugatch Mountains. Courtesy Ward Wells Collection, Anchorage Museum of History and Art.

warned, the oil boom might accentuate these factors unless the bonus money and other state revenues were used wisely and in the public interest.[35]

## THE QUESTION OF MOVING THE CAPITAL

Whether or not all the public monies will be used wisely is still pretty much up in the air. One example will suffice to illustrate the ever-present urge to spend tax dollars foolishly. Soon after Alaska achieved statehood, Robert B. Atwood, the wealthy, powerful, and influential publisher of Alaska's largest newspaper, the *Anchorage Daily Times,* began campaigning to move the state capital from Juneau, in southeastern Alaska, considered fairly inaccessible, somewhere closer to the state's population center. State

voters decisively rejected initiatives for the move in 1960 and again in 1962 because of competing needs and scarcity of money.

In 1974, however, the move was approved, though it provided that the new capital could not be within a thirty-mile radius of either Anchorage or Fairbanks. This provision was included because politicians and business people in the two cities did not trust each other's intentions and had lobbied hard to make certain that the other city would not get the new capital.[36]

The new capital was to be established in an undeveloped area, but no specific sites had been listed on the referendum ballot, and no cost estimates were available. In short, citizens had voted for a concept without considering the ultimate costs or benefits. When asked why they desired to move the capital, Alaskans most often stated

Jay S. Hammond, colorful governor of Alaska, 1974–82. Courtesy *Fairbanks Daily News–Miner.*

that they wanted to have the capital in a central and accessible location. Perhaps the post-Watergate distrust of government and the desire to have an open and visible government played a role in the vote as well.

Alaska's newly elected Republican governor, Jay S. Hammond, no friend of the move, acceded to the will of the voters and appointed a Capital Site Selection Committee headed by Willie Hensley, an Eskimo and former legislator from Kotzebue who had run for Alaska's lone seat in the U.S. House of Representatives in 1974. During his unsuccessful campaign the capital move initiative had been on the primary ballot, and Hensley had spoken against it wherever he went. He felt that Alaska had many urgent needs to meet before the capital should be moved. Hensley's committee was charged with proposing and evaluating possible capital sites. With a handsome budget and many consultants, and after much travel across the state, the committee came up with three possible sites: Willow, approxi-

mately 35 air miles north of Anchorage, with an estimated price tag of $2.46 billion; Larson Lake, about 80 air miles north of Anchorage, at a cost of some $2.56 billion; and Mount Yenlo, approximately 70 air miles northwest of Anchorage, with a price tag of $2.7 billion. Consultants pointed out that in each case the state would have to assume only about one-fifth of the estimated costs. They expected private developers to supply the difference.[37]

Some state legislators attempted to give voters a fourth choice by adding "none of the above" but failed in their efforts. In 1976 voters chose Willow, the least expensive of three proposed sites. The selected site is less than a mile east of the settlement of Willow and covers about 100 square miles of state-owned land. Even before the Willow site was selected by the voters, private land in the Matanuska-Susitna valleys, particularly that near Willow, rose enormously in paper value in anticipation of the move.[38]

After voters had selected the site, the Hammond administration had to decide how the move was to be financed. There were two possibilities: to use revenues accruing to the state from the Prudhoe Bay oil field, which had begun flowing in June, 1977; or to put the method of payment to the voters in the form of a bond proposition. Opponents of the move hoped for the latter course, assuming that a massive bond issue would force a rethinking of the issue. They therefore launched a petition drive in April, 1977, to place on the 1978 ballot an initiative requiring Alaska voters to approve a bond issue before the capital could be moved. In the same year a group calling itself FRANK (Frustrated Responsible Alaskans Needing Knowledge) launched a petition drive seeking to put the true cost of the move on the ballot. The petition drive closed on December 15, 1977, and Alaskans had a chance to do some rethinking in light of the costs involved.

In the meantime, however, a new committee had been established to plan for the capital. Like its predecessor, it had a handsome budget, and its members traveled throughout Alaska to solicit public thinking on how the new capital city should look.

Opponents of the move took heart in early 1977. Results of a survey conducted by the Anchorage-based Rowan Group, which was hired as part of the governor's Alaska Public Forum program, revealed that Alaskans still preferred Juneau, which has the most spectacular natural setting of any state capital, to any other site. A representative sample of urban and rural Alaskans, when asked where the capital should be, preferred Juneau by 41 percent; Anchorage received 15 percent, Willow 13 percent, and Wasilla 7 percent. The remainder were undecided or preferred other locations in the state.[39]

When Alaska voters trooped to the polls in the November, 1978, general election, they decisively rejected a bond issue in excess of $900 million for moving the capital. Clearly, modern means of electronic communication can accomplish the goals of the proposed move—easy accessibility and communication—at a fraction of the cost. At the end of 1978, then, the voters had given conflicting directions to their legislators and the governor. Still on the books from 1974 was the approved capital move— yet in 1978 they had voted down the necessary funds to get the move under way. It is clear that more will be heard in the future about the pros and cons of relocating the capital.

## THE UPSET VICTORY OF JAY S. HAMMOND

The capital-move issue has been just one of many major developments affecting the future of Alaska. One of the most interesting of these developments was the election of Jay S. Hammond to the governorship in 1974. Born in Troy, New York, on July 21, 1922, the son of a Methodist minis-

ter, Hammond attended Pennsylvania State University and the University of Alaska, where he received a baccalaureate degree in biological sciences in 1948. Hammond had been a U.S. Marine Corps fighter pilot in the South Pacific between 1942 and 1946. In 1952 he married Bella Gardiner, a part-Eskimo, in Palmer, Alaska. He was an apprentice guide, fisherman, hunter, and trapper in Rainy Pass in the Alaska Range between 1946 and 1949 and served with the U.S. Fish and Wildlife Service from 1949 to 1956 as pilot-agent. Hammond established his own air-taxi service, became a registered guide, and built a sportsmen's lodge on Lake Clark and a fishing lodge among the Wood River Lakes. First elected to the state house in 1959 as an independent, Hammond switched to the Republican party two years later. He served for six years in the house, becoming minority and majority whip. He became mayor of the Bristol Bay Borough in 1965 and was elected in 1966 to the state senate, where he served for the next six years, becoming majority party whip, majority leader, chairman of the rules and resources committee, and finally president of the senate. Because his district was drastically reapportioned in 1972, Hammond chose not to run again, but once again he was elected mayor of the Bristol Bay Borough. He held that position until his election to the governorship in 1974.

Hammond's campaign for the governorship was a formidable undertaking because he had to defeat two former governors in the Republican primary—Walter J. Hickel and Keith H. Miller—and then incumbent Democratic governor William A. Egan in the general election. Hammond and his supporters started pounding the pavement, literally ringing thousands of doorbells. Hammond asked Lowell Thomas, Jr., son of the famous broadcaster and himself a member of the Alaska legislature, to run as his lieutenant governor. This was a smart move, because Thomas had far better name recognition than did Hammond at that point. A simple campaign brochure proclaimed: "It takes teamwork. . . . They will work together for Alaska. . . . We have only one special interest . . . the Alaskan people."[40]

Hickel, Nixon's former secretary of the interior, was heavily favored in the Republican primary because of his name and substantial financial backing from development interests. Hickel underestimated Hammond's candidacy, saving his money for his anticipated battle with Egan. To the chagrin of many Republicans, Hammond defeated Hickel decisively in the primaries. Then, after a hard-fought campaign, he defeated Egan by a margin of 287 votes in the November general election.

Hammond readily admitted that he was an environmentalist, which is considered a political liability in Alaska because most important environmental lobbying efforts are identified with "outside" interests, particularly the California-based Sierra Club. These groups are accused by many Alaskans of desiring to "lock up" the state forever from economic development. Hammond offered a middle course between those "who would develop for the sake of development" and those "who would conserve for the sake of conservation." Hammond believed that each particular development project should be weighted individually and the question be asked: Will the people of Alaska really profit from this? Hammond proposed to formulate basic policy guidelines with the help of Alaska's voting public. These guidelines were to determine the "use of our resources which will insure that our nonrenewable resources are developed when they can offer long-term benefits to all Alaskans, and that our renewable resources be maintained so there is a continual base for Alaska's economy.[41]

Although Hammond was intensely disliked by the development forces, particularly the *Anchorage Times,* his rapport with the average voter seemed to be good.

In a state that is unimpressed by formality, the governor fitted well. By and large, he did not isolate himself from the public with numerous aides and press spokesmen; he remained accessible, as were his top administrators. Bearded, casually dressed, and a colorful speaker, he projected an image of the typical Alaskan. Hammond insisted that development pay its own way. He was a fiscal conservative and emphasized that Alaskans should not rely on oil-and-gas revenues for operating the state government, but rather should rely on income from renewable resources and general taxation. The governor repeatedly reminded Alaskans that of the $900 million the state received in the 1969 Prudhoe Bay lease sale, only $504 million was left by January, 1975, and that was going fast.

The state had been spending more than it had taken in, using the bonus money to make up the deficit. But this is not to say that the bonus money had been wasted; the monies had been used to increase spending for badly needed education, housing, welfare, and transportation. In fiscal year 1970 the state's general fund budget had grown to $160 million; and by 1975 the total budget had increased to about $725 million.[42] Despite the approximately $2 billion per year that would accrue to the state in the 1980s, Hammond emphasized that Alaska had to plan ahead and develop a sustaining economic structure not solely based on the extraction of nonrenewable resources. It was no surprise, therefore, when Hammond announced that he wished to run for a second term to complete his program.

In a crowded and confused election, Hammond reclaimed the governor's chair with 49,580 votes to Chancy Croft's 25,656 votes. Hickel, who had launched a write-in campaign, received an astounding 33,555 votes.[43] The election highlighted the general difficulties of conducting elections in such a far-flung state.

What about Alaska's future? Will history

Glaciers feed off 18,000-foot Mount Saint Elias in the world's greatest coastal range. The mountain is in the Wrangell–Saint Elias National Park and Preserve. Photograph by M. Woodbridge Williams. Courtesy U.S. National Park Service.

repeat itself to the extent that Alaska will be merely a supplier of raw material for various colonial nations? The Russians came for the furs, and ever since the 1740s the Great Land has experienced various booms and busts. Americans exploited the fisheries and mined for gold and copper in the nineteenth and twentieth centuries. In the twentieth century Alaska once again became important because of its strategic position in the Arctic. The oil boom emphasized Alaska's importance as a resource storehouse, and not only American corporations but also the Japanese, the British, the Koreans, the Chinese, and the West Germans lust after Alaska's wealth in oil, fisheries, timber, and minerals.

Unfortunately, Alaska has little control over world resource demands. It seems clear that most decisions affecting the life of the average Alaskan will continue to be made in Washington, D.C., and in corporate boardrooms from Tokyo to London and from Seoul to Bonn.

# 11. NATIVE LAND CLAIMS

While the 1968 Prudhoe Bay oil discovery captured public attention, of perhaps greater long-range importance for Alaska is the Alaska Native Claims Settlement Act of 1971, known as ANCSA. The provisions of this legislation embrace two basically unrelated causes: the fight of Native Alaskans for a greater share and role in Alaska's development and a national concern that the course of this development will not endanger lands of special conservation value.

There can be no doubt that the descendants of Alaska's aboriginal inhabitants historically have participated but little in Alaska's economic development and its attendant social benefits. As a consequence they have suffered loss of lands and resources essential to their traditional ways of life.[1] Organized protest has been weak, sporadic, and divided along ethnic and geographical lines. Actually there was little reason for protest in southeastern and interior Alaska during the first decade of American rule because there was little interference with traditional uses of the lands and waters.

## THE RUSH TO EXPLOIT ALASKA'S NATURAL RESOURCES

It was a different story along the Arctic coast, where Yankee whalemen had moved into the Bering Sea by 1848 either by way of the Sea of Okhotsk or by passage through the Aleutian Islands. Soon as many as 250 vessels cruised along the edge of the ice pack in pursuit of the bowhead whale. In 1848 the first American ship, the *Superior,* of Sag Harbor, New York, passed through Bering Strait and entered the Arctic Ocean. Others soon followed, and when whalemen found the bowhead in short supply, they often hunted the walrus for its oil and tusks.

The whalemen had a disastrous effect on the Natives who lived along the shores they frequented. Drunkenness and diseases soon ravaged the population. Ivan Petroff, Alaska's first census taker, reported the devastation of Saint Lawrence Island Eskimos that occurred in 1874, when four hundred or more people succumbed to famine and disease. Petroff observed that "living directly in the track of vessels bound for the Arctic for the purpose of whaling and trading, this situation has been a curse to them; for as long as the rum lasts they do nothing but drink and fight among themselves." John Murdock, an American scientist, and Captain Michael A. ("Hell Roaring Mike") Healy, of the Revenue Service, called attention to yet another problem stemming from whaling activities. In the course of trade with whalers, Natives acquired modern firearms, which immensely increased their hunting efficiency and probably helped deplete the vast caribou herds. In addition, whalers and Eskimos competed for the bowhead and walrus, soon resulting in reduced numbers and famine for the Eskimos. It has been estimated that approximately 200,000 walrus were killed between 1860 and 1880.[2]

By 1878 the Tlingits and Haidas were experiencing the encroachment of white commercial fishermen on their traditional fishing grounds. The various Pacific salmon species, one of the most important food resources for various Native groups, were soon harvested commercially. In 1878 canneries were established at Klawock and Old Sitka. The salmon-canning industry spread rapidly northward and westward into central and western Alaska between 1882 and 1884, affecting Eskimos and Aleuts as well. From an initial pack of 8,159 cases of 48 one-pound cans, annual production quickly rose to approximately 2,500,000 cases at the turn of the century and averaged 4,800,000 cases during the 1920s. Between 1934 and 1938 the salmon pack rose to an average of 6,905,843 cases, but overexploitation dropped the average annual yield to 2,787,600 between 1954 and 1958.[3] After statehood the salmon fishery began a slow but steady recovery.

Whereas Natives had always caught salmon for their immediate and winter needs as well as for some trade, commercial packers caught as many as could be processed and sold. Using a variety of deadly efficient gear, such as stationary fish traps and mobile seines, they soon overfished the salmon stocks. In short, the story was the same as that of Alaska's other natural resources. Intense and often wasteful exploitation of the sea mammal, fish, and fur resources of Alaska soon resulted in severe damage to the economic base of the North's varied Native cultures.

At first white exploitation was confined to the seas. In time, however, intrusions into Native lands inevitably occurred. Chilkat Indians had always jealously guarded their trade monopoly with the interior Indians. In the spring of 1880 a U.S. Navy commander sent a steam launch to escort a party of nineteen prospectors led by Edmund Bean to the Chilkat country. There the commander's emissary, Chief Sitka Jack, aided by a barrel of molasses, persuaded the Chilkats to open the Chilkoot Pass to the Bean party. The prospectors climbed the pass to the Yukon River but failed to find gold in sufficient quantities.[4] But once the doors had been opened, they could no longer be closed. White penetration had begun and would become increasingly disruptive of the aboriginal way of life.

Despite the paper assurances of both the Treaty of Cession of Russian America and the First Organic Act of 1884, which promised the continued use and occupancy of lands to holders of aboriginal rights, there was little actual regard for the act, which declared that "the Indians or other persons in said district shall not be disturbed in the possession of any lands actually in their use or occupation or now claimed by them, but the terms under which such persons may acquire title to such lands is reserved for future legislation by Congress."[5]

The non-Native population of Alaska grew slowly, and American citizens and others, in their quest for profits from the natural resources of the North, readily ignored whatever aboriginal land rights existed. It was the discovery of gold in sizable quantities in Alaska and in Canada's neighboring Yukon, however, that led to the first large-scale migration to Alaska. Population figures illustrate the changes that occurred. When in the early part of October, 1880, Joe Juneau and Richard Harris discovered gold in Silver Bow Basin near what later became Juneau, Alaska's population consisted of an estimated 430 non-Natives and some 32,996 Natives. By 1890 the number of non-Natives had grown to 4,298, while that of the Natives had declined to 25,354. In 1900 non-Natives outnumbered Natives for the first time, 30,450 of the former and 29,542 of the latter.[6]

The flood of argonauts spread from Dawson, in the Yukon Territory, along the Yukon River, and by 1900 the beaches of Nome swarmed with nearly 20,000 adventurers; thousands of others were scattered along rivers and creeks. In 1902, Felix Pedro discovered gold near what was to become Fairbanks, in Alaska's interior. Other prospectors went to Cook Inlet, the Kenai Peninsula, the Copper River area, and elsewhere. Soon the Eskimos of western Alaska and the Athapaskans of the interior experienced the impact of white fortune seekers. Prompted by the gold rush, Congress in 1898 extended the homestead laws to Alaska; among other provisions, those laws reserved suitable tracts of land along the shores for "landing places for canoes and other craft used by such Natives."[7]

In 1906 the passage of the Native Allotment Act enabled Alaska Natives to obtain legal title to 160-acre homesteads to be selected from the unappropriated and unreserved public domain.[8] Although it enabled Natives to gain title to land, it was a regressive piece of legislation since it endeavored to turn hunters and food-gatherers into homesteaders. Alaska lands for the most part were not suitable for agricultural pursuits. Only eighty allotments, and most of these in southeastern Alaska, were issued under the act between 1906 and 1960.

Between 1914 and 1917 the president of the United States made ten withdrawals for Alaskan Natives amounting to some 490,368 acres.[9] The primary goal of the first Native organization to be formed on a more than local basis was the winning of citizenship. The Alaska Native Brotherhood (ANB), founded by nine Tlingits and one Tsimshian in Sitka in 1912, was followed in 1915 by a woman's organization,

the Alaska Native Sisterhood, and within a decade chapters, called camps, existed in most towns and villages of southeastern Alaska.[10]

## NATIVES AND TERRITORIAL POLITICS

Along with the intention of winning citizenship, the ANB also concerned itself with Indian education and the abandonment of aboriginal customs considered "uncivilized" by whites. The latter concern was prompted by one of the provisions of the General Allotment Act of 1887, which provided for acquisition of citizenship by Indians who had "severed tribal relationship and adopted the habits of civilization."[11]

In part through ANB efforts, the 1915 Alaska territorial legislature passed an act enabling Indians to become citizens. To do so they had to demonstrate that they had given up their tribal ways and adopted the habits of "civilized" life. Despite the complicated qualifying procedures, increasing numbers of Natives used the territorial law to become citizens. In 1924, Congress followed suit when it made citizens of all American Indians.[12]

In the meantime, on July 5 and 6, 1915, a number of Athapaskan chiefs and headmen met at the Thomas Memorial Library, in Fairbanks, with Delegate James Wickersham and various officials, among them C. W. Richie and H. J. Atwell, the acting registrar and the receiver of the U.S. Land Office at Fairbanks, and the Reverend Guy H. Madara, minister in charge of all Episcopal missions in the Tanana Valley. Madara stated that the Athapaskan leaders represented some fifteen hundred of their followers and had come to discuss land questions and educational needs. Since none of the Athapaskan leaders spoke English, Paul Williams, of Fort Gibbon, acted as interpreter. Delegate Wickersham told the assembled leaders that he expected that in-

The founders of the Alaska Native Brotherhood, formed in 1911. Left to right: Paul Liberty, James Watson, Ralph Young, Eli Katinook, Peter Simpson, Frank Mercer, James C. Johnson, Chester Worthington, George Field, William Hobson, and Frank Price. Courtesy Walter Soboleff Collection, Alaska and Polar Regions Archives, Elmer E. Rasmuson Library, University of Alaska.

creasing homesteading activity would soon take up all the good land, and "when all the good land is gone . . . the Indians are going to have to move over." The delegate offered two alternatives: 160-acre homesteads or reservations.

Homesteads, the Indians argued, were incompatible with their seminomadic lifestyle. Chief Ivan of Crossjacket probably best expressed Indian opposition to reservations by stating, "[We] wish to stay perfectly free just as we are now and go about just the same as now. . . . We feel as if we had always gone as we pleased and the way they all feel is the same." Chief Joe of Salchaket said: "We want to be left alone. As the whole continent was made for you, God made Alaska for the Indian people, and all we hope is to be able to live here all the time." Paul Williams, the interpreter, eloquently summarized their plight:

Just as soon as you take us from the wild country and put us on reservations . . . we would soon all die off like rabbits. In times past our people did not wear cotton clothes and clothes like the white man wears, but we wore skins from the caribou. We lived on fish, the wild game, moose and caribou, and blueberries and roots. That is what we are made to live on—not vegetables, cattle and things like the white people eat. As soon as we are made to leave our customs and wild life, we will all get sick and soon die. We have moved into cabins. There is no such thing now as the underground living and as soon as we have done this the Natives begin to catch cold. You used to never hear anything of consumption or tuberculosis. The majority of people say that whiskey brings tuberculosis to the Indians, but this is not true. It is because we have changed our mode of living and are trying to live like the white man does.[13]

Delegate Wickersham promised to report the chiefs' opposition to reservations to Washington, though he himself disagreed with them: "I think that a reservation is excellent and the best thing that can be done for the Indians." The meeting adjourned with the delegate admonishing the Indians

Athapaskan chiefs of the villages in the Tanana Valley, who gathered in Fairbanks in 1915 to discuss with James Wickersham, Alaska's delegate to Congress, the problems of their people. Bottom row, left to right: Chief Alexander of Tolovana, Chief Thomas of Nenana, Chief Evan of Koschakat, and Chief Alexander William of Tanana; top row: Chief William of Tanana, Paul Williams of Tanana, and Chief Charlie of Minto. For this picture they posed in their chiefs' jackets of moosehide decorated with beadwork and beaver fur. Note the dentalium and bead decorations at the necks and supporting the sheaths, which held their curved-handle knives. Courtesy Charles E. Bunnell Collection, Alaska and Polar Regions Archives, Elmer E. Rasmuson Library, University of Alaska.

that "as soon as . . . [you] have established homes and live like the white men and assume the habits of civilization . . . [you] can have a vote."[14]

Wickersham no doubt did report the sentiments of the Athapaskans to the secretary of the interior. That is where the matter rested. A few years later, in 1926, Congress amended the Townsite Act which enabled Alaska Natives to receive restricted deeds to surveyed town lots. The legislation also exempted Indians and Eskimos of full or mixed blood from all forms of taxation on lots occupied and claimed by them. Between 1926 and 1971 the federal government surveyed only 28 of more than 175 Native villages and issued restricted deeds to their inhabitants.[15]

On June 18, 1934, Congress passed far-reaching legislation known as the Indian Reorganization Act, or the Howard-Wheeler Act. Its intent was to improve the lot of Native Americans in keeping with the spirit of the New Deal. In 1936, Congress extended the Indian Reorganization Act to Alaska, including the authority to create reservations if approved by a majority vote of not less than 30 percent of the Natives involved. Both Secretary of the Interior Harold L. Ickes and his commissioner of Indian affairs, John Collier, firmly believed that the revival and preservation of American Indian culture required the establishment of reservations.[16]

The act soon became embroiled in

An Athapaskan constructing a birchbark canoe. The birch tree provided many of the needs of the interior people. This view shows the careful light framing and the neat binding of the bark to the frame with split spruce root. The canoes were extremely light and could be portaged easily. Courtesy Eva Alvey Richards Collection, Alaska and Polar Regions Archives, Elmer E. Rasmuson Library, University of Alaska.

territory-wide controversy because of its reservation provisions. Both Natives and whites objected to that particular feature, the latter fearful that even more land would be closed to them, preventing the development of resources and therefore hampering economic growth. Natives feared that the reservations would repeat the miserable pattern of the "Lower 48." What especially startled Alaskans was the announcement that there would be approximately one hundred reservations from which all but local Native residents would be excluded. This announcement was coupled with the creation of the large Venetie Reservation just north of the Arctic Circle. If 1.4 million acres were to be withdrawn for the benefit of some twenty-five Athapaskan families, many reasoned, then perhaps as much as one-third to one-half of Alaska would eventually be enclosed within the one hundred reserves. Many Natives feared that they might be confined to small areas with limited resources.

Despite the controversy, however, by 1946 the secretary of the interior had included seven villages in six reservations. The Venetie Reservation, the largest, included the villages of Venetie, Arctic Village, Kachik, and Christian Village, while Unalakleet Reservation, the smallest, contained a mere 870 acres. The secretary established the other reservations at Akutan, Little Diomede, Hydaburg, Karluk, and Wales.[17] Many other villages prepared petitions for reservations, and three villages voted against them. After 1946 no others were created under the act. Later on, a court held that the Hydaburg Reservation had not been established legally. Native villages, however, continued to submit petitions to the secretary of the interior requesting reservations. By 1950 eight villages had submitted such petitions embracing approximately 100 million acres. The Department of the Interior, however, did not act on any of them, probably because by then public opinion seemed opposed to the reservation system because it represented racial segregation and discrimination.[18]

Reservations were not the only avenue for safeguarding Native land rights. After years of efforts by various of its members, Congress enacted the Tlingit and Haida Jurisdictional Act of June 15, 1935, which had been introduced by Alaska's delegate, Anthony J. Dimond. The measure authorized the Tlingit and Haida Indians of southeastern Alaska to bring suit in the U.S. Court of Claims for any claims they might have against the United States. The Tlingits filed a suit against the United States demanding $35 million "for the value of the land, hunting and fishing rights taken without compensation." The court of claims, however, dismissed the case in 1944 because the Tlingit-selected attorneys had not been approved by the secretary of the interior as the act required. Several times the deadline for filing claims expired, only to be extended by Congress.[19]

After two such extensions, the Tlingits and Haidas filed a claim for compensation for tribal property rights expropriated by the United States in southeastern Alaska. In a 1959 decision the court of claims decided that the Tlingits and Haidas had established aboriginal Indian title to six designated areas in southeastern Alaska. After the case dragged through the courts for another nine years, the court of claims awarded $7,546,053.80 to the Tlingits and Haidas on January 9, 1969. The court also found that, except for eight small parcels for which patents were granted, Indian title to an area of 2,634,744 acres had not been extinguished.

In 1946, Congress passed the Indian Claims Commission Act, which permitted Indian tribes to sue the United States for certain claims not previously allowed. Most of the claims involved compensation for loss and damages apart from the loss of Indian title lands.[21]

While Natives asserted their claims to the federal government, they also were determined to make political gains in Alaska. As early as 1924, Tlingit attorney William L. Paul won election to the territorial house of representatives. Twenty years later, in 1944, Frank Peratrovich of Klawock and Andrew Hope of Sitka won house seats; Frank G. Johnson of Kake was elected to the house and Peratrovich to the senate in 1946. In the legislative session beginning in 1952, seven Natives held seats.[22] From then on, Native political gains were slow but steady.

The 1950s also witnessed a fundamental change in Alaska's economy. By the mid-fifties the military, long a mainstay of the economy, was losing interest in the territory. At the same time, however, Alaska began to reestablish an economy based on natural resources. In 1957 the Richfield Oil Company discovered oil at Swanson River on the Kenai Peninsula, and by 1959 there were several producing wells on the Kenai Peninsula. Exploration and development extended to offshore Cook Inlet, where additional oil-and-gas fields were soon brought into production.

The First Organic Act of 1884 and the second act of 1912 had contained disclaimers for lands used and occupied by Natives. The statehood act of 1958 renewed this pledge, specifically stating that the new state and its people disclaimed all rights or title to lands "the right or title to which may be held by Eskimos, Indians, or Aleuts" or held in trust for them. It did not, however, define the "right or title" which Natives might have, correctly leaving this for future action by Congress or the courts. More important, Congress granted the new state the right to select 102.55 million acres from the "vacant, unappropriated, and unreserved" public lands of the United States, another 400,000 acres from the national forests, and 400,000 acres from other public lands for community expansion. Congress intended Alaska "to achieve full equality with existing states not only in a technical, judicial sense, but on political, economic terms as well . . . by making the new state master in fact of most of the natural resources within its boundaries."[23]

In 1959, among the first legislature's early actions, which included a variety of laws making possible the transition from territoriality to statehood, was the creation of a Department of Natural Resources. Through its Division of Lands the department would choose, manage, and dispose of the state's 103,350,000 acres from the public domain. While the legislature provided general guidelines for the Division of Lands to follow, it was up to that agency to determine state criteria in its land-selection program and to decide which among the many possible uses of the land was in the public interest. Ever so slowly and carefully, under the able direction of its first director, Roscoe Bell, the agency began to select tracts of land here and there. No one really knew what most of the land in Alaska contained, and, furthermore, the director was acutely aware of the state's limited financial resources and the strains on those resources that land management would impose.

In the meantime, Alaska Natives, who made up about one-fifth of the state's population in 1960, continued to live mostly where they constituted a majority—in the approximately two hundred villages and settlements widely scattered across rural Alaska. They confidently expected to continue using the land as their ancestors had used it for thousands of years.

Soon, however, threats to Native land rights emerged, to which Natives responded by forming local and regional organizations, eventually uniting statewide. The fear of losing their land aroused the Natives and radicalized them. An identity revolution occurred in villages across Alaska during the 1960s, and by 1968 the inhabitants of the most remote settlements understood what was at stake. A number of factors had contributed to that revolution: one was the es-

tablishment on October 1, 1962, of the *Tundra Times,* the first statewide Native newspaper, under the capable editorship of Point Hope Eskimo Howard Rock; another was the emergence of several energetic and able young Native leaders who were able to think simultaneously as United States citizens and as Natives.

## NEW THREATS TO NATIVE LANDS

The first government threat to Native lands occurred as early as 1957. On June 19 of that year the Atomic Energy Commission (AEC) established the Plowshare Program for utilizing the peaceful uses of atomic energy. In November scientists at the Lawrence Radiation Laboratory at the University of California recommended to the AEC that large earth excavations promised the earliest success in the Plowshare Program. By the end of the year they had designed a massive explosion equal to 2.4 million tons of TNT, known as "Project Chariot."[24]

After considering a number of ideas, the physicists decided "to blast an artificial harbor—or at least a hole that could be made to look like a harbor—at Cape Thompson," on Alaska's northwest coast. In 1958 the AEC asked the U.S. Geological Survey (USGS) for a study of the geological and oceanographic factors relevant to excavating a harbor on the Alaska coast between Nome and Point Barrow. Later it requested a detailed report on the twenty-mile coastal strip south of Cape Thompson, and the Lawrence Radiation Laboratory at the University of California contracted with the E. J. Longyear Company to study the economic potential of minerals along the coast. No travel money was authorized for either study.[25]

In April, 1958, both reports came back. The USGS found "the northwest coast of Alaska . . . relatively unknown geologically," while the Cape Thompson area was "largely unexplored" and ice-blocked nine

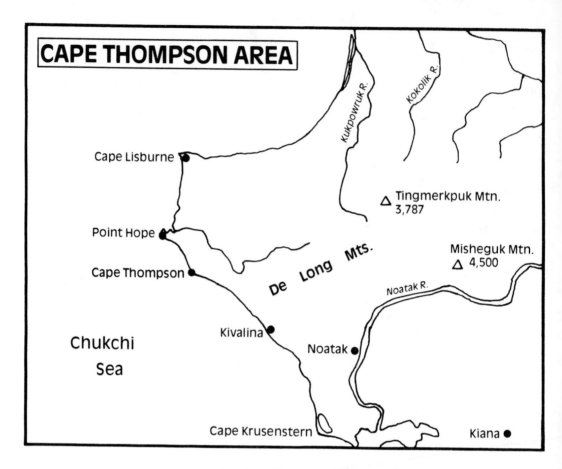

# CAPE THOMPSON AREA

Kukpowruk R.

Kokolik R.

Cape Lisburne

△ Tingmerkpuk Mtn.
3,787

Point Hope

De Long Mts.

Misheguk Mtn.
△ 4,500

Cape Thompson

Noatak R.

Chukchi
Sea

Kivalina

Noatak

Cape Krusenstern

Kiana

The Cape Thompson area

months of the year. Longyear reported optimistically that within twenty-five years a port at Cape Thompson would handle the "substantial" amounts of oil and coal believed to be abundant near the cape. Both reports had been based on literature searches for relevant data rather than on investigations on the spot. On June 5, 1958, Lewis Strauss, chairman of the AEC, requested a 1,600-square-mile withdrawal of land and water from the public domain in the Cape Thompson area. The explosion was scheduled for 1960.[26]

In July, 1958, Edward Teller, the famous Hungarian-born physicist and father of the hydrogen bomb, led a group of scientists and AEC officials to Alaska to sell "Project Chariot." Teller assured his Alaska audiences that two-thirds of the projected $5 million targeted for the project would be spent in Alaska. The Alaska press wholeheartedly supported the blast because it would funnel needed federal funds into the new state and put Alaska on the map, but business leaders were skeptical of the alleged mineral deposits and the need for a harbor. A few members of the science faculty of the University of Alaska, a handful of citizens, and a few key government officials questioned the alleged safety of the proposed blast.[27]

Alaska dissenters demanded that the AEC establish a scientific basis for its assertion that "Project Chariot" would harm neither human life nor livelihood. Faced with this task, the AEC lost faith in "Chariot" and announced the the project would have to be dropped for lack of support in the state. Lawrence Laboratory physicists quickly recognized that a crisis existed. The project had to be sold properly. Two of them toured the state warning that "Project Chariot's" fate depended on endorsement by chambers of commerce and the state legislature. Soon some chambers of commerce were backing the project, and others were falling into line, while the legislature gave its official blessing. Preparations resumed, but then the AEC announced that the project would be only an excavation experiment because the harbor likely would not be commercially useful.[28]

The AEC did finance biological studies which showed rich and varied flora and fauna. These were the first preexplosion surveys ever undertaken by the AEC, and their assessment triggered bitter disagreement. One botanist quit the project, maintaining that the environmental committee uncritically went along with the predetermined policy of the AEC, since the official press release stated that no biological reasons existed for stopping the project.[29]

Not until the spring of 1960 did AEC officials visit the villages to reassure the Natives, because the USGS report had shown that along the 1,600-mile coastline from Nome to Point Barrow there were only eleven locations as much as 20 miles away from any human habitation. The village council members of Point Hope listened politely and then voted unanimously to oppose "Project Chariot." On March 3, 1961, the Point Hope village Health Council wrote President John F. Kennedy in opposition to the proposed chain explosion of five atomic bombs. The blast, they objected, would be

too close to our hunting and fishing areas. We read about the cumulative and retained iso-

tope burden in man that must be considered. We also know about strontium 90, how it might harm people if too much of it gets into our body. We have seen the summary Reports of 1960, National Academy of Sciences, on "The Biological Effects of Atomic Radiation." We are deeply concerned about the health of our people now and for the future that is coming.[30]

The Point Hope residents had deep roots in the past and were unwilling to jeopardize the continued existence of their village. Archaeological records indicated a continued existence for at least 5,000 years of that village on a spit of land projecting like a finger into the Chukchi Sea, and for that same period of time the inhabitants had depended on the fish, seals, and whales of the sea and the game animals, chiefly caribou, of the immediate hinterland. An atomic explosion, they feared, could end the existence of Point Hope.

In addition to the Point Hope–"Project Chariot" controversy, another, concerning hunting rights, was brewing in Barrow, the northernmost settlement. State Representative John Nusinginya was arrested for shooting ducks outside the hunting season established by an international migratory bird treaty. Two days later 138 other men shot ducks and presented themselves to federal game wardens for arrest, but they were merely cited for their violations. By 1961 the charges against all of them had been dropped. Finally, in November, 1961, representatives from all along the coast met at Point Barrow for a conference on Native rights sponsored by the Association on American Indian Affairs, a private charitable organization based in New York City.

They discussed many of their mutual concerns. The Native representatives claimed that the proposed site for Project Chariot belonged to them and asked the Department of the Interior to revoke the research

Mr. and Mrs. Kignak, of Barrow, 1965. Photograph by Claus-M. Naske.

license the Bureau of Land Management had granted to the AEC. The representatives opened their report by saying:

> We the Inupiat have come together for the first time ever in all the years of our history. We had to come together in meeting from our far villages from Lower Kuskokwim to Point Barrow. We had to come from so far together for this reason. We always thought our Inupiat Paitot [the people's heritage] was safe to be passed down to our future generations as our fathers passed down to us. Our Inupiat Paitot is our land around the whole Arctic world where the Inupiat live.[31]

Eskimos and public opposition eventually forced the government to abandon "Project Chariot" at Cape Thompson. Furthermore, the conference won the attention of high officials of the Department of the Interior and also led to the development of the first regional Native organization to be established since the founding of the Alaska Native Brotherhood nearly half a century earlier. The new organization adopted the name Inupiat Paitot (the People's Heritage) and elected Guy Okakok, of Barrow, president.

"Project Chariot" had been aborted, but there were other dangers to Native land rights. The Alaska Statehood Act constituted the greatest threat because, while it recognized the right of Natives to lands which they used and occupied, it did not and could not provide any means of assuring such use and occupancy. State land selections proceeded cautiously but steadily, thereby endangering the continued use of lands by Natives.

It was in the Minto Lakes region of interior Alaska that state land selections first conflicted with Native hunting, fishing, and trapping activities. In 1961 the state wanted to establish a recreation area near the Athapaskan village of Minto and construct a road into the area to make it accessible to Fairbanks residents. State officials also had an eye on the future development of oil and other resources in the area.[32] Learning of these state plans, the village of Minto asked the U.S. Department of the Interior to protect their rights and reject the state's application for the land. In response late in 1961 the Bureau of Indian Affairs began filing protests on behalf of the Natives of Minto, Northway, Tanacross, and Lake Alegnagik over land totaling approximately 5,860,000 acres and conflicting with some 1,750,000 acres of state selection.[33]

As early as December, 1961, the Department of the Interior reacted by ordering the state director of the Bureau of Land Management (BLM) for Alaska to dismiss protests unless the claims clearly fell within the regulation that "lands occupied by Indians, Aleuts, and Eskimos in good faith are not subject to entry or appropriation by others." On February 20, 1962, the regional solicitor for the Department of the

Interior issued an opinion in which he asserted that "Indian title" was involved in the protest and that therefore a determination of the facts had to be made.

Subsequently BLM managers were told not to accept protests of this kind. The solicitor suggested that the protests be dismissed on jurisdictional grounds because the only occupancy recognized in BLM regulations was that which led to the issuance of allotments under the Alaska Native Allotment Act. Following instructions, BLM personnel in 1962 dismissed a number of Native protests, which the claimants appealed to the director of the BLM. Early in 1963 the director advised Alaska BLM offices to make no more decisions at the local level and instead to forward case records to Washington for consideration.[34]

While the Natives filed protests and the BLM weighed what steps to take next, the Alaska Conservation Society met in Fairbanks in February, 1963, to discuss the proposed Minto Lakes recreation area. Attending the meeting were about 150 local sportsmen and conservationists, as well as Richard Frank, chief of the Minto Flats people, who hunted and fished and found some seasonal employment with the river barge companies and as firefighters. Most of the people also used more than a million acres of land, including the lakes where the state planned its recreation area, in their search for food. Frank told his listeners that the lakes belonged to his people, that the area was their traditional hunting ground, and that without the use of the area his people would go hungry. Frank also told how the Bureau of Indian Affairs had asked his people in 1937 whether they wanted to go on a reservation. The village had rejected the idea, but Frank's father, then chief, had made a map showing the area where they hunted and fished. In 1951 the Minto Flats people had filed a land claim with the Fairbanks office of the BLM. The chief at that time had simply taken a map and indicated with a circle the approximate

area his people used. In the wake of oil and exploration around nearby Nenana in 1961, Frank took his father's map to the BLM office and indicated what lands his people claimed. Frank resented the fact that the state planned to build a road across village-claimed lands without consultation.[35]

Roscoe Bell, head of the Alaska State Division of Lands, suggested that the state and the Minto people resolve their differences. He proposed that the state select and patent the land and then sell parcels of it back to the Indians. Frank flatly refused to go along with that scheme: "As long as I'm chief, we won't give up our land. We have the same idea the state has. The state wants to develop this land and that's our aim, too." Thereupon the Minto people hired attorney Ted Stevens, who had just spent a number of years in the solicitor's office at the Department of the Interior. Stevens offered his services free.[36]

The *Tundra Times* spread Frank's fighting words to every Native community in the northern part of Alaska. Editor Howard Rock, commenting on what was happening in Minto, wrote: "We Natives should realize that we will not be able to compete fully with big business for a long time yet. Since we cannot do that now, we should try to hold on to our lands because that is the greatest insurance we can have. . . . Without land, we can become the poorest people in the world."[37]

Between 1962 and 1966 threats to Native-claimed lands multiplied, and the story of Minto was repeated over and over again. The most spectacular involved the proposal for building a dam 530 feet high and 4,700 feet long at the Rampart Canyon, on the Yukon River. At a cost of several billion dollars, the dam would generate 5 million kilowatts and would put the entire Yukon Flats—a vast network of sloughs, marshes, and potholes that is one of the largest wildfowl breeding grounds in North America—under several hundred feet of water. The proponents of the scheme, the U.S. Army

Corps of Engineers, intended to create a lake with a surface greater than that of Lake Erie or the state of New Jersey; it would take approximately twenty years to fill.

An organization named Yukon Power for America, armed with an initial budget of $100,000, intended to lobby the Rampart project through Congress. Businessmen, newspaper publishers, chambers of commerce, and mayors of Alaska's principal cities belonged to the group. Yukon Power for America published a colorful brochure entitled *The Rampart Story*, which extolled the benefits of cheap electrical power, namely, three mills per kilowatt-hour. This power would in turn attract industry, it was said, notably the aluminum industry. Alaska's junior U.S. senator, Ernest Gruening, wholeheartedly supported the project.[38]

The U.S. Fish and Wildlife Service, on the other hand, reported to the Army Corps of Engineers that "nowhere in the history of water development in North America have the fish and wildlife losses anticipated to result from a single project been so overwhelming." The authors of the report strongly opposed authorization of the Rampart Canyon Dam and Reservoir. Paul Brooks, a conservation writer, estimated that about twelve hundred Natives would have to be relocated elsewhere; that the livelihood of five to six thousand more in Alaska and approximately thirty-five hundred in Canada's Yukon Territory would be affected by the reduction in the salmon run; and that the moose range, with an estimated eventual carrying capacity of twelve thousand animals, would disappear, together with wildfowl breeding grounds and the smaller furbearers.[39]

Rampart Dam eventually died a quiet death for a variety of reasons, including adverse ecological and economic reports backed by the opposition of Alaska's Natives and an increasingly well-informed public.

## ALTERNATIVES FOR SETTLING NATIVE CLAIMS

During these controversies the state had continued to claim its allotted lands, and by 1968 it had selected 19.6 million acres, some 8.5 million acres of which had been tentatively approved and over 6 million acres had been patented. In the same year Alaska Natives had legal ownership of fewer than 500 acres and held in restricted title only 15,000 acres. Some nine hundred Native families lived on twenty-three reserves administered by the Bureau of Indian Affairs. These reserves, which included 1.25 million acres of reindeer lands, totaled 4 million acres. An estimated 270 million acres of land remained in the public domain. About 37,000 rural Alaska Natives lived on that land and the twenty-three Native reserves, while another 15,600 of their kin lived in Alaska's urban areas.[40]

The only recourse open to Natives consisted of filing protests to the state land selections, and between 1961 and April 1, 1968, Native protest filings covered some 296 million acres; by the middle of 1968 the filings covered almost 337 million acres.[41]

Early in 1963 the Alaska Task Force on Native Affairs established by the Department of the Interior issued a report that stated that a resolution of Native land rights was long overdue. The report cited the failure of the First Organic Act to provide the means by which Natives might obtain title to land and noted that in the following seventy-eight years Congress had "largely sidestepped the issue of aboriginal claims." If Congress ever was going to define Native rights, the report concluded, it should do so promptly. The Alaska Task Force also included specific recommendations for solving the Native land problem. It called for the prompt grant of up to 160 acres to individuals for homes, fish camps, and hunting sites; withdrawal of "small acreages" for village growth; and designation of areas for Native use—but not ownership—in traditional food-gathering activities.[42]

With the help of the Association on American Indian Affairs and its executive director, William Byler, Natives successfully opposed the implementation of the Alaska Task Force recommendations. Part of the opposition was based on the fact that there were no provisions for cash payment for land lost or for mineral rights for lands they would receive. Alaska's congressional delegation offered differing approaches as well. Senator Ernest Gruening favored settlement through the U.S. Court of Claims, while Representative Ralph Rivers felt that that would take too long. He favored congressional extinguishment of Native claims coupled with cash compensation. Senator Bob Bartlett urged that state land selections be allowed to proceed before a land settlement was reached. One million acres for villages would be sufficient, he suggested,

while cash payments should be made for other lands Natives claimed.[43]

At that point four basic courses of action seemed plausible: Natives might seek the establishment of reserves under existing laws, resolve their claims in the federal Court of Claims, obtain legislation at the state level to protect their land rights, or attempt a congressional settlement. Reserves would be held in trust for Natives by the federal government, and thus that option did not hold great appeal. The Tlingit-Haida experience with the courts made the judicial alternative unattractive. Congress had allowed the Tlingit-Haida to sue in 1935, but not until 1959 had the court of claims supported the case and decreed that their claims were compensable. Later the compensation was fixed at $7.5 million. State action was rejected because most state legislators agreed that Native land rights could be resolved only by Congress.[44]

Native leaders briefly considered state

Eskimo schoolchildren at lunch recess, playing in the drifting snow, Barrow, 1965. Photograph by Claus-M. Naske.

legislation that would protect their rights. One proposal would have created twenty-square-mile reservations surrounding villages. Natives rejected the proposal as inadequate. But most Native leaders also realized that congressional settlement was enormously uncertain, since, because Congress was sovereign, it could extinguish or recognize rights, grant little or no land, or decide to give compensation only for surrendered lands.

While the various alternatives were being examined and discussed, none was pursued. That would have to await the formation of a statewide Native organization with sufficient financial resources to pursue a settlement.

What made the organization of a statewide group difficult was the deeply rooted mistrust that many Natives harbored for people outside their own geographical regions. Yet throughout the 1960s various Native groups organized themselves, and in October, 1966, representatives of all the Native organizations and numerous individual villages met in Anchorage to form the organization that was to become the Alaska Federation of Natives (AFN). In the preamble to its constitution, adopted the following year, the AFN made its purpose clear. It was to secure the rights and benefits to which Natives were entitled under the laws of the United States and Alaska, enlighten the general public about Natives, preserve cultural values and seek an equitable solution to Native claims, promote the common welfare of Alaskan Natives, and foster continued loyalty and allegiance to Alaska and the United States.[45]

In the spring of 1967 a small group of Natives who had attended the Anchorage meeting the previous fall met again and formally established the AFN. Despite some disagreements with the Eskimos and the interior Athapaskans, the AFN began to function in 1967. Before it became a reality, however, Secretary of the Interior Stewart Udall stopped the transfer of lands claimed by the Natives until Congress had settled the land-claims issue. Udall's action followed Native protests against state plans to sell gas-and-oil leases on the North Slope on lands tentatively approved for patent to the state.[46]

In the meantime, Governor William A. Egan had lost to Republican Walter J. Hickel in the 1966 elections, while Republican Howard Pollock had defeated Representative Ralph Rivers, who had not favored a settlement. Before Hickel's election the Egan administration and the Democratic congressional delegation had maintained that the land claims were a federal problem. During his campaign Hickel had not stressed the claims issue but had concentrated on the theme of getting Alaska moving economically.[47]

After he became governor, Hickel promptly overrode a Bureau of Land Management decision not to allow the lease sale, which then proceeded as planned. In the meantime, the Natives tried to enlist the governor's support for a settlement. After initial resistance Hickel proposed the outlines of such a settlement, calling for granting Natives full title to some lands around their villages and surface rights to a larger acreage.[48]

In May, 1967, the Department of the Interior finally drafted a settlement bill for congressional consideration. In essence the measure proposed a grant of 50,000 acres to each Native village and the payment of a small amount of cash to each individual. The Department of the Interior, however, would maintain its paternalistic role and control both the land and the money.[49]

The AFN, learning of the proposal, met in Anchorage and voted to oppose it. They asked Senator Ernest Gruening to introduce legislation making possible a court of claims settlement instead. In the late fall the AFN met again, this time to listen to Hickel's attorney general, Edgar Paul Boyko, urge cooperation between the Natives and the state against the Department of the Interior, which he characterized as a common enemy. The state wanted to avoid lengthy litigation, afraid that the oil companies with leaseholdings in the Arctic would leave. Boyko promised to compensate the Natives for lands already taken on the basis of their value at the time of statehood in 1959 and to give full title to other lands as well. A few weeks later Hickel appointed thirty-seven members of a land-claims task force which was to write a mutually acceptable bill.[50]

Such action was desirable because the land area affected by Udall's freeze had rapidly grown as Natives had filed additional claims, ranging from a 640-acre claim by Chilkoot village to the 58 million acres claimed by the Arctic Slope Native Association. Because many of the claims were overlapping, the total acreage amounted to 380 million acres, more than the state's land area.[51]

Eskimo woman stretching a fishnet on the Kobuk River. Courtesy U.S. National Park Service.

In January, 1968, the land-claims task force delivered its report, recommending that legal possession of 40 million acres be given to Native villages, that all lands currently used for hunting and fishing activities be available for such purposes for one hundred years, that the Native Allotment Act remain in force, and that 10 percent of the income from the sale or lease of oil rights from certain lands be paid to Natives up to a total of at least $65 million. The settlement was to be carried out by business corporations, one of which would be statewide, the rest organized by villages and regions. The task force also recommended that the state legislature pass companion legislation providing $50 million to Natives from mineral revenues from certain lands, but only if the freeze was lifted before the end of 1968.[52]

In 1968, Senator Gruening introduced a bill recommended by the land-claims task force. The Senate Interior and Insular Affairs Committee promptly held a three-day hearing in Anchorage, which opened on February 8, 1968. A large crowd, including many Eskimos, Indians, and Aleuts from across the state, attended the hearing. Committee members listened to Native leaders explain the proposed settlement and urge prompt action on the measure.

The principal opposition came from the Alaska Sportsmen's Council, which objected to the granting of public lands but approved of cash payments. On the other hand, the Alaska Miners' Association, represented by George Moerlein, of its Land Use Committee, claimed that the U.S. government was "neither legally nor morally obligated to grant any of the claims put forth by the various Native groups or by the Native Land Claims Task Force." Quoting the Indian Claims Commission Act of 1946, which required that claims be either presented before 1951 or not presented at all, Moerlin stated that, except for claims filed by that deadline, "neither the United States, the State of Alaska, nor any of us here gathered as individuals owes the Natives 1 acre of ground or 1 cent of the taxpayers' money." Phil Holdsworth, the lobbyist of the Alaska Miners' Association, disagreed with Moerlein's assertion, stating that there indeed existed a moral responsibility to settle the claims.[52]

Committee members also listened to older village people describe why a settlement was needed. Peter John, of Minto, described how plentiful game used to be around his home but how increasing hunting pressure from whites had caused a steep decline. He said that there had been an abundance of furbearing animals, such as muskrats, mink, fox, beaver, and otter. Mining activities, however, had filled many of the lakes and creeks with silt, driven away the furbearing animals, and killed most of the fish. Walter Charley, of the Copper River Indians, said: "Game, up to a few years ago, was always plentiful. Some of my people still hunt moose as well as caribou. They have to live. We also fish. Two years ago the state put very strict limits on the number of fish that each family could take. We were only allowed 20 sockeye salmon and five king salmon." After much protest, however, this limit had been increased to two hundred fish. There were no jobs, and out of a total of five hundred people in the Copper River area, only twelve held full-time jobs. "The rest of our people live from hand to mouth and the living they can make from a little bit of trapping, fishing, and firefighting." George King, an Eskimo from Ninivak Island, complained that the federal government had reserved the island as a national wildlife refuge in the 1930s: "The island has apparently been set aside for ducks, musk ox, and reindeer. We have not even been able to get a townsite, and, according to the Executive Order establishing the reservation, we are not even there. It is hard for us to understand why the government reserves all of Nunivak Island for the animals and left none of it for

the people." The government, contrary to previous pledges, had deprived the Nunivak Islanders of all their land.[54]

The Hickel administration generally supported the proposed settlement but urged speedy lifting of the land freeze because it prevented oil leasing on federal lands. Since the state received 90 percent of the federal revenues from such leases, it was losing money. After the election of Republican Richard M. Nixon to the presidency in 1968, Native leaders worried about the continuation of the land freeze, which, in Udall's words, had "held everyone's feet to the fire." Just before giving up his office, Udall signed an executive order changing the informal freeze into law.[55]

President-elect Nixon chose Walter Hickel, a vocal critic of the land freeze, to replace Udall. Hickel, who had a reputation as a developer, needed all the support he could obtain, including that of the AFN, because powerful conservationist groups objected to his Senate confirmation. In return for AFN support, Hickel promised to extend the land freeze until 1971 or until the claims were settled. He was confirmed by the Senate as Nixon's new secretary of the interior.[56]

In 1968, Senator Henry Jackson, chairman of the Senate Interior and Insular Affairs Committee, asked the Federal Field Committee for Development Planning in Alaska to carry out a comprehensive study dealing with the social and economic status of the Natives. Headed by Joseph H. Fitzgerald, this small federal agency had been established following the 1964 Good Friday earthquake to coordinate planning among federal and state agencies.[57]

Early in 1969 the Federal Field Committee for Development Planning in Alaska completed its 565-page study of the Native land problem. The committee recommended a land grant of between 4 and 7 million acres, the right to use public lands for subsistence, a $100 million compensation for lands taken in the past, and a 10 percent royalty on mineral revenues from public lands in Alaska for ten years.[58]

Congressional hearings on proposed claims legislation were held in 1969, but no bill emerged from the committees. The Native cause was strengthened through the continuation of the land freeze, support from the Association on American Indian Affairs, and various national newspapers. Furthermore, former Supreme Court Justice Arthur Goldberg represented the AFN, enhancing its national image. Soon Ramsey Clark, former U.S. attorney general, joined Goldberg.[59]

In the meantime the Department of the Interior proposed a settlement differing considerably from that endorsed by Hickel's task force. The department proposed to give Natives about 12.5 million instead of 40 million acres of land, and $500 million instead of $20 million, but no royalty or any sort of revenue sharing. Soon the Natives presented their own proposal, which included full title to 40 million acres of land, allocated among the villages according to their size; $500 million and a 2 percent royalty in perpetuity on all revenues from all other public and state lands in Alaska; and the creation of a statewide Native development corporation and up to twelve regional corporations, coinciding with areas inhabited by various Native groups, who were to manage the land and money received in the settlement.[60]

It was a far-reaching proposal, designed to avoid problems that had arisen elsewhere with Indian claims settlements. It avoided a per capita distribution of cash—which could be quickly squandered—and also retained the Native concept of communally held land but adapted it to changing times.

The various interest groups responded quickly. The Department of the Interior recommended that all federal reservations, including Naval Petroleum Reserve no. 4, which Alaskans and the oil industry had long been trying to open for development, be used in settling the claims. The Forest Service objected to including any portions of the Chugach and Tongass national forests in the settlement. The conservationists wanted the Natives to receive as little federal refuge land as possible and also wanted guarantees that none of the land would pass out of Native hands. The Natives strenuously objected to any Department of the Interior trusteeship.

The oil-and-gas industry worried because the Federal Field Committee had suggested that competitive leasing should be required throughout the state, not just in areas known to contain oil. The various independent companies knew that this would mean bonus leasing, requiring large outlays of cash at the time leases were sold, and feared that they would be unable to compete with the major oil companies. Ten Canadian independent oil companies had a special problem because they had filed for noncompetitive federal oil-and-gas leases in Alaska between March, 1967, and November, 1968. The lease applications covered approximately 20 million acres and had cost $3 million altogether. But because of the Natives' protests and the land freeze, the Bureau of Land Management had not processed these applications. They wanted language in the bill protecting their priority rights.[61]

The Western Gas and Oil Association wanted to be sure that existing federal and state mineral leases were not changed, while other oil companies and the state wanted to make sure that tentative approval for patent, as well as actual patenting, would be considered an "existing right." The state had already leased some 2.4 million acres, mostly on the North Slope, which were only tentatively approved for patent by the BLM at the time of the land freeze. Furthermore, the state planned to offer more leases on tentatively approved land at its September 10, 1969, lease sale.

While the settlements proposed by the Department of the Interior recognized tentative approval as a valid right, the Natives
argued that their claims took precedence
over the statehood act and that they should
be allowed to take tentatively selected state
lands. This cast a shadow on the validity
of the state oil-and-gas leases on these
lands.[62]

The state also worried about Native
claims to tentatively approved lands, and
Governor Keith Miller's administration argued that mineral rights to any land given
to Natives remain under state control since
the statehood act had given the state control over all leasable minerals. Giving these
rights to individuals or corporations constituted a violation of that compact.[63]

On November 18, 1969, just after the
Senate Interior Committee had begun drafting one acceptable bill from the three proposals before it, Governor Miller wrote
Senator Henry Jackson objecting to the nine
townships for each village and suggesting
that two, or even fewer, would be appropriate. There should be no mineral rights in
the lands given to the Natives, and no 2 percent royalty provision or any other revenue
sharing.[64]

Over much opposition from the *Anchorage Daily Times* and much of the Alaska
business community, Alaska senators Mike
Gravel (Democrat) and Ted Stevens (Republican) worked out a compromise that would
give the Natives $500 million in congressio-
nal appropriations; title, including mineral
rights, to between 5 million and 10 million
acres around the villages; use of another 40
million acres for subsistence purposes; and
a 2 percent royalty for a specified number
of years.[65]

Chairman Henry Jackson, angry over the
bickering within his committee and leaks to
the press, announced that his committee
planned to disregard all previous settlement
proposals and start from scratch. The committee was back where it had been the pre-

vious summer, and a year had passed.[66]

In the meantime, the state held its twenty-
third competitive oil-lease sale in Anchorage
on September 10, 1969, bringing in over
$900 million in bonus bids. The sale was
the psychological high point for Alaskans
since the discovery of the Prudhoe Bay field
in 1968.

Soon the Trans-Alaska Pipeline System
(TAPS), the incorporated joint venture of
Atlantic-Richfield, British Petroleum, and
Humble Oil, applied to the Department of
the Interior to construct a hot-oil pipeline
from Prudhoe Bay, in the Arctic, to Valdez,
on Prince William Sound, a distance of 798
miles. Secretary Hickel was under pressure
from opposing interest groups: the oil companies and most Alaskans wanted the $900

Natives protesting the state of Alaska's twenty-
third competitive oil-lease sale at the Sydney
Laurence Auditorium in Anchorage, 1969.
Courtesy Ward Wells Collection, Anchorage
Museum of History and Art.

million project to get under way, while conservationists wanted it delayed because of
the innumerable environmental, technical,
and economic questions that the project
posed.[67]

After much negotiating—and when Secretary Hickel was just about to issue the permit for the construction of the North Slope
haul road—on March 9, 1970, five Native
villages asked the federal district court in
Washington to stop Secretary Hickel from
issuing the permit. The villages said they
were claiming the ground over which the
pipeline and the road would pass. Avoid-
ing the Native claims issue, Federal Judge
George L. Hart, Jr., enjoined the Interior
Department from issuing a construction
permit across 19.8 miles of the route over
the land claimed by sixty-six residents of
Stevens Village. A few days later three conservation groups sued the Department of
the Interior, asking for a halt in the TAPS
project because it violated stipulations of
the 1920 Mineral Leasing Act and the new
National Environmental Policy Act. On
April 13, 1970, Judge Hart issued a temporary injunction against the TAPS project.[68]

By now the oil companies realized that
there would be no pipeline unless the Native land claims were settled first. British Petroleum soon agreed to help lobby for a
Native claims bill and agreed to persuade
its partners to do likewise.

## ALASKA NATIVES FINALLY COMPENSATED

In mid-April, 1970, Senator Jackson outlined the provisions of a bill on which his
committee had tentatively agreed. It awarded
$1 billion to the Natives but authorized
revenue-sharing for only a limited number
of years. Natives would receive only a little
more than 40 million acres of land, and, instead of the twelve regional corporations
which the AFN sought, the measure authorized one for the Arctic Slope and two

statewide corporations, one for social services and another for investments. Within
five years of enactment the educational and
social programs of the Bureau of Indian Affairs would be terminated. Despite Native
protests the full Senate adopted the Jackson
measure. The AFN now had to look to the
House for a more favorable bill.[69]

But there had been gains. The AFN,
strapped for cash, had received a $100,000
loan from the Athapaskan village of Tyonek,
on Cook Inlet. Tyonek had earlier reached a
cash settlement with the federal government over land disputes and therefore had
been able to help bankroll the struggle. Still
there was not enough cash, and the AFN
appealed for voluntary contributions. At
that point the Yakima Indian Nation of the
State of Washington extended a $250,000
loan to the hard-pressed AFN, enabling it
to continue its congressional lobbying efforts. The lobbying apparently bore fruit:
soon thereafter the House Subcommittee
on Indian Affairs informally agreed that
Natives should be granted 40 million acres.[70]

There were other good omens. The National Congress of American Indians decided to give unqualified support to the
AFN's struggle to obtain a congressional
claims settlement. This action gave the AFN
a significant source of national support. In
Alaska, Keith H. Miller was defeated in the
gubernatorial election by former Governor
William A. Egan, who had expressed a willingness to work with the AFN. Nick Begich, a state senator who had stated that 10
million acres was an inadequate settlement,
was elected to Alaska's lone seat in the
House of Representatives. Furthermore, the
Arctic Slope Native Association, which had
earlier withdrawn from the AFN over a disagreement, rejoined by the end of the year.
With the AFN unified once again, its settlement proposal kept the twelve regions and
the $500 million initial compensation, plus
the 2 percent share in future revenues from
public lands. It raised the land provision to

60 million acres and accepted the Arctic Slope argument that the regions with the largest land area should also receive the most land and money.[71]

Soon after Congress convened in 1971, Senators Fred Harris (Democrat, Oklahoma) and Ted Kennedy (Democrat, Massachusetts) introduced the measure in the Senate, while Congressman Lloyd Meeds (Democrat, Washington) submitted the companion measure in the House. Senator Jackson's bill was also reintroduced in the Senate, and Wayne Aspinall, chairman of the House Committee on Interior and Insular Affairs, submitted still another measure that would grant a mere 100,000 acres.[72]

The final drive now started. Efforts centered on the bill's progress in the House because attempts to have the Jackson measure amended in the Senate had failed during the previous year. Lobbyists descended on Congress, but perhaps the most important factor in moving the White House and Congress toward a settlement was the continuing delay in construction of the Trans-Alaska Pipeline. Oil companies and contractors had made enormous investments and impatiently waited to recover them.

Early in April, 1971, the lobbying efforts bore fruit. President Richard M. Nixon, in a special message to Congress, presented a settlement scheme which provided for 40 million acres of absolute legal possession, $500 million in compensation from the federal treasury, and an additional $500 million in mineral revenues from lands given up. On the same day the administration bill was introduced, AFN President Donald Wright met with Nixon, who indicated that he would veto any bill with inadequate land provisions.[73]

Events now moved quickly, with Alaska Congressman Nick Begich playing the key role in the House in dealing with balky Chairman Wayne Aspinall. On August 3, 1971, the subcommittee reported its recommendations to the full House. They pro-

vided for 40 million acres of land, with 18 million acres available for immediate village selection and 22 million to be chosen after the state had completed its selections under the statehood act. About $425 million was to be paid from the federal treasury in compensation over a ten-year period, and $500 million would derive from the state's mineral revenues. Also included was the concept of regional corporations desired by the AFN. The bill, after clearing a strong challenge from conservationists, passed the House.[74]

The Senate also acted swiftly and reported a measure that would provide $500 million from the federal treasury and a like amount from mineral revenue sharing. It would provide 50 million acres of land, but 20 million would be for subsistence use, not ownership, and it established only seven regional corporations. Senator Mike Gravel of Alaska had proposed a land-use planning commission, which was also included. In November the Senate passed the measure with but little opposition.[75]

The conference committee reported its measure in early December, having compromised on several dozen items. There would be title to forty million acres, compensation amounting to $962.5 million, $462.5 million of which was to come from the federal treasury and the rest from mineral revenue sharing. Twelve regional corporations would administer the settlement. The compromise bill passed both houses, and after approval by the AFN, President Nixon signed the measure into law on December 18, 1971.

The land settlement act was a complex measure, hastily drawn so that Congress could pass it quickly before adjourning. The law extinguished Native claims based on aboriginal title in Alaska in return for legal title to 40 million acres. Except for Annette Island, existing reserves were revoked, as was the Native Allotment Act, which had allowed trust status. All U.S. citizens with one-fourth or more Alaska

Indian, Eskimo, or Aleut blood except members of the Metlakatla community on Annette Island who were living when the settlement became law were entitled to become beneficiaries. All eligible Natives were to become stockholders in the business corporations after registering and proving Native ancestry. A Native would be enrolled in the corporation of the region considered home and become the owner of 100 shares of stock. No rights or obligations of Natives as citizens or rights or obligations of the government toward Natives as citizens would be diminished, but federal programs affecting Natives were to be studied to determine whether changes were called for. Within three years the secretary of the interior was to deliver his recommendations to Congress regarding the future operations of these programs.[76]

The act also authorized the secretary of the interior to withdraw up to 80 million acres of land in Alaska for study and possible inclusion in existing national parks or forests, wildlife refuges, or wild or scenic river systems. Congress was then to decide which areas to include. The ten-member Joint Federal-State Land Use Planning Commission was to recommend how to dispose of Alaskan lands, keeping in mind the interests of various groups, such as Natives and other residents of Alaska, and the national interest as well.[77]

By the summer of 1972 land distribution had begun, and by midsummer twelve regional corporations had been established. On July 2 ten of the corporations received their first federal checks for $500,000 each. Most of this money had to be passed to the villages, which were to incorporate as soon as the enrollment of the Natives had been completed. Most of the money was to be used to make the land selections from the 100 million acres Secretary Rogers C. B. Morton had set aside. Villages were to pick their lands first, some 22 million acres. The acreage each village received depended on the enrollment; villages with an enrollment

of between 25 and 99 would receive 69,120 acres, while those with an enrollment of 100 or more would receive 161,280 acres. Villages would make their selections over a three-year period, and then regional corporations could make theirs over a four-year period.[78]

Regardless of size, villages in southeastern Alaska could choose only a single township, or 23,050 acres, because the Tlingit-Haida had earlier received a cash award from the federal government. In the rest of the state, villages were restricted from selecting land in national forests or wildlife refuges, land chosen by the state but not yet patented, and Naval Petroleum Reserve no. 4 on the North Slope. Instead, selections had to be made elsewhere from available lands.[79]

Villages would own the surface rights to their lands, while regional corporations owned the subsurface or mineral rights. Villages situated on revoked reserves had the choice of acquiring full ownership to surface—and subsurface—rights, but by so doing they were excluded from the monetary benefits of the act. The measure provided another 2 million acres to be distributed to special Native corporations organized in once historic Native places now largely occupied by white populations—Sitka, Kenai, Kodiak, and Juneau—and for various other special purposes, such as cemeteries and historic sites.[80]

The $462.5 million was to be paid into the Alaska Native Fund over an eleven-year period, while $500 million from mineral revenue sharing went into the same fund. Payments from this fund were to be made to regional corporations only, which in turn retained some monies and paid out others to individuals and village corporations.[81]

## THE REASONS FOR CLAIMS SETTLEMENT

As a result of the settlement act, neither the Natives nor Alaska will ever be the same again. Despite much rhetoric, the land-claims settlement has ended Native subsistence culture, which is the way Alaska Natives and their ancestors had lived from time immemorial. Numerous conferences have been held around the state in the last few years in which participants assure each other that they will be able to maintain the traditional ways and also fully participate in modern American life. The talk is illusory, however. Natives must learn to think like Western whites to succeed with their corporations. At best the claims settlement will make Native transition into the white world a bit easier.

The AFN displayed superb organization and exercised sophisticated political judgment in its dealing with the federal courts, bureaucracy, and Congress. It showed the proper amount of strength and yet knew when to compromise. But there is no question that the kind of settlement it achieved was largely because of the Prudhoe Bay oil discovery and the desire of industry to extract the oil and bring it to market. There was the widespread belief that if only Alaskan oil could be brought to market, most of America's energy problems would be solved. A quick settlement of Native claims was essential because they stood in the way of oil extraction.

In addition to the energy concerns, there also came into play a new consciousness of the environment. Various conservation groups were eager to settle the uncertain Alaska land question and preserve large areas of wilderness for the benefit of future generations. The civil-rights movement undoubtedly played an important part as well. After a long, hard fight, American blacks had succeeded in pressuring Congress into passing a modern civil-rights bill, long overdue. In the process they had succeeded in sensitizing American society as a whole to the plight of various minorities.

# 12. THE NATIVE REGIONAL CORPORATIONS

The Alaska Native Claims Settlement Act of 1971 provided that inhabitants of each of the Native villages were to be organized as a profit or nonprofit corporation to take title to the surface estate in the land conveyed to the village. These village corporations, totaling more than two hundred, were to administer the land and receive and manage part of the monetary settlement.

The act also directed that twelve regional corporations were to be organized to take title to the subsurface estate in the lands conveyed to the villages and full title to the additional acreage divided among the regional corporations. The latter were also to receive the $962.5 million grant, divided among them on a population basis. The U.S. Treasury was to pay $462.5 million over an eleven-year period, and the remaining $500 million was to come from a 2 percent royalty on production and 2 percent on bonuses and rentals from lands in Alaska thereafter conveyed to the state under the Statehood Act and from the remaining federal lands in Alaska, excluding, however, Naval Petroleum Reserve no. 4. Each regional corporation also had to divide among all twelve entities 70 percent of the mineral revenues received by it.[1]

Each regional corporation had the responsibility of distributing among the village corporations in the region no less than 50 percent of its share of the $962.5 million monetary award, as well as 50 percent of all revenues received from the subsurface estate. This provision did not, however, apply to revenues received by the regional corporations from their investment in business ventures.

For the first five years after the act became law, 10 percent of the revenues from the first two sources mentioned above were to be distributed among the individual Native stockholders of the corporation.

Still another section provided that Natives who had moved from the state and no longer were permanent Alaska residents could, if they so desired, organize a thirteenth regional corporation rather than receive stock in one of the twelve regional corporations. This thirteenth regional corporation would receive its pro rata share of the $962.5 million monetary award but no land and would not share in the mineral revenues of the other regional corporations.[2]

By the early summer of 1972 the twelve regional corporations had organized and soon thereafter rented office space and hired a cadre of professionals, including land planners, economists, and accountants, to begin their corporate existence. By 1975 there was no doubt that Native investments had already made a substantial impact on Alaska's economy. And although the cumber-

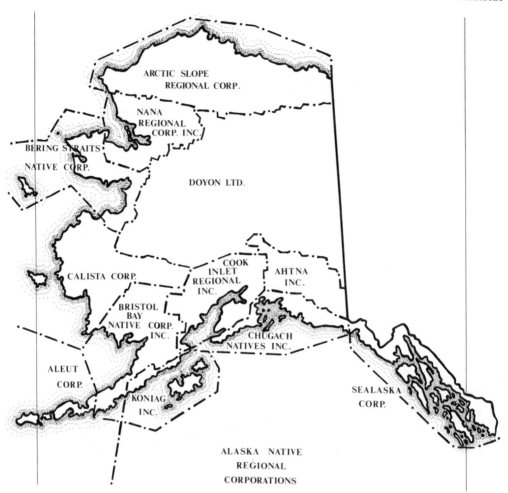

ARCTIC SLOPE
REGIONAL CORP.

NANA
REGIONAL
CORP. INC.

BERING STRAITS
NATIVE CORP.

DOYON LTD.

CALISTA CORP.

COOK
INLET
REGIONAL
INC.

AHTNA
INC.

BRISTOL
BAY
NATIVE CORP.
INC.

CHUGACH
NATIVES INC.

ALEUT
CORP.

KONIAG
INC.

SEALASKA
CORP.

ALASKA NATIVE
REGIONAL
CORPORATIONS

The boundaries of the twelve Native regional corporations. Map by Nancy Van Veeneu.

some federal bureaucracy had delayed transfer of most of the approximately 44 million acres of land that would eventually belong to the Native community, money from the settlement had been flowing steadily into corporate treasuries. By December, 1975, the regional corporations had received $270,306,168 of the monetary settlement.[3]

During 1975 the Bristol Bay Native Corporation, based in Dillingham, made the largest purchase to date of any corporation, acquiring the Peter Pan Seafoods Company for about $9 million. Included in the deal were canneries at Dillingham, King Cove, and Bellingham, Washington; shrimp-processing plants at Squaw Harbor and Coos Bay, Oregon; about 60 large and 120 small vessels; four fish camps in Alaska; a 5-acre boatyard in Seattle; and 1,000 acres of land in Alaska, Washington, and Oregon. In addition, five regional corporations pooled their resources and founded the United Bank of Alaska. Most regional corporations also explored for oil, gas, and hard-rock minerals.[4]

## THE ACTIVITIES OF THE REGIONAL CORPORATIONS

A look at the activities of the various corporations provides a view of their diversity, style of operation, opportunities, and difficulties. The Cook Inlet Region, Inc., a corporation with six thousand stockholders, paid some of the highest legal fees of any of the corporations; it also encountered difficulties in its land-selection process. Most of the Cook Inlet lands had already been preempted by the federal government, the state, the borough, and private landowners. Cook Inlet Region, Inc., therefore, had to make many alternate selections to take the place of such lands. Despite these difficulties the corporation spent a great deal of money in 1975. It purchased five hotels and motels in Anchorage, bought one of the largest warehouses in the state and an office building, and formed a joint venture to develop and sell single-family houses and townhouses. It also participated in two joint-venture contracts on the Trans-Alaska Pipeline project. Perhaps one of the most profitable possibilities may accrue to Cook Inlet Region, Inc., through the development of coal lands. An intricate land swap among the federal government, the state, and the corporation will enable the corporation to choose about 321,040 acres in the Beluga Coal Field.[5]

The Calista Corporation, centered in the Yukon-Kuskokwim region, second-largest of the regional corporations, spent several million dollars on various projects. These included a first-class hotel in Anchorage, a subdivision near Knik, an earth-science consulting firm, a mobile-home park in Valdez, and a 108-foot crabber trawler. With fifty-six villages in its region, Calista had received some $47.3 million from the Alaska Native Fund by December, 1975.[6]

Ahtna, Inc., has one thousand stockholders in the Cooper River basin. It received the smallest financial endowment of any of the corporations, yet corporate leadership put the money to good use. Since the Trans-Alaska Pipeline crosses the region's landholdings, Ahtna worked out a lease agreement with Alyeska Pipeline Service Company for the pipeline corridor, and the company also agreed to buy gravel from Ahtna. Early in 1974, Ahtna also negotiated one of several joint ventures for pipeline work with the construction firm of Rogers and Babler. Pooling monetary resources, the regional corporation and the eight village corporations formed a company called Ahtna Development Corporation to serve as the economic arm for the nine corporations. Their first joint venture was the construction of a $1.5 million lodge, restaurant, and bar complex in Glennallen to serve the tourist trade. Pending congressional approval of the Wrangell–Saint Elias National Park proposal, Ahtna hopes to become a codeveloper of the area in cooperation with the National Park Service.[7]

NANA Regional Corporation, a moderate-sized corporation based in Kotzebue, won a $15 million contract in 1974 for its Security Systems Division to guard the northern pipeline camps. It then acquired NANA Oilfield Services and NANA Environmental Systems, both involved in the North Slope oil fields. The corporation built a $2.6 million hotel in Kotzebue and owns a modern apartment building as well. The corporation acquired jade mining claims in the Brooks Range and also became involved in the reindeer business. The Aleut Corporation invested some of its funds in two 120-foot crabber draggers and another 222-foot fishing vessel and in a joint-venture exploration for copper.[8]

The Bering Straits Native Corporation invested in transportation, construction, and housing—industries most crucial to its Nome-based shareholders. It bought Pacific Alaska Airlines, a nonscheduled charter company; Alaska Truck Transport, a trucking firm based in Anchorage and Fairbanks;

Reindeer in a corral near Nome. Photograph by Laura Kosell, Nome, Alaska.

and Coastal Barge Lines. After the purchase of Coastal Barge Lines, Bering Straits formed a corporation called Grand Alaska, Inc., which includes Anchorage Trailer Sales and Fairbanks Mobile Home Sales, both of which use the barge line to ship their units to Alaska. Also under consideration was the possibility of building mobile homes on the Seward Peninsula, and after two years of joint ventures with Central Construction of Seattle, Bering Straits bought the company. Although Central Construction had operated almost exclusively in Alaska, corporate management planned to extend operations to Washington, Montana, Oregon, and Idaho. The corporation also bought a large block of stock in Alaska National Bank of the North and acquired half interest in the Alaska branch of the California-based engineering and surveying firm CH2M Hill, called CH2M Hill of Alaska.[9] Unfortunately, many of the investments were hastily made, and the corporation lost much money.

The Southeast Alaska Corporation, Sealaska, was the most cautious investor. While waiting for 400,000 acres of timberland to be conveyed by December, 1977, the corporation constructed a 30,000-square-foot office building in downtown Juneau.[10]

Koniag, Inc., limited its investment to Kodiak Island, buying the Shelikof Net Company and Kodiak Outboard, a retail marine supplier. It built a combination office and apartment building in downtown Kodiak and through its Kodiak Kwik Copy offered commercial printing. Still unsettled were the alternate land selections of Koniag, Inc., which it hoped to make on North Slope acreage with oil-and-gas potential.[11]

Doyon Corporation is based in Fairbanks and, with 12 million acres, is the largest regional corporation. It has concentrated on developing the natural resources of the region, such as oil and gas, asbestos, and gold. In 1975, Doyon concluded a contract with the Louisiana Land and Exploration Company for oil-and-gas exploration in the Kandik area, near the Canadian border east of Circle City. In addition, the consortium

A commercial salmon processing facility of the Bering Straits Regional Corporation. Photograph by Laura Kosell, Nome.

Doyon shareholders employed on Doyon rig no. 9, a development oil drilling rig owned by Doyon Drilling, Inc., a joint venture under contract to ARCO Alaska. Courtesy Doyon, Ltd., Fairbanks.

made up of BP Alaska Exploration, Inc., Ethyl Corporation, General Crude Oil Co., McIntyre Mines, and Union Carbide explored Doyon lands for oil-and-gas deposits. So far, however, no oil or gas has been found. Doyon also had a joint venture with Alaska International Construction for maintenance of the pipeline haul road north of the Yukon.[12]

Chugach Natives, Inc., based in Cordova, invested its money around the rim of the Gulf of Alaska in such ventures as the development of deep-water ports to service offshore oil-and-gas exploration. As one of the largest landowners in Seward, the corporation planned the development of subdivisions and also put money into the pioneer aquaculture efforts by the Cordova Aquatic Marketing Association.[13]

The preceding sketch briefly outlines the variety of economic activities and investments pursued by the regional corporations. The new corporations organized just in time to take advantage of one of Alaska's greatest boom periods. Pipeline construction enabled the new corporations to gain valuable business experience through contracts ranging from security to catering and from heavy construction to revegetation along the pipeline right-of-way. Many of these contracts were joint ventures and brought needed profits to the corporations during their early years.

## THE REGIONAL CORPORATIONS MATURE

By the summer of 1977 the pipeline was complete, and the Native corporations had to compete in a shrinking market. Mineral exploration continued on corporate lands, but generally the corporations began to consolidate their holdings in the post-pipeline period. Doyon Corporation invested a large amount of money in acquiring the historic Pioneer Inn hotel and shopping complex in Lahaina, on the island of Maui, Hawaii.

Mr. and Mrs. Andrew Isaac, of Dot Lake. Chief Isaac is the traditional Athapaskan chief of the Doyon Region. Courtesy Doyon, Ltd., Fairbanks.

Sealaska Corporation, which did not participate in pipeline activities, bought the Alaska Brick Company of Anchorage.[14]

This new acquisition conducts between $11 and $12 million worth of business a year and includes a concrete-block operation; Pacific Western Lines, a barge operation; and Alaska National Corporation, an import-export branch which imports building products from Japan. Development of the corporations' substantial timber resources is tied up by environmental regulations and the threat of lengthy lawsuits. The Bristol Bay Native Corporation, which had made the largest purchase with the acquisition of Peter Pan Seafoods, added to its investment by buying the Anchorage Westward Hotel, Alaska's largest hotel, with twenty-two stories and 546 rooms. The purchase price amounted to approximately $18 million.[15]

The Native regional corporations have become firmly established in Alaska's economy. They have contributed somewhat to diversifying the state's economy. Obviously, problems remain. The settlement act provided a twenty-year tax moratorium on Native lands, which has brought much pressure on corporate leadership to put lands into production. Village corporation permission is required before the regional corporations are allowed to explore and produce subsurface mineral deposits. It is already apparent to many that regional corporate profit goals are often incompatible with village subsistence goals. Perhaps a congressional extension of the tax moratorium will ease some of the development pressures.

Perhaps most important, most of the Native corporations have realized that they are business corporations first and foremost and Native corporations second. This has contributed to the split between the village Natives and the so-called Brooks Brothers Natives—individuals who have seen and experienced a much larger segment of the world than their village brothers and have assumed leadership in the corporations and in political life. It can be safely assumed that the corporate structure, just like the historic white incursions, will materially contribute to the disappearance of traditional Native life-styles. Before the settlement Alaskan Natives roamed over much of Alaska in search of subsistence; since the settlement they have become landowners, their domain defined by one stake in each of four corners. Now Natives worry about trespassing and rights-of-way just as their white neighbors do.

## THE 1975 OMNIBUS ACT

It was to be expected that a complex piece of legislation like ANCSA would be ambiguous in parts and that Congress would soon be asked to define its intent more clearly and rectify some of the apparent injustices. In 1975, Congress passed such an omnibus act, which became law in 1976. A major part of the new law concerns the Cook Inlet region, where not enough lands were available for regional and village corporation selections. The law authorized a complicated

exchange of lands among the United States, the Cook Inlet Region, Inc., and the state of Alaska as a means of satisfying the region's entitlement under the Alaska Native Claims Settlement Act of 1971.

To accomplish this land exchange, the governor and the Alaska legislature, after heated debate, reached some accord. The legislature then enacted the necessary legislation authorizing the exchange, to become effective March 12, 1977. The legislature had acted hurriedly to meet a congressionally mandated deadline and recognized that comprehensive legislation was needed for future land exchanges. After much deliberation and helpful guidance from the Joint Federal-State Land Use Planning Commission, the legislature enacted the necessary regulations that clearly spelled out the requirements to be met before land exchanges could be made by the executive branch.[16]

The Omnibus Act clarified many more sections. For example, it extended Native enrollment for one more year and provided that monies received under ANCSA were not to be used in lieu of various federal programs but only for extinguishing land claims.[17]

By the spring of 1977 only 3.5 million acres of land of some 44 million acres due the Native corporations had been conveyed. The federal bureaucracy was working very slowly indeed.

## PROBLEMS OF THE NATIVE REGIONAL CORPORATIONS

The regional corporations have now been operating for some time. One of the most troublesome issues affecting them was the dispute over the distribution of revenues derived from their large land entitlements. There was bitter fighting and much ill will as the corporations tried to determine how the revenue from oil, minerals, and forests could be distributed equitably to all Alaska

Natives. The "7i dispute," as it became known after the paragraph and subchapter in ANCSA, was finally settled in 1982. According to the agreement, each regional corporation retains 30 percent of its revenues from natural resources, while it pays the remaining 70 percent into a resource pool income from all of the regional corporations. These pool funds are then redistributed according to the number of shareholders each regional corporation has. The regional corporation then redistributes half of the funds to the village corporations in its region and to at-large shareholders, while the remainder is income for that regional corporation and its shareholders.[18]

Although the "7i dispute" has finally been resolved, many shareholders and regional corporation executives are worried about 1991, when Native shareholders will be able to sell their corporation stock to anyone they choose. The fear is that Caucasian investors will buy up much of the stock, thereby gaining control of the regional corporations. Recently the U.S. General Accounting Office surveyed the regional and village corporations and found that 62 of the 13 regional and 129 village corporations do not favor the opening of stock sales to outsiders and believe that this provision of ANCSA should be repealed outright, while 42 corporations believed that Congress should extend the deadline. Only 24 of the corporations believed that the stock-sale provision was appropriate, and two believed that the option should become available before 1991.[19]

At the request of Senator Ted Stevens (Re-

Eskimo dancers at the Alaska Federation of Natives convention in the Howard Rock Ballroom, named for the late Eskimo editor of the *Tundra Times,* in the Sheraton Calista Hotel. The Calista Corporation, second-largest of the regional corporations and centered in the Yukon–Kuskokwim region, owns the luxury Sheraton Hotel in Anchorage. Photograph courtesy Ross V. Soboleff/Sealaska Corporation, Juneau.

publican, Alaska) the General Accounting Office is in the process of reviewing the financial aspects of the Alaska Native Claims Settlement Act, and reviews of other aspects of the act will follow. In fact, there is much dissatisfaction with the settlement act among many members of Alaska's Native community. Jeanie Leask, the 1984 president of the Alaska Federation of Natives which originally took the lead in lobbying for passage of the act, has charged that ANCSA is surrounded by myths and misconceptions. For example, there is the belief that the settlement act was to address and solve all the problems Alaska Natives face, running the gamut from alcoholism to the inadequacies of village life. Leask stated that she often heard the remark that the "Natives were given all that land and money—why do they want more?" In reality, she continued, ANCSA was only a limited economic tool, a land settlement which did not affect the special relationship Natives enjoy with the federal government. Nor did it affect Native rights to self-government under the Indian Reorganization Act of 1934 and the Alaska Reorganization Act of 1936. As Native leaders and shareholders have come to realize the limitations of the corporate structure, they have begun to study the possibility of vesting control in the 44 million acres in tribal governments, represented by traditional councils or Indian Reorganization Act Councils, and membership organizations in which participation would not depend on stock ownership. Consideration of these alternatives, she concluded, was urgent because of the looming deadline of 1991, when shareholders will be able to sell their stock and other protections in ANCSA will expire as well.[20]

The whole question of tribal government charters, or the Native sovereignty issue, perplexes many Alaskans. In April, 1984, for example, Alaska's Governor Bill Sheffield asked the Department of the Interior to delay issuing a tribal government charter under the provisions of the Indian Reorganization Act of 1934 and its 1936 extension to Alaska to the Native village of Eagle on the Yukon River. Don Wright, a Fairbanks resident, the former president of the Alaska Federation of Natives and a long-term champion of Native self-government, immediately claimed that the governor's action broke a campaign promise he had made in 1982 to respect tribal sovereignty. Horace Biederman, Jr., the president of the Eagle village corporation, reminded Sheffield that he had promised the village not to oppose IRA governments. Obviously, Biederman concluded, Sheffield "speaks with a forked tongue." What is clear is that Sheffield, on the campaign trail, apparently was not acquainted with the Indian Reorganization Act or the 1936 Alaska Reorganization Act. Furthermore, it is easy to make promises on the campaign trail. Once the candidate is elected, issues become much more complex than imagined. This seems to be the case in this matter. John Shively, Sheffield's chief of staff and a former Native corporation executive, issued a statement clarifying the governor's intent. Sheffield had only asked for time to study the Eagle constitution because it is different in important respects from the approximately seventy IRA constitutions mostly issued in the 1940s. While those documents were general in nature, the Eagle constitution has some powers specifically identified, such as the taxing authority and the right to issue charters to businesses. In short, Sheffield continued to support the issuance of IRA constitutions but desired that they maintained the status quo.[21] Basically the whole issue is a federal responsibility and doubtlessly will eventually be settled by the courts.

As previously stated, many Natives have become dissatisfied with the Alaska Native Claims Settlement Act of 1971. A 1984 article in the magazine *Alaska Native News*, signed by "The Arctic Fox," was entitled "Who Signed for Me?" The author claimed that the federal government, the Alaska

Longshoremen loading the first shipment of logs from Sealaska Timber Corporation lands on the *Young Seagull,* 1980. Photograph courtesy Rafael Gonzales/Sealaska Corporation, Juneau.

state government, and the big oil companies "all gave a great sigh of relief" after President Nixon signed the legislation into law in December, 1971. Now the trans-Alaska pipeline could be constructed, issues of federal responsibility and Native sovereignty could be slowly terminated, the state treasury could swell with oil revenues, and fundamental diversity among Alaska's populations could be quietly erased. The author further argued that ANCSA

> was designed, written, debated, and signed by Congress and the president, not by me. I'm sure they had all of our best interests at heart because, in essence, they said, through the Act, "we are the best possible world, become like us. Organize your wealth into corporations, . . . be able to sell your corporate shares and lands in 1991, have some fun with the money or invest the money, and retire to Hawaii and Florida. If you can't, don't, or won't make a profit and sell the corporate

shares in 1991, learn what it is like to have your lands taken for tax default and sold to strangers."

The author concluded that "the Act is sure unsettling to me. Somehow it seems a permanent, implacable, and inescapable part of reality, like Judgment Day. Whatever happens in 1991 seems so final. When the title to fee simple lands passes into someone else's hands, there will be no way to recover it, short of military conquest." [22]

"The Arctic Fox" was correct, at least in part, because at the beginning of the congressional battle for ANCSA, the Alaska Federation of Natives outlined its demands for a settlement in a 1969 memorandum. The AFN plan included full title to 40 million acres of land, to be allocated among the villages according to their size; $500 million; a 2 percent royalty in perpetuity on all revenues from all other public and state lands in Alaska; and the creation of a state-wide Native development corporation and up to twelve regional development corporations to manage the land and money received in a settlement. Each Native was to receive stock in the development corporations. The charters of these corporations were to be very flexible so that they could make the most of the resources they had, the land, mineral rights to some of the land, and the revenues provided by the settlement. Villages would be able to convey their lands to their local regional corporation or the state corporation, provided the regional corporation agreed. Mineral rights on all village land was to be conveyed automatically to the regional corporations, and revenues derived from any minerals found there were to be divided fifty-fifty between the regional corporations controlling the rights and the other regional corporations. The $500 million in federal money and royalty revenues were to be distributed on the following basis: 75 percent to the villages (but only 20 percent distributed there on a per capita basis, while the rest would go for public projects), 20 percent to the regional corporations, and 5 percent to the state-wide corporation. It was an innovative approach, but the AFN had to accept compromises during the legislative battle. There would be no 2 percent royalty in perpetuity and no statewide corporation.[23] And there were other compromises as well.

## THE ALASKA NATIVE REVIEW COMMISSION

With the widespread uneasiness about ANCSA, the Innuit Circumpolar Conference in 1983 created the Alaska Native Review Commission to examine the intent of ANCSA and its consequences in the lives of Alaska Natives. It hired Thomas R. Berger, a former chief justice of British Columbia who had gained international recognition for his pursuit of Native rights issues in Canada, to chair the commission. The commission was to hold extensive hearings in Anchorage and Fairbanks and then move to the villages and elsewhere to listen to people discussing their expectations of and experiences with ANCSA. The commission's mandate was to examine the social and economic status of Alaska Natives; the Alaska Native Claims Settlement Act of 1971; the policies the United States has historically followed in settling claims by Native Americans; the functions of the Native corporations established by ANCSA; the social, cultural, economic, political, and environmental impact of ANCSA; and the significance of ANCSA to indigenous peoples throughout the world. At the conclusion Justice Berger was to prepare a report, developed from the testimony collected at the hearings, and recommendations to protect and promote Native interests.[24]

The commission held its first hearings in Anchorage over a three-week period from the end of February to the middle of March, 1984. It moved to Fairbanks at the end of April and then held hearings in the villages and elsewhere. Some of the comments made by those testifying in Fairbanks well expressed the dissatisfactions, anxieties, and ambiguities many Natives feel about ANCSA. For example, Jeff Oates, a member of Doyon Corporation, remarked that he would "like to see some of this land put in shareholders' hands so they can utilize it." Others thought that the 44 million acres and the nearly $1 billion settlement had been inadequate. Ron Silas of Minto testified that

Somehow I feel ripped off. I look at this piece of paper for my land from the village corporation, and I could just about throw a rock across it. It's just a little piece. I look at the map my grandfather made of the land they wanted, and it covered the whole Minto Flats. On the rest of it [state or federal land], if I go out hunting, I kind of feel like I'm trespassing on somebody else's land which should be mine. I don't feel we did receive enough land.

John Moses, a Calista Corporation share-holder, noted that his Native language did not include words for acre, square, or corporation. In fact, "American society through this act has already fenced our Native people into tiny square boxes. Above all, they have fenced our great grandchildren into tiny square boxes."[25]

Witnesses at the Fairbanks hearings, as elsewhere, both praised and criticized the Native corporations holding the land. Several speakers acknowledged the economic and political benefits the corporations had brought, but many complained that corporate management seemed to be out of touch with the average shareholder. Clara Johnson, a Doyon Corporation shareholder, was concerned that "the corporations have split us as people. There's no communication between the people who run the corporations and the shareholders." Johnson explained that traditional Native decision making was handled by consensus, which was absent from the corporate decision-making process. In fact, there existed "a real sense of disharmony in the way the system operates," she concluded.[26] Berger's report was published in 1985 in a volume entitled *Village Journey: The Report of the Alaska Native Review Commission.*

## NATIVE CORPORATIONS IN THEIR SECOND DECADE

How well had the regional corporations performed as they started their second decade of existence? No general statement can be made, but it is clear that all have had their ups and downs. Alex Raider, a Canadian citizen, assumed the presidency of the Calista Corporation in June, 1981. His predecessor, Oscar Kawagley, was fired in March of that year after the announcement that the corporation had lost $7.1 million the previous year. Worse, Calista had lost approximately $20 million since ANCSA established it and its sister corporations in 1971. After less than two years at the helm

as Calista's chief executive officer, Raider announced a dramatic turn-around, its first profit after ten years of successive losses. Raider, a lawyer with a background in real estate and management consulting, cut the corporation's losses to $1.5 million in 1981 and then announced a $4.2 million profit in 1982. In 1981, Calista Corporation owned six subsidiaries, but only one, the commercial fishing vessel *Calista Sea,* had earned a profit in 1980. Raider decided that the losing subsidiaries had to be eliminated. He sold Esca-Tech, a geophysical survey company, to the Ninilchik Native Corporation. It was a bad bargain for the latter, because Esca-Tech subsequently filed for bankruptcy. Raider eliminated other unprofitable operations, including R&R Travel; Bayport Mobile Homes, a Valdez Trailer Court; Pier 48, a tourist development in Seattle; and Cal-Mar Construction Company. Calista Corporation, however, reentered the building business with the creation of Calista Construction in 1982.[27]

Raider retained only two subsidiaries, the Sheraton Hotel in Anchorage, a first-class hostelry which lost money from the day it opened its doors in 1979 until 1982, when it earned a profit of more than $1 million, and Settler's Bay, a real estate development that consistently lost money before Raider assumed corporate management. Settler's Bay began selling homesites and condominiums in 1982, and Raider predicted that it would make a profit in 1983.[28]

After ridding Calista Corporation of its losing subsidiaries, Raider turned his attention toward the development of new and profitable ventures. In 1983 he announced the formation of several joint ventures, including construction and steel for heavy building jobs, airport design and construction, and export of Alaska and import of Japanese products. The ultimate goal is to build Calista Corporation into a large, profitable company that can help provide jobs and services for its shareholders.[29]

The remaining twelve regional Native

An unidentified Sealaska shareholder driving a truck for the Sealaska Timber Corporation. In 1980 and 1981 Sealaska Corporation maintained a training program for shareholders in logging and road-building projects. The company eventually discontinued the program as too costly for the number of people being trained. Photograph courtesy of Ross V. Soboleff/Sealaska Corporation.

corporations also experienced dramatic changes in 1983. A few examples will suffice. Sealaska Native Corporation, the largest, posted a profit of $1.17 for the first six months of 1983 after losing a staggering $7.65 million for the same period in the previous year, with huge 1982 year-end losses totaling $27.99 million.[30]

Sealaska Chairman and Chief Executive Officer Byron I. Mallott announced an operating profit of $2,608,000 for the first six months of 1983. He warned, however, that future prospects were not entirely rosy be-

cause of continuing low timber prices and an unstable seafood market, the two major commodities Sealaska produces.[31]

The Bristol Bay Native Corporation, the seventh-largest of Alaska's thirteen Native regional corporations, recorded a 375 percent increase in profits during the 1983 fiscal year, primarily because of the profitable operation of the Anchorage Westward Hilton Hotel and the Pacific Food Products Company. The corporation gladdened shareholder's hearts when it announced after-tax earnings of $3.47 million for the year ended March 31, 1983. In 1982 the corporation showed net profits of $729,817 and $63,302 for the fiscal year 1981. Obviously shareholders were pleased because earnings had increased steadily for the past three years. The Bristol Bay Native Corporation also held varying interests in numerous businesses, from a 10 percent interest in the United Bancorporation to a 33 percent interest in the Chignik Canning Company, and had also entered into a number of joint enterprises from building oil drilling rigs to providing support services for the petroleum industry.[32]

The Arctic Slope Native Corporation reported a $6.9 million loss for 1982. Most of the loss stemmed from the approximately $9.8 million it had to pay as a result of the previously mentioned so-called 7i settlement, which affected the Arctic Slope Native Corporation dramatically because of the region's large oil-income base. President Edward E. Hopson, Sr., and Executive Vice-President Lawrence A. Dineen told stockholders that, although they had hoped for a 7i settlement more favorable to the corporation, in actuality it was "a blessing," because the dispute had been costly and time-consuming for the past eight years. "Moreover, nobody knew the rules. Now we have more rules than we would like, but at least we know what they are."[33]

The Arctic Slope Native Corporation controlled numerous subsidiaries, among them the Arctic Slope Alaska General Construction Company. Some of the 1982 losses were attributed to General Construction of Hawaii, a division of ASAG, and there was also a considerable decline in construction activity at Prudhoe Bay and in the National Petroleum Reserve: Arctic Slope Native Corporation's other subsidiaries include Arctic Slope Consulting Engineers; Eskimos, Inc., which operates gravel pits in Barrow, rents and repairs heavy construction equipment, operates an auto service station, and stores and distributes locally used petroleum products; and Tundra Tours, Inc., which owns and operates the Top of the World Hotel at Barrow and also provides contract bus service to school districts in Fairbanks, Wasilla, and Palmer.[34]

Koniag, Inc., the regional corporation for Kodiak, has experienced particularly distressing times. In the spring of 1983 it announced that it might have to seek protection under chapter 11 of the federal bankruptcy laws. J. F. Morse, the executive officer whom shareholders blamed for some of the problems, resigned and left Alaska. As early as in the spring of 1982 some members of the boards of directors had already asked for a management change and had succeeded, in part.[35] If Koniag, Inc., avoids bankruptcy, it will have been a narrow escape.

The problems started soon after Morse assumed management responsibilities on July 1, 1979. By late 1980, Koniag, Inc., was ensnarled in a series of lawsuits over a scheme to merge the regional corporation with several village corporations. Koniag, Inc., obviously was interested in promising timberlands on Afognak Island held by the village corporations. Finally, in January, 1983, Anchorage Superior Court Judge Douglas Serdahely held that the management of Koniag, Inc., had made false and misleading statements in proxies sent to shareholders before the merger vote. The litigation cost Koniag, Inc., almost half a million dollars, and that was just one of the many financial woes besetting the corporation. It invested heavily in the seafood industry, but a few poor years led to losses, and in 1981 it invested $2 million to become a limited partner in an oil-refinery project in Phoenix, Arizona. This undertaking, however, also became entangled in legal controversies, and Koniag, Inc., sued to attempt to recover its investment.[36]

Doyon, Ltd., the interior Native corporation, for the eighth consecutive year reported a profit in 1982, a very good record indeed. The corporation has focused on resource developments in Alaska. In August, 1982, drilling rig no. 9, built by Doyon, Ltd., subcontractors, began operations under contract to ARCO Alaska, Inc., in the Kuparuk River oil field. Better yet, the drilling rig was built under budget and employed thirty stockholders.[37] In 1983, however, the corporation lost a large amount of money when an oil-refinery project at North Pole, Alaska, failed to gain the needed financing.

NANA, Inc., the Kotzebue-based Native corporation, reported total assets worth $67.6 million in 1982, up from $64.9 million in 1981. But it also showed a decline in income from $1,598 million in 1981 to $1,319 million in 1982. In 1982, NANA, Inc., also concluded an agreement with Cominco Alaska, Inc., which allows that mineral company to develop the Red Dog zinc and lead deposit north of Kotzebue, believed to be one of the largest zinc deposits in the world.[38]

The thirteenth Native corporation is also the smallest, representing Natives who no longer live in Alaska. Based in Seattle, it recently underwent a complete change in management. President and Chairman Kurt Engelstad from Portland, Oregon, believed that the corporation had a chance to succeed. It suffered a great loss, which, however, was fully insured, when its $14 million fish processing vessel *Al-Ind-Esk-A-Sea* burned and sank in 1982. Fish processing remains

Waterfront view of the Petersburg Chatham Strait Seafood processing facility, Sealaska Corporation's operation in Petersburg. Photograph courtesy of Betsy Brenneman/Sealaska Corporation.

the corporation's primary business; it continues to operate four multipurpose vessels mainly in salmon-rendering operations, and it also holds a 10 percent interest in dock facilities at Captain's Bay. With about 4,500 shareholders it reported total assets worth $7.2 million in 1982, a decline of 53.2 percent from a high of $15.4 million in 1981.[39]

The foregoing narrative gives examples of the changing fortunes of the Native corporations since they started operations in 1972. Undoubtedly the corporations will continue to change, and some may not survive at all. It is clear, however, that they have become important forces in Alaska's economy, and also in the lives of their stockholders.

# 13. LAND CLAIMS AND LAND CONSERVATION

Many different factors made possible the Alaska Native Claims Settlement Act of 1971. Among these must be counted the civil rights revolution of the 1950s, which led to the landmark Supreme Court decision in *Brown* v. *Board of Education of Topeka, Kansas* in 1954, which declared that "in the field of public education the doctrine of 'separate but equal' has no place. Separate educational facilities are inherently unequal." Subsequent to the 1954 Supreme Court decision, Congress passed Civil Rights Acts in 1957 and 1960 which modestly increased the number of black voters in 1960. Congress passed another Civil Rights Act in 1964 (P.L. 88-351), which, among other provisions, barred unequal application of voting registration requirements and made a sixth-grade education (if in English) a rebuttable presumption of literacy.[1]

## THE SCRAMBLE TO DIVIDE ALASKA

The court decision and federal legislation, together with the work of civil rights activists and women's rights advocates, sensitized Americans to the plight of minorities. Although Alaska was remote from the civil rights struggles in the contiguous states, modern communications media—television, radio, and newspapers and magazines—carried the news of the civil rights struggle into every town and village in the North. Indians, Aleuts, and Eskimos watched, listened, and in time became politicized, a development hastened by their long-standing demands for compensation for the lands taken from them. The state government's selections of acreage under the statehood grant conflicted with Native claims and speeded political awareness. In October, 1962, Natives found a statewide voice with the publication of *Tundra Times*, edited by Eskimo artist Howard Rock and modestly financed by Dr. Henry Forbes, a Massachusetts physician who was chairman of the Alaska Committee for the Association of American Indian Affairs. Native leaders established several new regional organizations, but it was not until 1966 that the Natives established a statewide organization, the Alaska Federation of Native Associations. They changed the name to Alaska Federation of Natives in early 1967.

In 1968, the Atlantic-Richfield Company discovered the huge Prudhoe Bay oil field. It soon became apparent that the pipeline necessary to transport the oil from the Arctic to tidewater at Valdez would have to cross lands claimed by Natives. The civil rights revolution had created a climate in which the majority now listened to minority concerns and demands. In addition, the necessity to get the oil to market resulted in a sustained and energetic effort to resolve the Native claims. An unlikely coalition of interest groups, each with its own agenda and goals, worked together to solve the Native claims issue. Included were the oil companies, the state of Alaska, various environmental organizations, the Natives, Congress, and the executive branch of the federal government. The combined efforts of these groups produced the Alaska Native Claims Settlement Act of 1971. But perhaps the problems had just begun, because now the Natives, the state, and the various executive agencies of the federal government scrambled to cut up Alaska.

## FURTHER PROTECTIVE LEGISLATION

As well as building on the momentum of the civil rights movement, there can be no question that Congress passed the Alaska Native Claims Settlement Act at a time when the nation had moved into a new era in federal land planning and management, which emphasized protection of natural and other environmental values on the remainder of the public domain. Several major pieces of legislation passed by Congress in the 1960s and 1970s reflected this changing national mood and had important bearing on the evolving controversy over Alaska lands.

The first of these was the Wilderness Act of 1964, which directed the major federal land-management agencies to conduct detailed reviews of roadless areas under their jurisdiction and to recommend which lands Congress should include in a national wilderness preservation system.[2]

On January 1, 1970, President Nixon signed into law the National Environmental Policy Act (NEPA) as the first measure in what he called the "environmental decade of the 1970s." Many commentators and observers originally thought the measure to be only a vague statement of environmental consciousness. It quickly became clear, however, that it was a firm directive requiring federal agencies to prepare lengthy and detailed environmental-impact statements on all federal actions that might significantly affect the quality of the environment.[3] Whenever a federal land-management agency in Alaska proposed to add to its landholdings, it became subject to the NEPA provisions, necessitating the development of full environmental-impact statements. Not only did these studies employ an army of consultants, but they also ensured that both economic and environmental values came under closer public scrutiny during the so-called d-2 controversy than for any previous major land-management decision in the United States. During the legislative battle for passage of ANCSA, Congress included section 17(d)(2) in the measure to gain the support of the conservation forces. It authorized the secretary of the interior to withdraw up to 80 million acres of vacant, unreserved, and unappropriated federal public lands for study as possible additions to the national park, forest, wildlife refuge, and wild and scenic river systems. Congress, however, reserved to itself the right to make final decisions on the lands withdrawn for study. Section 17(d)(2) created an uproar in Alaska, and in Congress as well, pitting conservation groups against development-minded interests.

The Joint Federal-State Land Use Planning Commission, not without dissent among its members, made its first recommendation in August, 1973. Established in 1972 by the state of Alaska and the federal government as part of ANCSA, it was to serve for nearly a decade in which major changes in landownership and land management took place. Its goal was to create a framework for the use and protection of Alaska lands and resources in the years to come.[4] Reflecting its largely Alaskan composition, it stressed the "multiple-use" concept for the 78 million acres the secretary had withdrawn in 1972. The commission

The Katmai National Park and Preserve, which provides protection of the habitat of the Alaska brown grizzly bear. These four are salmon-fishing in the McNeil River. Photograph by Keith Trexler. Courtesy U.S. National Park Service.

urged that more than 60 million acres be opened for limited mineral development.[5]

At the same time, conservation groups lobbied vigorously for the creation of parks, wilderness areas, and refuges, and an Alaska task force in the Department of the Interior formulated alternative proposals for the 80-odd million acres. The task force was subject to the varying pressures of the industry interests, the conservationists, and the state, all wanting the land for themselves. But it also had to deal with federal agencies: the Forest Service intended to create vast national forests, while the Bureau of Land Management desired to maintain its control.[6]

In December, 1973, Secretary Rogers C. B. Morton asked Congress to add 63.8 million acres to the national park and refuge systems. He proposed three new national parks: the Gates of the Arctic, in the Brooks Range; a park in the Wrangell Mountains; and a park centered around Lake Clark, in southwestern Alaska. Mount McKinley National Park was to be enlarged with parcels of land on both the north and the south. Morton further proposed nine new or expanded wildlife refuges encompassing 31.5 million acres and the creation of three new national forests and expansion of the Chugach National Forest, involving some 18.8 million acres.[7] Congress had until December, 1978, to decide precisely which lands were to be put into which categories. In the meantime, the conservationists, the state, and various extractive interests lobbied for their pet schemes.

As a result of increasing demands for

Steller Sea Lion Rookery in the Kenai Fjords National Park. Photograph by M. Woodbridge Williams. Courtesy U.S. National Park Service.

natural resources, such as timber, minerals, and energy from public lands, Congress passed several pieces of legislation designed to improve the land-planning and management functions of the Forest Service and the Bureau of Land Management. This legislation was also a response to the growing national concern for environmental quality, with an emphasis on protection, preservation, and recreational, nonexploitative uses of the land. In 1960 the Multiple Use–Sustained Yield Act gave the Forest Service its first statutory authority to manage the lands under its jurisdiction for a number of different uses simultaneously. It also gave the Forest Service the legal basis for fending off pressures from single-use advocates such as wildlife and wilderness champions and timber interests. Two other pieces of legislation extended and reemphasized that pol-

icy. The Forest and Rangeland Renewable Resources Planning Act of 1974 and the National Forest Management Act of 1976 required that national forest lands be managed on the basis of detailed inventories of the resources, future-demand projections, careful consideration of alternative land uses and management schemes, extended public participation in the planning process, and consultation and coordination with local, state, and federal agencies.[8]

With the passage of the Federal Land Policy and Management Act of 1976, also known as the Bureau of Land Management Organic Act, Congress established similar policies for that bureau. The Organic Act changed the bureau from primarily a land-disposal agency to a land-management agency. Congress instructed the BLM to manage the remaining public

domain lands for multiple uses. The BLM
was now included within the authority of
the Wilderness Act of 1964, which required
it to conduct wilderness studies of all its
roadless areas. In effect, the act marked the
closing of the public domain by ending land
disposals with but few exceptions.[9]

## THE BATTLE FOR LANDS BREWS

With the passage of the act of 1976 a battle
began for the control of the last of the nation's uncommitted lands in Alaska. Each of
the federal land-management agencies now
studied the d-2 lands and staked out large
acreages. The Forest Service proposed that
44 million acres be added to its holdings in
the form of fourteen new national forests.
The National Park Service claimed some
of the same lands and asked for 33 million
acres to establish several large new national
parks and to expand the boundaries of
existing parks. The Fish and Wildlife Service wanted 30 million acres for new wildlife refuges to protect waterfowl nesting
and breeding grounds as well as other habitats. About half of this acreage conflicted
with either National Park Service or Forest Service proposals. The Bureau of Land
Management had not officially become a
land-management agency until passage of
the act of 1976. Therefore, it was in a weak
position to claim lands for permanent management and watched practically helpless
as other federal land-management agencies
prepared proposals that would have left the
bureau with scattered parcels of marginal
lands that neither the state of Alaska and
the Natives nor the other federal agencies
wanted.

As the d-2 battle proceeded, each federal
agency sought political support for its particular proposals. Various interest groups
began to fall in line behind one or the other
agency in preparation for the upcoming congressional battle. Environmental groups in
Alaska and the contiguous states desired
that maximum acreage be placed under the

A magnificent wolf in its natural habitat in
Alaska. Courtesy Alaska Department of Fish
and Game.

management of the National Park Service
and the Fish and Wildlife Service, where
it would be managed almost exclusively
to safeguard natural values and wildlife
habitat or recreational uses that would
not impair the wild character of the land.
Development interests cried foul and described this kind of management as a "lock-
up" of America's last remaining storehouse
of resource wealth. They demanded that
the Forest Service and the Bureau of Land
Management, the two multiple-use agencies, obtain jurisdiction over the maximum
acreage.

The Native community was divided in
this battle. Many rural villagers favored the
conservationists, hoping to be provided
greater protection for their subsistence style
of living, while regional corporate leaders,

intent on maximizing income, more often joined those supporting the multiple use of federal lands.

When legislative proposals to resolve the d-2 land issue were introduced in Congress in 1977, officials of President Jimmy Carter's administration, members of Congress, Alaskans, conservationists, developers, and national lobbyists for varied interests joined in emphasizing the importance of the legislation.[10]

How much and which federal public lands in Alaska should be permanently reserved to protect their natural values and under what management systems were the problems that had to be resolved. Much of the most bitter fighting in Congress centered on this issue. But several other questions also had to be dealt with at the same time. What effect would wilderness preservation have on Alaska's and the nation's

economies? Should the state of Alaska play only an advisory role in the management of federal lands, or should it be given considerable powers to affect federal land-management policy? What actions were necessary to protect the subsistence lifestyles of Alaska Natives and other rural residents, and to what extent, if any, should sport hunting be allowed in the new units of the national park system? What impact would the fractured landownership patterns have on Alaska's wildlife, particularly species like the caribou that migrate over large areas? How would the new federal units affect state and Native land selection and management, and what could be done to ensure that the state of Alaska, the Natives, and other landowners would have access across new federal conservation units? Finally, how could the state's need for transportation corridors across Alaska's vast-

Archaeologists from the University of Alaska hunt for artifacts near the trans-Alaska pipeline construction workpad north of the Yukon River. Most of the artifacts recovered were stone tools and projectile points. Courtesy Alyeska Pipeline Service Company.

ness be satisfied without adversely affecting natural values in the areas crossed?

In the congressional hearings politicians received widely differing recommendations on how to solve these questions. Obviously the variance stemmed from the very dissimilar perceptions various interest groups had about what constituted the "national interest" in Alaska's lands and resources. Many Alaskans and those associated with resource-extractive industries viewed the lands as representing important economic opportunities that could benefit the whole nation—but only if a large percentage of the lands remained open to multiple use. These groups argued that not enough was known about the resources of the lands to make a wise decision about their potential. It was premature to "lock up" the lands in restrictive management units, because only further resource exploration could reveal their full potential.

Environmentalists had a totally different point of view. They argued that Alaska's national-interest lands represented the last opportunity to save intact a significant portion of the nation's wilderness. The state and the Natives had already selected the lands with the highest potential for development of oil, gas, mineral, and other resources, they claimed. Any resources found on national-interest lands should be left in place for eventual future use.

These widely divergent views were evident in a host of bills introduced in Congress in 1977. Congressman Morris Udall (Democrat, Arizona) sponsored H.R. 39, which quickly became known as the conservationist measure. Udall proposed to create a total of 116 million acres of new conservation-system units in the state. All the units were to be made a part of the national wilderness preservation system, effectively precluding any resource development. In June of the same year Senator Ted Stevens (Republican, Alaska) introduced S. 1787, representing the views of the Alaska state government and strongly supported by

development interests. At the opposite end of the Udall measure, it proposed to put 25 million acres in new conservation units without the protective wilderness designation. An additional 57 million acres were to be placed in a new category called Federal Cooperative Lands, to be managed on a multiple-use basis under joint commission oversight, somewhat along the lines proposed by the Joint Federal-State Land Use Planning Commission for Alaska. Secretary of the Interior Cecil Andrus presented the Carter administration plan, which fell within the two extremes, proposing to set aside 92 million acres in new conservation units. Of these, 43 million acres were to be protected with the wilderness designation.

Obviously, a significant departure from section 17(d)(2) of the Alaska Native Claims Settlement Act had taken place. That law had directed that 80 million acres be set aside for study, and there had been no intention of designating some or all of the new conservation units as wilderness. The wilderness issue, however, became centrally important in the congressional d-2 land debate. Resource development interests and Alaska state government officials rejected the proposed creation of these "instant wilderness" areas, maintaining that they bypassed the formal procedures required in the Wilderness Act, which mandated agency review, public hearings, and presidential recommendations to Congress. Supporters of the concept argued that the d-2 lands had already been studied extensively in the eight years that had passed since the passage of ANCSA and that this amounted to a de facto compliance with the Wilderness Act.

To mollify state and development interests, the House Interior Subcommittee revised H.R. 39 to include less acreage and wilderness. The compromise measure, which passed the House of Representatives on May 19, 1978, by a vote of 277 to 31, included about 100 million acres in new conservation units with only 66 million acres designated as wilderness. Conservationists were jubilant—but they had not reckoned with the Senate.

Alaska's two senators, Ted Stevens and Mike Gravel, rejected the House measure and worked closely with the Senate's Energy and Natural Resources Committee and its chairman, Senator Jackson of Washington to change it. In early October, 1978, the Senate committee reported out a measure that protected about one-third less in conservation units and designated just about half as much wilderness as H.R. 39 did. In the final hours before adjournment, House and Senate leaders tried to reach a compromise. Agreement on a measure that would have put 96 million acres in conservation units and designated 50 million acres of this total as wilderness emerged, but at the last moment Senator Gravel balked and threat-

ened to filibuster the bill if it reached the Senate floor. Thereupon negotiations fell apart, and the measure died. Unable to reach a compromise, congressional leaders introduced legislation to extend the d-2 land withdrawals for another year, but Senator Gravel threatened to filibuster that as well, and Congress adjourned without action on Alaska lands legislation.

Congress had given itself until December 18, 1978, to pass Alaska lands legislation. It had failed to do so. Shortly before the deadline the Carter administration acted. Using the emergency withdrawal authority provided by section 204-e of the Federal Land Policy and Development Act of 1976, Secretary Andrus withdrew 110 million acres of Alaska lands on November 16. This withdrawal renewed the protection

Dall ram in the Denali National Park and Preserve. Photograph by Robert Belous. Courtesy U.S. National Park Service.

for the original 80 million acres of d-2 lands together with an additional 30 million acres of new lands. On December 1, 1978, President Carter used his authority under the 1906 Antiquities Act to designate 56 million acres of Alaska lands as permanent new national monuments and also directed Secretary Andrus to administratively designate 40 million acres as permanent wildlife refuges. At the request of the president, Robert Bergland, the secretary of agriculture, closed to mining another 11 million acres of lands in the Tongass and Chugach national forests. Altogether about 120 million acres were included in the different withdrawals, and only Congress could reverse these executive actions.

The battle over Alaska's lands started anew when the Ninety-sixth Congress convened in 1979. Conservationist and development interests faced each other. On one side were the state and national environmental organizations, the so-called Alaska Coalition, which eventually included fifty-two nationwide organizations. Although representing differing philosophical views, these groups were able to come together on the Alaska lands issue and form a formidable power base in the capital. These organizations were supported by a constituency several hundred thousand strong around the country. On short notice they were able to put grass-roots pressure on their senators and congressmen. Reinforcing the coalition's efforts was Americans for Alaska, a small but vocal organization whose membership included prestigious individuals such as photographer Ansel Adams, scientist Jacques Cousteau, singer John Denver, and Lady Bird Johnson, to name but a few.

On the other side were the Citizens for Management of Alaska's Lands (CMAL), representing the state of Alaska and many of its citizens and business interests, as well as many of the nation's most important oil, timber, and mining corporations. The U.S. Chamber of Commerce, the national Association of Manufacturers, and the National Rifle Association supported CMAL, and the Alaska Legislature had appropriated $5.7 million for lobbying, possible litigation, and a national media campaign to publicize CMAL's views.

## THE PLANNING COMMISSION REPORTS

On May 30, 1979, the Joint Federal-State Land Use Planning Commission for Alaska issued its final report. Commission members were convinced that the issues to be decided were comparable in scope to those of the American West in the last century. Alaska, one-fifth the size of the rest of the United States, relatively underpopulated, with vast open spaces and potentially valuable resources largely undeveloped and frequently unexplored, had captured the nation's imagination. The federal government's approach to Alaska had differed markedly from the often imprudent expansion into the western states, because in the meantime a new land ethic had evolved. No longer would resources be exploited without attention to conservation and environmental protection. Wilderness had been recognized as a scarce national resource meriting protection and preservation. Most lands remaining in the public domain would be retained in public ownership. Federal policies toward the Natives sought to foster self-determination and avoid paternalism. The commission members stated that the public interest demanded that planning precede and regulations govern significant resource development and land use.[11]

The years of labor bore fruit in the recommendations contained in the commission's final report. Commission members had looked at the state as a whole and considered the myriad public goals and interests integrally related to the protection and use of Alaska's land and resources. Its recommendations reflected this viewpoint:

1. New national parks and national wildlife refuge systems should be added to those already existing, and also join complimentary areas adjacent to established national parks, wildlife refuges, and forests to these existing units.

2. Certain lands with high natural values as well as resource potential should be managed in a flexible manner compatible with the land's natural values and largely primitive character.

3. Boundaries of new national interest units and additions to existing ones should follow hydrologic, physiographic, or other natural features and exclude privately owned areas.

4. A statewide system of wild, scenic, and recreational rivers should be created on both federal and state lands.

5. The state legislature, by statute, should recognize the public value of recreation and direct agencies to provide public recreational opportunities.

6. The state should manage fish and wildlife. Hunting, fishing, and trapping should be allowed on all national interest units. Subsistence use of fish and wildlife, where scarce, should be given preference over sport and commercial use.

7. Boundaries of proposed national parks and wildlife refuges should avoid including Alaska's major natural transportation corridor routes where possible.

8. All federal lands remaining after selections by the state of Alaska and Native corporations should be retained in public ownership.[12]

The commission then made specific recommendations providing a policy framework for future land-use decisions affecting the Arctic. Together with the general recommendations, these were meant to apply to other regions as well.

There was a host of other recommendations, but those summarized above give a flavor of the commission's thinking. It is doubtful, however, that Congress made use of much of the commission's work.

## THE CONGRESS ACTS

In early 1979, Congressman Udall reintroduced H.R. 39, but by using a parliamentary maneuver the House Interior Committee substituted a measure more favorable to development interests. When the bill reached the House floor, however, Udall succeeded in having his measure substituted. The House passed it 360 to 65. Udall's bill included 127 million acres of conservation units, with 65 million acres carrying the wilderness designation.

As in the previous year, the Senate Energy and Natural Resources Committee approved a measure with much smaller acreages. At that point conservationists persuaded Senate leaders to negotiate anew. Out of these deliberations emerged a substitute bill representing a compromise between the Udall measure and the prodevelopment Senate measure. Not until a year later, on August 19, 1980, after several days of debate and frantic lobbying efforts, did the Senate vote on the Alaska Lands Bill, and it finally passed the substitute bill by a vote of 78 to 14. The measure put 104 million acres in new conservation units; of these, 57 million acres were designated as wilderness.

There existed significant differences between the House and Senate versions that would have required a conference committee for resolution. Senate leaders informed the House, however, that if the House made any important changes in the Senate version Alaska's two senators would filibuster the measure, thereby killing any chances of enacting an Alaska lands bill in that Congress.

Young bald eagle in its nest, Katmai National Park and Preserve. Photograph by Robert Belous. Courtesy U.S. National Park Service.

## THE ALASKA NATIONAL INTEREST LANDS CONSERVATION ACT

In November, 1980, American voters rejected Carter and swept Republican Ronald Reagan into the presidency. A conservative and a westerner, Reagan had aroused fears among conservationists that he would open the public domain to unbridled exploitation. Furthermore, the Senate gained a Republican majority, and the House, although still Democratic, was more conservative. Udall, House leaders, and the conservation lobby quickly realized that the Senate bill was better than nothing. They realized that if they put off the decision for the next Congress they would probably lose all the gains they had made in the four-year congressional battle. Thereupon the House quickly passed the Senate version on November 12, and President Carter signed the Alaska National Interest Lands Conservation Act into law on December 2, 1980.[13]

The 156-page Alaska National Interest Lands Conservation Act of 1980 (ANILCA) is a complex measure. It states that it

provides sufficient protection for the national interest in the scenic, natural, cultural and environmental values on the public lands in Alaska, and at the same time provides adequate opportunity for satisfaction of the economic and social needs of the State of Alaska and its people; accordingly, the designation and disposition of the public lands in Alaska pursuant to this act are found to represent a proper balance between the reservation of national conservation system units and those public lands necessary and appropriate for more intensive use and disposition, and thus Congress believes that the need for future legislation designating new conservation system units, new national conservation system units, new national conservation areas, or new national recreation areas, has been obviated thereby.

The last part reflected the wishes of the Alaska congressional delegation to end land withdrawals.[14]

ANILCA not only established the boundaries for federal, state, Native, and private lands but also created a framework for dealing with future conflicts in land use. Those supporting economic development and those favoring environmental protection had fought bitterly over practically every provision in the act, and although the act resolved many important issues, it hardly touched that basic conflict. The battleground now shifted from Congress to the land, and undoubtedly further legislative efforts will be made to modify ANILCA. Perhaps more important for Alaska's future will be the administrative actions taken to implement the act.

Specifically, ANILCA added 104.3 million acres to conservation systems in Alaska. Of these, 43.6 million are in national parks and preserves; 53.8 million are in wildlife refuges; 3.4 million are in national monuments within the Tongass National Forest; 2.2 million are in national conservation and recreation areas; and an additional 1.2 million are included in twenty-two wild and scenic rivers. Thirty-six conservation units are scattered throughout the state and are interspersed with large and scattered state and Native lands.[15]

Taken together, the conservation units es-

Migratory waterfowl at the Creamer's field sanctuary near Fairbanks, Alaska. Photograph by Dave Johnson. Courtesy Alaska Department of Fish and Game.

tablished in Alaska before 1980 and those added by ANILCA embrace 150.8 million acres, or about 41 percent of the total area of the state. Adding the Bureau of Land Management lands outside the conservation system brings federal holdings to 60 percent of the lands in Alaska. Of the remaining 40 percent, the state of Alaska, once it completes its statehood selections, will own about 28 percent, the Natives 12 percent, and private owners 1 percent.

Obviously, the federal government has significant landholdings in Alaska. In fact, when state and Native land selections are finally completed, federal holdings in Alaska will amount to 30 percent of all federal lands nationwide. Designating almost 57 million acres of new wilderness within various units of the conservation system was a highly controversial aspect of ANILCA.

With this legislation the size of the national wilderness preservation system throughout the United States was more than tripled, increasing from 24 million to 80 million acres. Alaska now contains about 71 percent of all federal lands classified as wilderness in the United States. When all land transfers have taken place, the state will own about 104 million acres, or approximately 28 percent of Alaska's land area; private lands will amount to about 2 million acres, or 1 percent; the federal government will own approximately 228 million acres, or 60 percent of Alaska's land area; the Native Regional Corporations will own about 44 million acres, approximately 12 percent of Alaska's land area.

All lands in the park and refuge systems not designated wilderness were to be studied for possible later inclusion in the na-

Hydroseeding was used to spread a mxture of water, grass seed, and mulch over a work area to prevent erosion during and after construction of the trans-Alaska pipeline. The work above was done near the pipeline's pump station no. 12. Courtesy Alyeska Pipeline Service Company.

tional wilderness preservation system, and Congress is to receive recommendations within seven years from the date of the passage of the lands act. ANILCA, however, provides for only one study area of roughly 1.5 million acres in the Chugach National Forest. Environmentalists are particularly bitter about the exclusion of about 150,000 acres from the Misty Fjords Wilderness Area, in the Tongass National Forest near Ketchikan, to accommodate a large molybdenum exploration undertaking. In addition, to pacify the lumber interests and avoid a possible reduction in timber production because of prohibitions on logging in national forest wilderness areas, ANILCA provided for maintaining a production of 4.5 billion board feet per decade, considered to be close to the maximum. To attain that goal, the act authorized an intensive forest-management program to be funded by Congress at $40 million a year.[16]

Conservationists are also unhappy that Congress excluded roughly 1 million acres in the Arctic National Wildlife Range to allow seismic exploration for oil and gas. Opponents argue that the Porcupine caribou herd, which calves on the coastal plain, the polar bears denning there, and other wildlife, as well as natural values, could be irreparably harmed. Since major oil deposits are suspected to lie under the coastal plain, it is clear that this area will remain one of contention.[17]

It is also clear that the land and resource issue will continue in Alaska well into the 1990s. The question is and will be how the new landownership patterns will affect the state's economic development. The percentage of the federal lands in Alaska open to a variety of commercial uses is fairly high. About 50 percent of all federal lands are open to new mining claims; about 12 percent to homesteading, settlement, and other land disposals; and 75 percent to all other uses, including oil-and-gas development. In fact, Congress excluded from the conservation units lands with known commercial value and allowed sport and trophy hunting in national preserves. This allows hunting on about 40 percent of the Alaska national park system classified as preserves. Only about 10 percent of all lands in Alaska are excluded from all commercial uses, namely, the national parks and parts of national preserves designated as wilderness.

There are other provisions favorable to development. For example, Title 15 gives the president the authority to recommend to Congress that mineral exploration and development be permitted on all Alaska federal lands except the national parks and Arctic National Wildlife Range if he determines that national needs dictate such a course of action. If Congress were then to enact a joint resolution supporting the presidential recommendation, it would take effect.

Other sections of ANILCA direct the secretary of the interior to study all federal lands on the North Slope for oil-and-gas potential, wilderness and wildlife values, and transportation requirements. Within eight years (in 1988) the secretary is to submit a final report to Congress on how national interests can best be served in the area. Other provisions of the act establish procedures allowing pipelines, highways, power lines, and other transportation systems to cross conservation units where existing law prohibits such uses.

ANILCA also guarantees subsistence and other traditional users access into and through conservation units, including parks, and also authorizes occupancy permits for cabins in national parks, salmon aquacultural activities in national forest wilderness and wilderness study areas, and public-use cabins and shelters in wilderness areas. Finally, Senator Ted Stevens inserted a clause declaring that no more executive land withdrawals of more than 5,000 acres may be made in Alaska without congressional consent.

A newborn bearded seal, held by Ed Muktoyuk, left, of the Alaska Department of Fish and Game, and Atmospheric Administration pilot Bill Harrigan. Muktoyuk and Harrigan were part of a team studying the biology of seals and seal movements in the Bering Sea in 1977. The information from this and similar studies will be used to minimize the effect of offshore development on marine mammals. Alaska and federal biologists cooperated in the study. Photograph by John J. Burns. Courtesy Alaska Department of Fish and Game.

## THE SUBSISTENCE QUESTION

Congress realized that the Alaska Native Claims Settlement Act of 1971 did not transfer enough land to maintain subsistence activities. It therefore included complex provisions in ANILCA to ensure the continuation of the subsistence life-style. Federal land managers were to give highest priority to subsistence use of resources by rural Alaskans, and the state was to continue to manage fish and wildlife on federal lands as long as it adhered to that basic priority. If the state failed to do so, the federal government would take over fish and wildlife management on federal lands. Many local and regional subsistence councils and commissions have been established throughout Alaska in compliance with ANILCA. This assures rural residents a voice in the decision process. The whole process, by necessity, has to be a cooperative one among the various landowners.

Not all has been smooth sailing: during the congressional debate over ANILCA, sport-hunting groups opposed the subsistence provisions, asserting that Natives relinquished subsistence rights with the passage of ANCSA. In 1982, Alaska sportsmen's groups undertook a statewide campaign to repeal the state subsistence law passed in 1978. The voters rejected the initiative, which, if passed, would have resulted in the federal assumption of fish and wildlife management. Subsistence, however, continues to be a divisive issue.

Congress also established an Alaska land bank designed to protect undeveloped lands and promote cooperative land management among the various landowners. This is a voluntary effort in which a Native corpo-ration or anyone else can cooperate with other landowners to shield unimproved and undeveloped land from taxation. It will be recalled that, under the provisions of the Alaska Native Claims Settlement Act, lands conveyed to Native corporations were not to be taxed for twenty years as long as they remained undeveloped. The land-bank program protects lands that many village corporations chose primarily to protect subsistence activities. Lands placed in the land-bank cannot be sold or developed except as provided in the agreement. Furthermore, management of those lands must be compatible with that of adjacent state or federal lands. Lands may be withdrawn again, but if they are then developed, they become taxable. The land-bank concept, an untried one, will take several years to become fully operable.

The division of Alaska's land has resulted

Mount McKinley, at 20,320 feet the highest mountain in North America and the centerpiece of Denali National Park and Preserve. Courtesy U.S. Bureau of Outdoor Recreation.

in an often confusing patchwork of ownership. Unfortunately, it has too often proved impossible to draw rational boundary lines. Various natural resources have been divided by mixed ownership, and wildlife, which requires extensive habitats, pays no attention to landownership. The Joint Federal-State Land Use Planning Commission anticipated many of these problems early in the 1970s and, as already related, analyzed a variety of institutional mechanisms suitable for cooperative planning and management after passage of ANILCA.

ANILCA established the Alaska Land Use Planning Council.[18] It is composed of Alaska's governor or someone he chooses to represent him, a federal cochairman appointed by the president, and members who are the heads of the federal and state land-management agencies and other agency officials with interest in lands, such as transportation, environmental protection, and energy. In addition, there are two representatives from Native corporations. Although the fifteen-member council is mainly advisory, it has important powers to recommend uses for state and federal lands; negotiate land exchanges; identify and encourage regional, state, Native, and federal cooperation; and provide for mutual consultation, review, and coordination of resource-management plans and programs. The council has existed only a few years, and it is too early to assess its effectiveness.

What is clear is that it will take years, much litigation, and also considerable goodwill among all of Alaska's landowners to implement the intent of the Alaska National Interest Lands Conservation Act of 1980.

# 14. THE OIL BOOM

No single event in Alaska's history has had an impact on the region of intensity comparable to that of Atlantic-Richfield's discovery of the gigantic 9.6-billion-barrel Prudhoe Bay oil field in 1968. The initial discoveries of oil deposits, however, were made long ago, many decades before phrases like "energy crisis" and "environmental degradation" became household terms.

Thomas Simpson, an officer of the Hudson's Bay Company, first observed oil deposits along the Canadian Arctic shore while engaged in his coastal survey of 1836–37. As the first traveler to reach Point Barrow from the east, he certainly could not foresee the later frenzy of oil exploration in North America's Arctic.[1]

Sometime during the nineteenth century Eskimo travelers along the Arctic Coast discovered natural oil seeps near Cape Simpson, 50 miles southeast of Barrow and 150 miles northwest of Prudhoe Bay, and at Angun Point, 30 miles southeast of the village of Kaktovik, on Barter Island. For many years inhabitants of the area traveled to these seeps to cut out blocks of oil-soaked tundra to take back to their homes for use as fuel.[2]

Somewhat later in the century Ens. W. L. Howard, a member of the U.S. Navy's 1886 exploration expedition headed by Lt. George M. Stoney, extensively explored the North Slope of Alaska. Howard found oil near the upper Colville River and took back a sample.[3]

In more recent times William Van Valin, a U.S. Bureau of Education teacher in the Arctic village of Wainwright, heard reports of an oil lake. In 1914 he traveled 550 miles to the east side of Smith Bay, 1 mile from the Arctic shore—now a part of the United States Naval Petroleum Reserve No. 4—where he found two springs of what appeared to be engine oil. Van Valin quickly staked his claim on the hill from which the streams oozed, as well as on the little lake into which they drained. Since he had but little time on this journey, he hastily put out his stakes and put up a sign naming the place Arctic Rim Mineral Oil Claim. Van Valin returned at a later date, built a cabin, and did some assessment work on his claim. He then left Alaska but did not forget the discovery, and in later lectures on the North and its wonders he mentioned the oil lake.[4]

In 1919 pioneering geologist and explorer Ernest de K. Leffingwell mentioned oil seepages in his report on his scientific studies of the Canning River region, more than 60 miles southeast of Prudhoe Bay. Leffingwell spent the years 1906 to 1914 mapping the geology of the area, and although he had not actually visited the seeps, he had heard reports of them and mentioned them in a general discussion of the economic potential of the area.[5] Tests had indicated oil of very high quality, and oil-men began to take notice of the region and its potential. There were other reports of similar seepages at various locations on the North Slope, and Natives told Alfred H. Brooks, head of the Alaska division of the U.S. Geological Survey, that the most extensive oil seepages occurred at a site 300 miles east of Point Barrow near the Canadian boundary.

Still later, in 1921, representatives of Standard Oil Company of California and General Petroleum Company examined the seepages at Cape Simpson, near Barrow, finding two flows that encouraged their hopes of finding oil in quantities suitable for commercial production, but that did not happen for economic reasons—namely the discoveries of oil on the West Coast, particularly in California. But favorable geological conditions also existed in other parts of Alaska.[6] As early as 1853 employees of the Russian-American Company found oil-and-gas seeps on the west shore of Cook Inlet near the Iniskin Peninsula. In 1892 a prospector named Edelman staked claims to the oil-and-gas seeps at that location. In 1896 oil seepages were noted in the Katalla and Yakataga areas on the Gulf of Alaska.[7]

Edelman abandoned his claims for unknown reasons, but in 1896 prospectors again staked claims on the Iniskin Peninsula and also in the Katalla and Yakataga districts. Operators began drilling for oil in the Iniskin area and in 1898 brought in a wildcat well at Oil Bay. The operators reported an oil flow of 50 barrels a day at 700 feet. After probing to 1,000 feet, the drill entered a water stratum that choked off the oil flow. In 1902 the Alaska Oil Company drilled a wildcat well at Puale Bay, on the east coast of the Alaska Peninsula. At about the same time the Chilkat Oil Company drilled another well in the Katalla district

Cudahy Oil Company drilling rig on the shore of Bering Lake, in the Katalla oil field. Courtesy Barrett Willoughby Collection, Alaska and Polar Regions Archives, Elmer E. Rasmuson Library, University of Alaska.

on the coast east of the mouth of the Copper River. Although both were unsuccessful, the operators had found enough encouragement to continue testing. In 1904 the Alaska Oil Company had drilled two more dry holes at Cold Bay. The Chilkat Oil Company was luckier at the time and found oil in the Katalla district. Between 1902 and 1931 it drilled thirty-six wells, eighteen of which produced oil. Production was low, however, ranging to 20 barrels a day. In 1911 the Chilkat Oil Company built a small topping plant at Katalla Slough. It began operating in 1912 and sold its products in Cordova. Katalla prospered, and its main street was lined with hotels, restaurants, and saloons. As many as 10,000 people may have called Katalla home during the boom year of 1907, but the number declined gradually. For twenty-one years the company supplied some of the local petroleum-product demands. Late in 1933 a fire destroyed the boiler house at the topping plant, and the company abandoned the entire operation. Katalla soon became a ghost town.[8]

During the twenty-nine years of its production history the Katalla field produced only a modest 154,000 barrels of oil—not enough to supply even local needs. The Katalla wells had been shallow, most not over 1,000 feet deep and none more than 2,000 feet deep.[9]

For all practical purposes oil exploration ended in 1904 because operators had failed to find oil in commercial quantities, exploration costs had been high, and it had been difficult to obtain title to oil lands under the placer-mining laws then in effect. Furthermore, oil discoveries and developments, particularly in California, supplied demands at reasonable prices.

In 1910 the federal government withdrew lands from oil-and-gas leasing. This halted exploratory work until passage of the oil-and-gas leasing act in 1920. This legislation once again spurred activities in Alaska which centered on the known oil-bearing areas of south-central Alaska, but prospectors also examined new regions, such as the Chignik district, on the Alaska Peninsula; the vicinity of Anchorage; the Cook Inlet-Susitna Valley area; and an area near Killisnoo, on Admiralty Island, in southeastern Alaska. Major companies drilled in the Kanatak district, on the Alaska Peninsula, between 1923 and 1926, and the first test well in the Yakataga district was drilled during 1926 and 1927. In 1920 entrepreneurs drilled a well to a shallow depth on the outskirts of Anchorage, an event recorded in the name Oil Well Road. From 1926 to 1930 a test well was drilled near Chickaloon in the Matanuska Valley, and between 1938 and 1940 operators sank two deep test wells, one on the Iniskin Peninsula and the other in the Kanatak district. Neither produced oil in commercial quantities. This and the advent of World War II, with its restrictions and withdrawals of public lands for leasing, temporarily ended oil exploration.[10]

## NAVAL PETROLEUM RESERVE NO. 4

Despite failures, geologist Alfred H. Brooks maintained his optimism regarding territorial oil. In June, 1922, the press quoted him as telling a Seattle group that he was confident that "oil will be found in Alaska, and the probabilities are that there are extensive [oil] areas in the Territory." Perhaps President Harding was influenced by Brooks's optimism when he created Naval Petroleum Reserve No. 4 (NPR-4) by executive order on February 27, 1923. The reserved area on the North Slope comprised approximately 37,000 square miles, a large area surrounding the seeps at Cape Simpson and extending to the Colville River on the east and south to the crest of the Brooks Range.[11]

The U.S. Navy subsequently asked the Geological Survey to conduct a topographic and geological reconnaissance of the entire area to map the petroleum reserves. Brooks submitted a detailed work plan spanning a

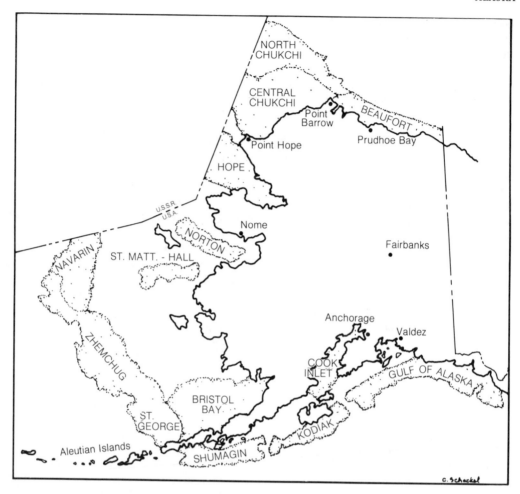

Alaska's sedimentary basins with possible oil-and-gas deposits. Map by Christie Schackel.

period of five years, and the Geological Survey accomplished its task. There was no follow-up work, and it was not until the summer of 1943 that the U.S. Bureau of Mines conducted field examinations on the Arctic Slope and recommended further and more definitive surveys.[12]

In March, 1944, Secretary of the Navy Frank Knox informed President Franklin D. Roosevelt that his department had formulated a definite and comprehensive program for the exploration of NPR-4. The president approved the proposal. Congress granted the Navy $1 million for the fiscal year ending June 30, 1945, to start exploration work on NPR-4. The Navy intended to drill six wells, and in testimony on the Navy appropriation bill, Secretary Knox told the congressmen that he "proposed to use Seabees [naval construction battalions], ideal men for that type of work," for the drilling operations. Before the Navy dispatched the Seabees, however, it sent a team of three officers under the command of Lt. W. T. Foran to survey conditions on the Arctic Coast of Alaska. The trio made a surface examination of the geological structure along the Colville River about 100 miles from its mouth and found promising indications of oil. In the meantime the Navy had obtained a light drilling outfit and shipped it by cargo vessel to Barrow, from where it had to be hauled overland to the proposed testing site.[13]

The Navy's activities soon gave rise to speculations and rumors. Early in September, 1944, Harold W. Snell, of Seattle, Washington, informed Secretary Ickes that he had received important information from a very competent source "whose identity I can not disclose." According to the informant, an individual with "world wide experience in the field of petroleum exploration," naval exploration work in

> the Point Barrow, Alaska, Oil Preserve Development will disclose it as one of the largest and richest oil fields in North America; that the route and size of the pipe line between the field and the refinery have been tentatively decided upon; that it is believed that a major refinery will be built at Fairbanks and that the representatives of most of the large companies are on the ground and that there is much oil outside of the boundaries of the Preserve.

The secretary dampened Snell's enthusiasm by pointing out "time alone will show whether there is oil . . . and, if so, what its quality and quantity may be."[14]

In the spring of 1945, Secretary of the Navy James Forrestal informed President Roosevelt that he had authorized a continuation of the exploratory program and sent the necessary personnel and equipment to Barrow to undertake a detailed geological study of the most promising part of NPR-4. In April, 1944, the reconnaissance party had found a good oil structure at Umiat Mountain, on the Colville River. Geological mapping of the area had "revealed a closed anticlinal structure with live gas and oil seeps." Forrestal had decided to start drilling at Umiat in the winter of 1945, while directing further geophysical exploration and core drilling at Cape Simpson to determine the oil-bearing structure. The secretary planned to have another drilling rig shipped to Barrow in the summer of 1946 and have it moved to Cape Simpson as soon as the frozen ground would bear its weight. Additionally, Seabees were surveying a prospective pipeline route and conducting reconnaissance work in the southeastern part of the reserve in the spring of 1945. Above all, the secretary was determined to have the Navy undertake a long-range exploratory program with a minimum expenditure of power, time, and effort "to determine the presence and quantity of oil in Naval Petroleum Reserve No. 4." The Naval Appropriations Bill for 1946 contained $1,620,000 to cover the work for the coming year.[15]

At the end of 1945, Secretary Forrestal informed the president that by the time the work in NPR-4 was finished "there will have been expended approximately $8,000,000, and if oil is found in justifiable volume, a development program for readiness involving an expenditure in the order of $150,000,000 may be indicated."[16]

Early in 1946, Secretary Forrestal once again reported to the president on the status of exploration in NPR-4. Much had changed since Secretary Knox had initiated the program in 1944. The end of the war and the demobilization of naval personnel had made necessary a redetermination of the Navy's future course in exploring the reserve. The Seabees, on NPR-4 since the spring of 1944, had been "mustered out of the service and no other qualified personnel is available." Therefore, contractors from the petroleum industry had to be found in order to continue the work. Exploration so far had been limited to the eastern third of the reserve and had included reconnaissance by airborne magnetometer, aerial photography, geological surface mapping, subsurface reconnaissance by gravity meter, seismography, core drilling, and drilling of test wells on carefully selected locations.

The Navy and the U.S. Geological Survey had collaborated on the work, and now these two and the photographic section of the Army were correlating the collected data and preparing maps for the use of surface geological parties in the summer of 1946. Some work had also been accomplished in the southern section of the reserve and at Cape Simpson. A test well at Umiat was approximately 1,900 feet deep and already had encountered five separate oil-bearing sands, but so far none had been of commercial value. The preliminary pipeline survey had been completed, and a study had shown that an extractable reserve of 400 to 500 million barrels with a potential production of 100,000 barrels a day was required to economically support such a venture.[17]

In support of the exploratory work, the Navy had established a base camp at Barrow with secondary camps at Umiat and Cape Simpson. During the summers of 1944 and 1945, approximately 26,000 tons of equipment and supplies had been landed at Barrow and taken to the secondary camps during the coldest winter months when the ground was frozen sufficiently to bear the weight of sled trains. The Navy had discovered that it was impossible to move freight during the summers because of the numerous lakes and rivers and the generally boggy tundra. The Navy had to rely almost entirely on air transport for logistic support. It had built landing fields at Barrow, Umiat, and Cape Simpson and emergency strips midway between Fairbanks and Barrow and Barrow and Umiat. The Naval Air Transport Service provided the necessary air transportation to Barrow and to some extent to Umiat. Wien Alaska Airways, a Fairbanks "bush carrier," provided the service necessary to maintain contact with the secondary camps, field parties, and tractor trains under contract to the Navy. Secretary Forrestal also informed the president that civilian contractors had been engaged to

continue the work. In 1947, Congress appropriated $9.6 million to continue the work until 1950 and eventually made funds available until 1953. Contractors and field parties of the U.S. Geological Survey ranged over the reserve from 1946 until 1953 and also explored a similarly large area of public land contiguous to the reserve. Seabees had drilled the first wildcat well in 1945. Although it showed light-gravity oil, it could not be completed as a producer because there was not enough oil. The same was true of a second well.[18]

In 1946, Arctic Contractors, a joint venture of three specially qualified firms, continued to carry out all phases of exploratory work except for geological research, which members of the U.S. Geological Survey performed. The contractors drilled eleven wells in the Umiat area, outlining a field that contained an estimated 100 million barrels of recoverable oil.[19]

Between 1944 and 1953, when the Navy suspended its exploration of the reserve, thirty-six wildcat wells had been drilled and forty-four core holes had been sunk, varying in depth from 2,000 to 11,800 feet. Arctic Contractors found two minor oil and three natural-gas fields but made no commercially significant discoveries. By 1953, however, the Navy's findings suggested that the area north of the Brooks Range might contain extensive reserves of both oil and gas. While the Navy could claim some success, in 1936 and 1939 the Havenstrite Oil Company had also found some oil and gas below 4,700 feet on the Fritz Creek anticline, but it could not get production under way.[20]

## THE OIL INDUSTRY'S INTEREST IN ALASKA

By 1957 more than 100 wells had been drilled in Alaska, financed by private capital. Outside of the few wells in the Katalla field, none had been commercially successful. Still, oilmen dreamed of sudden riches to be wrested from Alaska's promising oil structures. The year 1957 will be remembered for a long time by the industry. Humble Oil and Refining Company drilled the most promising dry hole ever in Alaska, the Bear Creek wildcat. Though it went to 14,900 feet and showed signs of both oil and gas, it was not a commercial find. It was, however, a very expensive well, at a cost of about $6 million.[21]

On July 23, 1957, Richfield Oil Corporation cored into the oil sands of what became the Swanson River field, establishing Alaska's first truly commercial oil production. It was Richfield's first wildcat in the territory, and the company had been lucky indeed, because the drilling rig, situated on the Swanson River oil structure, nearly missed the reservoir. Richfield completed its Swanson River Unit 1 on September 29, 1957, after drilling to a depth of 12,384 feet. Oil flowed from the discovery well at the rate of 900 barrels a day, and it also produced 122,000 cubic feet of gas a day. A second well was started in the same year and completed in 1958. Eventually, eleven dry wells were drilled in the task of outlining the boundaries of the Swanson River field.[22]

And although that discovery did not trigger an immediate oil rush, it did result in a leasing boom in the territory. By September 28, 1965, Alaska had held its fifteenth competitive lease since the first one, recorded on December 10, 1959. The state offered a total of 3,728,456 acres for lease during those six years, of which 66.9 percent, or 2,494,714 acres, were snapped up by the oil companies. The state had taken in a total of $66,134,155 in its fifteen lease sales which averaged $26.51 for every acre leased.[23]

By 1965 the oil industry had become an important part of Alaska's economy; five oil and eleven gas fields had been developed. Between 1958 and January 1, 1966, the state received a total of $122,223,000 in di-

rect cash payments from the oil industry—approximately $480 per person in Alaska—which compares to the $756,805 the territorial government had received between 1947 and 1957. Most of the money came from bonuses on competitive leases, which provided more than $66 million. In addition, the state received 90 percent of the rentals paid to the federal government for leases on federal lands. It also collected 90 percent of the royalty paid to the federal government for production from the Swanson River field.[24]

By 1966, in the short span of nine years since the first truly commercial discovery in 1957, the oil industry had become an integral part of Alaska's economy. Natural gas heated homes in Anchorage; a refinery on the Kenai Peninsula processsed Alaskan crude into heating oils and jet fuels; and Union Oil Company, through its subsidiary Collier Carbon and Chemical Corporation spent about $30 million in constructing the largest ammonia plant on the West Coast and another $20 million jointly with Tokyo Gas and Chemical Company in building the world's biggest urea plant—both located on the Kenai Peninsula.[25]

The oil industry and many Alaskans were optimistic about future prospects. Experts believed that the upper Cook Inlet area had not been fully explored and still held much promise; the lower Cook Inlet was virtually untouched; and Geophysical Services, Inc., had sent seismic crews into the Bristol Bay area and the Gulf of Alaska to check these two oil provinces for some twenty oil companies. Although oil men seemed almost certain that Alaska's North Slope contained sizable reserves, they were put off by the region's inaccessibility and climatic rigors. The industry estimated that it needed to discover between 200 million and 500 million barrels of recoverable oil before it could establish an economically viable field on the North Slope. In 1966 industry spokesmen estimated that producing and moving oil to markets even after the discovery of such a big field would "test the ingenuity of the American petroleum industry." They added that "there's nothing to be done with the gas."[26]

While geologists and seismic crews roamed Alaska's wide spaces, annual crude oil production rose from 187,000 barrels in 1959 to 74 million barrels in 1969; and natural gas, from 310 million cubic feet to 149 billion cubic feet. Wellhead value of this production, on which the state levied its taxes, had risen from $1.5 million in 1960 to $219 million in 1969—at which point the oil industry had become Alaska's foremost natural resource extractive industry.[27]

## THE PRUDHOE BAY DISCOVERY

On January 16, 1968, oil became big news when it was announced that a substantial flow of gas had been found in the Arctic. Various companies had been exploring the North Slope for some time, and geologists speculated that the Atlantic-Richfield Company's willingness to make the announcement at that time was an indication that the optimism about oil and gas development prospects on the North Slope was well founded. Two days later Atlantic-Richfield Company's exploration manager, Julius Babisak, described the gas well, known as Prudhoe Bay State No. 1, as "encouraging." He said: "This is a very rank wildcat. We are keeping information on it tight. I think you can understand why."[28]

Judging by subsequent events on Alaska's North Slope, it was indeed understandable that Atlantic-Richfield (ARCO), in partnership with Humble Oil and Refining Company, wanted to limit its disclosure on the strike. Alaskans speculated that Prudhoe Bay State No. 1 was the first nonmilitary oil discovery ever reported from the Arctic Slope and hoped that it would be but the forerunner of additional discoveries big enough to make commercial production possible. Drilling continued amid growing

industry optimism. In February, ARCO reported that it had cased the well at 8,708 feet and found oil-saturated sands in the lower 70 feet.[29]

Early in March, ARCO announced, amid much speculation, that the company had made a major find—that its discovery well flowed oil at the rate of 1,152 barrels a day. On June 25, ARCO announced that a second well, drilled about seven miles southeast of the discovery well, had also found oil. This supported the Prudhoe Bay discovery.[30]

While ARCO cautiously conceded that the discovery was significant, geologists in Fairbanks surmised that Alaska's North Slope might well contain one of the largest oil fields in the world. Expert opinion ranged from "evidently mammoth" to "almost certainly of Middle-Eastern proportions."[31]

ARCO's discovery had been largely a matter of luck, for in 1966 the company had decided to drill a wildcat well on the North Slope leases it had acquired in a state sale. Geologists proposed two drilling sites, one at Prudhoe Bay and the other inland near the Saganavirktok River. ARCO chose the latter, calling it Susie Unit No. 1, spent $4,500,000, and came up with a dry hole. That was an inauspicious beginning. The company decided to give it one more try— this time at Prudhoe Bay, called Prudhoe Bay State No. 1—and this time the oil gushed up and the great Alaska oil rush was on.[32]

In 1967, before the rush, Alaska's Governor Walter Hickel asked the state legislature to create a NORTH Commission, a body to ponder ways to develop Alaska's Arctic. In August of 1968 the NORTH Commission met, no longer to ponder ways to develop the Arctic but rather to devote its attention to planning for an orderly development. Governor Hickel, in private life a real estate developer and contractor, painted a bright picture of the Arctic's future for his NORTH Commission members. "We are going to see villages grow to towns and towns grow to cities and a vigorous, new breed of people working and playing and raising families and building libraries, schools, museums, universities, and theaters where there is nothing now but tundra." While many members of Alaska's business community applauded the governor's remarks, others, concerned with Alaska's unique wilderness and life-style, were dismayed. All could see, however, that momentous changes were coming.[33]

Conservationists predicted that development would play havoc with the finely balanced ecology of the Arctic, and they expected the state government to be insensitive to environmental concerns. Governor Hickel did not disappoint these groups. In order to give Alaska's trucking industry an opportunity to participate in the rush, Hickel approved the construction of a road approximately 400 miles long from Livengood, about 60 miles north of Fairbanks, across the frozen tundra to Sagwon, on the North Slope. Shortly after Governor Hickel ordered the construction of the winter road, President Nixon appointed him secretary of the interior. Hickel's successor, Governor Keith H. Miller, promptly named the project the Hickel Highway. From the beginning it was a mess. Instead of compacting the snow on the tundra without disturbing the permafrost under it, state bulldozers scraped off the snow and protective ground covering and gouged a road into the tundra. This made a trench, and much time was lost clearing windblown snow out of the roadway. Open only for about a month—from March to April— the road carried a total of 7,464 tons of freight. About 80 percent of that went to the oil fields. The cost of freight delivered to Sagwon, well short of the Prudhoe Bay exploration area, still amounted to $240 a ton—approximately the same as airfreight. The same tonnage could easily have been carried by three trips of the giant Hercules air transports, which require only a 5,000-foot runway at each end.[34]

The worst was yet to come. During the spring breakup, the Hickel Highway rapidly turned into a water-filled canal as the exposed permafrost melted and water from surrounding areas drained into the roadbed. But once committed to a particular project, no matter how impractical or expensive, governments tend to forge ahead. Prodding from the trucking companies helped also, and during the winter of 1969/ 70, the state highway department compounded its mistake and reconstructed the winter road. Since some sections had eroded badly, portions of the road had to be rerouted, resulting in two ditches instead of one.[35]

No matter what the state did or did not do, events moved forward. For weeks potential bidders for the approximately 450,000 acres of North Slope oil lands to be leased by the state of Alaska had been gathering in Anchorage. Texans in big hats and cowboy boots mingled with conservatively dressed New York investors and dapper and shrewd oil experts from London. The influx of outsiders strained accommodations in Anchorage; all hotels, from the Westward to the Captain Cook and Traveler's Inn, as well as every tiny motel and rooming house, were solidly booked. All over the city, oil-company men, executives, geologists, drilling experts, and accountants huddled together to plan strategy. Companies like ARCO, British Petroleum, Sinclair, Colorado Oil and Gas, and Union Oil, already holding leases on the North Slope, were anxious to guard the geological information on which they planned to base their bids for the remaining acreage, while those companies not so fortunate had to assemble every clue and bit of information they could in order to put together sensible bids on the various tracts.

Before the sale date of September 10, 1969, companies without actual lease holdings sent seismic crews to find prime unleased land, and scouts and spies repeatedly flew to the North Slope in an attempt to gain clues by observing equipment, watching the comings and goings of crews and supplies, and trying to estimate the depth of holes being drilled and analyze reports of test burn-offs. Tips were sold across bar counters in Fairbanks, and oil company and state employees were propositioned for information. As the lease sale date approached, widespread publicity built suspense. Articles appeared in the national magazines and newspapers, and television specials were made about the Prudhoe Bay oil strike, the coming sale, and the state of Alaska. Media crews from Japan, Europe, and Britain's BBC, in addition to ABC, CBS, and NBC crews, prepared to cover the bid openings. In addition to seats held by oil company representatives, there were extra ones for the general public. By 6:00 A.M. people lined up halfway around the block from the Sydney Lawrence Auditorium for these spots. Alaska was front-page news across the Western world for one day. Never had there been so much media coverage in Alaska as on that Wednesday morning.[36]

Those in attendance from the East Coast, Europe, and Japan may have been amused by the rather folksy opening ceremonies, but not the Alaskans present. After reciting the Pledge of Allegiance, everyone sang Alaska's state song, "Eight Stars of Gold on a Field of Blue." Commissioner of Natural Resources Tom Kelly, the master of ceremonies, next made some sprightly remarks about Alaska's resources and the widespread interest in both preserving and responsibly developing its wilderness. Next, Larry Beck, a local poet and self-proclaimed "Bard of the North," jauntily dressed in parka and mukluks, recited his own poem paying tribute to the oil industry. Governor Keith Miller reminded all to manage Alaska's birthright wisely and concluded that Alaska would never be the same again.[37]

After the opening ceremonies concluded at 10:30 A.M. in the auditorium, the serious business began. Dozens of oil men and their bankers, packing briefcases containing several hundred million dollars, quietly filed up and presented state officials with sealed envelopes containing their bid checks for 179 tracts of land. For the next several hours the bids were read off, tract by tract. The Gulf–British Petroleum consortium took the first six tracts at the mouth of the Colville River with bonus bids of $97 million. Each announcement was cheered, and by 5:15 P.M. the state had received a 20 percent down payment on the $900,220,590 in bonus monies. Loaded into bags, the money was taken to the airport and flown by chartered jet to the Bank of America in San Francisco for deposit so that not a penny of interest would be lost. Amerada Hess was the high bidder of the day with $272 million, followed by Union of California and Pan American Petroleum with $163 million and Gulf and British Petroleum with $97 million. Standard of California, Phillips, and Mobil, in consortium, were fourth with $96 million.[38]

Since statehood Alaska had held a total of twenty-two lease sales, which had netted less than $100 million. Then, in one day, the state sold oil leases on less than .001 percent of its total landmass and raised more than $900 million.[39] Those residents who had always claimed that Alaska would be the nation's treasure chest of natural resources finally had their proof. Others, interested in maintaining Alaska's open spaces, its magnificent wilderness, and their own life-styles, were apprehensive about the vast changes in the making.

All through that winter Alaskans debated what to do with their money. Many believed that Alaska's financial troubles were at an end, for there was speculation that the Prudhoe Bay discovery represented the mere tip of the iceberg. What other oil provinces, on land and offshore, many asked, awaited exploration? Many had visions of schools, hospitals, community centers, roads, pensions for all, and free scholarships and tuitions for those who wanted them. The legislative council hired the Brookings Institution, and Governor Miller bought advice from a team of twenty-four from Stanford Research Institute and from New York petroleum consultant Walter J. Levy. There was much talk about the best and wisest way to develop Alaska, and many assumed that the state should be developed. The Brookings Institution arranged four successive meetings in Anchorage, where a broad cross-section of urban Alaskans examined and discussed the financial foundations for the future of the state, the use of its human resources, the quality of the natural environment, and alternative futures for the state. What distinguished the Brookings sessions were the repeated calls by participants for preserving the "unique" Alaskan life-style, defining it as one which "affords the conveniences of technological innovation with the opportunity and values of living as close to nature as possible." Most

agreed that a compatibility between the oil industry and the Alaskan life-style could be achieved with "well-enforced, proper regulation." [40]

## PLANNING FOR THE TRANS-ALASKA PIPELINE

The lease sale and the subsequent debate over what to do with all the money were the highlights of that season. In the meantime, the Trans-Alaska Pipeline System (TAPS), an unincorporated joint venture of Atlantic-Richfield, British Petroleum, and Humble Oil, applied to the U.S. Department of the Interior in June, 1969, for a permit to construct a hot-oil pipeline across 800 miles of public domain from Prudhoe Bay on the North Slope to tidewater at Valdez on Prince William Sound. TAPS estimated that it would cost approximately $900 million to build the pipeline. Secretary of the Interior Walter J. Hickel, Alaska's former gover-

Valdez, now the terminus of the trans-Alaska pipeline, about 1900. Courtesy Charles E. Bunnell Collection, Alaska and Polar Regions Archives, Elmer E. Rasmuson Library, University of Alaska.

nor, was under great pressure to grant the construction permit promptly. Conservationist groups throughout the United States also applied pressure not to grant a construction permit. The giant project posed innumerable environmental, technical, and economic questions for which no one had yet furnished any answers.[41]

The oil companies, even without the permit in hand, already had made a number of decisions. The first one was to build a conventional buried pipeline; but the companies had not considered what effect oil at 160° F would have on Alaska's permafrost. Second, despite a number of feasibility studies investigating various routes for the pipeline, TAPS opted for an Alaskan one and announced in February of 1969 that it planned to build the pipeline from Prudhoe Bay to Valdez. TAPS sought and was given permission from the Department of the Interior to conduct geological and engineering investigations along the proposed route. This permission required that former Secretary Stewart Udall's land freeze order be modified. This the Senate Interior and Insular Affairs Committee approved, and investigations began. Third, the companies had decided that they needed 48-inch-diameter pipe in order to transport 2 million barrels of crude oil a day once the pipeline was operational. The companies also wanted to have the pipe by September, 1969, in order to start construction in July of that year. Since no American company made pipe of that size, the order went to three Japanese firms—Sunimomo Metal Industries, Ltd., Nippon Steel Corporation, and Nippon Kokan Kabushiki Kaisha. This move annoyed Secretary Hickel and other development-minded Alaskans because Kaiser Industries had offered to build a steel mill in Alaska. As it eventually turned out, the 800 miles of steel pipe at $100 million was probably the biggest bargain of the whole project.[42]

In April, 1969, Secretary Hickel an-

nounced the creation of a departmental task force to oversee North Slope oil development and designated Russel E. Train, an undersecretary, to head the new organization. Train, a former head of the Conservation Foundation who later became the first chairman of the Council on Environmental Quality, had been brought into the department to mute conservationist opposition to Hickel's appointment. A month after Hickel set up the task force, President Nixon, under pressure from conservation groups, expanded it to include a conservation-industry ad hoc committee as well as representatives of other government agencies. The expanded task force was to report on plans to protect the arctic environment by September 15, 1969.[43]

On June 6, 1969, TAPS filed a formal application for "an oil pipeline right-of-way together with two additional right-of-way and eleven pumping plant sites for the construction of a 48 inch diameter oil pipeline system." Undersecretary Train immediately sent TAPS Chairman R. E. Dulaney a list of questions to which satisfactory answers had to be found before construction could proceed.[44]

Dulaney quickly replied, reiterating that the pipeline should be constructed consistent with wise conservation practice and that a good pipeline dictated design and construction procedures that would cause a minimum of disturbance to the natural environment. Dulaney sent along a twenty-page document detailing the planning and research done to that date. TAPS planned to bury the hot-oil pipeline beneath the streambed of all the rivers it crossed. A system of block valves would shut off the oil should a break or leak occur. Crews and equipment would clean up the oil that did spill at various intervals. TAPS also had commissioned a number of studies to preserve and revegetate the tundra, and it also was taking core samples along the proposed route to determine what kind of permafrost it would encounter. This was the first of many such exchanges between TAPS and the Department of the Interior.[45]

In the meantime, the department sent its own personnel to Alaska to reconnoiter the route. After the survey, particularly after talking to specialists at the University of Alaska and to Dr. Max Brewer, an arctic expert and the director of the Naval Arctic Research Laboratory, the interior group concluded that the TAPS plan to bury most of the pipeline was not feasible.[46]

Although in June, 1969, there was as yet no National Environmental Policy Act, TAPS had to comply with the 1920 Mineral Leasing Act, which provided for the ground necessary for the pipe—4 feet in this case— and for 25 feet on either side of the pipe, for a total corridor of 54 feet. Yet TAPS asked for a 100-foot right-of-way. Additionally, since the land freeze would have to be modified, approval would have to be obtained from the interior committees of Congress in order to adhere to a promise which Senator Jackson and the Alaska Federation of Natives had extracted from Secretary Hickel.[47]

TAPS also planned to build a haul road to the North Slope paralleling the pipeline from Livengood, a ghost town north of Fairbanks. Subsequently, TAPS and the state of Alaska agreed that TAPS should build the road according to state secondary-road specifications and then, when it had completed the pipeline, turn the road over to the state. On July 22, 1969, the state asked for a modification of the land freeze to allow the construction of a state highway from Livengood to the Yukon River, a distance of 50 miles, where TAPS planned to have the oil pipeline cross the river. On July 29, Secretary Hickel asked the Senate Interior Committee to approve such a modification on the land freeze order. The committee complied and the secretary lifted the freeze for that particular purpose. TAPS promptly gave the contract to Burgess Con-

struction Company of Fairbanks, and work commenced on the first part of the Trans–Alaska Pipeline project.[48]

On September 15, 1969, Undersecretary Train's task force submitted its preliminary report to the president. After reporting on the status of the TAPS application, the task force also listed problems to which no solutions had yet been found. These included the permafrost, the questionable availability of gravel for insulating the pipeline from the ground, the earthquake danger along the route, waste disposal, water pollution from oil spills or tanker discharges, and the effects of so much human activity on wildlife. There were other problems that did not have to do with the environment, such as the Native claims and the size of the right-of-way.[49]

In the meantime, conservationist groups began organizing opposition to TAPS, and by the fall of 1969 the Sierra Club and the Wilderness Society were urging members to write their congressional delegations about the project. But conservationists also knew that the only time Congress would have any real control over the decision-making process would be when Secretary Hickel asked the Department of the Interior committees to approve a modification of the land freeze for the right-of-way. He was expected to do so sometime in the fall.[50]

While conservationist groups worried, the Department of the Interior and TAPS methodically removed the legal obstacles to the project one by one. On September 19 the various Native villages claiming land over which the pipeline would pass waived their claims to the right-of-way. On September 30 the Department of the Interior published the first of many sets of stipulations for construction of the pipeline, said to be the most rigid governmental controls ever imposed on a private construction project. Implementation of these controls was to be left to Bureau of Land Management (BLM) personnel in the field.[51]

On October 1, 1969, Secretary Hickel asked Congress to approve his lifting of the land freeze for the entire project. The House Interior and Insular Affairs Committee seemed willing to approve his request; however, unable to round up a quorum, it delayed any decision until the last week in October. During the interim, the House Indian Affairs Subcommittee was to tour Native villages in Alaska and also take a look at the proposed pipeline corridor. Senator Jackson's Interior Committee was more skeptical than the House's committee, and Jackson stated that he would have to hold hearings on the proposed modification of the land freeze before making a decision. Nevertheless, Under Secretary Train appeared before Jackson's committee and argued that the freeze should be lifted as a necessary preliminary step.[52]

When Train appeared before the House Interior and Insular Affairs Committee, he was surprised by the displeasure expressed by the two ranking members, who had just returned from their Alaskan tour. They had observed denuded hilltops, a swath cut in the wilderness for miles, and all sorts of drilling activities. The congressmen were particularly upset because this activity had occurred without their permission. Actually, the work the congressmen observed had been approved; Congress had allowed TAPS to build the road to the Yukon River and collect core samples of the soil along the pipeline route.[53]

On October 23, Senator Jackson sent Secretary Hickel a list of questions that had to be answered before his committee could approve any modification of the land freeze. These questions were exhaustive and dealt with almost every phase of the pipeline, from permafrost to Native rights. The House, learning of Jackson's questions, decided to wait until they had been answered.[54]

It took Hickel nearly a month to reply to the questions, and when he did so, his answers were ambiguous at best. He did state that TAPS had not solved the engineering problems to his satisfaction. In early December, Hickel told Senator Jackson that his department would do nothing until TAPS had solved its problems with permafrost, although he was certain that TAPS would find solutions to this problem. Still, Senator Jackson was concerned about the effect on the pipeline environment.

The Senate committee then notified the secretary that it had no objections to lifting the freeze, after pointing out that the National Environmental Policy Act, then in its final form, provided, among other things, for a public statement of the environmental impact of any federally financed project on federal lands, including an evaluation of alternatives to it. A few days later the House Interior and Insular Affairs Committee followed the Senate's lead in notifying Hickel that it did not object to lifting the land freeze for the pipeline. Secretary Hickel did not immediately grant the permit, although he modified the land freeze, allowing him to lift it entirely when called for. The BLM thereupon started to classify some 5 million acres along the proposed pipeline route as a transportation corridor, while TAPS refiled its permit application, requesting a 54-foot right-of-way and temporary special land-use permits for additional footage up to 146 feet in places along the route.[55]

Secretary Hickel intended to issue a permit for construction of the 390-mile haul road, and in January, 1970, TAPS issued letters of intent to contractors for the entire road from the Yukon River to Prudhoe Bay. The companies, anticipating firm contracts, soon hauled heavy equipment up portions of the old Hickel Highway and up a new winter road to convenient staging areas along the road's tentative route. The companies wanted to start construction immediately when the final permit was issued. At about the same time, the BLM authorized TAPS to proceed with the centerline survey for the haul road. But when Secretary Hickel was about to issue the haul road permit, Natives and conservationists asked a federal district court in Washington, D.C., to prevent him from doing so.[56]

What had occurred was that some of the villages that had signed a waiver of their claims to the pipeline right-of-way the previous fall were now reneging. The villagers wired Hickel and told him that TAPS, contrary to a prior promise, had not chosen any native contractors and furthermore had selected firms unlikely to give jobs to Natives. On March 9, before anything had happened in the case, five villages asked the federal district court in Washington, D.C., to stop Secretary Hickel from issuing the construction permit because they claimed the road right-of-way crossed their lands. And on April 1, 1970, Judge George L. Hart, Jr., enjoined the Department of the Interior from issuing a construction permit across 19.8 miles of the route, land claimed by the residents of Stevens Village. Judge Hart stated that he would reconsider the temporary restraining order in ten days.[57]

In the meantime, the Wilderness Society, the Friends of the Earth, and the Environmental Defense Fund sued the Department of the Interior in the same court on March 26, asking that the TAPS project be halted because it violated both the 1920 Mineral Leasing Act and the new National Environmental Policy Act. Judge Hart scheduled a hearing on this case for April 13, 1970.[58]

Alaska's Governor Keith Miller now decided to take matters into his own hands, and based on an 1866 statute that grants states rights-of-way over public lands "not reserved for public use," the governor authorized the haul road himself. TAPS, however, chose to wait for a federal permit. On April 13, Judge Hart, after listening to arguments from the lawyers employed by the various parties, issued a temporary injunction against the TAPS project.[59]

The oil industry suddenly realized that Alaska presented problems that would not easily be overcome. And British Petroleum, after much maneuvering, agreed to help lobby for a Native land claims settlement and also agreed to persuade other companies in TAPS to join in that effort. Nothing happened immediately, because TAPS was in the throes of reorganization: in the fall of 1970 it became a well-organized Delaware corporation named the Alyeska Pipeline Service Company, Inc. The new corporation included the same oil companies that had started TAPS. By mid-1970 the plans for construction of the Trans-Alaska Pipeline were stymied, and the oil companies realized that the real obstacle consisted of the Native land claims, which had to be resolved before any progress could be made (discussed in the preceding chapter).

## ALTERNATIVE METHODS FOR TRANSPORTING OIL

While that political drama was played out on the Washington and Alaska stage, several other methods for transporting the oil from the Arctic to commercial markets were considered. As early as 1968, the Humble Oil and Refining Company had committed itself to a $50 million experiment with the 115,000-ton S.S. *Manhattan*, the largest U.S. flag merchant ship. This supertanker was to navigate the Northwest Passage in an attempt to determine whether or not it would be commercially feasible to transport the oil via this route. To conquer the passage, Humble converted the *Manhattan* into a powerful icebreaker. The ship's hull was equipped with protective belts of steel plate; the bow was designed to attack the ice at a sharp 18-degree angle rather than at the 30-degree angle of most traditional icebreaker bows. In addition, the bow was sixteen feet wider than the rest of the hull so that the ship's hard nose could break a wide path in the ice. Equipped with a 43,000-horsepower plant, nearly one and one-half times larger than those on most other ships twice her size, the *Manhattan* during the summer of 1969 broke through the 6- to 18-foot-thick pack ice and through pressure ridges as thick as 100 feet. The ship was also equipped with two helicopters which scouted the route ahead, and it contained varied scientific equipment measuring stress and gathering data. The *Manhattan* had the help of a Canadian and an American icebreaker; once, when it became stuck in the ice-choked M'Clure Strait in the Canadian Arctic Archipelago, it was freed with some difficulty. On the way home it was carrying a single symbolic barrel of North Slope oil when the ice put a hole in one of the oil tanks (which was filled with seawater) "big enough to drive a truck through." In any event, by late 1970, following a second summer excursion by the *Manhattan*, Humble decided that it was impractical to construct larger icebreaking tankers.[60]

Other alternatives to the pipeline were considered during the early and even late planning stages; all were abandoned for reasons of logistics, cost, or safety. In 1972 there was talk of another version of the supertanker, this one a flying Boeing version. The Boeing Company earlier had suggested the possibility of using fleets of conventional jumbo aircraft for lifting the oil out of the Arctic. Boeing now unveiled a giant airplane that would be powered by twelve 747-type engines. With a 478-foot wingspan and an 83-foot tail, the plane would have a gross take-off weight of 3,500,000 pounds. A fleet of such aircraft would have been designed to carry oil, gas, or other natural resources in two wing-mounted removable pods, 150 feet long and 26 feet in diameter. The plane never advanced beyond the drawing board.[61]

In 1973 the idea was advanced of using giant, 900-foot nuclear-powered submarines carrying 170,000 tons of cargo for

The experimental oil tanker *Manhattan*, which negotiated the Northwest Passage from east to west in 1969, with the help of Canadian and U.S. Coast Guard icebreakers. Photograph courtesy of Merritt Helfferich.

transporting the oil. These submarines, it was suggested, could be redesigned as 300,000-ton subsea tankers. Made by General Dynamics Corporation and formally presented to the North Slope oil companies, the submarines would be 140 feet at the beam and have a hull depth of 85 feet. Twin screws would provide a cruising speed of eighteen knots. Roger Lewis, the president of General Dynamics, declared that his corporation had already formulated plans to build these submarine tankers at its Quincy, Massachusetts, shipyards. The oil companies, however, did not pursue the idea.[62]

There were other plans, such as extending the Alaska Railroad to Prudhoe Bay and carrying the oil to market in tank cars. But this idea did not get beyond the discussion stage either. Finally, Mark Wheeler, a cartoonist from Ketchikan, suggested that the oil companies use a 789-mile-long human bucket brigade to get the oil to tidewater at Valdez.[63]

## TAPS DEBATE AND APPROVAL

By late 1970, TAPS finally completed its metamorphosis and became the tightly organized Alyeska Pipeline Service Company, Inc., headed by Edward L. Patton, formerly of Humble Oil. At the urging of Hugh Gallagher, a representative of British Petroleum and a former administrative assistant to Senator E. L. "Bob" Bartlett, Patton hired William C. Foster as the company's chief lobbyist. Foster, a young Washington attorney with extensive federal and Alaskan connections, had also been a Bartlett staff member in the 1960s and had helped to codify the new state's laws after it attained statehood in 1959. Foster advised his client to push for a land claims settlement satisfactory to the natives so that there would be no subsequent lawsuits to further delay the pipeline. Such a settlement was achieved when President Richard M. Nixon signed the Alaska Native Claims Settlement Act into law in December, 1971.

While the Native claims settlement progressed through Congress, the Department of the Interior dealt with the pipeline issue. The land claims settlement cleared only one obstacle for the pipeline. The department still had to comply with the national environmental policy and mineral leasing acts.

After the Department of the Interior released its Draft Environmental Impact Statement on the pipeline in January, 1971, subsequent public hearings brought forth some twelve thousand pages of testimony. Permafrost was not the only problem. Another question raised was whether the pipeline should go through Canada rather than Alaska. The Department of the Interior was not eager to explore this alternative, insisting that it had to consider only the application for an Alaskan pipeline. The department changed its tune, however, after the appeals court for the District of Columbia ruled in January, 1972, that the National Environmental Policy Act required the broad considerations of alternatives to any proposed federal action.[64]

There were disadvantages and advantages to a Canadian route. A pipeline through the Arctic National Wildlife Range and up the Mackenzie River would be much longer, pose many of the same engineering problems, and, above all, pass through a foreign country. It would also take much longer to complete. On the other hand, it would avoid the numerous earthquake zones in Alaska, a point stressed by the conservationists; and it would not involve tanker traffic on Canada's rugged west coast, which would endanger Canadian and Alaskan fisheries. Most importantly, it would provide a means of delivering Prudhoe Bay's estimated 26 trillion cubic feet of natural gas to the American Middle West in an economical fashion.[65]

Conservationists were particularly effective in keeping several additional issues in public view. The above-ground portions of the line might hamper caribou migrations, and timber clearing, gravel excavation, and access-road construction would disrupt natural habitats, silt streams, and damage fish spawning grounds. Even with a carefully engineered and constructed, trouble-free pipeline, the conservationists contended, there would almost certainly be accidental oil spills from the tankers operating out of Valdez. Furthermore, the oil and construction boom, new access roads and airstrips, and temporary and permanent settlements would, without adequate planning and controls, result in haphazard land development, speculation, inflation, and intensified resource exploitation.[66]

As if these issues were not frustrating enough to the oil companies, the Cordova District Fisheries Union filed suit against the proposed Valdez terminal in April, 1971, contending that Alyeska had not met the requirements of the National Environmental Policy Act. Furthermore, Rogers C. B. Morton, the new secretary of the interior who assumed office in 1971 after the dismissal of Walter Hickel, was uncomfortable about the pipeline and disapproved of his predecessor's open advocacy of it. The new secretary not only disowned the draft impact statement the department had released before he came into office, but he also refused to be pinned down to any sort of timetable for approving the project.[67]

Throughout the spring of 1971, Secretary Morton was under considerable pressure from the industry to grant the permit and from conservationists to deny it. In June, 1971, the secretary visited and toured Alaska, and on his return to Washington he said that he now understood more about Alaska. Many Alaskans interpreted this remark to mean that the secretary favored the pipeline.[68]

On March 15, 1972, Secretary Morton, acting under the authority of Section 17(d)(1) of the Native Claims Settlement Act, withdrew some 80 million acres to be considered for inclusion in the natural conservation system and another 95 million acres for public-interest lands, including many forests and mineral deposits. He also set aside an additional 44 million acres for Native land selections, bringing total Native withdrawals to 99 million acres. Natives would eventually gain title to some 40 million acres.[69]

On March 20, 1972, the Department of the Interior released its nine-volume environmental impact statement on the Trans-Alaska Pipeline. Packed with detail, the volumes dealt with the possible environmental degradation but argued that Alaskan oil was needed on the U.S. West Coast. Alyeska, however, had indicated that when the line reached its full capacity of 2 million barrels per day, some 1.5 million would go to the West Coast, while another 500,000 barrels would go to "Panama," a catchall term for all markets outside the West Coast. Actually, as Alyeska president Patton admitted, some of the oil might be sold to Japan.[70]

In reality, the marketing of the oil was up to individual North Slope companies, and as early as 1970 British Petroleum had signed an agreement with a number of Japanese oil companies that included marketing an undisclosed number of barrels of crude oil there. Phillips Petroleum had proposed an import-export plan under which the companies would trade their excess Alaskan crude for Japanese rights to Middle Eastern oil, which could then be sold on the U.S. East Coast.[71]

Most important, perhaps, the impact statement asserted that the United States could not afford to wait two more years before developing the Alaskan reserves, for in the meantime the Arab countries, in an effort to force a change of American policy toward Israel, had cut off oil supplies to the United States. The pressures to develop reliable domestic energy supplies became almost irresistible. By the winter of 1973, Americans debated the energy crisis, and perhaps for the first time most people realized that the era of cheap and plentiful energy had come to an end. As former Secretary of Commerce Peter Peterson so very aptly put it, "Popeye is running out of cheap spinach."[72]

Amid much pressure from all sides, Secretary Morton announced on May 11, 1972, that it was "in the national interest of the United States to grant a right-of-way permit for the trans-Alaskan pipeline." Morton assured everyone that his decision was the result of much careful consideration of the nation's interest "in maintaining a secure and adequate supply of vitally needed energy resources."[73]

On August 15, 1972, Federal Judge George L. Hart, Jr., dissolved the temporary injunction against the Trans-Alaska Pipeline. After hearing the case, the appeals court in February of 1973 ruled that the rights-of-way and special land use permits which Secretary Morton proposed for the pipeline violated the mineral leasing law. The court ruled that Alyeska had to petition Congress if it intended to use a right-of-way exceeding 54 feet. The Justice Department appealed to the Supreme Court and asked it to expedite the case so construction could start as soon as possible. On April 7, 1973, however, the U.S. Supreme Court refused to review the lower court's decision. A couple of days later Secretary Morton urged Congress to act immediately on the necessary right-of-way legislation. After much political maneuvering, Congress finally decided to bypass NEPA and authorize the pipeline. President Nixon signed the measure into law on November 16, 1973.

## CONSTRUCTION BEGINS

On January 23, 1974, the secretary of the interior signed the primary federal right-of-way permit for construction of the Trans-Alaska Pipeline. Edward L. Patton, the president of Alyeska Pipeline Service Company, Inc., welcomed this action and assured the secretary that his company would endeavor to get all other permits and at the same time make all necessary prepara-

tions to "assure the earliest possible starting date of construction, so that Alaska oil can reach the U.S. West Coast market during 1977."[74]

But even before the signing of the permit gave Alyeska the green light, the company already had taken preliminary steps to get the construction phase underway. In mid-December, 1973, it had announced that contractors were building an ice bridge across the Yukon River as well as opening winter trails and ice airstrips to resupply the seven remote construction camps strung along the pipeline route north from the Yukon to Prudhoe Bay.[75]

A week before the signing of the permit, Alyeska requested bids for site work at Valdez and Prudhoe Bay and for camp housing to be used in construction of the tanker terminal and pump stations along the pipeline, and the company also awarded contracts, after competitive bidding, for the purchase of some $9.2 million worth of heavy construction equipment.[76]

After that, Alyeska moved at a fast pace. It named Bechtel, Inc., of San Francisco to manage the roads and pipeline construction for the project, and it named Fluor Alaska, a subsidiary of Fluor Corporation of Los Angeles, to manage construction of the marine tanker terminal at Valdez and of the pumping stations along the pipeline. A host of subcontractors received awards for various phases of the work as well, and in February, Mechanics Research, Inc., of Los Angeles was awarded a federal contract to provide third-party surveillance of pipeline construction. Working under federal coordinating officer Andrew Rollins, the company was authorized to make certain that adequate environmental safeguards were taken in design and construction of the line. Soon after Alyeska had selected the contractors for the haul road, the state gave the company the last necessary permit—a lease covering the 246 miles of state land which the pipeline would cross.[77]

By late summer construction had begun

in earnest on the Trans-Alaska Pipeline. Only a short five years before, in August, 1969, social and physical scientists had met on the University of Alaska campus for the twentieth Alaska Science Conference to discuss the state's future. Much had happened in those five years, and there had been a great deal of talk about planning for the future and anticipating change. Yet there had been few preparations, and the state government was no more ready for the oil boom than were the several communities about to be affected.

## THE IMPACT OF THE BOOM

One of the most strongly affected towns was Valdez. Before the boom it was a small community of about twelve hundred residents, located along the shore of the Valdez arm of Prince William Sound, the deep fjord in which the tankers would dock and load Prudhoe Bay oil. The oil would be collected at a tank farm across the bay from the town. Old Valdez had been almost totally destroyed and washed away in Alaska's catastrophic Good Friday earthquake on March 27, 1964. Residents decided to rebuild their town on more stable geological foundations four miles to the west of the old site. The construction of the Trans-Alaska Pipeline terminus across the bay from Valdez brought thousands of new residents to the town, swelling the population to approximately eight thousand. Valdez housing, public services, schools, and shopping facilities became totally inadequate. Prices soared, and the shelves at the town's two grocery stores often were all but empty, forcing families to drive 115 miles to Glennallen, a little highway community, or even more than 300 miles to Anchorage to do their shopping. To accommodate the new residents, Valdez began the construction of four trailer courts, new hotel and motel facilities, a new airport terminal building, an $11-million high school, and a U.S. Coast

Guard center to direct the tanker traffic in Prince William Sound.

Fairbanks, the other community to feel the direct impact of the Trans-Alaska Pipeline, is located in Alaska's interior plateau, in the broad Tanana Valley on the banks of a winding tributary, the Chena River. It is Alaska's second-largest city, with a population of approximately 69,633 (1984).

Named for Senator Charles Fairbanks of Indiana, later vice-president of the United States under President Theodore Roosevelt, the town became an administrative center in 1903 when the federal judge, James Wickersham, moved his third division court to Fairbanks from Eagle on the Yukon River. This move helped keep the town alive after other gold-mining boom towns had decayed and disappeared. The Fairbanks economy diversified over the years, linked to its role as a service and supply center for interior and arctic industrial activities, military bases, the University of Alaska, government offices, tourism, and, in recent years, construction of the Trans-Alaska Pipeline.

Fairbanks residents had grown cautious after the oil boom of 1969 collapsed. At that time, in anticipation of immediate construction of the Trans-Alaska Pipeline, many local businesses had laid in large inventories and made long-term financial commitments. When the boom did not materialize, there were numerous bankruptcies, and many others underwent drastic financial reorganization. By late summer of 1974, however, Fairbanks was about to experience the oil boom.

At the end of June, 1974, the influx of modern boomers hoping to land a pipeline job had swelled the population of Fairbanks. There were only twenty-seven listings under "furnished apartments" in the daily newspaper, with efficiencies renting for $200 per month and two-bedroom apartments going as high as $450. Most restaurants had doubled their prices from the fall of 1973; a cup of soup and a sandwich, for example, at an economical lunch counter cost $2.25. Everywhere there were lines, and it took fifteen or twenty minutes just to drive through the ten-block downtown area at rush hour. At certain times of the day, giant Hercules cargo jet planes roared overhead every ten minutes.

One graphic illustration of the dramatic increase in commerce spurred by the beginning of construction on the Trans-Alaska Pipeline is the number of operations at Fairbanks International Airport in 1974 as compared to 1973. In 1973 there were a total of 125,875 landing and take-off operations, of which 60,695 had been logged by the end of June. In 1974 total operations by the end of June had already reached 77,093, with the heaviest air traffic months still ahead. Perhaps even more striking is the increase in the number of air taxi operations and the volume of air cargo handled. Throughout all of 1973, some 24.5 million pounds of freight arrived. Through the end of May, 1974, the total volume of landed freight totaled 23.2 million pounds, nearly equal the total volume of 1973. Equally impressive is the number of travelers both originating and terminating in Fairbanks. Through May, 1973, 48,592 air travelers had terminated their flight in Fairbanks; 62,322 had arrived in the city through May of 1974. Likewise, 47,187 air passengers originated their flights in Fairbanks through May, 1973; this number sharply increased to 64,655 through May of 1974.[78]

By the summer of 1975, Fairbanks was humming with activity. Money flowed easily, and aggressive hookers populated Second Avenue—dubbed "two street" by the pipeliners—one of the town's main streets. Downtown Fairbanks is architecturally undistinguished, consisting of boxy buildings, many with false fronts, which were constructed more for utility than beauty. Concentrated within two or three blocks of Second Avenue are most of the town's bars, which remain open until 5 A.M. and reopen a few hours later for the early morning drinkers. There are also a few eating establishments, tourist gift shops full of novelties, and the Co-op Drug Store, which offers a large variety of sundry merchandise. It also seems to be the gathering place for many of the town's Eskimos and Athapaskan Indians and their visiting relatives, who may come from such faraway places as Barrow, Point Hope, Fort Yukon, and Allakaket.

For three hectic years Fairbanks experienced all the trauma and excitement of pipeline impact, including increased dollars and debts, increased population and deteriorating public services, increased crime and employment, and increased unemployment. As thousands of workers streamed into the state in quest of high-paying pipeline jobs, the biggest privately financed construction project ever undertaken got underway. On July 27, 1974, Alyeska announced that the first road link south from Prudhoe Bay had been established, and in September of that year the road was officially opened for truck traffic. On March 27, 1975, the first pipe was installed at the Tonsina River.

## MAIN PHASE OF CONSTRUCTION

By March, 1975 the Trans-Alaska Pipeline project, in the preliminary stages until then, was about to launch the main phase of construction all along the 789 miles from Prudhoe Bay to the tanker terminal at Valdez. Alyeska officials hoped to have oil flowing through the line by July 1, 1977. Operating on a tight schedule, Alyeska hoped to have 45 percent of all pipeline work, including the erection of storage tanks and buildings at most pump station sites and the tank and building construction at the Valdez terminal, completed at the end of 1975. A total of eighteen oil storage tanks, each having a capacity of 510,000 barrels, was to be built in that particular phase of construction, together with three ballast tanks and several

This crossing at the Tonsina River in the spring of 1975 was the first installation of pipe for the trans-Alaska pipeline. The pipe was weighted with concrete anchors for burial below the riverbed. Courtesy Alyeska Pipeline Service Company.

smaller tanks. At the same time, preparations were underway to start offshore work on the pilings at the Valdez terminal. At both Valdez and Fairbanks workers forklifted the 40-foot sections of the 48-inch-diameter pipe, in storage since 1969, from the stacks and cleaned and welded them together into 80-foot lengths. At other places along the line, crews drilled holes for erecting the 18-inch pipe vertical supports carrying the above-ground sections of the line[79]

The first construction year ended at the end of April, 1975. During that period an estimated 15 million man-hours had been expended on the effort, and hundreds of thousands of tons of cargo had been shipped

north. Furthermore, the first buried and elevated portions of the pipeline were in place about 85 miles north of Valdez, and three buried river crossings had been completed. The first installation of pipe and the successful completion of the 360-mile Yukon–Prudhoe Bay highway highlighted the first construction year.[80]

By October, 1975, trucks were rolling over the brand new Yukon River bridge connecting with the North Slope haul road. Five piers and two abutments supported the nearly half-mile-long span that had cost $30 million to build. Alyeska assumed one-half of the cost of the bridge, which is owned by the state. The opening of the bridge came just in time: that year's barge fleet of forty-seven vessels, carrying 160,000 tons of oil-field supplies from Puget Sound to Prudhoe Bay, was halted by heavy ice conditions. Only twenty-five of the barges reached their destination. The rest turned back, and most of them offloaded at Seward for shipment by rail north to Fairbanks and then by road to Prudhoe Bay. The bridge was an important link in the transportation chain.[81]

Thousands of workers were battling the climate and the calendar to complete this most costly and controversial of privately financed construction jobs in history. By late

Double joints of pipe for the northern section of the trans-Alaska pipeline being transported on railcars to Fairbanks. Courtesy Alyeska Pipeline Service Company.

1976 the price tag had escalated from $900 million to $7.7 billion. If nothing were to go wrong, the pipeline was to start up in mid-1977 and carry some 600,000 barrels of oil a day on a 789-mile journey across three mountain ranges, beneath 350 rivers and streams, and through highly active earthquake zones.

Unlike many other construction projects, the Trans-Alaska Pipeline was a cost-plus project in which money was not important at all. At the outset TAPS had no idea of how to build a pipeline in a region where temperatures fluctuated from 60° below zero to 100° above. TAPS was not only going to build a pipeline quickly, but also build it exactly as if it were located in Texas. They planned to weld it together, bury it, turn on the taps, and forget it. Vociferous objections from environmentalists and the sharp criticism of federal and state officials eventually forced Alyeska to design and build a line superior to any built before.

The Trans-Alaska Pipeline was also a wasteful project in terms of man-hours and material expended. Whenever there was a question of using more material or using less, invariably more was used. If there was the slightest chance that some machine was needed, it was bought. If management thought it might need additional laborers or craftsmen, they were hired, and pipeline wages were fantastically high—an average of $1,200 per week.

At the height of construction, Fairbanks International Airport hummed with activity. The terminal building and the parking lots were full. Each day the Alaska Airlines Pipeline Express, direct from Houston and Dallas, brought another contingent of

An aboveground section of the trans-Alaska pipeline in the interior of Alaska. The aboveground mode uses unique platforms that allow the pipe to move from side to side during thermal expansion and contraction and earthquakes. The coils mounted on the vertical support pipes are designed to dissipate heat. Courtesy Alyeska Pipeline Service Company.

"pointy-toes," so called for the cowboy boots many wore. These people were the soldiers of fortune of the oil industry, the professional troubleshooters, drillers, welders, and pipeline layers who have followed their calling from Kuwait to the North Sea, from Africa to Latin America. Motel and hotel rooms in town, if available, cost $50 per night.

Then, as suddenly as the boom had begun, it dropped off. By the summer of 1977 the line had been completed, Alyeska had laid off most of the workers, and the crowds at the airport had thinned considerably. The Fairbanks economy, buoyed by $800,000 a day in wages and purchases during the height of construction, slowed down once again.

## OIL FLOWS

At 10:05 A.M. on June 20, 1977, the first oil flowed into the pipeline, nine years after the initial discovery of oil at Prudhoe Bay. After receiving confirmation from the operations control center at Valdez that the pipeline system was ready to receive oil, Alyeska's pump station chief technician directed a station operator to open valves allowing the first barrels of oil to flow into the pipe under producer pressure. Later, a booster pump was activated, bringing crude oil from storage tanks to one of the station's large mainline pumps. Powered by a 13,500-horsepower aircraft-type turbine, the mainline centrifugal pump pushed oil out of the station on its trip to Valdez at an initial rate of 300,000 barrels a day. The only hitch at the beginning of the oil flow was a leak at the flange of a valve at Prudhoe, which was stopped when workers tightened a few bolts.

At the front of the flowing crude oil in the pipeline was a metal device known as a batching pig. Preceding the pig were approximately six million cubic feet of nitrogen gas. The gas purged the line of air, and thus its oxygen, to prevent the danger

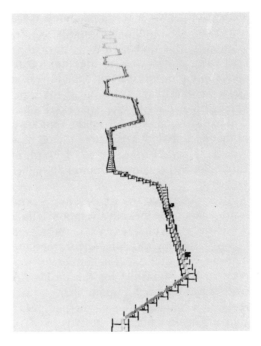

The trans-Alaska pipeline zigzags across the snow-covered North Slope. The design converts pipe thermal expansion and movement from other forces into a controlled sideways movement. Courtesy Alyeska Pipeline Service Company.

of an explosion caused by accumulations of crude oil vapor. The pig separated the nitrogen gas from the oil. A wheel attached to the batching pig emitted sounds as it traveled through the pipeline, enabling ground tracking teams to determine precisely where the oil front was located. Personnel equipped with hand-held receivers listened to signals transmitted from a battery-powered radio installed in the pig, checking for leaks, thermal stress, pipe movement, or anything else out of the ordinary.[82]

As the oil started to flow through the pipeline, headline followed headline. First a truck ran into the pipeline and dented it. Since oil had not yet reached that point, workers quickly replaced the damaged section. Then, on June 22, a false earthquake alarm shut down a mainline pump for a brief period. A spokesman for Alyeska explained that the shutdown was triggered by tolerances set too close in the line's earthquake monitoring system. On July 4 a crack in an L-shaped section of the pipe, apparently caused by the accidental injection of nitrogen, again forced the shutdown of the pipeline. Officials halted the oil flow between pipe miles 473 and 474, south of Fairbanks near Pump Station Number Eight.[83]

After the necessary repairs, oil flowed south again until the late afternoon of July 8, when a gigantic explosion destroyed Pump Station Eight, killing one worker and injuring five others.[84] Human error was once again responsible for the mishap. A worker had removed a pump filter and not replaced it before restarting the pump. Oil spraying against hot turbines triggered an explosion that destroyed the pump station. Ten days after the explosion and fire at Pump Station Eight, Alyeska restarted the line, bypassing the destroyed station and bringing Pump Station Nine on line earlier than planned to boost the oil over the mountains.

But the troubles were not over. On July 19 a front-end loader damaged the fitting on a check valve about twenty-three miles south of Prudhoe Bay. About 2,000 barrels of oil flowed onto the tundra before maintenance crews shut down the line for eight hours and repaired the damage. On July 20, the first sabotage attempt ripped a stretch of insulation off the pipeline north of Fairbanks and tore supporting pipe brackets from the line. The line itself was not damaged and the oil flow continued. State troopers soon arrested several individuals, and two men were later indicted, tried, and convicted on charges of malicious destruction of property.

The oil finally arrived at the Valdez tanker terminal on July 28, 1977, fulfilling Alyeska's promise three years earlier to deliver oil in Valdez by the first of August. Many Alaskans celebrated the event—particularly Jean Mahoney of Anchorage, who won the great Alaskan Pipeline Classic lottery of $30,000 for her guess that the oil would reach Valdez in 38 days, 12 hours, and 57 minutes, a mere 60 seconds off the actual time. Some fourteen thousand individuals entered that lottery sponsored by Saint Patrick's Catholic Church in Anchorage. The church profited as well.[85]

All went well until February 15, 1978, when a private pilot flying over the line just east of Fairbanks reported seeing a leak. Investigators soon discovered a length of fuse near the site and later concluded that a plastic charge had ripped a hole into the line, spilling 550,000 gallons of oil onto the tundra. Despite intensive efforts, the crime remains unsolved.[86]

But there were bright spots as well. In 1978 oil was flowing through the line at the rate of 1.16 million barrels per day. During the first year of operation 278 million barrels of oil reached Valdez, and with the construction of four additional pump stations along the route and more oil storage and tanker docking facilities at Valdez, the pipeline's capacity can be increased to carry 2 million barrels per day.

As many expected and feared, however, Alaskan oil has created a glut on the West Coast and necessitated the shipment of some of it through the Panama Canal to the East Coast of the United States; this has resulted in higher transportation charges. Since the state of Alaska taxes the sales price of the oil—about $13.50 per barrel— but not the transportation charges, it is generally in the companies' interest to have as high a charge as possible for the use of the pipeline. Before the pipeline opened, the oil industry and the federal government predicted an average wellhead—or state taxable—value of $7.50 per barrel for Prudhoe Bay oil. But when the oil companies began filing their first wellhead prices, they reported a weighted average price of $4.79 per barrel. In April, 1978, the average wellhead price per barrel of oil

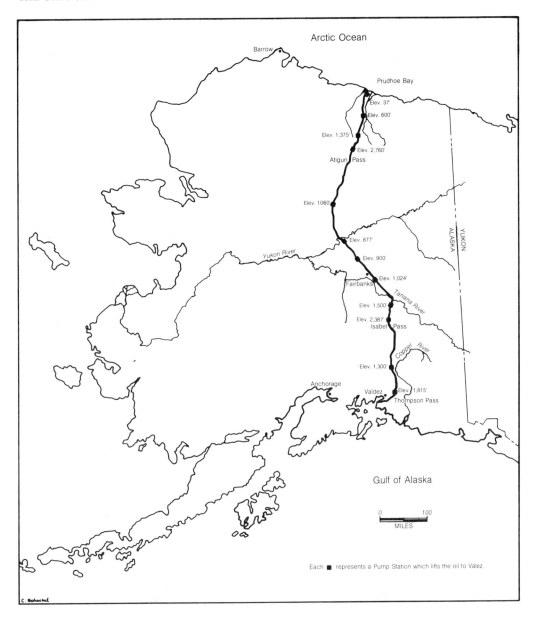

The trans-Alaska pipeline route, showing pump stations and their elevations. Map by Christie Schackel.

had further declined to $4.39. Even worse, one North Slope producer, Phillips Petroleum Company, shocked state officials with a wellhead price of $1.22 per barrel of oil shipped to the East Coast because of the West Coast surplus.[87]

Understandably, Alaskans and their officials were bitterly disappointed. Robert Le Resche, the state's commissioner of natural resources, most aptly summarized Alaskans' disappointments: "Here we are, having endured the negative impacts of construction of the Trans-Alaska Pipeline, and sitting back ready to reap our just rewards, suddenly confronted with a wellhead price far below what anyone ever suggested in the past." In fact, since North Slope oil began flowing through the pipeline in the late summer of 1977, state revenue department officials had been forced to reduce their royalty and severance tax income for the fiscal year 1979 by $308.5 million.

The state thereupon initiated a series of court challenges over producer-filed pipeline tariffs. In June, 1985, the Federal Energy Regulatory Commission (FERC) announced that it had revised its rate-making methods for pipelines located in the contiguous states. It was unclear whether that decision applied to Alaska as well, but there was hope that it would. In any event, the FERC decision altered the odds of the continued litigation in the state's favor. The plaintiffs in the suit were the state of Alaska and the U.S. Department of Justice. By 1985 the state had paid more than $35 million in legal fees. State revenue department officials estimated that if a settlement was reached in 1985 it would mean an additional $300 million for fiscal year 1986 and approximately another $200 million a year thereafter. Not long afterward all owners of the Trans-Alaska Pipeline except Sohio and Amarada Hess settled with the state out of court.[88]

In October, 1985, FERC approved the out-of-court settlement between the state and the owners of the pipeline on a 3–0

vote. Only Sohio and Amarada Hess still had not accepted the settlement, but they did so in 1986. The settlement ended the lawsuit that had begun in 1977. FERC found the agreement fair, reasonable, and in the public interest. Under the terms of the settlement tariff rates for shipping two-thirds of the oil through the pipeline would be set from 1982 to 2011. The complex agreement established shipping charges for oil delivered between January 1, 1983 and December 31, 1985, as follows: 1982, $6.05 per barrel; 1983, $5.93 per barrel; 1984, $5.63 per barrel, and 1985, $5.31 per barrel. Relatively low transportation rates are to be set in future years, encouraging the development of marginal oil resources and encouraging competitive exploration for oil. The pipeline owners also must reimburse the state for its legal expenses in the amount of $23 million. The state collected more than $700 million from the pipeline owners for past overcharges on the transportation of oil.[89]

Another plan designed to increase oil revenues called for an appeal to President Jimmy Carter to allow the shipment of Alaska crude oil to Japan in exchange for Middle East oil destined for that country, which would then be diverted to the East Coast of the United States. If the president had allowed such export, it would have relieved the West Coast oil surplus and the need for producers to ship Alaskan crude oil to the Gulf and East Coasts, resulting in lower wellhead values because of increased shipping costs.[90]

The Export Administration Act of 1969 granted the president the authority to impose export controls to deny the export of scarce domestic natural resources, including crude oil. Alaskans protested these limitations, but to no avail. The obstacles were too great.

To understand these prohibitions fully, one must return to the Trans-Alaska Pipeline System (TAPS) Authorization Act of 1973, which enabled pipeline construction to begin with the stipulation that North Slope crude oil production must be reserved for domestic use. In essence the TAPS Act reinforced the Export Administration Act of 1969 by borrowing from an earlier federal resource act. According to Section 28 of the Mineral Lands Leasing Act of 1920, crude oil transported through pipelines granted rights-of-way over federal lands (such as TAPS) is restricted from export. The 1977 amendments to the Export Administration Act contain the same restrictions. Those amendments and the TAPS Act further require a presidential finding that the proposed export would serve the national interest, and both allow for congressional review of the president's reported findings. In an identical exception, however, both statutes allowed for exchanges of crude oil in like quantities with adjacent foreign states "for convenience or increased efficiency of transportation."[91]

The Energy Policy and Conservation Act (EPCA) of 1975 directed the president to formulate regulations restricting crude-oil exports. Section 103(b) permits exceptions to be determined by the president on the basis of the national interest, but the accompanying Senate conference report directed the president "to assume that exemptions do not result in greater reliance on imports." Several other factors must also be considered in the export dilemma. The TAPS Act required that the proposed export not diminish the quantity or quality of crude oil entering the U.S. market. Additionally, the 1977 Export Administration Act amendments and Section 7(d) of the Export Administration Act of 1979 specified as follows:

1. The proposed export of exchange will benefit the consumer through reduced average refinery acquisition costs within a period of three months;

2. In case of an oil supply disruption, the proposed export or exchange will be terminated.

It is clear, therefore, that North Slope crude may be exported only in accordance with a set of rigorous limitations. State officials and Alaska's congressional delegation apparently have not succeeded in definining how the national interest will be served by lifting the export ban, how refinery acquisition costs can be lowered within three months, or how increased reliance on imports can be either avoided or rendered insignificant.[92]

In the meantime, the oil companies have continued to develop Prudhoe Bay, the world's twelfth-largest oil field and the largest ever discovered in North America, with recoverable reserves of approximately 10,014 billion barrels of crude oil and condensate and 26 trillion cubic feet of natural gas. In comparison, only two other fields discovered in the United States—the East Texas and the Wilmington—initially contained recoverable reserves in excess of 2 billion barrels. Except for these two, more oil had been removed from the Prudhoe Bay field during its first 4.5 years of production than from any other North American field. At the end of 1985 more than 4 billion barrels of oil had been pumped from the North Slope. By early 1986 approximately 6,000 tankers had berthed at the pipeline terminal at Valdez. For the week ending January 19, 1986, vessel cargo sizes ranged from 279,000 to 1,795,000 barrels a load.[93]

Industry sources estimate the total oil in place in the vicinity of the Prudhoe Bay field at about 60 billion barrels. This total includes 23 billion barrels of original oil in place at Prudhoe Bay, 5.5 billion in the Kuparuk River field, and 3 billion in the Lisburne formation underlying the Prudhoe Bay field. In addition, estimates of oil in place in the West Sak Sands and Ugnu heavy oil zones overlying the Kuparuk River field range between 21 and 36 million barrels. Known oil resources on the North Slope outside the immediate vicinity of Prudhoe Bay may bring the total oil in place in the region to 80 billion barrels. Unfortu-

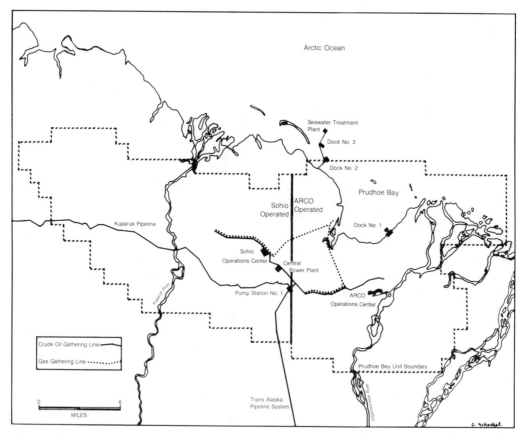

The Prudhoe Bay oil field, one half operated by ARCO and the other by Sohio. Map by Christie Schackel.

nately, however, industry can economically recover only a fraction of the oil in place, referred to as "recoverable reserves." Still, with the prevailing economic conditions during the mid-1970s the expected profitability of the Prudhoe Bay field was sufficient to finance the investment in the Trans-Alaska Pipeline System and the basic infrastructure on the North Slope without considering any potential production outside the Sadlerochit Reservoir at Prudhoe, the main oil pool.[94]

Oil prices declined after 1981, and tumbled as low as $12 a barrel in early 1986 and to below $10 a barrel during the summer. These declines have completely changed the outlook for profitable development of non-Prudhoe production on the North Slope. Although some of this development is already under way, future economic conditions will affect decisions on whether or not to go ahead with production. Technological problems are particularly challenging in the West Sak Sands at a depth of 3,500 to 4,000 feet and the Ugnu formation above West Sak Sands at about 2,500 to 3,000 feet. On much of the North Slope permafrost extends to depths of as much as 2,000 feet. Oil just below that depth is much cooler than reserves at greater depths. For example, oil from the Prudhoe Bay field flows at about 190°F, while the oil in West

Sak Sands is about 70°F. and Ugnu oil is between 40° and 50°F. In fact, if one had
Ugnu oil in a jar, it would not pour without
first being warmed. That is the crux of the
problem—how to add heat to the oil to decrease its viscosity. This calls for sophisticated tertiary recovery methods, such as
steam flooding or in situ combustion. Flow
rates illustrate the importance of the oil's
temperature to maximum recovery. Oil
from Prudhoe Bay's Sadlerochit formation
flows between 10,000 to 20,000 barrels a
well a day. Each Kuparuk well yields between 2,000 to 3,000 barrels a day, and

West Sak Sands would flow at a rate of up to
200 barrels a day.[95]

By the summer of 1984, Prudhoe Bay had
been producing oil since 1977. About 600
wells were flowing, and the field yielded an
average of 1.5 million barrels a day, the
maximum efficient rate established by the
Alaska Oil and Gas Conservation Commission. Sohio is of the opinion that the maximum efficient rate (MER) can be sustained
until 1987, but it also estimates that the
field's MER could drop by more than 50
percent by 1992 under conventional recovery methods. Producers can employ a vari-

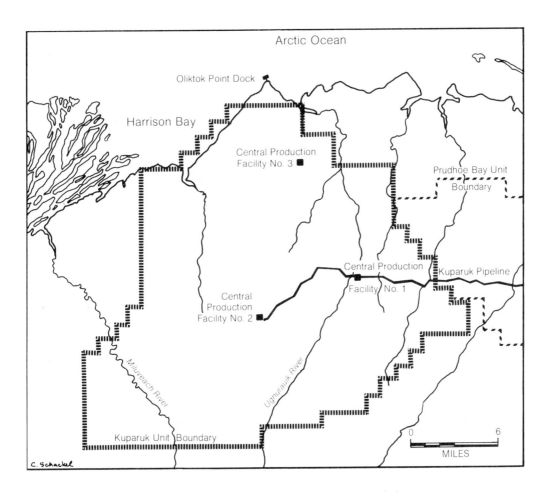

The Kuparuk oil field. Map by Christie Schackel.

ety of alternative methods to prolong the field's productive life into the 1990s and beyond and extract an additional 2 billion barrels of oil. At present there exists no system to export Prudhoe Bay's estimated 26 trillion cubic feet of gas—there is no market because the gas is too expensive. The gas produced is injected back into the reservoir rock to maintain sufficient pressure to push out more oil. The rest is used as fuel for field and Alyeska pipeline facilities. In 1984 operators began using secondary recovery techniques, including injection wells to force water (waterflooding) or gas (gas injection) into the reservoir to push out more oil through the reservoir rock to production wells. Operators invested $2 billion in a waterflood project in which Beaufort Sea water is processed in a treatment plant and pumped into the oil formation through injection wells. Water extracted simultaneously with oil from production wells is also used for injection. A seawater treatment plan with daily capacity in excess of 2 million barrels removes seawater impurities. Over the life of the field waterflooding is expected to account for production of about 1 billion of the 9.6 billion barrels of oil now deemed recoverable.[96]

A tertiary recovery program called the Prudhoe Bay Miscible Gas Project is designed to further maximize oil production ("miscibility" is the ability of two substances to mix perfectly). In this project the operators will combine waterflooding with injecting miscible mixtures of hydrocarbon gases into the reservoir. The project calls for some of the natural gas produced from the field to be enriched with propane and butane. The enriched mixture will then be injected into the reservoir, where it will mix with the oil, creating a solvent effect, helping the oil flow more easily through the reservoir to production wells. In addition, the gas-processing plant will also produce a natural-gas liquid stream in excess of 30,000 barrels daily, which will be blended with the crude oil entering the Trans-

Alaska Pipeline. The Miscible Gas Project is expected to cost more than $1 billion to install and will yield an additional 400 million barrels of oil and natural-gas liquids from the Prudhoe Bay reservoir.[97]

## THE FUTURE

The oil, gas, and pipeline story is far from over, for experts believe that fully one-third of the nation's undiscovered recoverable oil and gas may lie under Alaska and its continental shelf. Over the years the Department of the Interior has sold substantial lease acreage in the Gulf of Alaska and the Beaufort and Bering seas. For example, in 1983–84 leases for tracts in three offshore Alaska areas, the Navarin, Saint George, and Norton basins, netted the federal government about $1.4 billion in revenues. The oil industry, together with consultants and academic communities, has embarked on an ambitious research and exploration program to enable it eventually to extract oil and gas from these offshore areas.[98] In short, the federal government looks to Alaska and its outer continental shelf for the single largest increment of new oil-and-gas supplies to meet national energy needs in the 1980s, the 1990s, and beyond.

Unfortunately, the state of Alaska has become largely dependent on oil revenues for its operating and capital budgets. In 1978, Texas, Louisiana, and Oklahoma received 19.6, 29.2, and 15 percent, respectively, of their state revenues from the oil industry. In 1982 the state of Alaska received 86.5 percent of its revenues directly from the petroleum industry. Petroleum income fueled state spending, and for about a decade Alaska's labor force, population, and personal income increased faster than those of any other state. Very little of this growth would have occurred without the fivefold price increase for Middle Eastern crude oil in 1973–74 and the resulting threefold increase in the market value of U.S. domestic crude oil, which made it economically possible to develop the Prudhoe Bay field and construct the Trans-Alaska Pipeline.[99] World oil prices increased again in 1979–80, and at their peak in 1981 oil revenues flowed into the state treasury at an annual per capita rate of more than $10,000. State spending for government operations, transfer payments, loan programs, and public works kept pace with state revenues. In 1980 the state legislature abolished personal income taxes, and in 1982 it voted to distribute a "Permanent Fund dividend" check of $1,000 to each resident.[100]

By the second quarter of 1981 crude-oil prices began to decline, but most private and government planning had assumed that oil prices would keep rising. This implied that Prudhoe Bay would generate more and more revenues for the state, which in turn promised more public- and private-sector jobs and also a sustained high level of exploration activity on state and federal lands and on the federal outer continental shelf (OCS). This would undoubtedly bring about major new discoveries, and a few were made. Rising oil prices also convinced sponsors of the proposed Alaska gas pipeline that they could all but ignore the difficulty of marketing North Slope gas as a constraint on the project's economic feasibility.

Ever-increasing oil prices also seemed to assure Alaska a petrochemicals boom based on the growing cost advantage that North Slope natural-gas liquids would have over oil-based petrochemical feedstocks used elsewhere. It also seemed to guarantee development of Alaska's coal for export. Increasing oil prices also meant that natural gas and coal would soon be too valuable to use for generating electric power, and planners and lawmakers used this argument as a rationale for planning various hydroelectric generating plants, including a multibillion-dollar plant on the Susitna River.[101]

In November, 1982, the Governor's Council on Economic Policy focused a day of discussions and presentations of the question: "Is there life for the State of Alaska after Prudhoe Bay?" A diverse group of economists, oil-industry experts, and state officials concerned about the ominous Prudhoe Bay production curve met to share their views. State revenues from oil produced on state lands, primarily Prudhoe Bay (more than 1 billion barrels of oil were produced from Cook Inlet between 1959 and 1985) will peak in 1987 and then decline rapidly. How can state government be funded at present levels when the revenue flow from Alaska's oil industry begins its steep decline in the 1990s? Three points of view were identified in the roundtable briefing paper:

1. Projections of state oil revenues are unduly pessimistic; therefore state expenditures will continue to be important in bolstering Alaska's economy.

2. State oil revenues may decline, but other sources of revenue will be developed to make up the difference.

3. Oil revenues may decline, and no other significant sources of tax revenues may be found; but by the time revenues drop sharply, the unsubsidized private sector will have grown enough to offset the adverse economic impact of reduced state spending.

There was also a pessimistic view which maintained that the revenue projections were valid, that other significant sources of tax revenue either did not exist or could not be developed without damaging the private sector or precluding new investment, and that the private sector will not grow sufficiently to offset the decline in state spending. In fact, one economist predicted that Alaska's oil boom was short-lived and would be followed by the most severe depression experienced since statehood in 1959.[102]

No one knows what the future will bring, but by the spring of 1986 the economic bust had begun, and the future looks foreboding because of the low and unstable oil prices. Of course, Alaskans have argued heatedly among themselves and with others whether energy development has been a worthwhile trade-off for the increased economic activity and prosperity. There are those who maintain that the oil boom has irreparably harmed the delicately balanced ecology of the Arctic and has wrought havoc with the independent life-style of the state's residents. Those favoring economic growth point to the long-term economic benefits the state is reaping, including a vastly improved infrastructure made possible by abundant oil revenues. In any event, Alaskans themselves have had very little say in the decisions to develop the state's energy sources. The energy crisis of 1973–74, the subsequent explosion in crude-oil prices, and the national drive toward energy "self-sufficiency" have been the factors that combined to spur Alaska development.

What is certain is that oil activities temporarily brought more jobs, money, and people. Additional pipelines, roads, processing plants, and port facilities have been built. A larger population has put greater pressures on the state's land, water, and fish and wildlife resources. Above all, oil development has generated a momentum of its own, and it is largely unaffected by what the state may or may not do. A seasoned observer of Alaska has concluded that the state government, to have any control over the speed of development, will have to "rely primarily on policies other than the direct control of petroleum resources—on environmental regulations, tax policies, expenditure programs, and other policy actions that can both mitigate undesirable effects of petroleum development and distribute its benefits more equitably." But perhaps it was an old sourdough who best summed up the momentous changes in Alaska when he said: "They sure have gotta lotta things they never had before, ain't they?"[103]

# 15. LOOKING BACK

Between approximately 10,000 and 40,000 years ago, Asiatics drifted across the Bering Sea Land Bridge in pursuit of game. They came in small bands and slowly continued as far as the southern tip of South America. The ancestors of today's Indians came first, followed by the progenitors of the Aleuts and Eskimos. For thousands of years these various groups made Alaska their home. They used the resources of this subcontinent to sustain them and successfully adapted to the varied climates of the North. Then came the white man, who brought modern technology as well as disease. As elsewhere, upon contact with Europeans, thousands of Alaskan Natives died, most from unfamiliar European maladies.

For more than two centuries after the coming of the white man, Alaska was a remote and neglected province of little concern to either the Russian or, later, the American government. Russia, very large but sparsely populated, with a poorly developed political and economic system, had little need for new territory. After Peter the Great, who was the energy and vision behind Bering's voyage, its rulers—with the exception of Catherine the Great—were weak and incompetent and primarily concerned with European affairs. Those Russians who first came to Alaska were private individuals, interested only in the fur trade.

With little supervision from the government in Saint Petersburg, they reduced the Aleuts, the Native people with whom they first came into contact, to virtual slavery. By the end of the century the private traders had been ousted and a government-sponsored monopoly, the Russian-American Company, was given control. By the middle of the nineteenth century, however, the company was in a precarious economic position, subsisting on government favors and subsidies. Because Russian leaders believed that the country could not both defend Alaska and carry out an imperialistic policy in Asia, in 1867 they sold Alaska to the United States for $7,200,000.

Russian influence in Alaska was slight. The few Russians who came limited their stay to the islands and coastal areas, leaving the vast interior almost untouched. Even the Panhandle region, south of what is today Juneau, was leased to the Hudson's Bay Company. Baranov, the outstanding personality of Russian America, who came in 1790, was probably more affected by the ways of the Natives than they by the culture of the Russians. His successors as governors of Alaska were naval men, who were better educated and among whom were some explorers of note. They attempted to increase Russian influence among the Natives by establishing schools, improving their condi-

In 1847 the Hudson's Bay Company established Fort Yukon near the junction of the Porcupine and Yukon Rivers. At the end of June, 1867, Frederick Whymper, a young English adventurer, writer, and artist and a member of the Collins Overland Expedition visited the fort. He recounted that, on landing, "we found two young Scotchmen, and a French half-breed, the sole occupants of the Fort, the commander and many of his men being absent on the annual trip for supplies." From Frederick Whymper, *Travel and Adventure in the Territory of Alaska* (1868).

tions of livelihood, and furthering the efforts of the Orthodox church to bring Christianity. Father Ioann Veniaminov, a cleric of the Orthodox church, devised an alphabet and gave the Aleuts a written language. The Russians did introduce the Natives to the ways of the white man, and undoubtedly eased the contacts with them for the Americans. And they did develop New Archangel (Sitka) into the Pacific Coast's largest town, though by no means a metropolitan center, for a time. But aside from a few Russian Orthodox churches and Russian names among the Native population, little remains of the Russian presence in Alaska today.

American rule brought little change to Alaska. The United States in 1867 was not much better prepared than Russia to govern

Alaska. The Civil War had just ended; problems of the defeated South were foremost in the nation's mind, and those of Alaska held little interest. With no precedent to guide them in the administration of noncontiguous territories, Congress took the easiest course and turned Alaska over to the military. For the next seventeen years the territory was under the rule of the Army and, subsequently, the Navy. But even if the quality of American statesmanship had been greater and more thought been given to Alaska, there was little incentive for Americans to trek north.

In an era when the United States was undergoing great industrial expansion, those with money to invest found ample opportunities at home without incurring the risks

The U.S. marine revenue cutter *Bear* about 1900. The *Bear* was built in 1873 in Dundee, Scotland, for use in the Arctic sealing trade near Newfoundland. In 1883 it was called upon to rescue the Greely Expedition lost in the Arctic. The *Bear* subsequently spent forty years along the Alaska coasts. It was the first vessel to go north each spring, taking mail, medical services, and news and dispensing law and order. The *Bear* carried the first reindeer from Siberia to Alaska as part of the Reverend Sheldon Jackson's plan to relieve destitute Eskimos. The *Bear* was finally retired in the late 1920s. Courtesy Historical Photograph Collection, Alaska and Polar Regions Archives, Elmer E. Rasmuson Library, University of Alaska.

entailed in a distant land. Employment in the factories was high, and for those wishing to move, land was to be had almost for the asking in the sparsely settled West. When the Russian-American Company left Alaska, the population declined. Most Russians and those persons of mixed blood who had been given the option—under the treaty of purchase—to remain in Alaska either returned to their homeland or went to Canada or other parts of the United States where they felt their prospects were much better. A few Americans rushed to preempt land in Sitka, but they soon departed when the hoped-for boom failed to materialize.

Accounts differ concerning the Alaskan Natives' preference for the Russians or the Americans. Some altercations between soldiers and the aboriginal population took place, but no great wars such as occurred in the American West ever developed in Alaska.

Alaska's great size, remoteness, and formidable climate seemed to discourage small businesses and favor those possessing large capital. One thriving organization, the Alaska Commercial Company, which apparently had some political influence, was given the monopoly of the seal harvest of the Pribilof Islands. Under the auspices of this company, the Yukon Valley was also opened up for the fur trade. The exploita-

tion of the valuable salmon fisheries began
but with virtually no benefit to Alaska or
Alaskans. Needed capital for the industry
was provided by large packing firms from
the outside, who paid few taxes and brought
in not only the fishermen but also the crews
to work in the canneries.

## THE GOLD RUSHES

In the 1880s, Alaska was already becoming
something of a tourist attraction. The trip
to Alaska was long and expensive, however,
and tourists did not come in great numbers.
It was the lure of gold that began drawing
Americans to Alaska. Discoveries of gold in
the area of the Gastineau Channel led to
the founding of Juneau, the first town established under American rule. Gold was

also found on the American side of the
Yukon at Fortymile and then Birch Creek.
But far more important were the great discoveries on the Canadian side of the great
river near the banks of its tributary, the
Klondike. Alaska benefited greatly. Skagway, a port on Lynn Canal, became the
gateway to the Klondike, while the Canadian boom stimulated the search for the
precious metal in Alaska. Nome, where
twenty thousand men worked at one time
on its "golden sands," was the scene of
Alaska's greatest gold rush, followed by
Fairbanks and a host of others, including
Iditarod, Chandalar, and Livengood.

The gold rush marked a new discovery of
Alaska. Alaska was hailed as Eldorado.
Businessmen looked to it as a place for in-
vestment. Several government agencies be-

Charter members of the Yukon Order of Pioneers. Standing, left to right: Gordon Bettles, Pete Mc-
Donald, Jim Bender, Frank Buteau, G. Matlock, Al Mayo, Pete Nelson, Tom Lloyd, Bill Stewart;
seated, left to right: H. H. Hart, William McPhee, unknown, LeRoy Napoleon ("Jack") McQuesten,
G. Harrington, unknown, H. Albert; center: unknown. Courtesy Historical Photograph Collection,
Alaska and Polar Regions Archives, Elmer E. Rasmuson Library, University of Alaska.

gan work in Alaska. A start was made in road building and the surveying of the territory. The people of Alaska for the first time were given political rights of self-government, limited as they were. Towns were permitted to incorporate and elect their own officials. Alaskans were authorized to send a delegate to Congress in 1906. Six years later Congress granted a legislature to the territory, although it retained for the federal government control over Alaska's land and resources.

By 1910 the main effects of the gold rush had been achieved. The population of Alaska was stabilized at about 60,000, dropping a little during World War I and increasing slightly to a high of 72,000 just before the United States entered World War II. After the war population growth accelerated greatly. For a time the value of the copper mined exceeded that of gold, but minerals began to take second place in Alaska to the fisheries. The number of Alaska fishermen increased, but the control of the resource still remained outside Alaska.

## THE FIRST HALF OF THE TWENTIETH CENTURY

Many generalizations have been made about the people of Alaska. The population was highly transient, and men outnumbered women five to one. Few brought their families with them, and it was said that when they made their "pile," home they would go. But there were those who loved the "Great Land," as they called it, and many wrote lovingly about it. Henry W. Elliott pleaded for the conservation of the seals and for the protection of the Alaska Natives. William Healy Dall was excited by the wealth of its resources waiting to be developed. John Muir was entranced by Alaska's great beauty. The Reverend Sheldon Jackson saw it as a place for saving souls, and warned that the Natives should be protected from the corruption of the whites.

Alaskans, like residents of other territo-ries, constantly complained that their interests were being neglected and ignored. But, while neither Congress nor successive administrations ever made Alaskan affairs an item of priority, several presidents did give them some attention. Early in the twentieth century, a determined effort was made to keep Canadians from poaching for seals bound for Alaska in the Bering Sea. Theodore Roosevelt was most adamant in countering Canadian claims for part of the Alaskan Panhandle, and he closed the Alaska coal fields to further entry because, he claimed, the existing laws concerning coal mining in the territory were "defective." However, some Alaskans were highly critical of this action.

Woodrow Wilson, in his first presidential message, demanded that attention be given to Alaska's needs; and Congress, prompted by his urgings, passed laws allowing the leasing of the coal lands and authorized the building of a railroad at government expense but failed to make changes in the Alaska system of government which the president felt were most essential. Warren G. Harding, the first president to visit Alaska, promised much; but the only important piece of legislation coming from his corruption-ridden and ineffective administration concerned the Alaska fisheries, a law signed by his successor, Calvin Coolidge. For the first and only time in the American period, an attempt was made during the New Deal era of Franklin D. Roosevelt to bring people to Alaska, in the settlement program for the Matanuska Valley.

World War II revolutionized Alaska. The territory's strategic location made it a key factor in America's defense program. As thousands of troops were rushed north, Navy and Army bases were constructed in locations ranging from Unalaska to Kodiak, and from Sitka to Anchorage and Fairbanks. Finally, during the summer of 1942, Japanese forces invaded the Aleutian Chain. America's pride was hurt, and it began intense efforts to oust the enemy. In the spring of 1942 work also began on the Alaska-Canada Military Highway, the Alaska Highway, to link the territory with the lower states. The 1,671-mile highway was completed with almost incredible speed and opened for military traffic in November of that same year.

By the fall of 1943 the enemy had been expelled from Alaska. Ground forces were reduced from a high of 150,000 men in November, 1943, to 50,000 by March, 1945. Forts were closed, bases dismantled, and military airfields turned over to the Civil Aeronautics Administration.

The impact of the military activities irrevocably altered the pace and tenor of Alaskan life. The residual benefits to the civilian economy and the development of Alaska were tremendous. In addition to the influx of well over $1 billion in the territory between 1941 and 1945, Alaskans also benefited from the modernization of the Alaska Railroad and the expansion of airfields and the construction of roads.

Federal activity declined sharply after 1945, but it was the outbreak of the cold war in the late 1940s that once again caused the federal government to spend millions of dollars in defense-related activities. Federal projects became the primary base of the Alaska economy. Within two decades the population of Alaska more than tripled. Anchorage and Fairbanks—especially the former—became the new centers of population. Political demands of the "new" Alaska led to the achievement of statehood in 1958.

The Clear U.S. Air Force Ballistic Missile Early Warning (BMEW) site under construction in the early 1960s. One of three such installations (the other two are in England and Greenland), together they provide a protective screen for the Western Hemisphere, designed to give early warning of incoming long-range enemy missiles. Courtesy U.S. Army Corps of Engineers.

Alaska Oil and Gas Development Company Eureka no. 1 drilling rig. Courtesy Fred Machetanz Collection, Alaska and Polar Regions Archives, Elmer E. Rasmuson Library, University of Alaska.

## STATEHOOD, OIL, AND NATIVE CLAIMS

Although the new state stepped boldly into the new era, its finances and budget soon became major concerns. Alaskans quickly realized that it was expensive to provide the amenities of modern life to the sprawling subcontinent. In addition, military expenditures declined in the 1960s. Modest oil discoveries on the Kenai Peninsula in the late 1950s, a growing forest industry, and developments in the fisheries made up for some of the losses in federal spending. But not until the massive Prudhoe Bay oil discovery in 1968 was there reason to believe that Alaska's economy would become more stable.

The 1970s witnessed the passage of the Alaska Native Claims Settlement Act, which compensated the state's original inhabitants for losses suffered over many years. With land and money, Native Alaskans rapidly became influential in state politics and business. At the same time the construction of the Trans-Alaska Pipeline brought a measure of prosperity—and some problems—to the state. After oil began flowing in the summer of 1977, the state treasury and with it all Alaskans gained some financial stability and security. As the following table shows, however, the state has become dangerously dependent for its unrestricted general-fund revenues on oil-generated revenues:

Unrestricted General Fund Revenues,
State of Alaska,
Fiscal 1971 to 1985, and Forecast
(Millions of Dollars)

| Fiscal Year | Total General Fund Unrestricted Revenues | General Fund Unrestricted Petroleum Revenues | Percent |
|---|---|---|---|
| 1971 | 220.4 | 47.0 | 21 |
| 1972 | 219.2 | 48.4 | 22 |
| 1973 | 208.2 | 50.3 | 24 |
| 1974 | 254.9 | 80.2 | 31 |
| 1975 | 333.4 | 90.4 | 27 |
| 1976 | 709.8 | 391.5 | 55 |
| 1977 | 874.3 | 477.6 | 55 |
| 1978 | 764.9 | 441.5 | 58 |
| 1979 | 1,133.0 | 821.6 | 73 |
| 1980 | 2,501.2 | 2,256.5 | 90 |
| 1981 | 3,718.2 | 3,304.3 | 89 |
| 1982 | 4,108.4 | 3,574.8 | 87 |
| 1983 | 3,631.0 | 3,026.6 | 83 |
| 1984 | 3,390.1 | 2,861.6 | 84 |
| 1985 * | 3,234.3 | 2,707.9 | 84 |
| 1986† | 2,861.2 | 2,416.4 | 84 |
| 1987† | 2,394.2 | 1,941.7 | 81 |
| 1988† | 2,071.4 | 1,663.0 | 80 |

Source: Alaska Pacific Bank, *Alaska Business Trends: 1986 Economic Forecast* (Anchorage: Key Bancshares of Alaska, December 1985), p. 20.
 * Preliminary actuals.
 †Estimated as of September, 1985.

In the latter part of 1985 and during the first two months of 1986, world oil prices tumbled. In fact, the pricing structure of the Organization of Petroleum Exporting Countries collapsed. In January, 1986, for example, Texas light crude oil, a key grade, traded for $25 a barrel, down from $32 as recently as November, 1985. On the spot market, where oil is sold to the highest bid-

der, Texas light crude sold for less than $20 a barrel in January, 1986. The United States consumes about 5.7 billion barrels of oil a year, 30 percent of which is imported. Falling oil prices are beneficial for industrialized nations, because an average price cut of just $5 a barrel would free nearly $30 billion for increased investment and the purchase of consumer goods. It will also depress inflationary pressures. But there will also be many losers, among them oil-and-gas producers, pipeline companies, and banks that lent money to energy concerns and oil-exporting nations such as Mexico, Venezuela, and Nigeria. Falling oil prices also hurt producing states, such as Alaska, which in 1985 received 84 percent of its unrestricted general-fund revenues from petroleum revenues. At $22 a barrel, the state of Alaska shudders, and at $15 per barrel it would face a fiscal revolution. On February 17, 1986, a spokesman for Sohio in Cleveland confirmed that the company's negotiated contract price of crude oil from the North Slope fell $4 a barrel retroactive to February 1, 1986. Sohio owns about one half of the 1.5 million barrels of oil pumped from Prudhoe Bay each day. Sohio's Alaska crude sold for $20 a barrel on the West Coast and $21 a barrel on the Gulf Coast. The state receives a royalty payment of about 12.5 percent of the wellhead value of the oil. The wellhead value is calculated by subtracting the costs of transporting a barrel of oil from the amount the oil company receives for that barrel. Officials of the State of Alaska Department of Revenue have stated that every $1 drop in the price of oil costs the state $150 million a year in lost revenues.[1] In the summer of 1986 oil prices dropped below $10 a barrel and Alaska's economy plunged, bankruptcies abounded, and many panicked and left the state.

The precipitous drop in oil prices has hurt Alaska as well as other oil-producing states. Companies, faced with declining revenues, have deferred exploratory activities. For example, Conoco, Inc., announced in February, 1986, that it had suspended drilling operations at its Milne Point oil field on the North Slope because of plunging oil prices. A spokesman for the company stated that if crude oil prices continued to fall it would also shut down production from the field.[2] Milne Point is the newest and smallest of the three developed oil fields on the North Slope, producing about 20,000 barrels a day. The others are the Kuparuk River field, which produces about 190,000 barrels a day, and the Prudhoe Bay field, which produces 1,500,000 barrels a day for a daily total in excess of 1,700,000 barrels. The amount varies from day to day, however.

Obviously the declining crude-oil prices and the state's heavy reliance on oil-generated revenues worry many northern residents. Alternative sources of revenues must be found. Unfortunately, at a time of high crude-oil prices and record revenues for the state, the legislature decided to abandon Alaska's state income tax system. Many cautioned the lawmakers to suspend rather than abolish the tax. But with prospects of ever-rising oil revenues, these warnings were not heeded, and the legislature abolished it. No one seemed to remember that territorial Governor Ernest Gruening had struggled for ten years, from 1939 to 1949, to have the legislature fashion and adopt a modern tax system. His efforts were crowned with success in 1949. It took only one day to abolish what had taken ten years to create. Then Governor Jay S. Hammond failed to veto it, convinced that his veto would be overridden. It will be hard to reimpose the tax—as it must be, and soon.

As previously stated, voters created the Alaska Permanent Fund in 1976, when they approved an appropriate constitutional amendment. The original goal was to place part of the one-time oil wealth beyond the reach of day-to-day government spending. Then Governor Jay Hammond, among others, favored direct distribution of a portion of the oil revenues, thus giving each citizen

a personal stake in the oil revenues and protecting the permanent fund from possible raids by legislators. Others argued that government heavily subsidized various special-interest groups, as, for example, under the home-loan program, under which upper-income borrowers received monthly subsidies larger than the payments made by the federal government to recipients of aid for families with dependent children. Still others pointed out that direct distribution of part of the oil money would be more beneficial than government spending. In 1980 the legislature passed a Permanent Fund distribution measure. The bill provided that annual dividends would vary, increasing with length of residency.

Many supported the concept of richly rewarding those who claimed long residency and had helped build Alaska over those who had but recently arrived. In fact, this idea has deep roots in Alaska's history, going back to the establishment of the Pioneers' Home in 1913. After statehood other Pioneers' Homes were added, and residency was restricted to Alaskans over sixty-five who had resided in the state for at least ten years. There are other programs, such as the Alaska longevity bonus, which provides direct payments ($250 a month) to Alaskans over sixty-five who have lived in the state since 1969. Two Anchorage lawyers, Ronald and Patricia Zobel, maintained that the residency requirements embodied in these programs were unconstitutional. They filed suit against the dividend program, blocking all payments pending resolution of the litigation. The U.S. Supreme Court ruled 8 to 1 against the original proposal on June 14, 1982. In the meantime, the legislature had passed a bill without the objectionable residency requirements. In the summer of 1982 the computer in the State Office Building in Juneau began printing the first oversized blue-and-gold $1,000 checks, which were mailed to more than 400,000 Alaska residents. To stabilize income, lawmakers chose to base earnings on a five-year average, used to inflation-proof the fund and provide dividends. About half of the averaged earnings have been paid out as Permanent Fund dividends over the last several years. The program is much like a company sharing profits with stockholders. In this case the stockholders of the Permanent Fund include everyone who has lived in Alaska for at least six months. In 1985 the Permanent Fund dividend check amounted to $404, paid to more than 500,000 residents. In 1986 the check came to $556.26, reflecting astute investments by the fund's managers. There can be no question that the distribution of more than $200 million favorably affected the state's economy. At the end of 1986 the fund's principal approached $7 billion. In ten years the fund had earned $3.24 billion in net income. There has been much debate, however, over whether the distribution of Permanent Fund dividends represents the best use of these dollars. Suggestions have been made to discontinue the dividend program and use the income, after inflation-proofing, to fund large-scale development projects such as the Susitna Hydroelectric Dam or to support the state budget as Alaska's oil revenues decline. The debate will continue.

Alaska has also attempted to diversify its economy, an effort going back to the days of Russian America. It has not been crowned with overwhelming success. The timber industry in southeastern Alaska has fallen on hard times. Oversupply and soft markets have plagued it for a number of years, and there are fears that one of the two pulp mills in southeastern Alaska may shut down permanently within the next few years. Low mineral prices have obstructed large-scale developments in that industry, though there are promises that the world-class molybdenum deposit at Quartz Hill, near Ketchikan, will be developed once the economic conditions for this mineral have improved. The U.S. Borax Corporation holds the lease and has performed extensive de-

velopment work. COMINCO and NANA Regional Corporation, based at Kotzebue, plan to develop the huge zinc-and-lead deposit at Red Dog, about 120 miles north of Kotzebue. The state legislature appropriated approximately $200 million to build a road and port facilities to be used to transport the ore to the smelters. The state is to be fully reimbursed by the developers for this work.

The state government has carefully managed the salmon stocks since it assumed control of this resource in 1960. Nearly ruined under federal mismanagement, the salmon runs have increased substantially over the years and reached record levels in the 1970s and 1980s. The state and various nonprofit organizations have also developed a vigorous hatchery program, which has contributed to the revival of the salmon runs. When the federal government claimed a 200-mile economic zone off the coasts, the plan was to have American rather than foreign fishermen harvest the bountiful bottomfish, such as pollock and haddock, in the Bering Sea. Over the years foreign harvest quotas have been cut back, and American fishermen have entered into cooperative agreements with the Russians, Japanese, and Koreans. Americans catch the fish, and foreign factory ships process the catch. Increases in income from the fishing industry can be expected in the years ahead.

Estimates of Alaska's coal resources have varied through the years. In 1967, Farrell Barnes, a U.S. Geological Survey geologist, listed an identified resource of 120 billion short tons, but more recent and speculative estimates put the numbers at 1,800 to 5,000 billion tons. Whatever the exact magnitude, Alaska's coal resources are huge. Extensive coal fields lie in the Cook Inlet region and on the North Slope, and there are other fields of substantial size. Despite these mammoth reserves, by 1985 there was only one fairly large operating mine, the Usibelli Coal Mine at Healy, about 90 miles southwest of Fairbanks, and another small mine in the Matanuska Valley. The lack of activity is not caused by the newness of the industry. Eskimos began using coal on the North Slope in the nineteenth century after the whalers showed them how to utilize it. The Russian-American Company opened its first Alaska coal mine in 1855 at Port Graham, in Katchemak Bay, but this operation soon failed. Over the years many mines were opened, but all except the Usibelli coal mine failed. Usibelli supplies the fuel for the Healy coal-fired generating plant of the Fairbanks-based Golden Valley Electric Association. The proprietor, Joe Usibelli, has also been able to develop a modest export market to Korea. About 800,000 tons of coal are shipped to that country each year, transported by the Alaska Railroad to Seward, where a modern loading facility transfers it onto ships. The Usibelli Mine also supplies the limited private market, particularly in Fairbanks.

The visitor industry has increased every year since statehood, and about 750,000 tourists visited the state in 1986. Tourism has become an increasingly important factor in the Alaskan economy.

Agriculture has been and remains a problem in the state. The 1935 Matanuska colony did not meet expectations. The Hammond adminstration expended substantial state dollars to develop the Delta area, about 98 miles south of Fairbanks. The plan was to grow barley for export to the Far East, but it never materialized. The weather never cooperated fully, a buffalo herd at Delta grazed in the barley every fall, and the farmers were undercapitalized and heavily in debt to the state. The more modest plan now is to produce barley and feed it to cattle to develop a local red-meat industry. A projected dairy development at Point McKenzie, near Anchorage, has experienced difficulties as well, with farmers unable to meet the state development schedules.

Many Alaska Natives have become disillusioned with the Alaska Native Claims Settlement Act of 1971. Perhaps William ("Spud") Williams, president of the Tanana Chiefs Conference of 1981, put it best when he stated: "I get tired of these newspaper articles [that say] they gave us 44 million acres and a billion dollars. They didn't give us shit. They stole it [from us], and the only time they were interested in settling it [the claims] was when they found a few barrels of oil. And now they're trying to steal our identities."[3] Many Natives have voiced disappointment with the structure of the thirteen regional corporations. Many are also afraid of a section in ANCSA which allows shareholders to barter, trade, or sell stock in 1991. The fear is that multinational corporations will rush in and buy the stock from disaffected stockholders, eventually taking over the corporations. The Alaska Federation of Natives, Inc., has submitted draft legislation to Congress which, among other amendments to ANCSA, will eliminate the provision for allowing stock alienation after 1991.

Various Alaska Native villages and groups, spearheaded by the United Tribes of Alaska, headquartered in Unalakleet, have claimed sovereign tribal status. The legal status of Alaska Natives involves many complicated, controversial, and sometimes emotional issues. The relevant history is extensive and dates back to a time before the purchase of Alaska from Russia in 1867. Unfortunately, many of these issues have not yet been resolved to the satisfaction of all concerned. Often there is a state, a federal, and one or more Native positions on any specific question. In 1984, Undersecretary of the Interior William Horn addressed the sovereignty issue. There have been efforts to create a new reservation system in Alaska by establishing an Indian Reorganization Act Council, transferring Regional Corporation lands to this council, and then claiming that it has become an Indian reservation. Horn pointed out that section 2 of

ANCSA very clearly bars the creation of a new reservation system in Alaska and that it expresses a clear intent that there cannot be back-door transfers of the land to create such a system. The federal government did have a special relationship with the Alaska IRA Councils, but it differed from the relationship that it had with the Indian reservation system in the contiguous states. The Department of the Interior opposed the creation of more than 200 little governments, each on its own reservation, scattered throughout the state. He also pointed out that Congress clearly expressed its intent in ANCSA, namely, to compensate the Natives for losses suffered with 44 million acres of land and $1 billion—and there was to be no reservation system. Still, this is a

An Inupiak Eskimo whaling crew on a hunting trip near Barrow, in the traditional umiak, or large skin boat, which is found from Siberia across North America to Greenland. The frame is made of wooden stringers nailed and lashed together. It is approximately 20 to 25 feet long and about 5 feet wide at the gunwales. The sides slant inward to a narrow flat bottom, which is about 2 feet wide in the center. The design gives the boat excellent stability and a large capacity. It is covered with the skins of 6 or 7 bearded seals. Eskimos use nails and bolts in the construction of the umiak and have also added a small transom in the rear to accommodate an engine. Photograph by Claus-M. Naske.

The Glacier Creek area of the Alaska Range, Denali National Park and Monument. Photograph by John Kauffman. Courtesy U.S. National Park Service.

most complicated legal issue, which Congress eventually will have to resolve.[4]

Another problem concerns the Alaska National Interest Conservation Land Act of 1980 (ANICLA). The legislation divided Alaskan lands among various owners—the federal government, the state, and the Natives. It will take many years and expensive litigation before the new boundaries are firmly drawn and uses for the many land categories have been agreed upon.

In short, it is exciting and rewarding to live in a state where every major issue is still in the process of being settled. What is clear is that the state's residents will have to accommodate themselves to an ever-growing body of rules and regulations. With statehood the simple structure of territorial Alaska vanished forever. The last frontier of yesterday disappeared, to be replaced by a complex social and political system.

# APPENDICES

# APPENDIX A  THE GOVERNORS OF ALASKA

Alexsandr Andreevich Baranov, 1790–1818

Leonti Andreanovich Hagemeister, January–October, 1818

Semen Ivanovich Yanovski, 1818–20

Matvei I. Muraviev, 1820–25

Peter Egorovich Chistiakov, 1825–30

Baron F. P. Wrangell, 1830–35

Ivan Antonovich Kupreanov, 1835–40

Adolph Karlovich Etolin, 1840–45

Michael D. Tebenkov, 1845–50

Nikolai Y. Rosenberg, 1850–53

Alexandr Ilich Rudakov, 1853–54

Stephen Vasili Voevodski, 1854–59

Ivan V. Furnhelm, 1859–63

Prince Dmitri Maksutov, 1863–67

The United States purchased Alaska in 1867. Secretary of State William Henry Seward devised the structure of the federal presence in Alaska. The ink was hardly dry on the U.S. Senate approval of the treaty before he began to guide his cabinet colleagues in planning three essential actions: the extension of customs authority over Alaska to bring revenue into federal coffers and facilitate commerce; the execution of a formal ceremony for transferring dominion and the colony's public lands, buildings, and archives; and the establishment of a military occupation to show the flag and preserve order. Under Seward's leadership the cabinet members involved worked so quickly that the three moves had been accomplished long before the appropriation bill to pay for Alaska emerged from the House committee. Immediately after the transfer a military commandant was to exercise executive author-

ity. The officers exercising this authority were as follows:

Brevet Maj. Gen. Jefferson C. Davis (U.S. Army), 1867–69

Capt. W. H. Dennison (U.S. Army), 1868–69

Capt. G. K. Brady (U.S. Army), 1868–70

Maj. J. C. Tidball (U.S. Army), 1870–77

In 1877 the Army withdrew its troops. This left M. C. Berry, customs collector, the only federal official in Alaska from 1877 to 1879. In 1879 the Navy assumed control of Alaska, and a number of naval officers exercised executive authority. The U.S.S. *Alaska*, Capt. George Brown commanding, arrived at Sitka on April 3, 1879, and departed on June 16, 1879. The U.S.S. *Jamestown*, Capt. L. A. Beardslee, arrived at Sitka on June 14, 1879. Commander Henry Glass relieved Beardslee on September 13, 1880, and the *Jamestown* left Sitka on August 9, 1881.

The U.S.S. *Wachusetts*, Comdr. Edward P. Lull, arrived at Sitka on July 30, 1881. Commander Henry Glass relieved Lull on October 19, 1881. The *Wachusetts* left Sitka on January 11, 1882, but returned on March 4, and Comdr. Frederick Pearson took over on March 13 of that year. The *Wachusetts* finally left Sitka on October 3, 1882. The U.S.S. *Adams*, Comdr. Edgar C. Merriman, sailed from Mare Island for Sitka on September 11, 1882. Commander Joseph B. Coghlan took over the ship on September 14, 1884, when the *Adams* left for California.

The U.S.S. *Pinta*, Lt. Comdr. Albert G. Caldwell, arrived at Sitka on August 17, 1884, to relieve the *Adams*. Lieutenant Commander Henry E. Nichols assumed command on September 14, 1884, and on September 15 fired a salute of seventeen guns in honor of John H. Kinkead, the first civil governor of Alaska. The *Pinta* remained in Alaskan waters until June 30, 1897, commanded by the following officers:

Lt. Comdr. John S. Newell, November 27, 1887

Lt. Comdr. Oscar W. Farenholt, September 16, 1889

Lt. Comdr. Washburn Maynard, September 24, 1891

Lt. Comdr. William T. Burwell, February 25, 1894

Lt. Comdr. Albert L. Cowden, September 26, 1894

Lt. Comdr. Frederick M. Symonds, October 9, 1896

In 1884, Congress passed Alaska's First Organic Act, which provided, among other things, for a governor appointed by the president. The governors were:

John Henry Kinkead, 1884–84
Alfred P. Swineford, 1885–89
Lyman Enos Knapp, 1889–93
James Sheakley, 1893–97
John Green Brady, 1897–1906
Wilford Bacon Hoggatt, 1906–1909
Walter Eli Clark, 1909–13

In 1912, Congress passed Alaska's Second Organic Act, which gave the territory a legislative assembly. The president continued to appoint the territorial governors:

John Franklin Alexander Strong, 1913–18
Thomas Riggs, 1918–21
Scott Cordelle Bone, 1921–25
George Alexander Parks, 1925–33
John Weir Troy, 1933–39
Ernest Gruening, 1939–53
B. Frank Heintzleman, 1953–57
Michael Anthony Stepovich, 1957–58

In 1958, Congress passed the Alaska Statehood Act, providing for the admission of Alaska to the union as the forty-ninth state. On January 3, 1959, President Dwight D. Eisenhower signed the formal document admitting the state. Residents had gone to the polls in 1958 and had elected the state's first governor. The governors since statehood:

William Allen Egan, 1959–66
Walter Joseph Hickel, 1966–69
Keith Harvey Miller, 1969–70
William Allen Egan, 1970–74
Jay Sterner Hammond, 1974–82
William Sheffield, 1982–86
Steve Cowper, 1986–present

# IMPORTANT PLACER GOLD DISCOVERIES

First Alaska gold discovery by the Russians on the Russian River on the Kenai Peninsula, 1848

Stikine River near Telegraph Creek, British Columbia, 1861

Sumdum Bay, 1870

Indian River on the outskirts of Sitka, 1871

Cassiar district in Canada, in the Stikine River headwaters country, 1872

Silver Bay near Sitka, 1874

Juneau, 1880

Fortymile, 1886

Yakutat, 1887

Lituya, 1887

Resurrection, 1888

Rampart, 1893

Circle City (Birch Creek), 1893

Seventymile, 1895

Klondike, 1896

Sunrise, 1896

Chistochina, 1898

Shungnak, 1898

Manley Hot Springs, 1898

Nome, 1898

Fairbanks, 1902

Valdez Creek, 1903

Bonnifield, 1903

Kantishna, 1905

Richardson, 1906

Chandalar, 1906

Innoko, 1906

Ruby (Poorman), 1907

Aniak, 1907

Melotzitna, 1907

Iditarod, 1909

Kiana, 1909

Hughes (Indian River), 1910

Nelchina, 1912

Chisana (Shushana), 1912

Marshall, 1913

Livengood (Tolovana), 1914

APPENDIX C  **FEDERAL DISTRICT COURT JUDGES BEFORE STATEHOOD**

District of Alaska, headquartered in Sitka:

Ward McAllister, 1884–85
Edward J. Dawne, 1885 (August–December)
Lafayette Dawson, 1885–88
John H. Reatley, 1888–89
John S. Bugbee, 1889–92
Warren D. Truitt, 1892–97
Arthur K. Delaney, 1895–97
Charles D. Johnson, 1897–1900

On June 6, 1900, President Theodore Roosevelt signed a measure creating three judicial districts in Alaska. An additional district was added in 1909:

First District, Juneau:

Melville C. Brown, 1900–1904
Royal Arch Gunnison, 1904–1909
Thomas R. Lyons, 1909–13
Robert W. Jennings, 1913–21
Thomas Milburne Reed, 1921–28
Justin W. Harding, 1929–34
George Forest Alexander, 1934–47
George W. Folta, 1947–55
Raymond John Kelly, 1955–60

Second District, Nome:

Arthur H. Noyes, 1900–1902
Alfred S. Moore, 1902–10
Cornelius D. Murane, 1910–13
John Randolph Tucker, Jr., 1913–17

William A. Holzheimer, 1917–21
Gudbrand J. Lomen, 1921–32
Lester O. Gore, 1932–34
J. H. S. Morison, 1935–44
Joseph W. Kehoe, 1944–51
J. Earl Cooper, 1952–53
Walter H. Hodge, 1954–60

Third District, Eagle, Fairbanks, Valdez, Anchorage:

James Wickersham, 1900–1907
Silas H. Reid, 1908–1909
Edward E. Cushman, 1909–12
Peter D. Overfield, 1912–13
Frederick M. Brown, 1913–21
Elmer E. Ritchie, 1921–27
E. Coke Hill, 1927–32
Cecil H. Clegg, 1932–34
Simon Hellenthal, 1935–45
Anthony J. Dimond, 1945–53
J. L. McCarrey, 1953–60

Fourth District, Fairbanks:

Peter D. Overfield, 1909–12
Frederick E. Fuller, 1912–14
Charles E. Bunnell, 1915–21
Cecil H. Clegg, 1921–34 (moved to Third District in 1932)
E. Coke Hill, 1932–35
Harry Emerson Pratt, 1935–54
Vernon D. Forbes, 1954–60

294

# APPENDIX D  DELEGATES TO CONGRESS

In 1906, Congress authorized Alaska to send a voteless delegate to the House of Representatives. The following individuals served in that capacity:

Frank H. Waskey, 1906–1907
Thomas Cale, 1907–1909
James Wickersham, 1909–17
Charles A. Sulzer, 1917 (contested election)
James Wickersham, 1918 (seated as delegate)
Charles A. Sulzer, 1919 (elected, died before taking office)
George Grigsby, 1919–21 (appointed)
James Wickersham, 1921 (seated as delegate, having contested the 1919 election and resulting appointment)
Dan A. Sutherland, 1921–31
James Wickersham, 1931–33
Anthony J. Dimond, 1933–44
Edward Lewis (Bob) Bartlett, 1944–58

In 1955, Alaskans decided to hold a constitutional convention. The fifty-five delegates drafted a constitution for the future state in seventy-five working days. All but one of the delegates signed the document on February 5, 1956. When Alaskans went to the polls in April, 1956, they overwhelmingly approved their constitution, together with the Alaska Tennessee Plan. George H. Lehleitner, a businessman from New Orleans, proposed this scheme to the delegates. The plan was so named because Tennessee had been the first, though not the last, territory to gain admission by means of it. When Congress denied Tennessee statehood, it elected its congressional delegation and sent these men to Washington without waiting for an enabling act. There the Tennessee delegation made a strong plea for admission, and finally, on June 1, 1796, Tennessee became the sixteenth state of the Union. Six other territories elected senators and representatives to Congress before these territories were formally admitted to statehood. In each case, statehood was hastened by as much as a few months to several years.

*Alaska Tennessee Plan Delegation*

Senators
Ernest Gruening, 1956–58
William A. Egan, 1956–58

Representative
Ralph J. Rivers, 1956–58

*Alaska's Congressional Delegation*
(Statehood proclaimed, January 3, 1959)

U.S. senators:
Edward Lewis (Bob) Bartlett, 1959–68 (died in office, December 11, 1968)
Ernest Gruening, 1959–68
Mike Gravel, 1968–80
Theodore F. Stevens, December 11, 1968–present (appointed to E. L. [Bob] Bartlett's vacant seat; elected in 1972 in his own right; reelected in 1978 and 1984)
Frank Murkowski, 1980–86, reelected to another 6 year term

U.S. representatives:

Ralph J. Rivers, 1959–66
Howard Pollock, 1966–70
Nicholas Begich, 1970–72 (On October 16, 1972, Begich boarded a small plane to continue his campaign for reelection. The plane took off from Anchorage, bound for Juneau, and disappeared. Thirty-nine days of intensive air, land, and sea search revealed no trace of the aircraft, its passengers, or its pilot.)
Don Young, 1972–present

# POPULATION BY REGION, 1880–1980

| Year | Total Alaska | Southeast | South Central | Southwest | Interior | Northwest |
|------|------|------|------|------|------|------|
| 1880 | 33,426 | 7,748 | 4,352 | 13,914 | 2,568 | 4,844 |
| 1890 | 32,052 | 8,038 | 6,112 | 12,071 | 2,333 | 3,498 |
| 1900 | 63,592 | 14,350 | 10,000 | 13,000 | 5,600 | 20,642 |
| 1910 | 64,356 | 15,216 | 12,900 | 12,049 | 13,064 | 11,127 |
| 1920 | 55,036 | 17,402 | 11,173 | 11,541 | 7,964 | 6,956 |
| 1930 | 59,278 | 19,304 | 11,880 | 12,118 | 8,246 | 7,730 |
| 1940 | 72,524 | 25,241 | 14,881 | 12,846 | 10,345 | 9,211 |
| 1950 | 128,643 | 28,203 | 50,093 | 17,715 | 23,008 | 9,624 |
| 1960 | 226,167 | 35,403 | 108,851 | 21,001 | 49,128 | 11,784 |
| 1970 | 300,382 | 42,565 | 162,001 | 26,491 | 56,479 | 12,846 |
| 1974 | 351,159 | 50,232 | 194,569 | 28,165 | 63,151 | 15,042 |
| 1975 | 404,634 | 50,438 | 229,492 | 28,428 | 78,614 | 17,662 |
| 1976 | 413,289 | 51,172 | 244,056 | 28,488 | 68,572 | 21,041 |
| 1977 | 411,211 | 53,162 | 252,836 | 26,512 | 58,208 | 20,493 |
| 1980 | 400,331 | 53,613 | 235,465 | 28,659 | 67,154 | 15,440 |

Source: Alaska Department of Labor.

As the figures above show, population statistics for the territory and state of Alaska have historically been characterized by periods of expansion and contraction, dictated by the economic climate of the time. The net result has been an overall increase. Between 1983 and 1985, during a favorable economic period, Alaska's population increased from 495,300 to 523,048, a 5.6 percent increase.

Alaska's population growth was especially impressive from the end of World War II until 1952, the largest increase occurring during the military buildup for the Korean conflict. The average annual growth rate for this period amounted to 9.6 percent. From 1952 to 1965, Alaska experienced a slower annual growth rate, averaging 2.7 percent. Between 1965 and 1973 population growth increased gradually, producing an average annual growth rate of 3 percent.

Between 1973 and 1976 the construction of the Trans-Alaska Pipeline stimulated population growth, averaging 6.6 percent a year. The completion of the pipeline construction boom was followed by a bust during the period 1976–80. Between 1977 and 1978 the state experienced a net out-migration of about 6,400 individuals. The average annual growth rate over the four-year period, however, amounted to 0.6 percent, caused by natural increases which offset out-migration.

In 1981 another economic boom began, caused primarily by construction and infrastructure development fueled by state and private spending. Oil prices and state oil tax revenues caused a rapid increase in state spending and a resulting optimism in the private sector. Consequently, Alaska's population grew approximately 30 percent in 4.25 years. This made Alaska the fastest-growing state in the Union since the 1980 census. The average annual growth rate for the United States as a whole during the 1980–84 period was 1 percent. Indications are that growth will slow as it did in the 1976–80 period after the end of the pipeline boom. Drastically lower oil prices have slowed state and private capital spending as well.

Economic growth determines population growth. In Alaska this will depend on the demand for the state's resources in the other states and on world markets, as well as on the amount of federal spending in the state. Despite fluctuations, Alaska's population growth in the period since 1946 has resulted in a fivefold increase.

Population change is composed of births and deaths and migration. Between July 1, 1983, and July 1, 1984, 12,208 persons were born in Alaska and 1,903 died, making a net natural increase of 10,305. Alaska births are currently equivalent to about 2.5 percent and deaths about 0.4 percent of the population at the beginning of each year, resulting in a natural increase of 2.1 percent per year.

In about one-third of the years since 1945 migration was a larger component of change than natural increase. The highest post–World War II migration growth occurred during the buildup for the Korean conflict in 1950–51 (14.7 percent) and 1951–52 (13.6 percent). In 1945–46 migration accounted for a 12.3 percent increase. These high percentages were caused in part by the small population base. The net migration for 1982–83 was numerically larger than that for 1950–51 but was equivalent to only 5.3 percent of the 1982 population. The largest single numerical increase caused by migration (30,235, or 8.7 percent) occurred during the construction of the Trans-Alaska Pipeline in 1974–75. The largest numerical loss (13,356, or 3.2 percent) occurred at the end of the pipeline construction in 1977–78.

The rapid population growth that Alaska has experienced is tied to in- and out-migration. In fact, well over half of Alaska's population growth has been caused by migration as opposed to natural increase. What is usually reported as migration is the net balance of in- and out-migration, or net migration. Gross migration is reported as well; this is the total amount of movement that results from adding in- and out-migration. If the in-migration equals the out-migration, the net migration is zero. If the turnover is high, the gross migration may be substantial. This is true in both Anchorage and Fairbanks, areas with large military populations. Troop strengths may remain stable, but personnel are rotated on a regular basis.

Generally people move short distances more frequently than long distances. The West Coast and the mountain states nearest Alaska have contributed the largest percentage of migrants to the north. Of all the people who have moved to or from Alaska in the 1980s, about half moved to or from the following states: Washington (14 percent), California (12 percent), Oregon (7 percent), Texas (7 percent), Colorado (4 percent), Florida (4 percent), Idaho (3 percent), and Arizona (3 percent). The remaining states contributed 2 percent or less each to the migrant population. The migration from Texas tends to be related to the oil industry, and Florida migrants are mostly military and Coast Guard personnel.

Alaska once had the smallest population of any state in the Union, but with an estimated population of 523,048 in 1985 it apparently has surpassed Wyoming, which had a population of 469,557 in 1980 and has grown very little since then. Alaska certainly has matured significantly since statehood. The typically high male-to-female ratio of a frontier area has decreased from 132.3 men per 100 women in 1960 to 112.8 men per 100 women in 1980, still well above the national ratio of 94.5 men per 100 women. Continued decline in this ratio is expected. In the 1900 census the ration was 258.9 men per 100 women. Men, however, will probably always outnumber women in the state as long as there is a significant military population.

Alaska's age profile has reflected major historic and economic events. At the turn of the century, during the major gold rushes, males between the ages of 25 and 34 years predominated. From 1890 to 1910 the total population grew 100.8 percent, while the male age group 25–34 grew by 160.9 percent. With the establishment of military bases in the 1940s the male population age 20–30 grew 180 percent, while the territory's population grew 77.4 percent. From 1960 to 1980 the state's population grew 77.7 percent; males 20–24, by 51.2 percent; males 25–29, by 115.7 percent; and males 30–34, by 108.2 percent. The same female age groups show much smaller increases.

With a median age of 26 years in 1980, Alaska had the second-youngest population of the fifty states: 32.5 percent of its population was under the age of 18. In 1960, 39.3 percent of Alaska's population was under 18, with a median age of 23.3. At the other end of the scale, Alaska is the state with the lowest percentage of individuals over the age of 65, namely 2.9 percent in 1980 and 2.4 percent in 1960. This may be changing in the years ahead, because the state has created financial incentives to retain its older citizens. In the 1890 census only 393 persons over 65 lived in Alaska. As in the rest of the country, however, Alaska's population has also aged.

Coinciding with national trends, fertility rates have decreased in Alaska. In 1960 there were 692 children under the age of 5 per 1,000 women 15–49 years of age. By 1980 there were 343 children, a drastic decrease. There was a slight rise in the number of children born to women age 15–24 in 1980, which may give Alaska a small population boom in the late 1980s. Still there was a marked decrease in that portion of the population under age 5 between 1960 and 1980. In 1960, 15.2 percent of the state's population was under age 5, while in 1980 this had decreased to 9.7 percent. Births per thousand dropped from 33.4 percent in 1960 to 22.9 percent in 1980. If these trends continue, the state's population will age significantly.

Alaskans, like their fellow citizens in the contiguous states, are living longer. In 1959–61 the average life expectancy for an Alaskan was 67.5 years; by 1980 it had increased to 72.7 years. Alaska still trails the U.S. life expectancy of 73.7 years in 1979. Demographers have examined this phenomenon and concluded that the shorter Alaska life-span is probably a statistical fact rather than an actuality. Many Alaskans retire in the contiguous states and therefore do not show up in the mortality statistics.

Alaskans are well educated, 21.1 percent, or one in five, having earned a college degree. This is second only to Colorado and more than double the 1960 percentage. Much higher education is attained outside the state. Alaska was second only to Nevada in 1979 in the percentage of first-time freshmen enrolling out of state, 47.1 percent. Only 5.7 percent of first-time freshmen come to Alaska for their education. This leaves Alaska with the highest percentage of out-migration for postsecondary education. This is slowly changing, however, because the state's university system and the two private colleges have recruited aggressively in Alaska in the last few years.

The median number of school years completed in 1960 was 12.1 and rose to 12.8 in 1980. In the latter year 82.8 percent of individuals 25 years and older had completed high school, up from 54.7 percent in 1960. For the entire United States, the median number of school years completed was 10.6 in 1960 and 12.5 in 1980. In 1980 a total of 66.3 percent completed high school in the United States as a whole.

Women have found greater employment opportunities in Alaska since statehood. In 1960, 39.3 percent of women 14 years and older were in the labor force. By 1980, 57.9 percent of women 16 years and older were in the labor force. Nationally the percentage of women age 16 and older in the labor force rose from 37.8 in 1960 to 52.9 percent in 1982. Alaska's continually higher female participation in the labor force is remarkable because it is a state where mining, construction, fishing, and lumbering are major industries, which have traditionally been male-dominated. Employment growth in services and trade has helped increase female employment in the last few years.

Contrary to popular belief, employment in local, state, and federal government has not changed significantly since 1960. In that year the three entities employed 33.1 percent of the total labor force. The 1980 census found that 33.5 percent of those employed in government in Alaska were state-government workers. After statehood the federal government shifted responsibilities to state or local government agencies, and employment also followed. The following table illustrates the breakdown of government employment:

| Percentage of Total Government Employment | | |
|---|---|---|
| Government | 1970 (Percent) | 1980 (Percent) |
| Federal | 46.7 | 35.8 |
| State | 27.9 | 34.9 |
| Local | 25.4 | 29.3 |

Additionally, the public administration and construction sectors have declined in their percentages of industry employment. Since 1970 the most significant change in major-industry employment has been the increase in the professional services. Employment there has risen from 14.7 percent in 1960 to 21.9 percent in 1980.

When the July 1, 1982, population estimate series from the Bureau of Census became available, they showed Alaska to have the largest rate of in-migration, placed at 10.3 percent between April 1, 1980, and July 1, 1982. The composition of this in-migration will determine whether or not the state's demographics will again reflect its economic trends. As the state shifts away from the frontier economic configuration, one should see even more women present, more families forming, more middle-aged persons (35–55) staying, and a general shift to the demographic profile of an older state. The 1990 census will furnish the next demographic profile.

# APPENDIX F MAJOR COMPONENTS OF POPULATION GROWTH, 1880–1970

| Year | Alaska | Native | Nonnative | Military |
|------|--------|--------|-----------|----------|
| 1880 | 33,426 | 32,996 | 430 | — |
| 1890 | 32,052 | 25,354 | 4,298 | — |
| 1900 | 63,592 | 29,542 | 30,450 | — |
| 1910 | 64,356 | 25,331 | 36,400 | — |
| 1920 | 55,036 | 26,558 | 28,228 | 250 |
| 1930 | 59,278 | 29,983 | 29,045 | 250 |
| 1940 | 72,524 | 32,458 | 39,566 | 500 |
| 1950 | 128,643 | 33,863 | 74,373 | 20,407 |
| 1960 | 226,167 | 43,081 | 150,394 | 32,692 |
| 1967 | 277,906 | 52,000 | 192,227 | 33,679 |
| 1970 | 300,382 | 50,554 | 219,828 | 30,000 |
| 1980* | 402,000 | | | |

*No breakdown into Native, nonnative and military available. An estimated 523,000 people were living in Alaska on July 1, 1984. The oil bust in 1986 resulted in an out-migration, but no numbers are yet available.

APPENDIX G  # DISTRIBUTION OF TOTAL POPULATION BY SIZE OF PLACE, 1950–1980

| Size of Place | Number of Places | Pop. | Percentage of Total Pop. | Number of Places | Pop. | Percentage of Total Pop. | Number of Places | Pop. | Percentage of Total Pop. | Number of Places | Pop. | Percentage of Total Pop. |
|---|---|---|---|---|---|---|---|---|---|---|---|---|
| Places of less than 1,000 | — | 79,394 | 61.7 | — | 116,446 | 51.5 | — | 117,017 | 39.0 | — | 107,120 | 26.8 |
| 1,000–1,500 | 3 | 3,575 | 2.8 | 10 | 12,444 | 5.5 | 13 | 15,170 | 5.1 | 3 | 3,783 | 1.0 |
| 1,500–2,000 | 4 | 7,190 | 5.6 | 4 | 7,032 | 3.1 | 4 | 6,918 | 2.3 | 7 | 11,914 | 3.0 |
| 2,000–2,500 | 2 | 4,222 | 3.3 | 2 | 4,478 | 2.0 | 7 | 15,765 | 5.2 | 7 | 15,355 | 3.8 |
| 2,500–5,000 | 2 | 5,976 | 4.6 | 2 | 5,865 | 2.6 | 6 | 21,355 | 7.1 | 7 | 25,923 | 6.5 |
| 5,000–10,000 | 3 | 17,032 | 13.2 | 3 | 22,354 | 9.9 | 6 | 43,268 | 14.4 | 3 | 20,223 | 5.1 |
| 10,000–25,000 | 1 | 11,254 | 8.7 | 1 | 13,311 | 5.9 | 2 | 32,860 | 10.9 | 2 | 42,021 | 10.5 |
| 25,000 or more | — | — | — | 1 | 44,237 | 19.6 | 1 | 48,029 | 16.0 | 1 | 173,992 | 43.5 |

Sources: U.S. Bureau of the Census and Alaska Department of Commerce and Economic Development, Department of Community and Regional Affairs.

## APPENDIX H THUMBNAIL PROFILES OF THE THIRTEEN NATIVE REGIONAL CORPORATIONS

| Corporation | ANCSA Entitlement (Land) | ANCSA Entitlement (Millions of Dollars) | Investments | Number of Shareholders | Number of Villages | Net Worth (1980) (Millions of Dollars) | Net Profit/Loss (1979) | Net Profit/Loss (1980) |
|---|---|---|---|---|---|---|---|---|
| Ahtna, Inc. | 1.7 million acres | 13.3 | Maintenance of pipeline, investments | 1,074 | 8 | 7.0 | $168,093 | $361,623 |
| Aleut Corp. | 1.25 million acres, sub-surface rights; 52,000 surface rights | 40.1 | Money-market funds, freight, fishing | 3,249 | 14 | 13.7 | −$2.7 million | $636,000 |
| Arctic Slope Regional Corp. | 4.6 million acres | 46.5 | Oil-field service, construction | 3,738 | 8 | 24.3 | −$184,000 | $1.1 million |
| Bering Straits Native Corp. | 2.9 million acres | 79.5 | Natural resource development, real estate | 6,333 | 20 | 4.6 | −$3.6 million | −$2 million |
| Bristol Bay Native Corp. | 2.2 million acres, 2.9 million subsurface rights | 67.0 | Hotel, banking, drilling, food processing, mineral exploration | 5,400 | 29 | 34.1 | $1.9 million | $ 63,300 |
| Calista Corp. | 5.9 million acres | 165.0 | Sheraton Anchorage, Settlers Bay, Calista Fisheries | 13,308 | 56 | 57.8 | −$4.2 million | −$7.3 million |

(Continued)

| Corporation | ANCSA Entitlement (Land) | ANCSA Entitlement (Millions of Dollars) | Investments | Number of Shareholders | Number of Villages | Net Worth (1980) (Millions of Dollars) | Net Profit/Loss (1979) | Net Profit/Loss (1980) |
|---|---|---|---|---|---|---|---|---|
| Chugach Natives, Inc. | 1 million acres | 24.0 | Timber, fisheries | 1,912 | 5 | 8.8 | −$618,541 | −$1.5 million |
| Cook Inlet Region, Inc. | 1.2 million acres subsurface and subsurface rights, 1.3 million acres subsurface rights | 77.2 | Natural resource development, real estate, construction drilling | 6,264 | 8 villages, 2 certified groups, 1 historic village | 46.1 | $3.4 million | $5.7 million |
| Doyon, Ltd. | 9 million acres surface and subsurface rights, 3.5 million acres, subsurface rights only | 112.3 | Securities, real estate, banking, oil, construction | 9,061 | 28 | 54.1 | $1.03 million | $445,089 |
| Koniag, Inc. | 1 million acres | 41.3 | Timber, oil, fisheries | 3,344 | 9 | 15.5 | −$2.3 million | −$245,000 |
| NANA Regional Corp. | 2.3 million acres | 59.9 | Oil-field service, construction, tourism, reindeer | 4,838 | 11 | 44 | $635,932 | $207,324 |
| Sealaska Corp. | 280,000 acres | 196.9 | Sealaska Timber, Alaska Brick Co., banking, seafoods, oil and gas | 15,819 | 12 | 198.9 | $575,000 | $5.94 million |
| 13th Regional Corp. | None | 45.6 | Fishing | 4,435 | None | Unavailable | −$3.7 million | −$6.8 million |

Source: *Anchorage Daily News*, prepared with information from Alaska Pacific Bancorporation, Bureau of Indian Affairs, and Native regional corporations.

# NOTES

## Chapter 1

1. Alfred H. Brooks, *The Geography and Geology of Alaska,* U.S. Geological Survey Professional Paper no. 45 (Washington, D.C.: Government Printing Office, 1906), p. 11.

2. Bernard R. Hubbard, S.J., *Mush, You Malemutes* (New York: American Press, 1943), pp. 70–71.

3. Arthur Grantz et al., *Alaska's Good Friday Earthquake, March 27, 1964,* Geological Survey Circular no. 491 (Washington, D.C.: Department of the Interior, 1964), p. 1; Edwin B. Eckel, *The Alaska Earthquake, March 27, 1964: Lessons and Conclusions,* Geological Survey Professional Paper no. 546 (Washington, D.C.: Government Printing Office, 1970), p. 1.

4. T. Neil Davis and Carol Echols, *A Table of Alaskan Earthquakes, 1788–1961,* Geophysical Research Report no. 8 (College: University of Alaska, 1962).

5. Based on information supplied by David Stone, of the Geophysical Institute of the University of Alaska, and on Clyde Wahrhaftig, *Physiographic Divisions of Alaska,* U.S. Geological Survey Professional Paper no. 482 (Washington, D.C.: Government Printing Office, 1965).

6. J. E. Ransom, "Derivation of the Word Alaska," *American Anthropologist,* July, 1940, pp. 550–51.

7. Map no. 55, by Ivan Lvou (about 1710), in A. V. Yefimov, ed., *Atlas of Geographical Discoveries in Siberia and North-Western America, XVII–XVIII* (Moscow: Nauka, 1964).

8. A. L. Seeman, "Regions and Resources of Alaska," *Economic Geography,* October, 1937,

p. 334; "The Aleutians," *Alaska Geographic* 7, no. 3 (1980): 30.

9. The discussion of Alaska's geography and climate is based on U.S. Department of the Interior, Bureau of Reclamation, *Alaska: Reconnaissance Report on the Potential Development of Water Resources in the Territory of Alaska,* H. Doc. 197, 82d Cong., 1st sess. (Washington, D.C.: Government Printing Office, 1950); and National Resources Committee, *Alaska: Its Resources and Development* (Washington, D.C.: Government Printing Office, 1938). For those interested in further reading, the following publications are very helpful: Resource Planning Team, Joint Federal-State Land Use Planning Commission for Alaska, *Resources of Alaska: A Regional Summary,* rev. ed. (Anchorage: Joint Federal-State Land Use Planning Commission for Alaska, 1975); and Lidia L. Selkregg, *Alaska Regional Profiles,* sponsored by State of Alaska, Office of the Governor, in cooperation with Joint Federal-State Land Use Planning Commission for Alaska, 6 vols. (Fairbanks: Arctic Environmental Information and Data Center, University of Alaska, 1974–ca. 1980). The volumes deal exhaustively with Alaska's six geographical regions.

10. T. D. Stewart, *The People of America* (New York: Charles Scribner's Sons, 1973), pp. 51–55; based on information supplied by Jean Aigner, professor, Department of Anthropology, University of Alaska, Fairbanks.

11. Philip Drucker, *Indians of the Northwest Coast* (Garden City, N.Y.: Natural History Press, 1963), pp. 1–176.

12. James Van Stone, *Athapaskan Adaptations* (Chicago: Aldine Publishing Co., 1974),

pp. 1–89; based on information from Aigner; Marie-Françoise Guedon, *People of Tetlin, Why Are You Singing?* (Ottawa: National Museum of Man, National Museum of Canada, 1974), pp. 204–208.

13. Vladimir Jochelson, "People of the Foggy Seas," *Natural History* 4 (1928): 413.

14. Margaret Lantis, "The Aleut Social System, 1750 to 1810, from Early Historical Sources," in Margaret Lantis, ed., *Ethnohistory in Southwestern Alaska and the Southern Yukon: Method and Content* (Lexington: University of Kentucky Press, 1970), p. 179.

15. Federal Field Committee for Development Planning in Alaska, *Alaska Natives and the Land* (Washington, D.C.: Government Printing Office, 1968). p. 238.

16. Based on information from Aigner.

17. Lantis, "Aleut Social System," pp. 292–95; Don E. Dumond, *The Eskimos and Aleuts* (London: Thames and Hudson, 1977), pp. 55–56.

18. Lantis, "Aleut Social System," pp. 292–95.

19. Hans-Georg Bandi, *Eskimo Prehistory*, trans. Ann E. Keep (College, Alaska: University of Alaska Press, 1969), pp. 7–8.

20. Based on information from Michael E. Krauss, professor of linguistics and director, Alaska Native Language Center, University of Alaska, Fairbanks; and Aigner.

21. Bandi, *Eskimo Prehistory*, p. 8.

22. Ibid., pp. 9–11.

23. Based on information from Krauss.

24. William C. Sturtevant, gen. ed., *Handbook of North American Indians*, vol. 5, *Arctic*, ed. David Damas (Washington, D.C.: Smithsonian Institution, 1984), pp. 14–16.

25. Based on information from Aigner.

### Chapter 2

1. Raymond H. Fisher, *Bering's Voyages: Whither and Why* (Seattle: University of Washington Press, 1977), pp. 25–26; Svetlana G. Fedorova, *The Russian Population in Alaska and California: Late 18th Century–1867*, trans. and ed. Richard A. Pierce and Alton S. Donnelly (Kingston, Ontario: Limestone Press, 1973), pp. 48–49. Fedorova devotes a chapter to the question of lost settlements; see pp. 39–97.

2. Fisher, *Bering's Voyages*, pp. 11–17.

3. Ibid., pp. 22–23.

4. Ibid., pp. 94–95.

5. Ibid., pp. 112–13.

6. Ibid., pp. 111–12.

7. Ibid., pp. 120–22.

8. "The Aleutians," *Alaska Geographic* 7, no. 3 (1980): 105.

9. Glenn Barratt, *Russia in Pacific Waters, 1715–1825: A Survey of the Origins of Russia's Naval Presence in the North and South Pacific* (Vancouver: University of British Columbia Press, 1981), pp. 58–59.

10. Semon B. Okun, *The Russian-American Company*, ed. E. B. Grekov, trans. from the Russian by Carl Ginsburg (Cambridge, Mass.: Harvard University Press, 1951), p. 14. See also Terence Armstrong, "Cook's Reputation in Russia," in Robin Fisher and Hugh Johnson, eds., *Captain Cook and His Times* (Seattle: University of Washington Press, 1979), p. 125.

11. Barratt, *Russia in Pacific Waters*, pp. 78–79, 84–87.

12. Ibid., pp. 93–95.

13. Fedorova, *The Russian Population*, p. 114, believes that Unalaska, not Kodiak, was the first permanent Russian settlement. Unalaska, however, was much smaller, never more than a trading post, while Kodiak became an administrative center where dwellings and fortifications were erected. See also James R. Gibson, *Imperial Russia in Frontier America* (New York: Oxford University Press, 1976), p. 4.

14. Barratt, *Russia in Pacific Waters*, pp. 101–102. See also Raisa V. Makarova, *Russians on the Pacific*, trans. and ed. Richard A. Pierce and Alton S. Donnelly (Kingston, Ontario: Limestone Press, 1975), p. 127; P. A. Tikhmenev, *A History of the Russian-American Company*, trans. and ed. Richard A. Pierce and Alton S. Donnelly (Seattle: University of Washington Press, 1978), pp. 21–24; Okun, *The Russian-American Company*, p. 29.

15. Gibson, *Imperial Russia*, p. 4.

16. Hector Chevigny, *Russian America: The Great Alaskan Adventure, 1741–1867* (New York: Viking Press, 1965), pp. 81–83.

17. Tikhmenev, *A History of the Russian-American Company*, pp. 54–56; Okun, *The Russian-American Company*, pp. 44–45.

18. Tikhmenev, *A History of the Russian-American Company*, pp. 91–94.

19. Ibid., pp. 92–94.

20. Ibid., p. 94.

21. Ibid., pp. 98–99.

22. Ibid., pp. 95–100.

23. Okun, *The Russian-American Company*, pp. 189–92.

24. Kyrill T. T. Klebnikov, *Colonial Russian*

*America: Kyrill T. Klebnikov's Reports, 1817–1832*, trans. Basil Dmytryshyn and E. A. P. Crownhart-Vaughan (Portland: Oregon Historical Society, 1976), pp. 4–5, 101–102; Tikhmenev, *A History of the Russian-American Company*, p. 99.

25. Howard I. Kushner, *Conflict on the Northwest Coast: American-Russian Rivalry in the Pacific Northwest, 1790–1867* (Westport, Conn.: Greenwood Press, pp. 11–17; Gibson, *Imperial Russia*, pp.158–59.

26. Gibson, *Imperial Russia*, pp. 158, 160–61.

27. Barratt, *Russia in Pacific Waters*, pp. 173–74.

28. Quoted in Okun, *The Russian-American Company*, p. 120.

29. Gibson, *Imperial Russia*, pp. 129, 132.

30. Ibid., pp. 181–83, 191–93.

31. Ibid., p. 142; Richard A. Pierce, "George Anton Schaffer, Russia's Man in Hawaii, 1815–1857," in Morgan B. Sherwood, ed., *Alaska and Its History* (Seattle: University of Washington Press, 1967), pp. 73, 77, 79–80.

32. Barratt, *Russia in Pacific Waters*, pp. 186–88; Tikhmenev, *A History of the Russian-American Company*, p. 155.

33. Tikhmenev, *A History of the Russian-American Company*, p. 156.

34. Chevigny, *Russian America*, pp. 72–73.

### Chapter 3

1. Okun, *The Russian-American Company*, pp. 44–45.

2. Kushner, *Conflict on the Northwest Coast*, pp. 31–32.

3. Barratt, *Russia in Pacific Waters*, p. 217.

4. Ibid., pp. 273–74; Gibson, *Imperial Russia*, pp. 162–165.

5. The boundary south of 56° north latitude was imprecisely drawn and remained in dispute until the issue was finally settled in 1903.

6. John S. Galbraith, *The Hudson's Bay Company as an Imperial Factor* (Berkeley and Los Angeles: University of California Press, 1957), pp. 139–40.

7. Ibid., pp. 144–47.

8. Ibid., p. 154.

9. Ibid., pp. 161–62.

10. Ibid., pp. 157–58; Sir George Simpson, *Narrative of a Journey Round the World During the Years 1841 and 1842* (London: Henry Colborn, 1847), 2:182, 200–13.

11. Galbraith, *The Hudson's Bay Company*, p. 156.

12. Gibson, *Imperial Russia*, p. 205.

13. Ibid., p. 206.

14. Galbraith, *The Hudson's Bay Company*, p. 161; Gibson, *Imperial Russia*, pp. 207–208.

15. Galbraith, *The Hudson's Bay Company*, pp. 169–71.

16. Barratt, *Russia in Pacific Waters*, p. 211.

17. Henry N. Michael, ed., *Lieutenant Zagoskin's Travels in Russian America* (Toronto: University of Toronto Press, 1967), p. xii.

18. Alfred H. Brooks, *Blazing Alaska's Trails* (Fairbanks: University of Alaska, 1953), p. 237.

19. Federova, *The Russian Population*, pp. 148–49; Okun, *The Russian-American Company*, pp. 172–73.

20. Captain P. N. Golovin, *The End of Russian America: Captain P. N. Golovin's Last Report, 1862*, trans. Basil Dmytryshyn and E. A. P. Crownhard-Vaughan (Portland: Oregon Historical Society, 1979), pp. 13–14.

21. Federova, *The Russian Population*, p. 156.

22. Golovin, *The End of Russian America*, pp. 14–16.

23. Federova, *The Russian Population*, pp. 157–58.

24. Ibid., p. 212.

25. Ibid., p. 278.

26. Tikhmenev, *A History of the Russian-American Company*, p. 470n.

27. Golovin, *The End of Russian America*, pp. 21–22; "The Aleutians," *Alaska Geographic* 7, no. 2 (1980): 100.

28. Golovin, *The End of Russian America*, pp. 21–22; Okun, *The Russian-American Company*, p. 198.

29. Golovin, *The End of Russian America*, p. 23.

30. Quoted in Okun, *The Russian-American Company*, p. 200.

31. Golovin, *The End of Russian America*, pp. 54–55.

32. Simpson, *Narrative*, vol. 2, p. 190.

33. Okun, *The Russian-American Company*, pp. 226–27.

34. Ibid., p. 220.

35. Ibid., pp. 230–32.

36. Gibson, *Imperial Russia, p. 42.*

37. *Ronald J. Jensen, The Alaska Purchase and Russian-American Relations* (Seattle: University of Washington Press, 1975), p. 15.

38. Ibid., pp. 18–19.

39. Ibid., p. 13.

40. Golovin, *The End of Russian America,* passim.

41. Jensen, *The Alaska Purchase,* pp. 48–50.

42. Ibid., pp. 57–60.

43. Ibid., pp. 70–74.

44. Ibid., pp. 75–78; F. A. Golder, "The Purchase of Alaska," *American Historical Review* 25 (1919–20): 419, 423.

*Chapter 4*

1. Charles Vevier, "The Collins Overland Line and American Continentalism," in Sherwood, ed., *Alaska and Its History,* pp. 226–29.

2. James Alton James, *The First Scientific Exploration of Russian America and the Purchase of Alaska* (Evanston, Ill.: Northwestern University, 1942), p. 45.

3. Jensen, *The Alaska Purchase,* p. 80.

4. Thomas A. Bailey, *A Diplomatic History of the American People* (New York: Appleton-Century-Crofts, 1950), pp. 397–404.

5. Jensen, *The Alaska Purchase,* pp. 85–87.

6. Ibid., p. 92.

7. Morgan B. Sherwood, *Exploration of Alaska* (New Haven, Conn.: Yale University Press, 1965), p. 312.

8. Jensen, *The Alaska Purchase,* p. 117.

9. Richard A. Pierce, "Alaska's Russian Governors: Prince D. P. Maksutov, the Chief Manager of the Russian-American Company," *Alaska Journal* 3, no. 1 (1973): 20–30.

10. Ibid., p. 405.

11. Ted C. Hinckley, "Alaska as an American Botany Bay," *Pacific Historical Review* 42, no. 1 (1973): 8.

12. Ibid., pp. 1–11.

13. Ted C. Hinckley, *The Americanization of Alaska* (Palo Alto, Calif.: Pacific Books, 1972), p. 34.

14. Ibid., pp. 40–57.

15. Ibid., pp. 49–52.

16. Ernest Gruening, *The State of Alaska,* 2d ed. (New York: Random House, 1968), pp. 555–56.

17. Ibid., p. 36.

18. Brooks, *Blazing Alaska's Trails,* pp. 270–71.

19. Sherwood, *Exploration of Alaska,* pp. 45–46.

20. Ibid.

21. Gruening, *The State of Alaska,* pp. 67–70; Hinckley, *The Americanization of Alaska,* p. 92; Brooks, *Blazing Alaska's Trails,* pp. 270–71; Jeannette P. Nichols, *Alaska: A History of Its Administration, Exploitation, and Industrial Development During Its First Half Century Under the Rule of the United States* (Cleveland, Ohio: Arthur H. Clark, 1924), pp. 47–49.

22. Sherwood, *Exploration of Alaska,* p. 44.

23. Lawrence W. Rakestraw, *A History of the United States Forest Service in Alaska* (Anchorage: Alaska Historical Commission, Department of Education, State of Alaska; and Alaska Region, U.S. Forest Service, Department of Agriculture, with the assistance of the Alaska Historical Society, 1981), p. 7.

24. Richard A. Cooley, *Politics and Conservation* (New York: Harper & Row, 1963), pp. 25–26.

25. Brooks, *Blazing Alaska's Trails,* pp. 300–301.

26. Robert N. DeArmond, *The Founding of Juneau* (Juneau: Gastineau Channel Centennial Association, 1967), p. 74.

27. According to DeArmond (ibid., p. 89), Juneau was the only mining district in the United States that was developed under the auspices of the navy.

28. Brooks, *Blazing Alaska's Trails,* pp. 303–306.

29. Gruening, *The State of Alaska,* p. 72.

30. DeArmond, *The Founding of Juneau,* p. 110.

31. Ted C. Hinckley, "Prospectors, Profits, and Prejudice," *American West* 2 (Spring, 1965): 59–63.

32. Brooks, *Blazing Alaska's Trails,* pp. 327–28.

33. Ibid., pp. 332–34.

34. Ibid., p. 334.

35. Nichols, *Alaska,* pp. 67–68.

36. Gruening, *The State of Alaska,* pp. 565–66.

37. Hinckley, *The Americanization of Alaska,* pp. 153–56.

38. Ibid., pp. 160–66.

39. Ibid., p. 166.

40. Ted C. Hinckley, "Sheldon Jackson and Benjamin Harrison," in Sherwood, ed., *Alaska and Its History,* pp. 306–307.

41. Hinckley, *The Americanization of Alaska,* p. 167.

42. Ibid., pp. 81–82.

43. Ibid., pp. 115–16.

44. Ibid., pp. 98–99; Brooks, *Blazing Alaska's Trails,* pp. 488–92.

45. Bailey, *A Diplomatic History of the American People,* pp. 446–49.

## Chapter 5

1. Brooks, *Blazing Alaska's Trails*, p. 335.
2. William R. Hunt, *North of 53°: The Wild Days of the Alaska-Yukon Gold Rush* (New York: Macmillan, 1974), pp. 37–43.
3. Brooks, *Blazing Alaska's Trails*, p. 376.
4. Ibid., pp. 390–91.
5. Hunt, *North of 53°*, p. 113; Brooks, *Blazing Alaska's Trails*, pp. 397–98; "Nome," *Alaska Geographic* 11, no. 1 (1984): 73–79.
6. "Nome," pp. 79–89.
7. Terrence Cole, *E. T. Barnette and the Founding of Fairbanks* (Anchorage: Alaska Northwest Publishing Co., 1981), pp. 38–44.
8. Ibid., p. 139.
9. David B. Wharton, *The Alaska Gold Rush* (Bloomington: Indiana University Press, 1972), pp. 264–66.
10. Ibid., pp. 131–34.
11. Nichols, *Alaska*, pp. 159–62.
12. Gruening, *The State of Alaska*, p. 113.
13. Bailey, *A Diplomatic History of the American People*, pp. 507–10.
14. Orlando W. Miller, *The Frontier in Alaska and the Matanuska Colony* (New Haven, Conn.: Yale University Press, 1975), p. 17.
15. Ibid., pp. 17–18.
16. William H. Wilson, *Railroad in the Clouds: The Alaska Railroad in the Age of Steam* (Boulder, Colo.: Pruett Publishing Co., 1977), pp. 4–15. For a good source on railroad development, consult Frank W. Burch, "Alaska's Railroad Frontier: Railroads and Federal Development Policy, 1898–1915" (Ph.D. diss., Catholic University of America, 1965).
17. Gruening, *The State of Alaska*, p. 144; Nichols, *Alaska*, p. 251.
18. Nichols, Alaska, pp. 330–32.
19. Herman E. Slotnick, "The Ballinger-Pinchot Affair in Alaska," *Journal of the West* 10, no. 2 (1971): 337–47.
20. Nichols, *Alaska*, pp. 283–84, 308–309; Gruening, *The State of Alaska*, pp. 142–45.
21. Nichols, *Alaska*, pp. 385–89.
22. Gruening, *The State of Alaska*, pp. 151–52.
23. Ibid., pp. 159–63, 173–74.
24. *Congressional Record*, vol. 51, pt. 1, 63 Cong., 2d sess. (December 2, 1913), p. 43; Edward Fitch, *The Alaska Railroad* (New York: Frederick A. Praeger, 1967), p. 43.
25. Fitch, *The Alaska Railroad*, pp. 49–52.
26. *Alaska v. Troy*, 258 U.S. 101 (February 27, 1922).

## Chapter 6

1. Gruening, *The State of Alaska*, pp. 270, 272.
2. Cooley, *Politics and Conservation*, p. 26.
3. Ibid., p. 73.
4. Ibid., pp. 75–76, 78–82.
5. Ibid., pp. 97–98.
6. Ibid., p. 96.
7. Ibid., pp. 87–89. For the definitive study of the hatchery program, see Patricia Roppel, *Alaska's Salmon Hatcheries, 1891–1959*, Studies in History no. 20 (Anchorage: Alaska Historical Commission, 1982).
8. Cooley, *Politics and Conservation*, pp. 104–105.
9. Ibid., pp. 106–108.
10. Ibid., p. 118.
11. Ibid., pp. 125–27, 129.
12. George W. Rogers, *The Future of Alaska: Economic Consequences of Statehood* (Baltimore: Johns Hopkins Press, 1962), p. 91.
13. National Resources Committee, *Alaska*, pp. 170–77.
14. U.S. Department of the Interior, Bureau of Reclamation, *Alaska*, pp. 65–66.
15. Gruening, *The State of Alaska*, p. 271.
16. Rogers, *The Future of Alaska*, p. 62.
17. Rakestraw, *A History of the United States Forest Service*, pp. 108–109.
18. Mary C. Mangusso, "Anthony J. Dimond: A Political Biography" (Ph.D. diss., Texas Tech University, 1978), pp. 166–68, 183.
19. Rakestraw, *A History of the United States Forest Service*, pp. 95–100.
20. Cooley, *Politics and Conservation*, pp. 136–39.
21. Ibid., pp. 147–49.
22. Ibid., pp. 151, 156.
23. Miller, *The Frontier in Alaska*, pp. 38–45.
24. Ibid., pp. 62, 69–71.
25. Ibid., pp. 83–87, 98–99.
26. Ibid., pp. 88–89.
27. Ibid., pp. 102–104.
28. Mangusso, "Anthony J. Dimond," p. 186.
29. Ibid., pp. 188–95; Miller, *The Frontier in Alaska*, pp. 166–75.
30. Compare Rogers, *The Future of Alaska*, pp. 248–50; and Gruening, *The State of Alaska*, pp. 255–59, 364–68.
31. National Resources Committee, *Alaska*, p. 19; Harold Ickes, *The Secret Diary of Harold Ickes* (New York: Simon and Schuster, 1954), 2:449–50.

32. Ernest Gruening, *Many Battles: The Autobiography of Ernest Gruening* (New York: Liveright, 1973), p. 283.

## Chapter 7

1. U.S. Army, Alaska, *The Army's Role in the Building of Alaska*, Pamphlet 360-5, April 1, 1959 (Headquarters, U.S. Army, Alaska, 1969), pp. 3–7 (hereafter cited as USARAL Pamphlet 360-5).

2. Ibid., pp. 9–16.

3. Ibid., pp. 20–22.

4. Morgan R. Sherwood, *Exploration of Alaska, 1865–1900* (New Haven, Conn.: Yale University Press, 1965), pp. 93–118.

5. USARAL Pamphlet 360-5, pp. 26–28.

6. Ibid., pp. 32–34.

7. Ibid., pp. 34–44.

8. Ibid., pp. 45–47.

9. Ibid., pp. 47–62.

10. Ibid., p. 74.

11. Ibid., p. 70.

12. Ibid., p. 71.

13. Ibid.

14. Claus-M. Naske, *An Interpretative History of Alaskan Statehood* (Anchorage: Alaska Northwest Publishing Co., 1973), p. 56.

15. USARAL Pamphlet 360-5, p. 73.

16. Ibid., p. 74.

17. Naske, *An Interpretative History*, pp. 56–57; USARAL Pamphlet 360-5, p. 74.

18. Samuel Eliot Morison, *History of United States Naval Operations in World War II*, vol. 4, *Coral Sea, Midway, and Submarine Actions* (Boston: Little, Brown, 1962), pp. 163–65.

19. Brian Garfield, *The Thousand-Mile War: World War II in Alaska and the Aleutians* (Garden City, N.Y.: Doubleday, 1969), p. 12.

20. Morison, *The Coral Sea*, p. 75.

21. Ibid., pp. 3–7.

22. Ibid., pp. 17–28.

23. Ibid., pp. 7, 25.

24. Ibid., pp. 180–81.

25. Ibid., pp. 169, 181.

26. Ibid., p. 183.

27. Ibid., p. 4.

28. Ibid., p. 5.

29. Ibid., pp. 7–8.

30. Ibid., pp. 12–13.

31. Garfield, *The Thousand Mile War*, pp. 146–47.

32. Ibid., pp. 149–50.

33. USARAL Pamphlet 360-5, p. 90; Garfield, *The Thousand Mile War*, pp. 150–51.

34. Claus-M. Naske, "The Alcan: Its Impact on Alaska," *Northern Engineer* 8, no. 1 (Spring 1976): 12–18.

35. Deane R. Brandon, "War Planes to Russia," *Alaska Magazine*, May, 1976, pp. 14–17.

36. Garfield, *The Thousand Mile War*, pp. 153–55.

37. Morison, *Naval Operations*, vol. 7, *The Aleutians, Gilberts, and Marshalls*, p. 17.

38. Ibid., p. 22; Garfield, *The Thousand Mile War*, pp. 178–79.

39. Garfield, *The Thousand Mile War*, pp. 251–52.

40. Ibid., p. 256.

41. Ibid.

42. Morison, *The Coral Sea*, pp. 54, 57–59.

43. Ibid., pp. 59–60.

44. Ibid., pp. 63–64.

45. USARAL Pamphlet 360-5, p. 96.

46. Rogers, *The Future of Alaska*, p. 95.

47. USARAL Pamphlet 360-5, pp. 68, 70–74, 85–89, 97–98.

48. *New York Times*, March 13 and 16, 1949.

49. Ibid., March 19, 1949, p. 7.

50. Ibid.

51. Ibid.

52. Ibid., March 21, 1949, p. 9.

53. Ibid., March 26, 1949, p. 7; January 3, 1949, p. 92.

54. Ibid., June 25, 1950, p. 15; June 26, 1950, p. 18.

55. Brent R. Bowen, "Defense Spending in Alaska," *Alaska Review of Business and Economic Conditions* (Fairbanks: Institute of Social, Economic, and Government Research, July, 1971), p. 4.

56. *New York Times*, June 25, 1950, p. 15.

57. Ibid., June 27, 1950, p. 37.

58. Ibid., June 25, 1950, p. 15; June 26, 1950, p. 18; June 27, 1950, p. 37.

59. Ibid., August 31, 1952, pp. 1–4.

60. Ibid., November 2, 1952, p. 14.

61. Ibid., January 6, 1954, p. 59; July 27, 1954, p. 12.

62. Jonathon Macauley Nielson, "Armed Forces on the Last Frontier" (MS, copy in author Naske's files), p. 139–41.

63. Ibid., p. 142.

64. Naske, *An Interpretative History*, p. 168.

65. Nielson, "Armed Forces," pp. 147–49.

66. Ibid., pp. 158, 155–56.

67. Ibid., p. 156.
68. Ibid., pp. 156–57.
69. Ibid., pp. 157–58.
70. Ibid., pp. 161–62.

*Chapter 8*

1. Hinckley, *The Americanization of Alaska*, pp. 41–42.
2. *Speech of William H. Seward, at Sitka, August 12, 1869* (Washington, D.C.: Philip & Solomons, 1869), pp. 15–16.
3. Jack E. Eblen, *The First and Second United States Empires: Governors and Territorial Government, 1784–1912* (Pittsburgh: University of Pittsburgh Press, 1968), pp. 151, 8.
4. James D. Richardson, ed., *A Compilation of the Messages and Papers of the Presidents* (New York: Bureau of National Literature, 1897–1922), 15:7019–20.
5. Naske, *An Interpretative History*, p. 7.
6. George Washington Spicer, *The Constitutional Status and Government of Alaska* (Baltimore, Md.: Johns Hopkins University Press, 1927), pp. 27–32; Marcos E. Kirnevan, "Alaska and Hawaii: From Territoriality to Statehood," *California Law Review* 38 (1950): 279.
7. Robert H. Wiebe, *The Search for Order, 1877–1920* (New York: Hill and Wang, 1967), p. 288.
8. Naske, *An Interpretative History*, pp. 8–9.
9. Territorial Senate, *Senate Journal*, 1915, pp. 4–5, 95; *Alaska Daily Empire*, March 31, 1915; *Senate Journal*, 1915, pp. 100, 150; *Senate Journal*, 1915, pp. 98, 100; *Alaska Daily Empire*, April 9, 13, 1915; *Senate Journal*, 1915, pp. 137, 192–93.
10. 64th Cong., 1st sess., H.R. 6887 (January 4, 1916).
11. U.S. Congress, *Congressional Record*, 64th Cong., 1st sess., p. A1520.
12. James Wickersham, "The Forty Ninth Star," *Collier's*, August 6, 1910, p. 17.
13. Naske, *An Interpretative History*, p. 37.
14. 64th Cong., 1st sess., H.R. 13978.
15. Naske, *An Interpretative History*, pp. 38–39.
16. *Daily Alaska Dispatch*, September 1, 1916.
17. *Alaska Daily Empire*, July 13, 1921.
18. Ibid., p. 43.
19. U.S. Congress, House, Committee on the Territories, *Reapportionment of the Alaska Leg-*

*islature: Hearings on H.R. 8114*, 68th Cong., 1st sess., pp. 1, 3.
20. Naske, *An Interpretative History*, p. 52.
21. Author Naske's interview with Sister Marie Therese, Dimond's eldest daughter, Trinity College, Washington, D.C., April 20, 1975. The commissioner was the lowest-ranking federal judge. Miners within an area recorded their claims in the appropriate recording district, where the commissioner served as recorder of claims.
22. Gruening, *The State of Alaska*, p. 316.
23. Gruening, *Many Battles*, pp. 3–87, 210–28.
24. *Alaska Daily Times*, September 2, 1939.
25. *Daily Alaska Empire,*, December 6, 1939.
26. Ibid., Progress Edition, March 23, 1941.
27. *Anchorage Daily Times*, June 25, 1942; *Daily Alaska Empire*, June 23 and April 24, 1943; S. 951, 78th Cong., 1st sess. (April 2, 1943).
28. *Daily Alaska Empire*, July 9, 15, and 29 and September 2, 1943; Juneau Chamber of Commerce, Legislative Committee, *Report of Legislative Committee, Juneau Chamber of Commerce, on Senate Bill No. 951, Entitled "A Bill to Provide Admission of Alaska into the Union"* (Juneau, Alaska: Juneau Chamber of Commerce, 1943).
29. H.R. 3768, 78th Cong., 1st sess. (December 2, 1943).
30. Dean Sherman, "The Statehood Question," *Alaska Life*, June, 1944, pp. 15–18.
31. *Daily Alaska Empire*, January 18 and 24, 1944; State of Alaska, Territorial Canvassing Board, "Alaska General Election, September 12, 1944."
32. Alaska Legislature, House, *Journal* (1945) pp. 46–47.
33. U.S. Congress, House, Subcommittee of the Committee on Appropriations, *Official Trip of Examination of Federal Activities in Alaska and the Pacific Coast States*, 79th Cong., 1st sess., p. 11; *Washington Post*, August 14, 1945; *Ketchikan Alaska Chronicle*, August 25, 1945.
34. *Daily Alaska Empire*, August 13, 1945.
35. Ibid.
36. *Anchorage Daily Times*, November 2, 1945; E. Atwood to Gruening, December 26, 1945, E. L. Bartlett Papers (University of Alaska Archives, Fairbanks), Statehood File, folder Correspondence, General, 1944–45, box 6; *Daily Alaska Empire*, March 12, 1946.
37. U.S. President, *Public Papers of the Presi-*

*dents of the United States, Harry S Truman, 1946* (Washington, D.C.: Office of the Federal Register, National Archives and Records Service, 1962–66), p. 66; *Anchorage Daily Times,* February 13, 1946; *Daily Alaska Empire,* February 26, 1946.

38. *Daily Alaska Empire,* August 20 and 22, 1946; *Ketchikan Alaska Chronicle,* August 21, 1946.

39. George Sundborg, *Statehood for Alaska: The Issues Involved and the Facts About the Issues* (Anchorage: Alaska Statehood Association, August, 1946), pp. 5–55.

40. Territory of Alaska, Territorial Canvassing Board, "Official Returns, General Election, October 8, 1946."

41. *Fairbanks Daily News-Miner,* July 22, 1952.

42. *Anchorage Daily Times,* October 5, 1946.

43. *Jessen's Weekly,* December 28, 1945.

44. *Anchorage Daily Times,* September 26, 1946; U.S. Congress, House, Subcommittee on Territories and Insular Possessions of the Committee on Interior and Insular Affairs, *Statehood for Alaska: Hearings on H.R. 20, H.R. 207, H.R. 1746, H.R. 2684, H.R. 2982, and H.R. 1916,* 83d Cong., 1st sess. (April 14–17, 1953), p. 138; *Daily Alaska Empire,* April 28, 1944.

45. Edward Latham, ed., *Statehood for Hawaii and Alaska,* Reference Shelf, vol. 25, no. 5 (New York: H. W. Wilson, 1953), p. 68; *Congressional Record,* 81st Cong., 2d sess., p. 2748.

46. Ernest Gruening, *The Battle for Alaska Statehood* (College, Alaska: University of Alaska Press, 1967), pp. 5–6.

47. U. S. Bureau of the Census, *Census of Population, 1950,* vol. 2, pt. 56, pp. 5–6; U.S. Congress, *Hearings Pursuant to H. Res. 93,* pp. 356–60.

48. U.S. Congress, *Hearings on H.R. 206 and H.R. 1808,* p. 428.

49. Ernest Gruening, *Message to the People of Alaska: A Report on the Eighteenth Territorial Legislature from Governor Ernest Gruening* (Juneau, 1947), p. 4; *Daily Alaska Empire,* April 9 and 21 and May 2, 1947; *Jessen's Weekly,* May 9, 1947.

50. U.S. Congress, *Hearings Pursuant to H. Res. 93,* pp. 374–75, 115; *Anchorage Daily Times,* August 30 and September 13, 1947; *Ketchikan Alaska Chronicle,* September 13, 1947; U.S. Congress, *Hearings Pursuant to H. Res. 93,* pp. 120, 155–56, 159, 166, 160, 169.

51. *Daily Alaska Empire,* December 10,

1946; *Anchorage Daily Times,* July 1, 1947; *Ketchikan Alaska Chronicle,* August 1 and September 3, 1947; U.S. Congress, *Hearings Pursuant to H. Res. 93,* p. 374; *Anchorage Daily Times,* September 5, 1947; *Jessen's Weekly,* September 12, 1947; *Daily Alaska Empire,* September 12, 1947; *Anchorage Daily Times,* September 5, 1947; *Ketchikan Alaska Chronicle,* September 15, 1947.

52. *Daily Alaska Empire,* February 21, 1948.

53. Bartlett to Burke Riley, March 1, 1948, Bartlett Papers, Statehood File, box 7, folder Correspondence, General, 1948; *Daily Alaska Empire,* March 3, 1948; *Ketchikan Alaska Chronicle,* March 3, 1948; H.R. 5626, 80th Cong., 2d sess. (February 27, 1948); Bartlett to Burke Riley, March 1, 1948, Bartlett Papers; *Daily Alaska Empire,* March 5 and 26, 1948; *Ketchikan Alaska Chronicle,* April 17, 1948; Bartlett to Friend, April 8, 1948, D'Ewart to Felix S. Cohen, March 29, 1948, Bartlett Papers, Statehood File, box 16, folder Legislative History, 1948; *Ketchikan Alaska Chronicle,* April 17, 1948; Frances Lopinski to Friend, April 26, 1948, Bartlett Papers, Statehood File, box 16, folder Legislative History, 1948; U.S. Congress, *Congressional Record,* 85th Cong., 2d sess., pp. 13734–35.

54. *Ketchikan Alaska Chronicle,* February 6, 1948.

55. *Fairbanks Daily News-Miner,* May 13, 1954; U.S. Congress, *Congressional Record,* 85th Cong., 2d sess., pp. 13734–35.

56. Kirk H. Porter and Donald Bruce Johnson, *National Party Platforms, 1840–1960* (Urbana: University of Illinois Press, 1961), pp. 435, 453; *Ketchikan Alaska Chronicle,* November 6 and 8, 1948.

57. Alaska Legislature, House, *Journal,* 1949, p. 49; *Daily Alaska Empire,* June 24, 1949; *Anchorage Daily Times,* December 18, 1948.

58. *Daily Alaska Empire,* January 23, and February 14 and 20, 1947; *Ketchikan Alaska Chronicle,* February 22, 1947; Alaska Legislature, House, *Journal,* 1947, p. 320; Senate, *Journal,* 1949, pp. 432, 541, 614–16; House, *Journal,* 1949, pp. 1022–23; Territory of Alaska, *Session Laws,* 1949, pp. 270–71.

59. U.S. Congress, H.R. 331, 81st Cong., 1st sess. (January 3, 1949); U.S. Congress, *Hearings on H.R. 206 and H.R. 1808,* pp. 393–94.

60. *Daily Alaska Empire,* March 4, 1949; U.S. Congress, House, Subcommittee on Territorial and Insular Possessions of the Committee on

Public Lands, *Statehood for Alaska: Hearings on H.R. 331 and Related Bills,* 81st Cong., 1st sess. (March 4 and 8, 1949), pp. 31, 34–35; U.S. Congress, House, *Providing for the Admission of Alaska into the Union,* H. Rept. 225 to accompany H.R. 331, 81st Cong., 1st sess., pp. 36–52; George B. Galloway, *The Legislative Process in Congress* (New York: Thomas Y. Crowell Co., 1955), pp. 343–45; *Congressional Record,* 81st Cong., 2d sess., pp. 2780–81.

61. *Ketchikan Alaska Chronicle,* January 24, 1949; March 27, 1950; U.S. Congress, S. 513 (January 17, 1949), S. 727 (January 31, 1949), and S. 2036 (June 10, 1949), 81st Cong., 1st sess.

62. *Anchorage Daily Times,* April 11, 1950; *Ketchikan Alaska Chronicle,* April 24 and 27, 1950.

63. U.S. Congress, Senate, Committee on Interior and Insular Affairs, *Alaska Statehood: Hearings on H.R. 331 and S. 2036,* 81st Cong., 1st sess. (April 24–29, 1950), pp. 1, 26, 49, 79, 160, 164.

64. Ibid., pp. 317–18.

65. Author Naske's Interview with Mary Lee Council, Washington, D.C., July 20, 1969.

66. U.S. Congress, Senate, *Providing for the Admission of Alaska into the Union,* S. Rept. 1929, 81st Cong., 2d sess.; transcript of E. L. Bartlett radio address, recorded for KINY, Juneau, July 5, 1950, Bartlett Papers, Statehood file, Legislative History, June–July, 1950, box 16; S. Rept. 1929, p. 11; E. L. Bartlett Memorandum, "Public Land Provisions in Modern Alaska Statehood Legislation," June 27, 1957, Bartlett Papers, Statehood file, Legislative History, June–July, 1950, box 16; S. Rept. 1929, p. 11; E. L. Bartlett Memorandum, "Public Land Provisions in Modern Alaska Statehood Legislation," June 27, 1957, Bartlett Papers Statehood file, Legislative History, June–December, 1957, box 19.

67. *Congressional Record,* 81st Cong., 2d sess., pp. 15919–16035.

68. *Congressional Record,* Index, 82d Cong., 1st sess., p. 658; H.R. 1493, H.R. 1510, and H.R. 1863, 82d Cong., 1st sess.; *New York Times,* January 24, 1951; U.S. Congress, Senate, *Providing for the Admission of Alaska into the Union,* S. Rept. 315, 82d Cong., 1st sess.

69. E. L. Bartlett Memorandum, "Public Land Provisions in Modern Alaska Statehood Legislation," June 27, 1957, Bartlett Papers, Statehood file, Legislative History, June–

December, 1957, box 19; U.S. Congress, House, *Providing for the Admission of Alaska into the Union,* H. Rept. 675, 83d Cong., 1st sess., pp. 1–7, 14–22.

70. *Anchorage Daily Times,* May 17, 1954.

71. *Congressional Record,* 83d Cong., 2d sess., p. 3501, 4069–71; U.S. Congress, House, *Alaska, 1955: Hearings Before the Subcommittee on Territorial and Insular Affairs of the Committee on Interior and Insular Affairs Pursuant to H. Res. 30,* 84th Cong., 1st sess., p. 279.

72. U.S. Congress, House, Committee on Interior and Insular Affairs, *Hawaii-Alaska Statehood: Hearings on H.R. 2535 and H.R. 2536 and H.R. 49, H.R. 185, H.R. 187, H.R. 248, H.R. 511, H.R. 555, and H.R. 2531,* 84th Cong., 1st sess. (January 25–February 16, 1955), pp. 91–98, 111–12, 337–42; E. L. Bartlett Memorandum, "Memorandum Seeking to Preserve for the Benefit of History Certain of the Events Which Took Place During the Week Starting February 13 as They Related to Alaska Statehood," February 18, 1955, Bartlett Papers, Statehood file, Legislative History, January–February 1955, box 18; U.S. Congress, *Hearings on H.R. 2535,* pp. 337–47.

73. U.S. Congress, *Hearings on H.R. 2535,* pp. 397, 350–55; E. L. Bartlett Memorandum, "Seeking to Preserve . . . ," Bartlett Papers.

74. *Anchorage Daily Times,* February 22, 1955; *Hearings on H.R. 2535,* pp. 395–96, 421–32; U.S. Congress, Senate, Committee on Interior and Insular Affairs, *Alaska-Hawaii Statehood, Elective Governorship, and Commonwealth Status: Hearings on S. 49, S. 399, and S. 402,* 84th Cong., 1st sess. (February 21–28, 1955), p. 26; Bartlett Memorandum, "Seeking to Preserve . . . ," Bartlett Papers.

75. U.S. Congress, 84th Cong., 1st sess., S. 49 (January 6, 1955); U.S. Congress, *Hearings on S. 49, S. 399, and S. 402,* pp. 20–21; U.S. Congress, Senate, Committee on Interior and Insular Affairs, *Alaska Statehood: Hearings on H.R. 331 and S. 2036,* 81st Cong., 2d sess. (April 24–29, 1950), pp. 36–47.

76. U.S. Congress, *Hearings on S. 49, S. 399, and S. 402,* pp. 89–90; *Congressional Record,* 84th Cong., 1st sess., p. 5880.

77. *Fairbanks Daily News-Miner,* March 17, 1955; *Anchorage Daily Times,* April 25, 1955; *Congressional Record,* 84th Cong., 1st sess., pp. 5878–80; *Daily Alaska Empire,* May 10 and May 2, 1955; *Congressional Record,* 84th Cong., 1st sess., p. 5927; *Anchorage Daily*

*Times,* May 16, 1955; *Congressional Record,* 84th Cong., 1st sess., pp. 5974–76.

78. For the story of the convention see Victor Fischer, *Alaska's Constitutional Convention* (Fairbanks: University of Alaska Press, 1975).

79. Ibid., pp. 52–53; Gruening, *The Battle for Statehood,* p. 383.

80. Territory of Alaska, "Official Canvass of Results, Alaska General Election, Tuesday, October 9, 1956."

81. Naske, *An Interpretative History,* p. 106; U.S. Congress, Senate, Committee on Interior and Insular Affairs, *Nomination of Frederick A. Seaton to Be Secretary of the Interior,* 84th Cong., 2d sess. (June 5, 1956), pp. 2–30.

82. *Congressional Record,* 85th Cong., 1st sess., p. A4651.

83. U.S. Congress, S. 49 and S. 50, January 7, 1957, and H.R. 49 and H.R. 50, January 3, 1957, 85th Cong., 1st sess.

84. Naske, *An Interpretative History,* p. 159.

85. Ibid., pp. 159–60.

86. Ibid., pp. 160–61.

87. E. L. Bartlett interview with Val Trimble and Scott Hart, Washington, D.C., August 1, 1965, Vide Bartlett, Private Papers.

88. Naske, *An Interpretative History,* pp. 98–99.

89. Ibid., p. 162.

90. *Fairbanks Daily News-Miner,* March 3, 1958; *Congressional Record,* 85th Cong., 2d sess., p. 5041.

91. Naske, *An Interpretative History,* pp. 163–64.

92. *Congressional Record,* 85th Cong., 2d sess., pp. 9217–18, 9368.

93. Naske, *An Interpretative History,* pp. 164–65.

94. Ibid., p. 166.

95. Bartlett interview with Val Trimble and Scott Hart, August 1, 1965.

96. Claus-M. Naske, "103,350,000 Acres . . . the Land Grant Provisions of Alaska Statehood Bills from 1916 Onward," *Alaska Journal,* Autumn, 1972; pp. 11–12.


*Chapter 9*

1. Richard A. Cooley, *Alaska: A Challenge in Conservation* (Madison: University of Wisconsin Press, 1967), pp. 21–23.

2. Ibid., p. 24.

3. Rogers, *Alaska in Transition,* pp. 74–75; Rakestraw, *A History of the United States Forest Service,* p. 128.

4. Rogers, *The Future of Alaska,* p. 266.

5. Ibid.

6. Ibid.

7. Ibid., pp. 266–67.

8. Ibid., pp. 267–68.

9. Ibid., p. 269.

10. "The 49th State," *Time,* July 14, 1958, p. 16.

11. Mary Lee Council to E. L. Bartlett, July 12, 1958, Statehood file, box 2, folder Alaska Statehood Committee, 1958–59, Bartlett Papers.

12. *Fairbanks Daily News-Miner,* August 14, 9, and 25, 1958; Robert B. Atwood, "Alaska's Struggle for Statehood," *State Government,* Autumn, 1958; p. 208.

13. *Fairbanks Daily News-Miner,* July 16 and 19, 1958; George Sundborg to E. L. Bartlett, July 4, 1958, Vide Bartlett, Private Papers.

14. *Anchorage Daily Times,* July 15 and 24, August 20, 1958; Donald R. Moberg, "The 1958 Election in Alaska," *Western Political Quarterly* 12 (1950): 259–60.

15. *Fairbanks Daily News-Miner,* August 19 and 25, 1958; *Daily Alaska Empire,* July 13 and August 16, 1958.

16. "Statehood Primary Election Results," Alaska Historical Library, Juneau.

17. Ibid.

18. *Fairbanks Daily News-Miner,* August 2, 1958; November 4 and 28, 1958; "Fred and the 49th," *Time,* November 24, 1958; Moberg, "The 1958 Election in Alaska," pp. 260–62; *Daily Alaska Empire,* December 1, 1958.

19. "Alaska Official Returns of the Special Statehood Referendum Election, August 26, 1958, and the General Election, November 25, 1958," copy in author Naske's files.

20. Thomas B. Stewart to E. L. Bartlett, May 25, 1957, Bartlett Papers, Statehood File, box 12, folder Correspondence, General, May, 1957; "Minutes of the Meeting of the Alaska Statehood Committee," March 7–8, 1958; "Minutes of Meeting, Executive Committee of the Alaska Statehood Committee," July 12–13, 1958, and "Contract Amendment," Bartlett Papers, box 2, folder Alaska Statehood Committee, 1958–59; Territory of Alaska, *Session Laws,* 1957, p. 471; Public Administration Service, *Proposed Organization of the Executive Branch, State of Alaska: A Summary Report* (Chicago: Public Administration Service, 1958); Public Administration Service, *Proposed Organization of the Judicial Branch, State of Alaska* (Chicago: Public Administration Service, 1959); Public Administration Service, *Local Government Under the*

*Alaska Constitution: A Survey Report* (Chicago: Public Administration Service, 1959); Public Administration Service, *Functional and Staffing Charts for the Proposed Organization of the Executive Branch, State of Alaska* (Chicago: Public Administration Service, 1959).

21. *Fairbanks Daily News-Miner*, January 3, 12, 1959.

22. *Congressional Record*, 86th Cong., 1st sess., p. 8737.

23. U.S. Congress, House, Subcommittee on Territorial and Insular Affairs, *Alaska Omnibus Bill: Hearings on H.R. 6091 and H.R. 6112*, 86th Cong., 1st sess., pp. 25–36, 55–56; U.S. Congress, Senate, Committee on Interior and Insular Affairs, *Alaska Omnibus Bill: Hearings on S. 1541*, 86th Cong., 1st sess.

24. U.S. Congress, *Hearings on H.R. 6091*, pp. 67–73; *Congressional Record*, 86th Cong., 1st sess., p. 9473; U.S. Congress, *Hearings on S. 1541*, p. 11.

25. U.S. Congress, *Hearings on H.R. 6091*, p. 45; U.S. Congress, *Hearings on S. 1541*, pp. 10–11; Paul F. Royster to Ralph Rivers, September 25, 1959, Ralph J. Rivers Papers (University of Alaska Archives, Fairbanks), Legislative File, 1959–66, box 18, folder Omnibus Bill; U.S. Congress, *Hearings on H.R. 6091*, p. 59–63.

26. U.S. Congress, *Hearings on H.R. 6091*, pp. 61–78.

27. U.S. Congress, *Hearings on S. 1541*, p. 11; U.S. Congress, *Hearings on H.R. 6091*, pp. 26–35.

28. U.S. Congress, *Hearings on H.R. 6091*, pp. 27–39; *Anchorage Daily Times*, March 25, 1959.

29. U.S. Congress, *Hearings on H.R. 6091*, pp. 56–58; U.S. Congress, 1958 ed., Title 23, sec. 103.

30. U.S. Congress, *Hearings on S. 1541*, pp. 5–8, 74.

31. *Anchorage Daily Times*, May 11, 1959, U.S. Congress, *Hearings on H.R. 6091*, pp. 79–80.

32. State of Alaska, *Session Laws*, 1959, pp. 89–104; *Anchorage Daily Times*, April 21 and 28, May 11, 1959.

33. U.S. Congress, H.R. 7120, 86th Cong., 1st sess. (May 14, 1959); *Anchorage Daily Times*, May 28, 1959; *Congressional Record*, 86th Cong., 1st sess., pp. 9470, 9480, 9482–84; *Anchorage Daily Times*, June 15, 1959; E. L. Bartlett to Hugh Wade, June 4, 1959, Bartlett Papers, Alaska Statehood File, folder 1959–62; Omnibus Act, 1959, May–June.

34. *Congressional Record*, 86th Cong., 1st sess., pp. 9470, 10568, 9678–79, 10594.

### Chapter 10

1. State of Alaska, Constitution, art. 10.

2. Ibid., Thomas A. Morehouse, Gerald A. McBeath, and Linda Leask, *Alaska's Urban and Rural Governments* (Lanham, Md.: University Press of America, 1984), p. 26.

3. Ibid., p. 39.

4. Ibid., p. 42.

5. Ibid., pp. 43–44.

6. Ibid., p. 45.

7. State of Alaska, Constitution, art. 10, sec. 1.

8. Ibid., art. 13.

9. Ibid., art. 15.

10. Ibid., art. 8; State of Alaska, Department of Education, Division of State Libraries, *Alaska Blue Book* (Juneau, 1973), p. 148.

11. State of Alaska, Constitution, art. 8, sec. 15.

12. Naske, *An Interpretative History*, p. 142.

13. Author Naske's interview with Hugh J. Wade, Anchorage, Alaska, December 30, 1976.

14. State of Alaska, Department of Education, Division of State Libraries, *Alaska Blue Book, 1975*, 2d ed., ed. Elaine Mitchell (Juneau, 1975), pp. 196–97.

15. State of Alaska, Department of Economic Enterprise, *Alaska Statistical Review* (Juneau), December, 1972, pp. 15–16.

16. Patrick O'Donovan, "The Forty-Ninth Star on the U.S. Flag," *London Observer*, July 13, 1958.

17. Author Naske's interview with Herbert L. Faulkner, Juneau, Alaska, August 11, 1969.

18. "Message of Governor William A. Egan to the Second Session, First Alaska State Legislature, Recommending Appropriations for Fiscal Year 1961," in *State of Alaska Budget Document, 1960–61* (Juneau), January 27, 1960, pp. 1–4.

19. Ray J. Schrick, "Alaska's Ordeal," *Wall Street Journal*, March 16, 1960.

20. Ibid.

21. "Main Trails and Bypaths," *Alaska Sportsman*, January, 1960; p. 7; Schrick, "Alaska's Ordeal."

22. "Main Trails and Bypaths," p. 7.

23. "Message of Governor William A. Egan to the Second Session," pp. 1–4.

24. Ibid., pp. 7, 20; Alaska State Planning Commission, *State of Alaska Capital Improve-*

ment Program, 1960–1966, January 29, 1960, pp. C-4–C-7.

25. State of Alaska, Department of Economic Development, Industrial Development Division, *Alaska Statistical Review, 1968* (Juneau, 1969), pp. 3, 23, 28, 56; "Bob" Bartlett, "Big Gains in Fish, Timber," *Fairbanks Daily News-Miner,* March 17, 1966.

26. Herman E. Slotnick, "The 1960 Election in Alaska," *Western Political Quarterly,* March, 1961; p. 300; Thomas A. Morehouse and Gordon A. Harrison, *An Electoral Profile of Alaska* (Fairbanks, Alaska: Institute of Social, Economic, and Government Research, 1973), pp. 2–3.

27. Jan Juran and Daniel Raff, "Theodore F. Stevens, Republican Senator from Alaska," *Ralph Nader Congress Project: Citizens Look at Congress,* p. 8; Tom Brown, *Oil on Ice: Alaskan Wilderness at the Crossroads* (San Francisco: Sierra Club, 1971), pp. 42–43.

28. State of Alaska, Office of the Governor, "Alaska Earthquake Disaster Damage Report" (preliminary), April 4, 1964, in author Naske's files.

29. *Washington Daily News,* March 30, 1964.

30. Ibid.,; *Washington Post,* March 31, 1964.

31. *Washington Post,* March 31, 1964.

32. E. L. Bartlett Press Release, April 3, 1964, in author Naske's files.

33. E. L. Bartlett to Clinton B. Anderson, April 11, 1964, in author Naske's files; *Fairbanks Daily News-Miner,* May 20, 1964; Public Law 88-451; 88th Cong., 2d sess., S. 2881 (August 19, 1964).

34. Brookings Institution, Advanced Study Program, in Association with the Legislative Council of the State of Alaska, "Conference on the Future of Alaska," fall, 1969.

35. *Planning Guidelines for the State of Alaska,* prepared for the Office of the Governor, State of Alaska (Menlo Park, Calif.: Stanford Research Institute, December, 1969).

36. Capital Site Selection Committee, "Information for Participants," 1974.

37. "Alaska Review," monthly television program funded by the Alaska State Legislature and the Alaska Humanities Forum.

38. Ibid.

39. *Ketchikan Daily News,* January 15, 1977.

40. Hammond campaign brochure, in author Naske's files.

41. Ibid.

42. State of Alaska, Department of Revenue, *Alaska '75: Facing the Crunch.*

43. *All Alaska Weekly,* December 22, 1978.

## Chapter 11

1. Joseph H. Fitzgerald et al., *Alaska Natives and the Land* (Washington, D.C.: Federal Field Committee for Development Planning in Alaska, 1968), pp. 19–22.

2. William R. Hunt, *Arctic Passage* (New York: Charles Scribner's Sons, 1975), pp. 117, 132–33, 122.

3. Rogers, *The Future of Alaska,* p. 89.

4. Bobby Dave Lain, "North of Fifty-three: Army, Treasury Department, and Navy Administration of Alaska, 1867–1884" (Ph.D. diss., University of Texas, Austin, 1974), pp. 121–56.

5. U.S. Congress, House, Committee on the Territories, *Civil Government for Alaska: Report to Accompany S. 153,* 48th Cong., 1st sess., 1884, H.R. 476, p. 2.

6. George W. Rogers and Richard A. Cooley, *Alaska's Population and Economy: Regional Growth, Development and Future Outlook,* vol. 2, *Statistical Handbook* (College, Alaska: Institute of Social, Economic, and Government Research, 1963), p. 7.

7. Fitzgerald et al., *Alaska Natives and the Land,* p. 433.

8. Ibid., pp. 434–35.

9. Ibid., p. 435.

10. Robert D. Arnold et al., *Alaska Native Land Claims* (Anchorage: Alaska Native Foundation, 1976), p. 83.

11. Ibid.

12. Gruening, *The State of Alaska,* pp. 355–81; U.S. Congress, Senate, *Alaska Native Claims Settlement Act of 1971: Report Together with Additional and Supplemental Views to Accompany S. 35,* 92d Cong., 1st sess. (October 21, 1971), p. 91.

13. Stanton H. Patty, "A Conference with the Tanana Chiefs," *Alaska Journal,* Spring, 1971, pp. 2–10.

14. Ibid., pp. 11, 18.

15. U.S. Congress, Senate, *Alaska Native Claims Settlement Act of 1971,* p. 91.

16. 48 Stat. 984; 49 Stat. 1250, sec. 2; Gruening, *State of Alaska,* pp. 364–65.

17. Gruening, *The State of Alaska,* p. 367; Arnold, *Alaska Native Land Claims,* pp. 86–87.

18. Arnold, *Alaska Native Land Claims,* p. 88.

19. Gruening, *The State of Alaska,* p. 370.

20. U.S. Congress, Senate, *Alaska Native Claims Settlement Act of 1971,* p. 93.

21. Ibid.

22. Arnold, *Alaska Native Land Claims,* pp. 85, 88–89, 91.

23. U.S. Congress, Senate, *Alaska Native Claims Settlement Act of 1971,* p. 94.

24. Paul Brooks, *The Pursuit of Wilderness* (Boston: Houghton Mifflin Co., 1971), p. 64.

25. Ibid., p. 66.

26. Ibid.

27. Ibid., p. 67.

28. Ibid., pp. 68–69.

29. Ibid., p. 72.

30. Ibid., pp. 62–63.

31. Arnold, *Alaska Native Land Claims,* pp. 95–96; Brooks, *The Pursuit of Wilderness,* pp. 72–73.

32. Arnold, *Alaska Native Land Claims,* p. 100.

33. U.S. Congress, Senate, *Alaska Native Claims Settlement Act of 1971,* p. 96.

34. Ibid., pp. 96–97.

35. Mary Clay Berry, *The Alaska Pipeline: The Politics of Oil and Native Land Claims* (Bloomington: Indiana University Press), pp. 34–35.

36. Ibid., p. 37.

37. Ibid.

38. Brooks, *The Pursuit of Wilderness,* pp. 78–90.

39. Ibid., pp. 91–92.

40. U.S. Congress, Senate, *Alaska Native Claims Settlement Act of 1917,* p. 96.

41. Ibid.; Berry, *The Alaska Pipeline,* p. 44.

42. Arnold, *Alaska Native Land Claims,* pp. 103–105.

43. Ibid.

44. Ibid., pp. 106–107.

45. Berry, *The Alaska Pipeline,* p. 47.

46. Ibid., pp. 48, 49.

47. Ibid., pp. 48–49.

48. Ibid., p. 50.

49. Ibid.

50. Ibid., p. 51.

51. Arnold, *Alaska Native Land Claims,* p. 119.

52. Ibid., p. 120.

53. U.S. Congress, Senate, *Alaska Native Land Claims: Hearings Before the Committee on Interior and Insular Affairs on S. 2906, S. 1964, S. 2690, and S. 2020,* 90th Cong., 2d sess., pp. 441, 189, 237.

54. Ibid., pp. 45–46, 289–90, 371–72.

55. Arnold, *Alaska Native Land Claims,* pp. 123–25.

56. Berry, *The Alaska Pipeline,* pp. 60–61.

57. Arnold, *Alaska Native Land Claims,* p. 126.

58. Berry, *The Alaska Pipeline,* p. 62.

59. Arnold, *Alaska Native Land Claims,* p. 132.

60. Berry, *The Alaska Pipeline,* p. 65.

61. Ibid., pp. 67–68.

62. Ibid., p. 69.

63. Ibid.

64. Ibid., pp. 76–77.

65. Ibid., p. 80.

66. Ibid., p. 81.

67. Ibid., pp. 102–103.

68. Ibid., pp. 117–18, 121.

69. Arnold, *Alaska Native Land Claims,* p. 134.

70. Ibid.

71. Ibid., pp. 135–36.

72. Ibid., p. 137.

73. Ibid., pp. 139–40.

74. Ibid., pp. 141–42.

75. Ibid.

76. Ibid., pp. 146–47.

77. Ibid.

78. Berry, *The Alaska Pipeline,* pp. 240–41; Arnold, *Alaska Native Land Claims,* pp. 148–49.

79. Arnold, *Alaska Native Land Claims,* p. 150.

80. Ibid., pp. 150–51.

81. Ibid., p. 152.

*Chapter 12*

1. P.L. 92-203, 85 Stat. 692, sec. 7; 85 Stat. 694, sec. 8; 85 Stat. 695, sec. 9; 85 Stat. 691, sec. 6.

2. Ibid., 85 Stat. 692, sec. 7(c).

3. Rosemary Shinohara and Virginia McKinney, "Natives Taking Leadership in Business Community," *Alaska Industry,* January, 1976, pp. 37–38, 40–47, 53–54.

4. Ibid., pp. 37, 39–40.

5. Ibid., pp. 37–38.

6. Ibid., p. 38.

7. Ibid.; *Alaska Magazine,* June, 1976, p. 45.

8. *Alaska Magazine,* pp. 41–43.

9. Ibid., pp. 43–45.

10. Ibid., p. 45.

11. Ibid., pp. 45–47, 53.

12. Ibid., p. 53.
13. Ibid., pp. 53–54.
14. Ibid., p. 54.
15. Virginia McKinney, "Native Regional Firms Enter New, Post-Pipeline Era," *Alaska Industry,* January, 1977, pp. 29–32.
16. Chapter 19, State of Alaska, *Session Laws,* 1976, chap. 240; State of Alaska, *Session Laws,* 1976.
17. P.L. 94-204, 94th cong., 1st sess. (January 2, 1976).
18. "A Year of Change for Alaska's Regional Native Companies," *Alaska Business and Industry,* September 1983, p. 24.
19. Ibid.
20. *Fairbanks Daily News-Miner,* April 25, 1984.
21. Ibid., April 20, 1984.
22. Arctic Fox, "Who Signed for Me?" *Alaska Native News,* March, 1984, p. 11.
23. Berry, *The Alaska Pipeline,* pp. 66–67.
24. "Alaska Native Review Commission Overview Hearings Agenda," *Alaska Native News,* March, 1984, p. 26.
25. *Fairbanks Daily News-Miner,* April 16, 1984.
26. Ibid.
27. "Alex Raider: Leading Calista to Profitable Ventures," *Alaska Business and Industry,* September, 1983, p. 15.
28. Ibid.
29. Ibid.
30. "A Year of Change for Alaska's Regional Native Companies," p. 24.
31. Ibid.
32. Ibid., pp. 24–25.
33. Ibid., p. 25.
34. Ibid., pp. 25–26.
35. Ibid., pp. 26–27.
36. Ibid.
37. Ibid., pp. 27–28.
38. Ibid., pp. 26–28.
39. Ibid.

### Chapter 13

1. Congressional Quarterly Service, *Congress and the Nation, 1945–1964: A Review of Government and Politics in the Postwar Years* (Washington, D.C.: Congressional Quarterly Service, 1965), pp. 1597, 1606, 1530.
2. 16 U.S.C. 530. The major federal agencies to conduct these reviews were the Forest Service, the Fish and Wildlife Service, and the National Park Service. Congress included the Bureau of Land Management in 1976 when it passed the Federal Land Policy and Management Act (P.L. 94-579). During this period Congress also passed legislation establishing national wild and scenic river and national trail systems, an act protecting endangered animal and plant species, and several measures dealing with air and water quality.
3. 42 U.S.C. 4321.
4. Joint Federal-State Land Use Planning Commission for Alaska, *The Final Report of the Joint Federal-State Land Use Planning Commisson for Alaska: Some Guidelines for Deciding Alaska's Future* (Anchorage: Joint Federal-State Land Use Planning Commission for Alaska, May 30, 1979), p. 1.
5. Mary Clay Berry, *The Alaska Pipeline: The Politics of Oil and Native Land Claims* (Bloomington: Indiana University Press, 1975), p. 250.
6. Ibid., p. 251.
7. Ibid., pp. 252–54.
8. 16 U.S.C. 528-31; 16 U.S.C. 1600-14; P.L. 94-588, codified in various sections of 16 U.S.C.
9. P.L. 94-579, 90 Stat. 2743.
10. U.S. Congress, House, *Inclusion of Alaska Lands in National Park, Forest, Wildlife Refuge, and Wild and Scenic River Systems: Hearings Before the Subcommittee on General Oversight and Alaska Lands of the Committee on Interior and Insular Affairs on H.R. 39, H.R. 1974, H.R. 2876, H.R. 5505, to Designate Certain Lands in the State of Alaska as Units of the National Park, National Wildlife Refuge, Wild and Scenic Rivers, and National Wilderness Preservation Systems, and for Other Purposes; H.R. 1454, to Establish the Lake Clark National Park in the State of Alaska, and for Other Purposes; H.R. 5605 and H.R. 8651, to Establish Admiralty Island National Preserve in the State of Alaska,* 95th Cong., 1st sess. (1977). Hearings were held on various dates starting on April 21, 1977, and ending on September 21, 1977. The hearings comprise sixteen volumes. Testimony given in Alaska is contained in vols. 8–13, and that in Washington, D.C., in vols. 1–3 and 14–16; testimonies given in Chicago, Atlanta, Denver, and Seattle are found in vols. 4–7, respectively.
11. Joint Federal-State Land Use Planning commission for Alaska, *The Final Report of the Joint Federal-State Land Use Planning Commission for Alaska,* p. 1.
12. Ibid., pp. 13–15.
13. P.L. 96-487, 94 Stat. 2371.
14. Ibid.

15. Ibid.

16. Ibid., sec. 708, sec. 705.

17. Ibid., sec. 1002.

18. Ibid., sec. 1202.

*Chapter 14*

1. William R. Hunt, "Notes on the History of North Slope Oil," *Alaska Magazine*, February 1970; pp. 8–10; herafter cited as Hunt, "History of North Slope Oil."

2. Gil Mull, "History of Arctic Slope Oil Exploration," in *Alaska's Oil/Gas and Minerals Industry, Alaska Geographic Quarterly* 9, no. 4 (1982): 188.

3. Hunt, "History of the North Slope Oil," pp. 8–10.

4. Ibid.

5. Mull, "History of Arctic Slope Oil Exploration," p. 188.

6. Ted A. Armstrong, "Alaskan Oil," *Oil and Gas Journal*, August 22, 1966, pp. 95–96.

7. *Anchorage Daily Times*, November 9, 1981.

8. Ibid.

9. Armstrong, "Alaskan Oil," pp. 95–96.

10. *Anchorage Daily Times*, November 9, 1981; Armstrong, "Alaskan Oil," pp. 95–96.

11. Hunt, "History of North Slope Oil," pp. 8–10. Ruth Hampton to Abe Fortas, Under Secretary of the Interior, January 21, 1944 Files of Under Secretary Abe Fortas, Territories, Alaska, RG 48, National Archives.

12. Frank Knox to President Roosevelt, March 14, 1944, Van Valin to Roosevelt, May 20, 1944, OF 400—Alaska, container 3, folder Appointments, Alaska, 1944–45, Franklin D. Roosevelt Papers (FDR Library, Hyde Park, N.Y.)

13. William B. Heroy to R. K. Davies, Deputy Petroleum Administrator, September 22, 1944 Harold L. Ickes Papers (Library of Congress).

14. Harold W. Snell to Harold L. Ickes, September 11, 1944, Ickes to Snell, September 25, 1944, Harold L. Ickes Papers.

15. James Forrestal to the President, March 31, 1945, Official Files 400, Alaska, Oil-Naval Petroleum Reserve (1), Harry S. Truman Papers (Harry S. Truman Library, Independence, Mo.).

16. Forrestal to Harry S. Truman, December 10, 1945, Ickes to Harold D. Smith, Director, Bureau of the Budget, January 17, 1946, Official Files 400, Alaska, Oil-Naval Petroleum Reserve (1), Harry S. Truman Papers.

17. Forrestal to President Truman, January 22, 1946, Official Files 400, Alaska, Oil-Naval Petroleum Reserve (1), Harry S. Truman Papers.

18. Ibid., Forrestal to Truman, March 10, 1947, General File, Alaska, box 112, Harry S. Truman Papers; Memorandum from director, Naval Petroleum Reserves, November 26, 1952, Records of John C. Reed, Staff Geologist for Territories and Island Possession, Correspondence with Navy, 6.3, RG 57, National Archives.

19. Armstrong, "Alaskan Oil," p. 96.

20. Ibid.

21. Ibid.

22. Ibid.

23. Ibid., p. 91.

24. Ibid.

25. Ibid., pp. 77, 81.

26. Ibid., p. 86.

27. Ibid., pp. 82–83.

28. *Fairbanks Daily News-Miner*, January 16 and 18, 1968.

29. Ibid.; Brown, *Oil on Ice*, p. 27.

30. Brown, *Oil on Ice*, p. 27.

31. *Fairbanks Daily News-Miner*, June 26, 1968.

32. Brown, *Oil on Ice*, p. 29.

33. *Fairbanks Daily News-Miner*, August 22, 1968.

34. Brown, *Oil on Ice*, pp. 42–45.

35. Ibid., pp. 45–46.

36. Hugh G. Gallagher, *Etok: A Story of Eskimo Power* (New York: G. P. Putnam's Sons, 1974), p. 181

37. Ibid., pp. 181–82.

38. Berry, *The Alaska Pipeline*, pp. 99–100.

39. Gallagher, *Etok*, p. 182.

40. Brookings Institution, Advanced Study Program, in Association with the Legislative Council of the State of Alaska, "Conference on the Future of Alaska," fall, 1969.

41. Ibid., p. 102.

42. Ibid., p. 104; "Special Pipeline Report," *Alaska Construction and Oil*, September, 1985, p. 5.

43. Berry, *The Alaska Pipeline*, p. 105.

44. Ibid., p. 106.

45. Ibid.

46. Ibid., p. 106–107.

47. Ibid., p. 108.

48. Ibid., pp. 108–109.

49. Ibid., pp. 109–10.

50. Ibid.

51. Ibid., p. 111.

52. Ibid., pp. 111–12.

53. Ibid., p. 113.

54. Ibid.

55. Ibid., pp. 115–16.

56. Ibid., pp. 116–17.
57. Ibid., pp. 117–18.
58. Ibid., p. 118.
59. Ibid., p. 118–21.
60. Brown, pp. 86–91.
61. "Special Pipeline Report," p. 8.
62. Ibid.
63. Ibid.; Mark Wheeler, *Half-baked Alaska* (Ketchikan, Alaska: Mark Wheeler, Publisher, 1972), p. 103.
64. Berry, *The Alaska Pipeline,* p. 215.
65. Ibid., pp. 215–16.
66. Thomas A. Morehouse and Gordon Scott Harrison, "State Government and Economic Development in Alaska," in Gordon Scott Harrison, ed., *Alaska Public Policy,* ed. Gordon Scott Harrison (College: Universisty of Alaska, Institute of Social, Economic, and Government Research, 1971), p. 35.
67. "Special Pipeline Report," p. 32; Berry, *The Alaska Pipeline,* p. 217.
68. Berry, *The Alaska Pipeline,* pp. 222–23.
69. Ibid., pp. 226–27.
70. Ibid., pp. 229–30.
71. Ibid., p. 230.
72. *Newsweek,* January 23, 1973, p. 52.
73. "Morton Announces Intention to Issue Pipeline Permit," *Alaska Industry,* June, 1972, p. 17.
74. Robert G. Knox, "Pipeline Progress Report: Road Construction Gets Off to Early Start," *Alaska Industry,* June, 1974, pp. 48–49.
75. Ibid.
76. Ibid.
77. Ibid., pp. 50–51.
78. Mary Clare Langan, "The Boom Is Still Awaited," *Alaska Industry,* August, 1974, pp. 39–40; *Fairbanks North Star Borough Pipeline Impact Office Report No. One,* July 11, 1974.
79. "All-Out Push Starting on Pipeline Job," *Alaska Industry,* March, 1975), pp. 33–34.
80. Ibid., June, 1975, pp. 39–40.
81. Ibid., December, 1975, p. 40.
82. *Fairbanks Daily News-Miner,* June 20 and 21, 1977.
83. Ibid., June 20, 1978.
84. Ibid., July 9, 1977.
85. Ibid., June 20, 1978.
86. Ibid.
87. Ibid., June 8, 1978.
88. Ibid., June 8, 1978, and September 6, 1985.
89. Ibid., October 23, 1985; *Pioneer All-Alaska Weekly,* February 28, 1986.
90. *Fairbanks Daily News-Miner,* June 8, 1978.

91. Charles Ebinger, "The Background," in *The Alaska Oil Export Ban: Special Interest Legislation That Hurts America,* briefing paper (Juneau, Alaska: Legislative Budget and Audit Committee, 1983), p. 6.
92. Ibid., pp. 6–7.
93. Scott Goldsmith, "Sustainable Spending Levels form Alaska State Revenues," *Alaska Review of Social and Economic Conditions,* February, 1983, p. 3; *The Insider,* January 24, 1986; interview with Kay Herring, Public Relations Department, Alyeska Pipeline Service Company, January 24, 1986, Anchorage, Alaska.
94. Matthew Berman, "Alaska North Slope Oil Production and Revenue Projections," *Alaska Review of Social and Economic Conditions,* February, 1985, p. 1–2.
95. Paul Laird, "North Slope's shallow crude defies technology, economics," *Alaska Business Monthly,* March, 1985, pp. 16–17.
96. Richard Wheatley, "Getting The Most out of Prudhoe Bay," *Sohio,* Summer, 1984, pp. 2–4.
97. Ibid.; "One-Billion-Barrrel Increase Is Goal of North Slope Projects," *Sohio,* Winter, 1985, p. 25.
98. "Results of Recent Alaskan Offshore Leasing by the U.S. Government," *Alaskan Update,* Spring, 1984, p. 1.
99. Goldsmith, "Sustainable Spending Levels," p. 1.
100. Arlon R. Tussing and Gregg K. Erickson, "Reflections on the End of the OPEC Era," *Alaska Review of Social and Economic Conditions,* December, 1982, p. 1.
101. Ibid.
102. Bob Dixon, "Experts View State's Fiscal Future When Oil Revenues Begin to Decline," *Alaska Business and Industry,* January, 1983, pp. 10–11.
103. Thomas A. Morehouse, "Petroleum Development in Alaska," *Alaska Review of Social and Economic Conditions,* March, 1977, p. 15; *Fairbanks Daily News-Miner,* July 18, 1977.

*Chapter 15*

1. *Fairbanks Daily News-Miner,* February 17, 1986.
2. Ibid., February 4, 1986.
3. *The Council,* January, 1982.
4. Transcription from the Alaska Public Radio Broadcast, May 17, 1984, in author Naske's files.

# BIBLIOGRAPHICAL ESSAY:
## THE SOURCES OF ALASKA'S HISTORY

The sources of Alaska's history are rich and varied. Anthropologists and archaeologists have long been fascinated with the Native cultures of Alaska, and bookshelves are heavy with the many studies produced over the years. In *Eskimo Prehistory* (1969), Hans-Georg Bandi, a Swiss scholar, discusses the various theories of the origin of the Eskimos and the sites, artifacts, and prehistoric cultures in the Eskimo area, extending from Alaska across Canada to Greenland. Wendell H. Oswalt, a prolific academician, has ably summarized the state of knowledge about Eskimos in his *Alaskan Eskimos* (1967) and has traced the contacts explorers made with these northern peoples from the Viking settlements in Greenland through the long history of Arctic exploration to modern times in his fascinating *Eskimos and Explorers* (1979).

Dorothy Jean Ray has added much to our knowledge about the Eskimos. Two outstanding books are her *Eskimos of Bering Strait, 1650–1898* (1975) and her *Ethnohistory in the Arctic: The Bering Strait Eskimo* (1983). Norman Chance gives the reader an overview of the richness and complexity of Eskimo culture in *The Eskimo of North Alaska*. Richard K. Nelson, a gifted writer, offers an absorbing account of Eskimo hunting methods in *Hunters of the Northern Ice* (1969), and in his poetic *Shadow of the Hunter* (1982) he portrays the Eskimo yearly hunting cycles.

Nicholas Gubser spent much time among the caribou-hunting Eskimos of Anaktuvuk Pass. *The Nunamiut Eskimos: Hunters of Caribou* (1965) is the outgrowth of his studies among these people. Ann Fienup-Riordan has written a fine book on Yupik Eskimos entitled *The Nel-son Island Eskimo: Social Structure and Ritual Distribution* (1983), and James W. VanStone, who has performed much field work in Alaska, has written an outstanding volume on the Eskimos in the Nushagak River region of southwestern Alaska, using research methods of history and anthropology, entitled *Eskimos of the Nushagak River: An Ethnographic History* (1967). Don E. Dumond presents the prehistory of the Eskaleut peoples in the area between the Bering Strait on the north and the Aleutian Islands and the Alaska Peninsula on the south in *The Eskimos and Aleuts* (1977). Charles Campbell Hughes has written a fine study of the Siberian Eskimos of Gambell, or Sivokak, on Saint Lawrence Island based on fieldwork he conducted there in 1954–1955. The title of his work is *An Eskimo Village in the Modern World* (1960).

Robert F. Spencer has written a volume entitled *The North Alaskan Eskimo: A Study in Ecology and Society,* based on fieldwork he conducted in 1952 and 1953. Originally published in 1959, it was reprinted in 1969 and has become a classic in its field, offering a very full and detailed account of the culture of the North Alaskan Eskimo. Spencer analyzes the way in which two different modes of earning a livelihood, caribou-hunting by the inland peoples and whaling by coastal Eskimos, represent ecological adaptations within the framework of a common Eskimo culture.

Dorothy Jean Ray has produced still another valuable volume entitled *Aleut and Eskimo Art: Tradition and Innovation in South Alaska* (1981), while Diamond Jenness, a Canadian anthropologist, has produced a series of studies on the way in which governments have dealt with Eskimo populations: *Eskimo Administration: Alaska* (1962), *Eskimo Administration: Canada* (1964), *Eskimo Administration: Labrador (1965), Eskimo Administration: Greenland* (1967), and *Eskimo Administration: Analysis and Reflections* (1968). For readers who wish to explore further the rich literature dealing with the Eskimos, Arthur E. Hippler and John R. Wood, both of the Institute of Social and Economic Research of the University of Alaska in Anchorage, have prepared a useful bibliography entitled *The Alaska Eskimos: A Selected, Annotated Bibliography* (1977).

Alaskan Natives are publishing their own oral-history accounts. A good example is *Puiguitkaat* (1981), a transcription and translation of a 1978 elders' conference. The North Slope Borough Commission on History and Culture funded the conference and the preparation of the volume, transcribed and translated by Leona Okakok, and Gary Kean edited the volume and furnished the photographs. The sponsors of the conference intended to talk about and record on tape and in books those things which the Inupiaq people know before they become lost, things which must be passed on to the younger generation. This knowledge is deemed essential if the young are to subsist on the land which their ancestors have occupied since time immemorial. Successful survival depends on a knowledge of the land and its history as well as that of its people.

Another volume by the North Slope Borough Commission on History and Culture, *The Traditional Land Use Inventory for the Mid-Beaufort Sea*, volume 1 (1980), is based on interviews with North Slope residents and is richly illustrated with historical photographs. Helen Slwooko Carius wrote and illustrated a slender volume entitled *Sevukakmet: Ways of Life on St. Lawrence Island* (1979). After living successfully in the contiguous states, she realised that she wanted to remember and record her heritage as a Saint Lawrence Islander. The volume is evidence of her acknowledgment of that heritage and her recognition that it continues to play an important part in her life and that of her family.

Yupiktak Bista commissioned Art Davidson to edit a pamphlet dealing with subsistence and the conservation of the Yupik life-style: *Does One Way of Life Have to Die So Another Can Live?* (1974). Ticasuk, or Emily Ivanoff Brown, an Eskimo woman who graduated from the University of Alaska, Fairbanks, later wrote *The Roots of Ticasuk: An Eskimo Woman's Family Story* (1981), a revision of an earlier work entitled *Grandfather of Unalakleet: The Lineage of Alluyagnak* (1974). Ann Vick edited *The Cama-i Book: Kayaks, Dogsleds, Bear Hunting, Bush Pilots, Smoked Fish, Mukluks, and Other Traditions of Southwestern Alaska* (1983), a volume in the *Foxfire* tradition made popular by Eliot Wigginton. High school students in southwestern Alaska interviewed and photographed the older members of their communities, documenting their folklore, legends, crafts, and skills, and published the material they collecteed in their school magazines. *The Cama-i Book* brings together the best of this material.

Margaret Lantis, an anthropologist, has ably summarized existing knowledge about the Aleuts in "The Aleut Social System, 1750 to 1810, from early Historical Sources," in *Ethnohistory in Southwestern Alaska and the Southern Yukon: Method and Content* (1970). William Laughlin, an archaeologist, has performed considerable fieldwork in the Aleutian Islands; one result of that work is his *Aleuts: Survivors of the Bering Land Bridge* (1980). Dorothy Jones, a sociologist, has written *Aleuts in Transition: A Comparison of Two Villages* (1976), a study of Aleut adaptions to white contact, and *A Century of Servitude: Pribilof Aleuts Under U.S. Rule* (1980), an indictment of federal adminstration of the Pribilof Islands.

Richard A. Pierce has earned the gratitude of historians, social scientists, and laymen alike for his series of translations issued by the Limestone Press, of Kingston, Ontario, entitled "Materials for the Study of Alaska History." To date Pierce has published twenty-five volumes. Included are Vasilii Nikolaevich Berkh's *Chronological History of the Discovery of the Aleutian Islands, or, The Exploits of Russian Merchants* (1974), translated by Dmitri Krenov and edited by Pierce. This classic was first published in Saint Petersburg in 1823. Berkh visited Russian America during the colonial period and talked to veteran seafarers, hunters, and merchants. His account acquainted the public of his day with the exploration and early exploitation of the Aleutian Islands. Another volume in the series is Grigorii I. Shelikov's *A Voyage to America, 1783–1786* (1981), translated by Marina Ramsay and edited, with an introduction, by Pierce. Shelikov established the first permanent Russian settlement at Three Saints Bay on Kodiak Island in 1784. Other volumes are *The Russian Orthodox Religious Mission in America, 1794–1837, with Materials Concerning the Life and Works of the Monk German, and Ethnographic Notes by the Hieromonk Gedeon* (1978), translated by Colin Bearne and edited by Pierce; and *The Journals of Iakov Netsvetov: The Atkha Years, 1828–1844* (1980), translated with an introduction and supplementary material by Lydia T. Black.

The Aleuts, like the Eskimos, have also begun publishing historical materials. The Aleutian/ Pribilov Islands Association, Inc., prepared a study entitled *The Aleut Relocation and Internment During World War II: A Preliminary Examination* (1981) and sponsored a handsome volume by Lydia T. Black called *Aleut Art* (1982). For those wishing to read more about the Aleuts, Dorothy M. Jones and John R. Wood, of the Institute of Social and Economic Research of the University of Alaska, have prepared *An Aleut Bibliography* (1975), an excellent guide.

The most useful and important single book on northern Athapaskans is *Subarctic* (1981), volume 6 in the Smithsonian Institution's *Handbook of North American Indians* series, under the general editorship of William C. Sturtevant. It contains many excellent articles on the environment, prehistory, and modern conditions of the Athapaskans and on the history of research on them. The volume also contains hundreds of photographs, illustrations, and maps, many published for the first time. Each article contains references for further reading.

The Alaska Historical Commission sponsored a volume by William E. Simeone entitled *A History of Alaskan Athapaskans* (1982), a summary from written materials, divided into sections on culture, and for each group a history of the contact period from 1785 to 1971. James Van Stone has summarized existing knowledge about the northern Athapaskans in his readable volume *Athapaskan Adaptations: Hunters and Fishermen of the Subarctic Forests* (1974), and Richard K. Nelson's *Hunters of the Northern Forest: Designs for Survival among the Alaska Kutchin* (1973) is a well-written account based on fieldwork he conducted among the Kutchin and Koyukon Indians of interior subarctic Alaska in the villages of Chalkyitsik, Huslia, and Hughes from August, 1969, to July, 1970, and from April to June, 1971. He followed that book with another volume, entitled *Make Prayers to the Raven* (1983). A gifted observer and writer, Nelson will undoubtedly continue his contribu-

tions to the understanding of Alaska's complex and rich Native cultures.

Poldine Carlo, a Fairbanks resident and Athapaskan Indian, has written a fine autobiographical volume entitled *Nulato: An Indian Life on the Yukon* (1978). In *Shandaa: In My Lifetime* (1982), Belle Herbert, a resident of Chalkyitsik and Alaska's oldest resident, probably born about 1861, near the dawn of white exploration of interior Alaska, tells of her own and her people's lives and customs, recorded and edited by Bill Pfisterer with the assistance of Katherine Peter.

The Yukon-Koyukuk School District has sponsored a series of biographies of Athapaskans who live in the eleven villages serviced by the district. These books are designed for upper-elementary students living in rural Alaska, but they make good reading for anyone interested in Athapaskan life-styles. Published by Hancock House Publishers, Ltd., of Vancouver, British Columbia, *Moses Henzie: A Biography Allakaket* (1979) is the first volume in this series. For anyone interested in the Athapaskans, Arthur E. Hippler and John R. Wood, of the Institute of Social and Economic Research of the University of Alaska, have prepared an excellent volume entitled *The Subarctic Athapaskans: A Selected Annotated Bibliography* (1974).

Philip Drucker has written the standard introduction to the Northwest Coast Indians, entitled *Indians of the Northwest Coast* (1963). Anthropologist Frederica de Laguna has written the three-volume *Under Mount Saint Elias: The History and Culture of the Yakutat Tlingit* (1972), which has become a classic. Aurel Krause and his brother Arthur were geographers sent by the Geographical Society of Bremen to follow up the work done by Nordenskiold on the Chukchee Peninsula in 1878 and 1879. This was the third Arctic expedition undertaken by the society. After the completion of their Siberian research Arthur departed for Europe, while Aurel settled at Klukwan, in southeastern Alaska, and worked intensively with the Tlingits. Subsequently he wrote an excellent ethnographic study, translated by Erna Gunther, entitled *The Tlingit Indians: Results of a Trip to the Northwest Coast of America and the Bering Straits* (1956). In 1933, Kalervo Oberg completed a study of Tlingit economic and social life. Unfortunately, his doctoral dissertation was not published until 1973. Wendell Oswalt, a noted anthropologist, observed that "Oberg's discussion of the social system and economy are outstanding for their clarity and breadth; and it is little short of amazing that this work has never been published." That has now been remedied. Wilson Duff, who wrote the foreword to Oberg's book, predicts that the period of university-initiated field research is ending and that there will be a shift in the locus of field research from the universities to the people themselves. "The topics, phrasings, and interpretations will increasingly be their own," he states, and "along with this will come an examination and testing of the previous work of anthropologists; not just of their ethnographic descriptions, but also the concepts which they, as expert witnesses in court cases, have helped harden into law."

A more general study that evaluates most aspects of historical and contemporary Native life can be found in a magnificent volume entitled *Alaska Natives and the Land* (1969), written by the Federal Field Committee for Development Planning in Alaska to provide Congress with information in its efforts to draft a Native land claims settlement measure.

For a number of years until the early 1980s the federal government maintained the Anthropology and Historic Preservation Cooperative Park Studies Unit at the University of Alaska in Fairbanks. Headed by the energetic and enthusiastic Zorro A. Bradley, the unit produced an enormous number of highly informative and interesting studies. A few titles will give an idea of the breadth of the studies undertaken: William R. and Carrie K. Uhl, *Tagiumsinaaqmiit: Ocean Beach Dwellers of the Cape Krusenstern Area, Subsistence Patterns* (1977); Gary C. Stein, *Cultural Resources of the Aleutian Region,* volumes 1 and 2 (1977); Russell Sackett, *The Chilkat Tlingit: A General Overview* (1979); Grant Spearman, *Anaktuvuk Pass: Land Use Values through Time* (1980); and William S. Schneider and Peter M. Bowers, *Assessment of the Known Cultural Resources in the National Petroleum Reserve in Alaska* (1977).

In 1966 the *Anchorage Daily News* ran a series of articles entitled "The Village People." The public reaction was favorable. To meet the demand for copies, the newspaper republished the eleven-part series, together with comments by Philleo Nash, commissioner of the Bureau of Indian Affairs, and comments by Governor William A. Egan. In 1981 the same newspaper published a five-part series of articles entitled "The Village People Revisited" (1981), discuss-

ing the changes that had swept through Alaska in the 1970s, changes that often stemmed directly from the Alaska Native Claims Settlement Act of 1971, and the impact of the Prudhoe Bay discovery, the construction of the Trans-Alaska Pipeline, the arrival of television in the bush, and urbanization and growth.

Joseph E. Senungetuk, an artist who was born in the village of Wales, northwest of Cape Prince of Wales, has written an interesting book entitled *Give or Take a Century: An Eskimo Chronicle* (1971). The author maintains that the Eskimo people had a complex, satisfying, technologically developed culture before white contact, a culture that rapidly deteriorated after contact.

A vast literature dealing with Native education has developed. Typical of the modern studies is Michael S. Cline's *Tannik School: The Impact of Education on the Eskimos of Anaktuvuk Pass* (1975), which deals with the impact of a school on an Eskimo community. Cline, who taught for two years at Anaktuvuk Pass, uses standard anthropological fieldwork to examine the white man's (or *tannik*) school and its effect on the Nunamiut villagers. Charles K. Ray, professor of education in the University of Alaska, conducted a study of Native education in the 1950s; published in 1958, it is entitled *A Program of Education for Alaska Natives*. It gives a convenient summary of educational history in Alaska and deals at length with the curriculum and educational objectives of Native elementary schools and secondary and post-high school education of Alaska Native youths. Although many of the ideas in this volume may seem outdated in the 1980s, they represented the best thinking on the subject in the 1950s.

Judith Smilg Kleinfeld, professor of psychology in the University of Alaska, Fairbanks, has written widely in the area of cross-cultural education. One of her books, *Eskimo School on the Andreafsky: A Study of Effective Bicultural Education* (1979), deals with Saint Mary's High school, a Catholic boarding school that enrolls Eskimo adolescents from remote villages that are undergoing rapid cultural change. It produces graduates with the skills needed for access to the opportunities of the majority culture.

Finally, Michael E. Krauss, head of the Alaska Native Language Center linguistic staff in the University of Alaska, Fairbanks, has long been concerned with the survival of Alaska's Native languages. In a long paper published in 1980, Krauss dealt with "Alaska Native Languages:

Past, Present, and Future." He concluded that Alaska Native languages are entering a period of final crisis for their future as living languages and that "most of them are about to die."

For those readers who want to pursue Native studies, the National Museum of Man, in Ottawa, Canada, which has both ethnology and archaeology divisions, publishes scholarly monographs. Journals dealing with peoples and cultures of the north include *Arctic Anthropology* (University of Wisconsin). *Anthropological Papers of the University of Alaska* (Fairbanks), and the *Canadian Journal of Archaeology* (Canadian Archaeological Association).

Much remains to be done on the history of Alaska's Russian period, but much excellent work has been accomplished in recent years. The Russian L. A. Zagoskin wrote a unique and interesting account of his travels in the Yukon and Kuskokwim valleys in 1842–1844 which the Arctic Institute of North America published in 1967. With some modifications a translation of the 1956 Soviet edition was published in 1967, edited by Henry N. Michael. It is an excellent early account of the riverine Eskimos of the Yukon and Kuskokwim rivers. Frank Golder, an American historian, worked extensively in Russian archives. One result was his volume *Russian Expansion to the Pacific, 1641–1850,* reprinted in 1960. Hector Chevigny, a blind scholar, produced three fast-paced accounts of Russian America, *Lost Empire: The Life and Adventures of Nikolai Rezanov* (1937, 1958); *Lord of Alaska: The Story of Baranov and the Russian Adventure* (1965); and *Russian America: The Great Alaskan Venture, 1741–1867* (1965). S. B. Okun, a Soviet scholar, in *The Russian-American Company* (1951) furnishes a Marxist interpretation of the formation and activities of that organization.

Richard A. Pierce, of Queens University, Kingston, Ontario, has translated or edited many Russian and other foreign classics on Alaska and published them in his series "Materials for the Study of Alaska History." In this series is K. T. Khlebnikov's biography of Alexsandr Baranov, entitled *Baranov: Chief Manager of the Russian Colonies in America* (1973), translated by Colin Bearne and edited by Pierce. Khlebnikov joined the Russian-American Company as an employee in 1800 and served his first seventeen years in Siberia. Arriving in Sitka in 1817, he helped the retiring Baranov wind up his affairs. For the next sixteen years he served under Baranov's succes-

sors. He retired to Russia in 1833, but his connections with the company continued until his death in 1838. His biography of Baranov—though sketchy in places—provides an essential source for later scholarship.

Pierce has included recent Soviet scholarship in the series. Raisa V. Makarova's *Russians on the Pacific, 1743–1799* (1975), translated and edited by Pierce and Alton S. Donnelly, adds much new material to the history of the Russian approach to North America. Svetlana G. Fedorova's *The Russian Population in Alaska and California: Late 18th Century–1867* (1973), translated and edited by Pierce and Donnelly, is an important new contribution to the history of Alaska, providing the most thorough study to date of Russian activities in the region. Derived from careful research in widely scattered printed sources and in archival materials, it illuminates many aspects of the history of Alaska before 1867 hiterhto untouched by scholars.

Pierce and Donnelly have translated and edited yet another important volume, written at the request of the Russian–American Company a few years before the sale of Alaska to the United States. P. A. Tikhmenev undertook the writing of the company's history to glorify its activities in the mistaken hope of winning a renewal of the monopoly charter. He based *A History of the Russian-American Company* (1965) on primary materials, many subsequently lost in the destruction of the company archives in the 1870s. It consists of an introduction and antique letters, journals, and agreements. It is a unique work.

James R. Gibson has written an important volume entitled *Imperial Russia in Frontier America: The Changing Geography of Supply of Russian America, 1784–1867* (1976), in which he maintains that Russia's occupancy of Alaska from the late eighteenth century was neither sudden nor novel; it was simply the latest and farthest phase of a protracted and extensive process of eastward expansion that had been launched by Muscovy in the mid-sixteenth century.

In 1972 the Oregon Historical Society inaugurated a publishing venture entitled North Pacific Studies. Its purpose is to make available in English little-known or hitherto unpublished works on the early history of the North Pacific Ocean and littorals. The first volume in the series, *Explorations of Kamchatka, 1735–1741* (1972), is by a young Russian explorer-scientist, Stepan P. Krasheninnikov, of the famous Bering expedition to Kamchatka and the shores of northwest America. It was translated with introduction and notes by E. A. P. Crownhart-Vaughan. The second volume is by Kirill Timofeevich Khlebnikov, also a Russian, who in his service as an official of the Russian–American Company left a rich account of the North Pacific. The volume's title is *Colonial Russian America: Kyrill T. Khlebnikov's Reports, 1817–1832* (1976), translated with introduction and notes by Basil Dmytryshyn and Crownhart-Vaughan. Other volumes have followed.

Mention should also be made of the University of British Columbia Press's Pacific Maritime Studies. Five volumes have appeared in this series. Representative is Glynn Barratt's *Russia in Pacific Waters, 1715–1825: A Survey of the Origins of Russia's Naval Presence in the North and South Pacific* (1981). The Hawaiian Historical Society in collaboration with the University Press of Hawaii has published V. M. Golovnin's *Around the World on the Kamchatka, 1817–1819* (1979), translated with an introduction and notes by Ella Lury Wiswell. Between 1803 and 1833 thirty voyages embarked from the Baltic port of Kronstadt to the Pacific, an average of one voyage a year. Sixteen of these were naval expeditions, while the remainder had a mixed character, involving Russian–American Company vessels manned by naval personnel. Commanders such as Kruzenshtern, Lisiansky, Golovnin, Lazarev, Kotzebue, and Lutke wrote accounts that won international recognition. Notwithstanding their historical and scientific value, some of these works have escaped translation. Until Wiswell translated Golovnin's account, this was true of his report.

Peter Lauridsen, a Dane, wrote a biography of his famous countryman Vitus Bering. Entitled *Vitus Bering: The Discoverer of Bering Strait* (1889), it was translated by Julius E. Olson. There also is the account by Sven Waxell, Bering's second-in-command, entitled *The Russian Expedition to America* (1962). Waxell had finished writing his report probably by 1756. He wrote it in German, but when his vocabulary failed him , he had recourse to Swedish or English words and phrases or Germanized versions of them. He doubtless wrote for publication, but it was almost two hundred years before the book was published. Waxell probably submitted the manuscript to the Admiralty Council, and various officials handed it up the hierarchical ladder. That is not certain, however, because it was not generally known until 1891 that Waxell had written the account. In that year a zoologist

writing on the sea cow in a scientific journal referred to the manuscript and mentioned that it was in the czar's private library in Tsarskoye Selo (today Pushkin).

There it presumably remained, only to disappear in the upheavals of the Bolshevik revolution. In 1938 someone discovered it displayed for sale in a bookshop; subsequently the State Library in Leningrad bought it. A few years later the Danish publishing house Rosenkilde and Bagger acquired a photostatic copy of the manuscript together with the only known portrait of Vitus Bering. Johan Skalberg translated the manuscript into Danish. Later translated into English, it is a valuable document which sketches Bering's second expedition, and it is particularly good in describing the voyage of Bering's vessel, the packet boat *Saint Peter,* and its wreck on Bering Island in 1741. Waxell then describes the winter on the island; the construction of a second, smaller ship from the wreck; and the return of the survivors to Russia in 1742.

Raymond H. Fischer, professor emeritus of history in the University of California at Los Angeles, has written two books dealing with Russian voyages of discovery. In *The Voyage of Semen Dezhnev in 1648: Bering's Precursor* (1981) he describes Dezhnev's voyage in the summer of 1648 around the eastern tip of Asia, from the Kolyma River, which empties into the Arctic Ocean, to a point south of the mouth of the Anadyr River, which empties into the Pacific Ocean. Dezhnev thereby anticipated by eighty years the voyage of Bering through the strait separating Asia and America. In *Bering's Voyages: Whither and Why* (1977), Fischer presents an examination of the purposes of the voyages. Valerian Lada-Mocarski, the adviser to the Russian Collection, Yale University, compiled a useful publication entitled *Bibliography of Books on Alaska Published Before 1868* (1969).

One of the earliest works in English on the Russian activities in North America was that of a young British clergyman, William Coxe, who toured Russia and in 1780 published his *Account of the Russian Discoveries between Asia and America,* reprinted in 1966. Coxe describes the movement of the Russian fur hunters along the Aleutian Islands which commenced during the 1740s. After the publication of Coxe's work the various explorers who were sent to investigate the Russian efforts wrote accounts of their own. There are, for example, volumes by the famous British explorer Captain James Cook and his colleagues George A. Vancouver, W. R.

Broughton, G. Dixon, Nathaniel Portlock, and J. Meares.

Numerous scholarly journals contain articles dealing with Russian activities in North America. The Alaska historian Clarence L. Andrews published a number of articles in the *Washington Historical Quarterly*, the predecessor of the *Pacific Northwest Quarterly*. His "Alaska Under the Russians—Baranof the Builder," appeared in *Washington Historical Quarterly* 7 (1916). A look at the index yields many other useful contributions. "The Condition of the Orthodox Church in Russian America: Innokentii Veniaminov's History of the Russian Church in Alaska," translated and edited by Robert Nichols and Robert Croskey, appeared in *Pacific Northwest Quarterly* 63 (April, 1972). The index to that journal also lists many fine articles on Russian America. Other journals which have published material on Russian America and Alaska include *North American Review, Mississippi Valley Historical Review, Pacific Historical Review, National Geographic, British Columbia Historical Quarterly, American Heritage, Quarterly of the California Historical Society, Journal of American History, Journal of the West, American Scholar, Pacific Historian, Beaver, Alaska Journal, Alaska Review*, and *Orthodox Alaska*.

The National Archives hold 77 microfilm reels of the records of the Russian-American Company (1802–1867), and 66 rolls of dispatches addressed to the Department of State by U.S. diplomatic representatives to Russia between September, 1808, and August, 1906. The Library of Congress houses the Alaska Russian Orthodox church files, consisting of approximately 1,000 boxes. During the early 1970s officials of the Alaska Diocese of the Orthodox Church in America discovered a large number of old documents, rare books, and periodicals in the basements and attics of several churches in their vast domain. Most of the findings came from the Kvikhpak (Yukon) River Mission, dating from its beginnings in 1845 through 1966. A search on the island of Unalaska, in the Aleutian chain; on Kodiak Island, at Saint George Church, in the Pribilof Islands; and at Nushagak, on Bristol Bay, also turned up a number of documents. Subsequently, Barbara S. Smith, of the history department of the University of Alaska, Anchorage, began inventorying, arranging, and describing these records and published a useful finding aid entitled *Russian Orthodoxy in Alaska: A History Inventory and Analysis of the Church Archives in Alaska with an Annotated Bibliography (1980).* The Alaska State Library in Juneau possesses an important collection of Russian books, as does the Elmer E. Rasmuson Library, at the University of Alaska in Fairbanks.

The members of the Western Union Telegraph expedition, 1865–67, published accounts of their labors. Among them was Frederick Whymper, an English artist, whose *Travel and Adventure in the Territory of Alaska* first appeared in London in 1868. Still a useful volume for the Russian as well as early American period is Hubert Howe Bancroft's *History of Alaska, 1730–1885* (1886), reprinted by Arno Press. A wide variety of government publications and documents on the American period fill libraries and archives. They include reports on hearings before various congressional committees and specific research studies. In short, Alaska has been discussed, debated, agonized over, and studied for a long time.

Congressional hearings have served as a means of investigating conditions in Alaska and provide the forum in which interested groups and individuals have been heard. What to do with Alaska's coal lands, as well as questions concerning oil-and-gas leases on public lands, prompted hearings in 1910, 1912 (two volumes), 1913, 1915, and 1917 (three volumes). The subject of fisheries—their exploitation, conservation, and regulation—fills many volumes; between 1906 and the 1950s and since, hearings on this concern alone have filled thousands of pages. Between 1947 and 1956 hearings on Alaska statehood were conducted on seven different occasions in Washington and three times in Alaska. The printed record of these investigations amounts to approximately 4,000 pages. Although congressional concern over Alaska's natural resources has exceeded its interest in health, education, and various other social problems in the territory and later state, the latter have also attracted attention.

Alaska, first as a district and later as a territory, had a long, close relationship with the federal government. Over the years an enormous documentation of federal activities in Alaska developed. Much of this material is housed in the National Archives, in Washington, D.C., and in various federal record centers. Working in this gold mine of information was difficult, at best, but fortunately there are always dedicated staff members of the National Archives to help researchers find their way to the Alaska-related holdings. Finally, researchers enjoy the luxury of being able to use a published guide for a comprehensive description of the major record groups, series, and subseries of records pertaining to Alaska. Although the manuscript was in preparation for many years, George S. Ulibarri, formerly of the National Archives staff, compiled the final form; it is entitled *Documenting Alaskan History: Guide to Federal Archives Relating to Alaska* (1982).

There are other finding aids. James Wickersham, Federal District Court judge and territorial delegate to Congress, prepared an excellent volume entitled *A Bibliography of Alaskan Literature, 1724–1924* (1927). The volume, according to its author, "is supposed to contain a complete list of the titles of all printed books of history, travels, voyages, newspapers, periodicals, and public documents, in English, Russian, German, French, Spanish, etc., relating to, descriptive of, or published in Russian–America, now called Alaska, from 1724 to and including 1924." Wickersham may have missed a few printed accounts, but he was thorough, and this is a helpful volume even today. Over a number of years the Arctic Institute of North America prepared and published the multivolume work *The Arctic Bibliography,* which primarily lists scientific entries but also has many important historical items. Also useful is Elsie Tourville's *Alaska: A Bibliography, 1570–1970* (1975).

For more than twenty-five years Melvin B. Ricks gathered references to books, articles, pamphlets, and other written records on Alaska's history. For years investigators used typescripts of his material in several forms. It was a useful reference tool. In 1977 the Alaska Historical Commission issued Ricks's *Alaska Bibliography: An Introductory Guide to Alaskan Historical Literature,* edited by Stephen W. and Betty J. Haycox. Although updated, the typescript manuscript is a much more valuable reference tool than the abbreviated volume produced by the Alaska Historical Commission. Last but not least, the Smithsonian Institution issued its *Guide to the Smithsonian Archives* (1978), valuable because many of its collections pertain to Alaska; an example is the papers of William Healy Dall, a scientist who went to Russian America as a member of the Western Union Telegraph expedition in 1865. Since 1867, the year of purchase, the federal government has commissioned scientific studies of Alaska. Obviously since that time a vast amount of such scientific work has accumulated, representing a valuable source of information for the historian.

Other government sources of historical inter-est include the innumerable annual and special reports and studies by federal executive departments operating in Alaska. It is a long list, and a few examples must suffice: the national census of 1880, in which Alaska was included for the first time; annual reports of the governor of Alaska, 1884 to 1958; annual reports of the Alaska Road Commission, 1905 to 1956; U.S. Geological Survey bulletins and professional papers, such as the indispensable *Dictionary of Alaska Place Names,* U.S. Geological Survey Professional Paper 567 (1967), by Donald J. Orth; and commercial statistics and weather reports. Much of the material is related to the development of one or another natural resource.

Obviously there is an abundance of material for political, social, and economic historians; but there are other resources as well. The personal-narrative literature about the North is rich and varied. Explorers, missionaries, traders, trappers, miners, tourists, and others have felt compelled to describe their experiences. The men and women who rushed north during the gold rushes probably produced a disproportionate share of these narratives, partly because the world at large was fascinated by the gold rushes and because adventurous accounts, especially those that promised quick and easy riches, were well received.

The Klondike, in Canada's Yukon Territory, drew the largest number of argonauts, and many narratives deal with that spectacular strike; but many miners went on to other stampedes in Alaska. One of the best accounts by a journalist, a sharp observer, is *The Klondike Stampede of 1897–98* (1900), by Tappan Adney. Those who participated in the gold rush as teamsters or miners rather than observers and recorders gave their narratives a distinctive flavor. A good example of such a book is Arthur T. Walden's *A Dog Puncher on the Yukon* (1928), which fully expresses the excitement and adventure the participants felt.

Many authors, however, exaggerated, boasted, and even told outright lies, because of forgetfulness or prompting from ghost writers who wanted to spice up the tales. Edward C. Trelawny-Ansell's *I Followed Gold* (1939) abounds with exaggerated descriptions of actual events at Saint Michael, Skagway, and Nome and of impossible sled journeys. A colorful fantasy attributed to Jan Welzl, *Thirty Years in the Golden North* (1932), became a best seller.

Basil Austin, a stampeder, kept a diary which fully conveys the joys and hardships the stampeders experienced. Published in 1968, it is entitled *The Diary of a Ninety-eighter.* Herbert L. Heller gathered firsthand accounts of life in Alaska and the Klondike from those who participated in these events in *Sourdough Sagas: Pioneering and Gold in Alaska, 1883–1923 (1967).*

It was not until a quarter of a century after the Klondike and Nome rushes, however, that a trained historian examined the documents and wrote a monograph about pioneer Alaska. In the mid-1920s, Jeannette Paddock Nichols, working on her doctoral dissertation under William Dunning, completed *Alaska: A History of Its Administration, Exploitation and Industrial Development During Its First Half Century Under the Rule of the United States* (1924). Republished in 1963, the book remains an indispensable source for Alaska's territorial political development. Since most of Alaska's population lived in the territory's southeastern section, the Panhandle, Nichols dealt with that area. During her work she received much help and encouragement from Wickersham. Nichols's central assumption, that Alaska received unnecessarily shoddy treatment from Uncle Sam, has been questioned by a number of contemporary historians.

In 1938, Clarence L. Andrews's *The Story of Alaska* appeared and was reprinted eight times. Andrews knew the pioneer period from experience, because during its heyday he had served in the U.S. Customs Service at Sitka, Skagway, and Eagle. Originally from the Midwest, Andrews became fond of the territory and spent the rest of his life telling its story. He was more versatile than most other historians, for he mastered the Russian language, which allowed him to explore and write about the period before 1867. A prolific researcher and writer, he produced a steady stream of articles and books both popular and scholarly. Although his work lacks critical perspective, it has retained its value.

In the years after World War II, three textbooks appeared. Stuart Ramsay Tompkins's *Alaska: Promyshlennik and Sourdough* (1945) long remained the recommended general survey. He carefully researched his book and compiled a useful bibliography. In 1953 the University of Alaska Press published posthumously Alfred Hulse Brooks's *Blazing Alaska's Trails.* Brooks, one-time head of the U.S. Geological Survey in Alaska, always had a strong interest in the territory. Edited by Burton L. Fryxell, the volume retains its value today. It is wide-ranging, dealing with Alaska's geography and climate, Natives, the Russians and the Americans, and resource development. Particularly useful are his chapters on the history of mining. The University of Alaska Press reprinted the book in 1973.

Early in the century Wickersham adopted Alaska and became its foremost politician, and he used pen as well as the political forum to advance the territory's interests. Late in his life appeared his delightful *Old Yukon: Tales—Trails—and Trials* (1938). Based in part on his diaries, the volume contains much social history. Ernest Gruening, after a distinguished career as a journalist, entered federal service and became the first director of the Interior Department's Office of Territories and Island Possessions. In 1939, President Franklin D. Roosevelt appointed him governor of Alaska, a position he occupied until 1953. Actively involved in Alaska's struggle for statehood, Gruening eventually was elected to one of the two U.S. Senate seats from the new state. He served as U.S. senator from 1959 until 1968 and then continued his career, championing birth control and advocating U.S. withdrawal from Vietnam. Throughout a long and eventful life, he, like Wickersham, used the pen as well as the political forum to advocate his ideas. Gruening, a Democrat, left the governorship after Dwight D. Eisenhower became president in 1953. With admirable singlemindedness he spent the year 1953–54 researching and writing *The State of Alaska* (1954), in which he told his fellow Americans how the United States had neglected the territory. He concentrated his narrative on the twentieth century but outlined earlier events. Gruening stated his ideas forcefully, and his footnotes are valuable for the researcher.

For Alaska's centennial celebration in 1967, Gruening wrote a legislative account of the Alaska statehood struggle entitled *The Battle for Alaska Statehood,* and in the same year appeared *An Alaskan Reader,* a selection of articles which he had edited. In 1973, one year before he died at age eighty-seven, Liveright of New York published his *Many Battles: The Autobiography of Ernest Gruening.* In that description of his long, rich life, Alaska occupies approximately 115 of a total of 543 pages. To write the section on Alaska, Gruening relied heavily on a diary he had kept intermittently. It is a useful book, though the reader should be aware of the author's strong opinions on a variety of Alaska topics.

Scholars have spent a disproportionate amount of time on the questions surrounding the purchase and annexation of Russian America. They have written many articles on the question, including William A. Dunning, "Paying for Alaska: Some Unfamiliar Incidents in the Process," *Political Science Quarterly* 27 (September, 1912); and Richard E. Welch, Jr., "American Public Opinion and the Purchase of Russian America," *American Slavic and East European Review* 17 (December, 1958). In the early 1940s, David Hunter Miller, a diplomat and specialist on international law, summed up the Alaska Purchase for the Department of State's series "Treaties and Other International Acts of the United States of America," of which he was editor. Completed in 1944 as volume 9 in the series, *The Alaska Treaty* was not published in the series, which was discontinued because of budget problems, but in 1981 the Limestone Press published Miller's book. It is an authoritative and thorough work.

Ronald J. Jensen wrote a doctoral dissertation on the purchase entitled "The Alaska Purchase and Russian-American Relations," which appeared in 1975. In the same year appeared Howard I. Kushner's *Conflict on the Northwest Coast: American-Russian Rivalry in the Pacific Northwest, 1790–1867*, which is broader in scope. Kushner argues that American expansion of fishing, whaling, and commerce led to conflict and that Russia ceded the territory to avoid its seizure by the United States.

Over the years many graduate students in American universities have completed master's theses and doctoral dissertations on Alaska topics. The titles of some of the dissertations demonstrate the range of subjects: Franklin Ward Burch, "Alaska's Railroad Frontier: Railroads and Federal Development Policy, 1898–1915" (Catholic University of America, 1965); Stanley Ray Remsberg, "United States Administration of Alaska: The Army Phase, 1867–1877" (University of Wisconsin—Madison, 1975); Bobby Dave Lain, "North of Fifty-three: Army, Treasury Department, and Navy Administration of Alaska, 1867–1884" (University of Texas, 1974); Marilyn Jody, "Alaska Literary History of Frontier Alaska with a Bibliographical Guide to the Study of Alaskan Literature" (Indiana University, 1969); and Terrence Michael Cole, "A History of the Nome Gold Rush: The Poor Man's Paradise" (University of Washington, 1983).

There has also been an increase in both the number of authors and the diversity of subjects of journal articles dealing with Alaska in the postwar period. A few examples are Ted C.

Hinckley, "The Presbyterian Leadership in Pioneer Alaska," *Journal of American History* 52 (March, 1966); John Sherman Long, "Webb's Frontier and Alaska," *Southwest Review* 56 (October, 1971); Thomas G. Smith, "The Treatment of the Mentally Ill in Alaska, 1884–1912," *Pacific Northwest Quarterly* 65 (January, 1974); Claus-M. Naske, "Jewish Immigration and Alaskan Economic Development: A Study in Futility," *Western States Jewish Historical Quarterly* 8 (January, 1976); Claus-M. Naske, "The Relocation of Alaska's Japanese Residents," *Pacific Northwest Quarterly* 74 (July, 1983); Herman Slotnick, "The Ballinger-Pinchot Affair in Alaska," *Journal of the West* 10 (April, 1971); William R. Hunt, "A Soldier on the Yukon," *Journal of the West* 10 (April, 1971); and Charles Hendricks, "The Eskimos and the Defense of Alaska," *Pacific Historical Review* (1985).

In 1965, Yale University Press published Morgan Sherwood's *Exploration of Alaska, 1865–1900*. Two years later, during the Centennial year, appeared Robert N. DeArmond's *The Founding of Juneau*. Both books are well written and opened up a variety of topics, including mining, politics, town building, and scientific activity in the North. Also worthy of mention is William H. Wilson's splendid book *Railroad in the Clouds: The Alaska Railroad in the Age of Steam, 1914–1945* (1977).

Since statehood events in Alaska have confirmed that history will increasingly find its strongest support in the state itself. In 1966, Robert A. Frederick, of Alaska Methodist University; George Hall, of the National Park Service; Robert N. DeArmond, of Juneau; and other interested citizens formed the Alaska Historical Society. Conferences, preservation projects, and various historical undertakings followed. In 1984 the society launched its own history journal. In 1985 the Alaska Historical Commission published a useful list of projects it had supported: *Publications, Research Reports and Other Projects Supported by the Alaska Historical Commission, 1973–1985*. In 1971, Robert A. Henning, owner of Alaska Northwest Publishing Company, and Robert N. DeArmond launched Alaska's first state historical magazine, the *Alaska Journal*. A very handsome publication, it combined some of the best features of *National Geographic* with traditional, scholarly, well-researched historical quarterlies. Unfortunately it ceased publication with the Autumn, 1985, issue.

Since statehood Alaska's historical fraternity has steadily increased. Historian Orlando Miller, formerly of the University of Alaska, Fairbanks, has analyzed Alaska agricultural failures in *The Frontier in Alaska and the Matanuska Colony* (1975). His conclusions destroyed cherished myths and upset many local boosters. Claus-M. Naske has analyzed and recounted Alaska's struggle for self-determination in *A History of Alaskan Statehood* (1985) and has written a biography of Alaska's last territorial delegate and the state's first senior U.S. senator, *Edward Lewis Bob Bartlett of Alaska: A Life in Politics* (1979).

Brian Garfield well described the only military campaign fought on American soil during World War II, that in the Aleutian Islands, in *The Thousand Mile War* (1969), and Ted C. Hinckley has added two welcome contributions to the growing historical literature of the North, a lively account entitled *The Americanization of Alaska, 1867–1897* (1973) and a colorful biography, *Alaskan John G. Brady: Missionary, Businessman, Judge, and Governor, 1878–1918* (1982).

William S. Hanable, executive director of the Alaska Historical Commission, created by the legislature in the early 1970s to foster historical research, writing, and publication, has produced a valuable regional history entitled *Alaska's Cooper River: The 18th and 19th Centuries* (1982). Patricia Roppel, an able amateur historian distinguished for her many articles on the Panhandle's mining history, which appeared with regularity in the *Alaska Journal*, has produced a fine book on a little-known facet of northern history entitled *Alaska's Salmon Hatcheries, 1891–1959* (1982). Morgan Sherwood produced *Big Game in Alaska: A History of Wildlife and People* (1981), and Richard A. Cooley's *Politics and Conservation: The Decline of the Alaska Salmon* (1963) has become the standard reference on that topic. Evangeline Atwood wrote an uncritical biography of James Wickersham, Alaska's political giant during the first three decades of the twentieth century, *Frontier Politics: Alaska's James Wickersham* (1979). Terrence Michael Cole produced *E. T. Barnette: The Strange Story of the Man Who Founded Fairbanks* (1981) and, more recently, *Nome: City of the Golden Beaches* (1984).

William R. Hunt, formerly of the Department of History of the University of Alaska in Fairbanks, produced a number of highly readable books. His *North of 53 Degrees: The Wild Days of the Alaska-Yukon Mining Frontier, 1870–1914* (1974) emphasized colorful personalities and episodes but also provided a much-needed overview of the far-flung region that attracted Alaskans and North Americans alike for almost half a century. His highly readable *Arctic Passage: The Turbulent History of the Land and People of the Bering Sea, 1697–1975* (1975) is a fine regional history.

George W. Rogers, a political economist and productive scholar, wrote a valuable regional study entitled *Alaska in Transition: The Southeast Region* (1960), which was followed by his thoughtful book *The Future of Alaska: Economic Consequences of Statehood* (1962).

Canada and Alaska are closely linked in many ways. Their historians have been attracted to northern history, and Pierre Berton, son of a stampeder who spent his childhood in Dawson, in the Yukon Territory, wrote what has since become a classic, *The Klondike Fever* (1958). Melody Webb, formerly of the National Park Service Studies Unit in the University of Alaska and now regional historian for the Southwest Region of the National Park Service, produced a fine volume entitled *The Last Frontier: A History of the Yukon Basin of Canada and Alaska* (1985). The author took a difficult subject and neatly tied it together by using Frederick Jackson Turner's thesis of successive frontiers. The author has done thorough research and is a fine writer.

For years travel writers have scribbled away in their attempts to portray Alaska. The results have been as varied as the people who steamed up the Inland Passage or to Saint Michael and up the Yukon River. Many tall tales and trivia have filled notebooks, and Alaskans reading the results have often been pained by the exaggerations and outright falsehoods. It must be remembered that it is difficult to encounter the vastness and variety of Alaska and describe them accurately. Yet some have managed to do so. T. A. Rickard, geologist, mining engineer, and editor, visited Alaska's important mining areas in the summer of 1908. His description of Alaska miners and their difficulties in *Through the Yukon and Alaska* (1909) is sympathetic and perceptive; he understood the appeal the country had for those who wrested a living from its soil. The charm of the land lay in its vastness, its freedom from restraints, and its uncomplicated life. The Reverend Hudson Stuck thoroughly enjoyed his life in the North. He contributed *Voyages on the*

*Yukon and Its Tributaries* (1917), which gives a good picture of travel and life along that great river.

Other good sources for the historian are the old gold-town newspapers and the back files of journals edited by men and women who knew the North and tolerated no nonsense. Among these are *Alaska Sportsman, Alaska Weekly, Alaska-Yukon Magazine,* and *Alaska Life.*

The Seattle Federal Records Service files contain vitally important Alaska manuscript materials, such as those of the U.S. Forest Service, the U.S. district courts, the Bureau of Land Management, the Alaska Road Commission, the Bureau of Indian Affairs, and the Bureau of Commercial Statistics. Archivists there eventually determine which records are of historical value and will be retained. During the 1960s, Elmer W. Lindgard, archivist of the National Archives and Records Service (NARS), inventoried a number of collections, among them the Sir Henry Wellcome Papers and the records of the Alaska territorial government. The former include written and pictorial evidence both on the missionary leader William Duncan and on the socioeconomic changes occurring among his Tsimshian parishioners. The records of the Alaska territorial government, spanning the period from 1884 to 1958, document Alaska's major government activities during the territorial period. These rich papers include the executive office central files, which reflect the varied roles Alaska's governors have played in their formal relations with other states and territories and the federal government. The General Correspondence file, from 1909 to 1958, is 176 feet long, and there are the annual reports of the governor; letters received and letters sent by the secretary of Alaska, 1900–13; the Territorial Legislative file, 1913–39, and reports of surveys and studies, 1910–58. The National Archives Trust Fund Board and the NARS microfilmed the "General Correspondence of Alaskan Territorial Governors, 1909–1958" on 378 rolls of microfilm and in 1980 published a pamphlet describing the series.

Much work remains to be done to chronicle Alaska's maritime history. An important volume is *Lewis and Dryden's Marine History of the Pacific Northwest* (1895), edited by Lewis Wright. Louis H. Sloss, a retired San Francisco attorney and descendant of one of the founders of the Alaska Commercial Company, has written two fine articles on that organization, which was important in the latter part of the nineteenth century in helping keep Alaska "tied together." His first article, with coauthor Richard A. Pierce, entitled "The Hutchison, Kohl Story: A Fresh Look," appeared in the January, 1971, issue of the *Pacific Northwest Quarterly;* a later piece by Sloss, entitled "Who Owned the Alaska Commercial Company?" appeared in the same journal in its July, 1977, issue.

A number of books on Alaska's maritime history have been published. Among them is *Children of the Light: The Rise and Fall of New Bedford Whaling and the Death of the Arctic Fleet* (1975), by Everett S. Allen. It relates the calamity which befell thirty-two of the thirty-nine vessels of the Arctic whaling fleet in 1871. John R. Bockstoce has written a useful summary entitled *Steam Whaling in the Western Arctic* (1977), with contributions by William A. Baker and Charles F. Batchelder. Sections of the volume describe the design and construction of steam whalers and give biographies of ships and a chronological list of commercial wintering voyages, 1850–1910. He followed this work with *Whales, Ice, and Men: The History of Whaling in the Western Arctic* (1986). *The Princess Story: A Century and a Half of West Coast Shipping* (1976), by Norman R. Hucking and W. Kaye Lamb, traces the ups and downs of a shipping line for more than a hundred years. The line began operating a steamship in Alaska waters in the late 1830s.

The use of Alaska's resources and the effect on Alaska of America's conservation movement have yet to be explored in depth. Lawrence W. Rakestraw has written a useful article, "Conservation Historiography: An Assessment," *Pacific Historical Review* 41 (August, 1972); and Ted C. Hinckley followed with a fine piece entitled "Alaska and the Emergence of America's Conservation Consciousness," in *Prairie Scout* 2 (1974). Rakestraw also wrote *A History of the United States Forest Service in Alaska* (1981), and Richard A. Cooley has produced *Alaska: A Challenge in Conservation* (1966). Hugh A. Johnson and Harold T. Jorgenson produced a fine, though now outdated, reference work entitled *The Land Resources of Alaska* (1963). Robert B. Weeden, professor of resource management in the University of Alaska, wrote a fascinating volume entitled *Alaska: Promises to Keep* (1978), in which he states that Alaska confronts the United States with a last chance to create new and viabale relationships between people and nature. Thomas A. Morehouse, professor of political science in the Institute of Social and Economic Research, University of

Alaska at Anchorage, has edited and contributed to a highly useful volume entitled *Alaska Resources Development: Issues of the 1980s* (1984). Claus-M. Naske and Don M. Triplehorn have addressed the topic of federal policies and the development of Alaskan coal in "The Federal Government and Alaska's Coal," *Northern Engineer* 12 (Fall, 1980); and Claus-M. Naske has dealt with "The Navy's Coal Investigating Expedition in Alaska," *Northern Engineer* 14 (Spring, 1982). Neil Davis addressed the whole range of energy issues in his comprehensive *Energy Alaska* (1984). Julia H. Triplehorn has compiled *Alaska Coal: A Bibliography* (1982), an exhaustive guide to one of the state's major resources. Through the years the Alaska Historical Library, part of the Division of State Libraries and Museums, led by its energetic and personable director, Richard B. Engen, has been publishing useful inventories of various of its collections. A sampling of these inventories will give readers some idea of the treasures in the Alaska Historical Library: *An Inventory of the Papers and Personal Correspondence, 1933–1939, of Governor John W. Troy* (1982); *An Inventory of the Lyman Brewster Papers and Photographs Concerning the Reindeer Industry and Life in Nome, Alaska, 1932–1934* (1982); *The Southeast Alaska Salmon Fishers: A Guide to Interviews with Men and Women Engaged in Commercial Fishing, 1913–1978* (1979); *A Guide to Alaska Native Corporation Publications* (1976); and *A Guide to the Alaska Packers' Association Records and to the APA Library* (1972). Robert N. DeArmond, Alaska's best-known historian, has compiled the excellent *Subject Index to the* Alaskan, *1885–1907, a Sitka Newspaper* (1974). The Elmer E. Rasmuson Library of the University of Alaska, Fairbanks, issues occasional papers; three examples must suffice: *An Index to the Early History of Alaska as Reported in the 1903–1907 Fairbanks Newspapers* (1980); *Alaskan Environmental Impact Statements: A Bibliography* (1980); and *Alaska Newspaper Tree* (1975), all frequently revised and updated.

A number of manuscript depositories in the United States contain Alaska materials. Among the useful guides is *Guide to the Archives and the Manuscripts in the United States* (1961), edited by Philip M. Hamer. This work, continued with *The National Union Catalog on Manuscript Collections,* enables the researcher to spot recently accessioned papers dealing with Alaska, while *America: History and Life* makes it possible to keep track of current journal scholarship on the North.

Patricia L. Davis has provided a useful introduction to the rich missionary records: "The Alaska Papers, 1884–1939," *Historical Magazine of the Protestant Episcopal Church,* June, 1971; and Harrison A. Brann has compiled "A Bibliography of the Sheldon Jackson Collection in the Presbyterian Historical Society," *Journal of Presbyterian History* 30 (September, 1952).

The discovery in 1968 of the giant Prudhoe Bay oil field on Alaska's North Slope moved Alaska once again into the American consciousness, just as the gold discoveries had in the late nineteenth and early twentieth centuries and the Japanese invasions of Kiska and Attu had in 1942. Once again national magazines pay attention to the North, and one can expect that national and international needs for raw materials will keep Alaska at center stage for years to come. *National Geographic* well reflects the nation's intermittent interest in Alaska. Between 1888 and 1940 it published 111 articles dealing with Alaska, most of them between 1890 and 1910. From 1940 to 1945 a mere 9 articles appeared, but the number increased to 36 between 1945 and 1968. From 1968 to January, 1984, the magazine published 31 articles on Alaska.

The sheer bulk of modern historical materials is overwhelming. Hearings on Alaska problems are voluminous. They provide insights into the views of witnesses and committee members and often expose conflicts between Alaskans and the federal government, between different interest groups, and between competing federal agencies. Long draft environmental statements concerning the use of millions of acres of land furnish excellent examples. Until the passage in 1980 of the Alaska National Interest Lands Conservation Act (94 Stat. 2371) for the time being settled the disposition and use of lands, several federal agencies struggled over the control of land in the wake of the Alaska Native Claims Settlement Act of 1971 and the subsequent need to classify 80 million acres for primary and secondary uses.

The voluminous draft environmental statements concerning the use of those 80 million acres contain much information. The U.S. Forest Service proposed to put most of the area into national forests; the Bureau of Outdoor Recreation wanted to include most areas in the national system of wild and scenic rivers; and the National Park Service had expansive plans for national wilderness parks as well as national wild lands.

Environmental statements and studies produced by federal, state, and local government bodies, Native groups, and private industry fill whole shelves. The reports reflect Alaska's growing economic development in the wake of oil discoveries and state and Native land selection. These bulky studies employ a small army of consulting firms, university research institutes, environmentalists, planners, anthropologists and archaeologists, engineers, scientists, draftsmen, and writers. And since the history of a region is related to its environent, they offer at least sketchy historical assessments. The impact statements must also evaluate the environmental changes that a particular development will produce and offer alternative methods of reducing environmental disruption. The statements are designed to inform the public and to enable governments to act wisely.

The final six-volume environmental impact statement on the then proposed Trans-Alaska Pipeline furnishes a good example of these fast-accumulating studies. Prepared by a special interagency task force for the Federal Task Force on Alaskan Oil Development under the auspices of the U.S. Department of the Interior, it was published in 1972.

There were other studies, hearings, and comments, among them two volumes of "Hearings on Proposed Pipeline Legislation, March 6–10, 1972, State of Alaska," and "Comments on the Proposed Trans-Alaska Pipeline" (1971), prepared under the direction of the Alaska Department of Law.

On March 27, 1964, before Alaska became an oil state, it experienced a devastating earthquake that left much of south-central Alaska in shambles. In response, the federal government created the Federal Field Committee for Development Planning in Alaska, designed to help the state get back on its feet. It also prepared studies designed to facilitate the settlement of Native claims. Over a period of several years the committee staff released more than forty studies, ranging from *An Approach to Marine Resource Development in Alaska* (1969) to the comprehensive, magnificent *Alaska Natives and the Land* (1968).

In the wake of the Alaska Native Claims Settlement Act of 1971, the state of Alaska and the federal government established the Joint Federal-State Land Use Planning Commission for Alaska in 1972. The commission was to serve during a decade of major change in land-ownership and land management in Alaska. Its goal was to create a framework for the use and protection of the state's lands and resources in the years to come. On May 30, 1979, the commission delivered its final report. During its existence it had published dozens of valuable studies, compiled a long list of recommendations and inquiries, made formal presentations, and conducted symposia. The commission issued much valuable historical material.

An eneretic group of political scientists, economists, and historians of the University of Alaska, Fairbanks, has addressed political developments in the state. George W. Rogers, a perceptive student of Alaska, has written much on the Forty-ninth State. His "Party Politics or Protest Politics: Current Political Trends in Alaska," *Polar Record* 14, no. 91 (1969), examines political developments in Native and non-Native Alaska. Herman E. Slotnick wrote on "The 1960 Election in Alaska," *Western Political Quarterly*, March, 1961; "The 1964 Election in Alaska," *Western Political Quarterly*, June, 1965; and "The 1966 Election in Alaska," *Western Political Quarterly*, June, 1967. Ronald E. Chinn covered "The 1968 Election in Alaska," *Western Political Quarterly*, June, 1971. Thomas A. Morehouse, Gerald A. McBeath, and Linda Leask have written a fine study entitled *Alaska's Urban and Rural Governments* (1984), and Gerald A. McBeath and Thomas A. Morehouse have addressed *The Dynamics of Alaska Native Self-Government* (1980). Victor Fischer, has written a useful study on *Alaska's Constitutional Convention* (1975).

Economic development has been uppermost in the minds of most politicians and many citizens as well. Gordon Scott Harrison edited a very useful volume entitled *Alaska Public Policy: Current Problems and Issues* (1971, 1973). Divided into five parts, it gives the reader an overview and then deals with land, petroleum development, environmental quality and rural development. At the end of each section are suggestions for further reading. Harrison is also the author of the useful volume entitled *A Citizen's Guide to the Constitution of the State of Alaska* (1982). David T. Kresge, Thomas A. Morehouse, and Geogre W. Rogers pooled their talents in *Issues in Alaska Development* (1977), which contains both basic and applied policy research on current social and economic problems of northern development. Peter G. Cornwall and Gerald McBeath edited *Alaska's Rural Develop-*

*ment* (1982), which examines the social, economic, political, and cultural concerns surrounding the development of rural Alaska.

Obviously, there is much more. This essay is designed not to be exhaustive but to whet the reader's appetite for further inquiries. Historians will have to wade through all these materials, make sense of them all, and then interpret Alaska's history. If they do their job well, they will discard the persistent romantic notions about Alaska that historian Jeannette P. Nichols has recognized as a barrier in making use of the historical experience as a guide to solving present problems, but also it can, and should, entertain and instruct all of us in numerous ways. Perhaps in the years ahead history will also be used as a basis for fictional creations. Jack London and Rex Beach focused on the gold-rush era. Edna Ferber dealt with modern-day Alaska. The material exists, and Alaska's spectacular scenery and varied cultures undoubtedly will challenge writers in the future. On the other hand, it may just be that Americans will respond to Alaska solely in economic terms—as a supplier of needed resources—as they have in the past. Or perhaps they will see Alaska only as a military bastion or respond only to spectacular events as in the past: gold rushes, foreign invasions, or construction of history's largest project, the nearly 800-mile-long oil pipeline. Only the future will tell.

# INDEX